CHAPEL OF DAWSON,

Good Time Girls

OF THE ALASKA-YUKON GOLD RUSH

by Lael Morgan

EPICENTER PRESS

Fairbanks ▪ Seattle

Epicenter Press, Inc., is a regional press founded in Alaska whose interests include but are not limited to the arts, history, environment, and diverse cultures and lifestyles of the North Pacific and high latitudes. We seek both the traditional and innovative in publishing quality nonfiction tradebooks, contemporary art and photography giftbooks, and destination travel guides emphasizing Alaska, Washington, Oregon, and California.

Editor: Christine Ummel
Cover and inside design: Elizabeth Watson
Proofreader: Lois Kelly
Maps: L.W. Nelson
Printer: Transcontinental Printing, Inc.

ISBN 0-945397-63-1

Library of Congress Cataloging-in-Publication Data

Morgan, Lael.
     Good time girls of the Alaska-Yukon gold rush / by Lael Morgan.
          p.   cm.
     Includes bibliographical references and index.
     ISBN 0-945397-63-1
          1. Women pioneers—Alaska—History.   2. Women pioneers—Yukon Territory—Klondike River Valley—History.   3. Prostitutes—Alaska—History.   4. Prostitutes—Yukon Territory—Klondike River Valley—History.   5. Prostitutes—Alaska—Biography.   6. Prostitutes—Yukon Territory—Klondike River Valley—Biography.   7. Alaska—Gold discoveries.   8. Klondike River Valley (Yukon) Gold discoveries.   9. Frontier and pioneer life—Alaska.   10. Frontier and pioneer life—Yukon Territory—Klondike River Valley.   I.   Title.
     F908.M67   1998
     971.9' 1—dc21   97-51815
                                                                                                                           CIP

To order single copies of GOOD TIME GIRLS, send $24.95 (Washington residents add $2.15 state sales tax) plus $5 for priority mail shipping to: Epicenter Press, Box 82368, Kenmore, WA 98028.

Booksellers: Retail discounts are available from our trade distributor, Graphic Arts Center Publishing, Portland, Oregon (phone 800-452-3032) and from major wholesalers.

Printed in CANADA
First printing, March 1998
10 9 8 7 6 5 4 3 2 1

Photos: Title page, "The Charm of Dishabille"—This Dawson charmer was identified by her photographer as an "actress." Coyly she used only her working name, "The Belgium Queen," which probably meant her "acting" was mainly for private audiences. YA #815. Endsheets, "Red Lights Under the Midnight Sun"—This photo of Dawson's restricted district is sometimes labeled "White Chapel" after a similar institution in London, but the Klondike's White Chapel was a late development built outside the population center. Some historians believe this is actually a picture of the stampede's pioneering effort on Fourth Avenue in downtown Dawson. NAC C20314, Larss and Duclos photograph.

Michael Carey Collection.

"Guys, if you're not ready, don't stand in line!"

Lillian of the Fairbanks Line

Contents

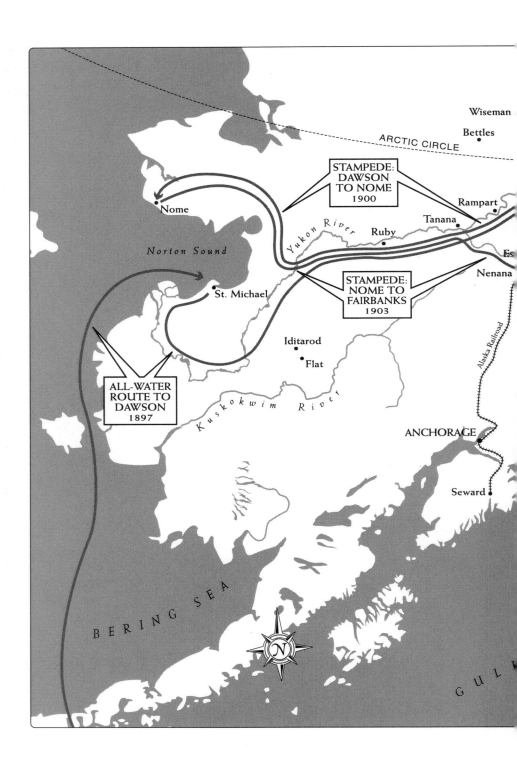

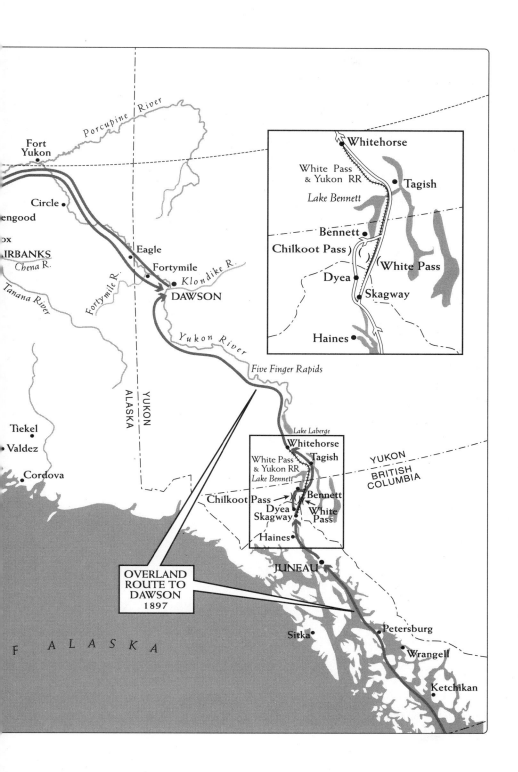

Preface

A Fairbanks prostitute, 1906.
Michael Carey Collection.

In 1965 I spent many hours going through the late Judge James Wickersham's collection of photos, now at the Rasmuson Library in Fairbanks, but then in his home in Juneau, Alaska, which he'd left to his niece, Ruth Coffin Allman. What I liked best was Scrapbook #1 (of more than a dozen), which contained wonderful portraits of Klondike dance hall girls and prostitutes. At the time it didn't occur to me to wonder why Wickersham—a scholar with a Renaissance mind—had collected them. The judge knew he was making history and he collected *everything*.

Only in researching this book did I realize how important it was that the images were pasted into Scrapbook #1. Judge Wickersham arrived in the Far North early, when dance hall girls and prostitutes were still a major part of the female population. The women of the demimonde were in his first scrapbook *because they were pioneers!*

"A little later, to be sure, the canvas-covered wagons brought the wives and children of the permanent settlers, but the early rush was the unencumbered, adventurous, strong-bodied youth of the East," historian Howard B. Woolston noted in *Prostitution in the United States*. "The characteristics of the mining camps and the towns were those universally found under such circumstances in South Africa, in Australia, and later in Alaska. The women who followed the miners were not their wives and mothers and daughters, but those women who everywhere are drawn to the lure of money easily found and easily spent."[1]

Another glimpse into the lives of these women came from the

portraits taken in the Fairbanks red light district in 1906, probably the best collection of its kind in the United States, saved from oblivion by the late Fabian Carey. Some of the subjects were young and clear-eyed, staring straight at the camera with an oddly innocent candor. Most were beautiful, all elegantly coiffed and gowned, yet they were living in some of the wildest country on the globe, under ruggedly primitive circumstances. What were their stories? Why had they come to this harsh land at a time when women were encouraged to stay home? And why had they worked as prostitutes when they could easily have found husbands—especially in the North, where the population is *still* predominantly male?

Then I learned that the Fairbanks red light district, started by an Episcopal archdeacon and one of the town's leading businessmen, was considered the best in the West, and I became intrigued. But while voluminous accounts had been written about respectable women pioneers in the North, nothing of any depth and scope had been written on the good time girls who generally preceded them. Most women of the demimonde avoided the limelight. The few who could write letters and keep diaries found it prudent not to do so. Many old-timers who had known them, especially those who had enjoyed their services or were related to them, were reluctant to admit it. And researching the topic in my home state, where many "pros" married in, was a delicate task at best.

Throughout my research, I've looked for patterns and found surprisingly few. Perhaps because so many of these ladies of the evening were "amateurs," their backgrounds and dreams mirrored those of respectable women of that post-Victorian era. However, one thing that the pioneering good time girls of the Far North did have in common was that all of them had to have vast courage and stamina. They often labored harder, under more unpleasant circumstances, than their respectable sisters to help carve a civilized niche into unforgiving wilderness. And most were extraordinarily independent women, not only for their time but by today's standards as well.

Moralists tend to think of prostitutes as parasites on society, but that stereotype falls away in situations where men heavily outnumber women and are forced to share them, and where conditions are so difficult that all must fight to survive. Thus the pioneering whores of yore of the Far North were accorded unusual license and respect. And whatever their motives in entering the trade, they definitely earned both.

Lael Morgan
Fairbanks, Alaska

Acknowledgments

PROSTITUTES EXPORTED

*In 1909 federal immigration inspector Kazis Krauczunas arrested nine Interior
Alaska prostitutes on charges of white slavery, and transported them to jail in Seattle,
only to learn they could only be tried in Fairbanks. From the left were (1) Germain C. Montbrun,
a.k.a. Lily Davies, (2) Marie Kesterlyn, (3) Camille Leonard, (4) Jennie Dutailly,
(5) Lily DeVarley, a.k.a. Rachel Couti, (6) Mrs. Felix Duplan, (7) Carman Dubois,
(8) Marcel Romet, a.k.a. Debiscop, and (9) Rachael Bursoin, a.k.a. Burgois.
Most were veterans from the Dawson red light district who had worked in Fairbanks quite
peacefully for a couple of years. Because they were foreigners, Krauczunas eventually
succeeded in deporting all but Camille Leonard, who outwitted him by hiring a
Fairbanks man to marry her, thus becoming an American citizen.*

NA, File #52484-28, RC85, with grateful thanks to Claus Naske who discovered the photo.

I would particularly like to thank the friends and brave descendants of our sporting women who forthrightly admitted they were connected and took the time to set the record (and my thinking) straight.

In addition, I owe a great deal to the historians, archivists, librarians, museum keepers, collectors of memorabilia, interested citizens, and fellow writers who helped me track what was thought to be untrackable. Many of you will find yourselves in my footnotes. In the three decades it took to

ACKNOWLEDGMENTS

research *Good Time Girls*, I have learned that some would prefer not to have their names mentioned. For the help of those who will remain anonymous, I am most grateful!

It is appropriate to address a hearty thank-you to Rosalie L'Ecuyer, my research assistant since 1989. She has been enthusiastic from Day One, and her insights greatly broadened the scope of this project.

My editor, Christine Ummel, and publisher Kent Sturgis of Epicenter Press have been incredibly helpful, patient, and supportive, even when my own spirits lagged. Catherine Breslin has proved a fine coach, despite the fact that she lives in New York City. Starry Kruger, also a New York resident, has been most helpful. Pat and Earl Cook, Orea and Clifford Haydon, the late John and Grace Butrovich, Candace Waugaman, Kathleen Dalton, Rene Blahuta, and Claire Fejes helped me unlock some of Fairbanks's mysteries and were more than generous with their time. Historians R. N. DeArmond of Sitka, Diane Brenner of Anchorage, Paul Solka of Fairbanks and Eugene, and Terrence Cole, Claus Naske, and Gretchen Lake of Fairbanks filled gaps I didn't always know I had. Michael Gates, with the Klondike National Historic Sites in Dawson, and David Neufeld, the Yukon historian in Whitehorse, were helpful on Canadian sources. Pierre Berton's *Klondike* provided wonderful background. David Richardson's biography of Richard Geoghegan and Richardson's painstaking translation of Geoghegan's diaries proved a wonderful resource that I hope one day will see publication. Thanks also to the Alaska Humanities Forum.

I would also like to acknowledge the encouragement of the late William Warren, a free-thinking priest of the Fairbanks Diocese of the Episcopal Church, who had privy to church records (later destroyed) that documented the founding of the Fairbanks Line by a fellow churchman, the late Archdeacon Hudson Stuck. And I'm more than grateful to Stuck himself for sticking his neck out in an era when he was hanged in effigy — and damn near in the flesh — for undertaking a radical social experiment. It stood the test of time for half a century and should not be written out of history.

Finally, I wish to express my appreciation of the good time girls of the Far North—for their courage, the entertaining charm of their antics, and their amazing endurance. Bets were placed that I'd never finish this book because I too much enjoyed the research . . . but I want to put the record straight in their memory.

MADAM BURNET

*In 1906 this veteran posed willingly for a photographer in her small but
lavishly decorated "crib" in the Fairbanks restricted district. Even though the subarctic
gold camp was still being pioneered, prostitutes of the region dressed in expensive
gowns and displayed astonishing social graces.*

Michael Carey Collection.

The red light district of Fairbanks, Alaska, was once hailed as the best
in the West. In older cities farther south, patrons of houses of ill
repute kept an eye on their wallets or lived to regret not doing so, but in
the early gold rush town of Fairbanks there was no worry. A customer

simply handed his gold poke to a lady of the evening, who took only what was fair and guarded the rest with her life. The honor of Fairbanks prostitutes was such that miners sometimes left gold with them for safekeeping. And many sporting women financed prospectors, playing a major part in developing this frontier.[1]

Fairbanks's restricted district was innovative in that its residents had a chance to buy the houses in which they worked—an option not generally afforded ladies of the night, almost universally the victims of rent gouging. The unusually progressive Fairbanks City Council also outlawed pimps,[2] making it possible—perhaps for the first time under the American flag—for the average woman without wealth to become truly independent.

The Fairbanks Line, or "Row" as it was called early on, was established in 1906 during a continuation of the turn-of-the-century Klondike gold rush that attracted about 200,000 stampeders to the Far North.[3] Ironically, the Line flowered, along with similar experiments in other frontier settlements like Dawson and Nome, during one of Western society's most zealous campaigns against prostitution. In what would later be called the Progressive Era (1900-1918), churchmen and reformers attacked the "Social Evil" with committee reports, surveys, studies, sweeping legislation, and police action.[4] Yet despite national crusades to halt the sale of love, gold rush settlements throughout Alaska and Canada quietly experimented with quasi-legal red light districts with considerable success.

In the mid-1890s, outside the gold-rich northern territories, times were tough. Financial panics had paralyzed industry and thrown millions out of work. Coxey's Army of hungry and homeless had marched on Washington, D.C. There had been riots in Chicago railroad yards and protests in the Pennsylvania coal fields, but the depression was worldwide and enduring. So international headlines were made when, in July of 1897, two ships carrying the first of the successful Klondike miners (who took their moniker from the mispronounced Indian name of the Yukon River near Dawson) docked in Seattle and San Francisco with more than two tons of gold.

Stampeders flooded north: professional miners fresh from diggings in Australia and South America, hopeful amateurs from all over the world, Americans from every state. John Muir, a naturalist who knew well the hardships of the harsh subarctic region where the gold had been found, labeled them a "horde of fools," but there was more to this rush than dodging the depression or risking one's neck for money.

Richard O'Connor, who spent many hours with old Klondike hands, saw it as a dash for freedom. "Never before or since have so many American men had such a hell of a good time, without the perils of war, provided they stayed fairly healthy and had a fair amount of luck," he declared in *High Jinks on the Klondike*. "Back home they had been singing, 'There'll Be a Hot Time in the Old Town Tonight,' but the Klondikers knew what a pallid falsehood that was; the 'hot time' was to be found right where they were, far removed from Victorian restraint and the lavender delicacies of their womenfolk."[5]

With women agitating for suffrage and contesting the double standard whereby men were allowed to sow their "wild oats" while those of the "fairer sex" were considered ruined if they were sexually promiscuous, O'Connor suggested the mass migration north was a "flight from home, wife, and mother."

Not only were Alaska and the Yukon Territory isolated from polite society by thousands of miles and lack of timely communication, but they were also amazingly self-sufficient—not only gold-rich but boasting enough natural resources that men could live off the land if Dame Fortune failed to smile at their diggings. And although this was the largest gold rush in the history of North America, if not the world, the Far North's population remained so small that its moral lapses were of little concern to administrators in Washington, D.C., and Ottawa.

Even normally sober, conservative citizens were capable of squandering hundreds of dollars on wine, women, and song when caught up in the excitement of the remote gold rush communities.

". . . The problem is, without doubt, that an atmosphere of vice and of license exists in Dawson which amounts to contagion, and, under its influence, men [are] not really themselves," philosophized Mrs. La Belle Brooks-Vincent, a stampeding "businesswoman" (with an interesting police record) who penned a melodramatic history titled *The Scarlet Life of Dawson and the Roseate Dawn of Nome*. "Vice, in its overpower, exercises a hypnotic influence that paralyzes the judgment and neutralizes the more refined tastes. This is proved by the fact that some men do publicly in Dawson what they could not be induced to do privately outside. Steamers have stood at their wharves in Dawson, their decks disgraced by conduct on the part of departing passengers which the same persons would disavow outside. The same crowd would land in Seattle with utmost decorum."[6]

Given the fact that about 80 percent of the citizens of early gold rush settlements were male, it is not surprising prostitution was viewed as a "necessary evil." Obviously "wedded bliss" was not an option for everyone, and therefore could not provide much-needed sexual restraint in the face of such a heavy gender imbalance.

While those embracing "The Progressive Era" outside the territory blamed the "Social Evil" for America's moral decay, attempting to outlaw prostitution as a national menace,[7] founding fathers in the Far North found legitimizing that institution a practical solution, not only to satisfy the natural lust of most citizens but to protect "respectable women" from the potential violence of a woman-hungry society.

Nor was there much opposition from the female contingent of those early frontier settlements. Most women observed the constraints of the late Victorian Era, which dictated that a whalebone corset, at least two ankle-length petticoats, and high-buttoned shoes were the uniform for proper feminine decorum, even while bucking high seas and struggling through icy mountain passes. But the emerging Women's Rights Movement was already proving effective. Many women had enjoyed freedom when left to fend for themselves during the Civil War. The Industrial Revolution made it possible (and mildly profitable) for women to work outside the home.[8] The male domination of the Victorian Era was being challenged, and women of the Klondike gold rush challenged it just by being there, despite their conventional trappings.

Female motives for coming north were mixed, according to Klondike veteran O'Connor: ". . . some of them [were] intent on profit, others on sharing the risks of their men, still others gallantly determined to prove themselves as men's equals; few of these were eager to be placed on any sort of pedestal."[9]

Women rushed north for the same reasons men did, according to writer Frances Backhouse—because they were seeking wealth or adventure or both. While adventure was there for all who sought it, wealth was hard to come by. There were two approaches to making a Klondike fortune: mining gold or mining the miners. The first was less accessible to women because it required brute strength and because polite society disapproved of an unmarried woman staking claims, while a wife was expected to file in her husband's name.[10]

Therefore a large percentage of early female arrivals were either prostitutes or professional entertainers who supplemented their incomes through the trade. An 1899 police census of Dawson showed 3,659 men to

786 women. The town had dozens of dance halls and, while estimates are unreliable, about 400 prostitutes were thought to be working the area. Today's feminists question this high count, arguing that many more "respectable" women were among the stampeders than were given credit, but there could have been no less than 150 prostitutes early on, since that's how many the police assessed with mild fines during one single sweep of the Dawson red light district in 1898.[11] Even that conservative count reflects a serious shortage of respectable women.

Nor did everyone within those hallowed ranks *remain* respectable for long. Some women were tempted by the unusually high wages of sin and the fact that few people back home would ever learn how their gold rush fortunes had been made. Others turned to prostitution out of necessity.

Jeremiah Lynch in his autobiography claimed cynically that "some women had a history and some not before they [came] but all had a history after arrival. There was no honest occupation for women. Many went professionally as housekeepers to miners who were rich enough to employ one, but it was only another name."[12]

However, one must look carefully at women's status in society at the turn of the last century to understand the desperation they must have felt when left on their own without resources. In many states the legal age of consent was ten years old, which allowed men to sexually exploit young girls. Business transactions, including purchasing property with money belonging to a wife, were automatically conducted in a husband's name. Considered the "weaker sex," females were discouraged from seeking higher education and generally excluded from lucrative jobs where they might compete with men. The Industrial Revolution only recently had made female independence possible, but those who sought it were paid inferior wages for horrendously long hours of dull, boring work. Studies done during the period indicate that while urban girls needed a minimum of eight dollars per week to live on their own, the minimum wage was only six dollars a week—and the gap was even wider in the Far North.[13]

In *The Lost Sisterhood: Prostitution in America 1900-1981*, Ruth Rosen warns, "When I look closely at the life stories of poor women during the early years of this century, I am struck again and again by most prostitutes' view of their work as 'easier' and less oppressive than other survival strategies they might have chosen. The statement that prostitution offered certain opportunities and advantages for some women, however, should not be interpreted as a positive or romanticized assessment of the life of a prostitute. *Instead it should be read as an indication of the limited range of opportunities that early twentieth-century women faced in their daily struggle for economic, social and psychological well-being."*[14]

Some single, respectable women did exceptionally well during the Klondike rush—women like Belinda Mulrooney, who made a fortune in the hotel trade and even more by investing in mining; Martha Black, who got her start running a successful sawmill; and numerous laundresses who scrubbed their way to small fortunes.[15] But most female entrepreneurs had capital or male backers or both. Without support, it was almost impossible for a woman to survive on the straight and narrow.

Earning one's living by prostitution was dangerous, both mentally and physically, but the odds of survival for those who entered the trade during the Far North gold rushes were improved over years past. A harsh but reliable treatment for syphilis recently had been invented, and knowledge of birth control was improving. Many prostitutes in the North had the benefit of health inspections which, combined with the region's complete isolation for much of the year when the severe winters shut down easy transport, greatly simplified disease control. And most could count on police protection.

In addition to good money, prostitutes were given an edge in the Far North. "For a number of years during the earlier part of the Klondike and Nome excitement, such women were encountered everywhere. Since they always had plenty of money, the best accommodations on the steamers and in hotels were reserved for them," observed geologist Alfred Brooks, who traveled to all the stampedes. "This condition made it very trying for the better class of women to travel."[16]

And, while mainstream society condemned women of easy virtue, hordes of miners were more than grateful for their companionship or just a chance to watch them from afar. In one classic photo of a crowd waiting outside the Dawson post office, not a single female form can be spotted in a solid sea of men. Nor did conditions improve much in the decade that followed.

"I don't think I had ever seen so many men before. The dock was packed with them: tall, ruddy-faced, broad-shouldered men mostly, all of them young or in their early prime, and in every conceivable kind of costume," wrote Laura Berton, recalling her arrival at Dawson in 1907. "There were miners in mukluks and mackinaws, jumpers and parkas, surveyors in neat khaki togs, Englishmen in riding britches, police officers in immaculate blue and gold, police constables in the familiar Mountie scarlet, and on the edge of the throng clusters of Indians in beaded skin coats and moccasins. There were perhaps only a dozen women on the dock."[17]

Early prospectors were not anxious to bring their wives to virtually unexplored subarctic territory. Just getting to the Klondike was a formidable task, even for those who were fit. The overland route demanded more than thirty miles of hiking through mountain passes, then a 500-mile trip over lakes and down the Yukon in rafts, over two sets of fearsome rapids. Or stampeders could take the supposedly easier but more time-consuming and expensive 1,600-mile "all water" route to the Yukon River via St. Michael, Alaska, a long sea voyage under incredibly crowded conditions. Either way, women—then universally considered the weaker sex—were warned away, so strong motivation was a prerequisite for the trip.

"Girls were very scarce in that country, and if a man wanted to get married he took no chances with time," observed Anna DeGraf, who in 1894 pioneered Chilkoot Pass at age fifty-three in an unsuccessful search for her son, and later lived in all the major gold camps. "Even a woman past the heyday of youth was not exempt," she wrote. "It was that way all through Alaska and Yukon Territory. A girl would come in on a boat and sometimes be engaged, or even married, within a week. If she was not, it was not on account of lack of proposals."[18]

It may seem astonishing that so many women chose prostitution over the legitimate option of matrimony, until that choice is viewed in the realistic context of the era. "All too often, a woman had to choose from an array of dehumanizing alternatives," Ruth Rosen pointed out, "to sell her body in a loveless marriage contracted solely for economic protection; to sell her body for starvation wages as an unskilled worker; or to sell her body as a 'sporting woman.' Whatever choice, some form of prostitution was likely to be involved."[19] And since only a small percentage of prospectors actually hit pay dirt, marriage was not usually the soundest economic option for women who had come north in search of wealth.

A few disgruntled gold rush participants gave Far North prostitutes short shrift. Retired stampeder E. C. Trelawney-Ansell bitterly insisted that "of all the predatory, gold-digging, disease-eaten, crooked female devils this side of hell, the worst were in the Klondike in the early days."[20] Writer Cy Martin, echoing others he had researched, declared that "a Dawson City girl did not need good looks. She needed stamina, a cold, calculating eye, and utter ruthlessness."[21]

Yet James Wickersham, an Alaska district federal judge with a no-nonsense stance on crime, spoke surprisingly well of this group. "The sporting women were of a more robust class than usual among their kind, hence there were fewer cases of venereal disease among them," he wrote in *Old Yukon*. "The women were also younger, more vigorous and independent than those of the same class in the older, more crowded communities in the states. . . ."[22]

The best possible accounts of the good time girls and their lives would come from the women themselves, but such personal glimpses are extremely rare. As far as we know, only two prostitutes published accounts of their adventures in the Far North.[23] The majority, however, had everything to gain from remaining anonymous and keeping their opinions to themselves.

What we do know about these women comes from census, cemetery, court, and police records; government reports; newspaper stories (which varied in accuracy and were too often prompted by publicity-seeking theater and dance hall performers); and personal accounts from those who claimed to have known them—most of whom virtuously denied all carnal knowledge.

As for the recollections of stampeders on which this book often relies, it must be remembered that most were recorded in later years when memories sometimes blur harshness with romance. However, one fact is certain: restricted districts flourished in the Far North for five decades. When they were finally closed, it was by the federal government, not by local vote. So it is safe to speculate that the gold stampeders' candid approach to prostitution worked well for the majority of citizens, who either backed or ignored the institution instead of campaigning against it.

Elmer John "Stroller" White, who lamented the passing of the era, best sized up its vitality in a column he wrote for the *Whitehorse Star* in 1912:

"The spirit of '98 is still extant all over the Yukon, but it takes more than three cents to the pan to awaken it. Back then good and reliable men, horny-handed sons of toil, many in moccasins, others in hob-nailed boots, would indulge in the 'long, juicy waltz' at three o'clock in the afternoon as readily as they would when the gloaming gloamed several hours later. Daylight next morning would find them promenading to the bar with more gusto than can now be found within the entire Klondike watershed to say nothing of Livingston and Kluane.

"Never again in the Yukon will dance halls advertise 'Fresh cheechako girls, just in over the ice.'"[24]

1

Pioneering Prostitutes

SLIM PICKINGS AND TOUGH TRAILS

The Far North has two histories, a secret one in which—just like life—anything goes, and a conventional "on the record" version where propriety is prerequisite for starring roles. So credit for making the harsh frontier more livable and civilized is generally given only to a handful of "respectable" female pioneers. Emilie Tremblay proudly claimed the honor of being the first white woman to take the Native route over Chilkoot Pass to the great northern gold fields. A very respectable twenty-one-year-old French Canadian bride, in 1894 she had followed her husband, Pierre-Nolasque, to Miller Creek in Alaska, about 200 miles north of Fortymile.[1] Church historians gave Mrs. T. H. Canham credit for being the first white woman into Yukon Territory, which she and her husband, an Anglican missionary, crossed during their five-month journey to Tanana Station to establish a mission in the summer of 1888.[2] Charlotte Bompas, wife of the Anglican bishop at Buxton Mission, was presented the gift of a splendid gold nugget by Fortymile miners in 1894 for being the "first white lady who has wintered among us."[3]

All these "firsts," however, actually belonged to a well-known prostitute, "Dutch Kate" Wilson, who beat Mrs. Canham by one full year and Bompas and Tremblay by six. Traveling on her own initiative in 1887, she exhibited both fortitude and feminine whimsy.

THE DUTCH KID

Federal Judge James Wickersham saved a photo of this Far North beauty, noting only her nickname and the fact that she later became a nurse. She may also have been Dutch Kate, the first good time girl to brave Alaska's rugged Interior.

ASL, Wickersham Collection, PCA 277-1-186.

Kate Wilson's trip over Chilkoot Pass was recorded by William McFee, who the following year would become the first man to bring in horses via that route.[4] Her personal and financial arrangements with the small party of prospectors who accompanied her are not known, but John Rogers, a Yukon miner who fell in with them on the lower Yukon, clearly identifies her as "one of those poor, fallen women who are often found casting their lot with the mining class," adding with disapproval that "the poor creature, in order to better enable her to undergo the hardships of the trip, had donned male attire."

Yet, to Rogers's bemusement, just before reaching a large, isolated Native village, Kate "arrayed herself in her finest apparel, powdered her face, and arranged her bangs in her most bewitching style."[5]

The Indians had never before gazed upon a pale-faced woman, "and this apparition of loveliness had an astonishing effect upon the gentle creatures," Rogers conceded. "They greeted her with exclamations of delight and the Chief detained her at the boat until the women and children could run to the lodges with armloads of their wild goat wool blankets which they spread for Kate to walk upon the whole distance to the village."

Kate had difficulty evading the persistent demands of the old chief, who "pressed her to share his lodge and the exalted position as chieftain of a great tribe. This unfortunate woman had a series of adventures during the summer that would read like a romance," Rogers reported, leaving the reader hanging for details.

⁂

Prostitutes were usually the first women to reach early gold rush sites, but the Far North had been slow to attract them. Although Alaska was always wonderfully rich in natural resources, in the century that followed the Russian discovery of 1741 it offered little market for the sale of virtue. Early wealth in the form of sea otter and fur seal skins went to Russian freebooters, who initially took Native women by force. The majority of the invaders were Siberian outcasts with no motivation to return to their mother country, and most settled in the areas where they hunted with Native crews, ultimately becoming accepted by the locals and marrying in.

Whaling and sealing crews from many other nations followed, but few spent much time ashore in any one location. Nor was there a major center for the fur traders who spread throughout the country. And while some outsiders made romantic alliances, they tended to favor legal or quasi-legal marriages with Natives as had the Russians, because in addition to their charms, Indian and Eskimo women were adept at living off the rugged land and could help them survive.

Native women, whose societies openly accepted human sexuality, occasionally "traded" their favors, but there was no shortage of wives, no stigma in divorce, and little ready cash. Thus prostitution as we know it did not exist in the Far North until Alaska was purchased by the United States. Even then it was slim pickings for professionals because of low population density and a decline in the lucrative sea mammal fur business. About the only ready cash came from the American military, a minor presence on a tight budget.

"In spite of the total absence of any kind of serious work, and consequently earnings, almost all of Sitka [the capital] gets drunk daily, is unruly, fights, and so on. Another contamination is raging here, not any less than inebriation—that is chasing the women," lamented Stephan Mikhailovich Ushin, a Russian clerk who stayed in the largest city in the Far North—population about 500 with 250 soldiers—after the Alaska purchase in 1867. "Prostitution is spreading here very rapidly and thanks to this development the social life does not have a family order. Until the arrival of the Americans, and especially of their soldiers, there was here some kind of balance in this respect, but with the raising of the American flag, the entire life of Sitka has been refashioned to the detriment of the whole population."[6]

Most of the American women in the area were married, for there was little to lure single women several thousand miles from civilization into country where the only real economy was minimum wages paid to a small detachment of soldiers, soon to be withdrawn. The troops moved south in 1871, and gold would not be discovered in paying quantities for nearly another decade.

The first prospectors in the Far North were described as a breed of lonely, restless men. "The vanguard of them came in time through Sitka and Wrangell to the Stikine, and followed that river inland into Robert Campbell's unhappy, hungry country [northwestern Canada]," Allen Wright wrote in *Prelude to Bonanza*. Since the California rush of 1849, these men had drifted north through the mining camps of Arizona, Colorado, Nevada, and Idaho.[7]

Footloose, driven by "gold fever," few were the marrying kind. Most were reconciled to living without women, since success eluded them and prospects took them not only far from "civilization" but beyond Native population centers as well. Those inclined to matrimony generally took Native wives, who were used to a migratory lifestyle and knew how to live off the harsh land.

An unfortunate exception was James M. Bean, who brought his wife to help set up a trading post at Harper's Bend on the Tanana River in 1878. Local Athabascans, unhappy with the Beans' prices, lay in wait for the couple, ambushing them at their campfire one night. James Bean managed to escape, but Mrs. Bean was murdered, and apparently neither the government nor Mr. Bean himself made any attempt at reprisal.[8]

While few females cared to follow in Mrs. Bean's bloody footsteps into the Interior, several minor rushes occurred in British Columbia, reached via the former army post of Wrangell on Alaska's southeastern coast. This community spasmodically supported a few professional prostitutes, but most of the females there were Indian women, who were often brutally assaulted by the men.

"In 1877 and 1878 several hundred miners from the British mines in the Cassiar district came down to Fort Wrangell to spend the winter, and spend their earnings of the summer in intemperance, gambling, and licentiousness," stated a congressional report.[9] "They turned the place into a perfect pandemonium, debauching the Native women. They went into one Native house, made the Indian woman drunk, and then set fire to the house without any effort to rescue her from the flames, so that she was burned to death."

Wrangell was quickly upstaged by a major gold discovery on Gold Creek in the Silverbow Basin (about 150 miles north on the same coast), which led to the founding of Juneau in 1880. Diggings near this Alaska port at the headwaters of Gastineau and Lynn Canals were so productive that a "beer tent" immediately went in business in nearby Miner's Cove, followed by establishment of the Missouri (later named "The Louvre"), which was Alaska's "first and finest saloon." James Carroll, Alaska's first mailboat captain and later a delegate to Congress, bought the Occidental Saloon (established there in 1881), decorated it with mirrors, and turned it into the Crystal Palace and Ballroom, which became the centerpiece for Alaska's first major red light and bootlegging district. According to early accounts, liquor was brought into the Palace (which was built on pilings) through a trapdoor in the floor at high tide, while upstairs ladies of the

JUNEAU

The scene of one of Alaska's earliest gold rushes, Juneau was a well-developed
town by the time of the Klondike strike. Its sheltered anchorage made it a
gateway city to the interior of Alaska and Canada.

UW #18027.

evening entertained in "Kinsington Rooms," which actually remained in
operation until 1954.[10]

An 1887 newspaper account listed the assets of the town as "forty
white ladies and 1,000 dogs,"[11] and occasional discreet referrals were made
to "ladies" from visiting variety shows and dance halls.

Miners kept early gold strikes relatively quiet, not wanting competition, but rumors of extraordinary prospects in the Interior began to circu-
late. Chilkoot Pass, the Indian route into this country, had been blocked
by hostile Tlingits until 1880, when the U.S. Navy helped negotiate safe
access for miners.[12] Several prospectors who also traded furs—Edmund
Bean, Arthur Harper, Napoleon "Jack" McQuesten, William Moore, and
Joseph Ladue—scouted the country via both the pass and river routes, and
also financed others to prospect the vast, unexplored region. Yet although
Jack McQuesten was headquartered for years at Fort Reliance, only six
miles from the later site of gold-rich Dawson,[13] no major strike would be
made there for another decade. Frustrated, McQuesten abandoned that
area in 1887 and moved about seventy miles west to Fortymile, where two
brothers named Day began panning out about $200 a week.[14]

The Fortymile River proved treacherous, taking at least seven lives during the initial stampede.[15] Food was so scarce that some worried about starvation. Unlike Southeast Alaska with its relatively mild climate, in Fortymile country winter claimed eight months of the year, with heavy snows and temperatures that dropped as low as 70 degrees below zero and routinely hung in at -50 Fahrenheit.

Yet, at last, there was incentive for white women—both those who were respectable and those who were not—to move north. Gordon Bettles, traveling with George "Tuck" Lambert, one of the Fortymile discoverers, found "Dutch Kate" Wilson ensconced there in the spring of 1888, and noted that she was the first white woman to reach the newly built Canadian boomtown.

"She had come in the summer of 1887 via the summit and had landed one ton of provisions, expecting to remain for some time," he wrote. "After her experience in the winter of '87-'88, she decided to dispose of what remained of the ton of provisions she had landed with and return to Dyea."[16]

Bettles reported that men in the area were panning from twenty to one hundred dollars per day, and he gave no inkling of what had discouraged the seemingly unflappable Kate Wilson. About 250 men had been in the makeshift camp of log hovels the summer she arrived. Fifty wintered over, and any man who did not have gold to purchase a winter's supply of food by August 1 had been allowed to set up his rocker on paying claims.[17] Obviously this economy could have supported at least one prostitute, but then it was a rough camp, answering only to miners' law.

Whatever Kate's reason for wanting out—the tough crowd, personal reasons, or perhaps just the rotten living conditions and fearsome climate—she had sold all but ten pounds of beans by the time Bettles returned to Fortymile after losing his own outfit. "We bought the beans and sometime later she left for outside," he noted.[18]

When Kate's mining companions descended the Yukon that fall, they had difficulty obtaining passage on the revenue cutter that visited St. Michael. According to one Oregon newspaper account, the captain of that U.S. government ship "absolutely refused the girl passage and she was left on the bleak Arctic shore at the mercy of the Indians and the missionaries. The following spring a sealing vessel which sprang a leak off the mouth of the Yukon and put into harbor for repairs, picked her up, and she returned to Southeastern."[19]

That Kate Wilson survived to pursue other ventures is borne out by a later newspaper account about the town of Douglas (near Juneau), recalling when "Dutch Kate's dance hall and the little Friend's Mission on the hill contended with grim aloofness for the grip on the souls of men."[20] And Kate may well have gone north again, for in the Wickersham Collection there is a photograph of a beautiful Dawson prostitute known only as the "Dutch Kid." The usually thorough Judge James Wickersham, perhaps purposely, included no last name in his caption, but noted with satisfaction that the woman had done well enough in her trade to go back to school and become a nurse.[21]

The tempo of the gold rush picked up in the Interior when Fortymile miners began moving to Circle, an American boomtown with better prospects, some 200 miles northwest. Established in 1892 following gold discovery by two Creole Natives that produced $400,000 during its first season, Circle City soon became the largest log cabin town in the world.[22]

Its success spawned the Far North's first bona fide demimonde, that strange "half world" of dance hall girls, legitimate actresses, and prostitutes, women who elsewhere would have been relegated to the outskirts of society but in that nearly wifeless community became the center of the social whirl. Theatrical promoter George T. Snow, a dedicated family man, may have inadvertently introduced its first contingent when he imported a troupe of "dance hall girls" to Circle from San Francisco.[23] Others began to trickle in from Juneau to work both Circle and Fortymile.

"These women had a hard time in the wilds of the subarctic forest, but they were also amply rewarded by the miners for the 'display of their talents,'" noted historian Michael Gates. "They were certainly a change from the Native women, to whom most of the miners were accustomed. One of these women boasted of receiving a gold nugget from a miner for agreeing to have a date with him. To her embarrassment, the nugget weighed out at a value of eighty-five cents, and she was forever after known as 'Six Bits.' Another, the youngest of the troupe, was lovingly known as 'The Virgin' because, the miners thought, she had actually seen one."[24]

Anna DeGraf, whose arrival in 1895, just before the dance hall girls, swelled the number of respectable women in Circle to eight, noted that white men sometimes "purchased wives from the chief of the [neighboring] tribe, giving provisions and blankets in exchange. Some of the young girls were sold when they were twelve years old, and many of them had sweet faces."[25]

Anna DeGraf voiced concern that, by attracting the attention of local men, the showgirls caused otherwise faithful husbands to neglect their Native wives. However, the outsiders also became the focus of violence and exploitation that previously had been committed mainly against Native women.

Anna once protected a dance hall girl from a gang of six miners, wielding a gun to stand them off. The girl had angered the men by objecting when they began to "roughhouse" in her cabin. "Because she protested, they had set her on her cook stove, which was red hot," Anna recounted, "... as a result she was painfully burned and was groaning and suffering terribly." And, although Anna was fifty-six at the time, the attractive seamstress barely escaped molestation herself.[26]

Early accounts show that Circle "miners' courts" sometimes dealt unfairly with women of the night, and the American government provided no protection for them. However, one reason the whores had been attracted to the camp in the first place was because of its lawlessness. Their pimps, the bar owners, gamblers, and confidence men—even the miners themselves—preferred Circle because, unlike Fortymile, it wasn't under the jurisdiction of Canada's watchful Northwest Mounted Police. With the enthusiastic patronage of this pioneer underworld, the American camp grew sophisticated enough to be called "the Paris of the North."[27]

"Of course, few miners on the Yukon River in the mid-1890s had seen Paris recently," history professor Terrence Cole observed dryly. "After one winter in the arctic bush, however, when a prospector discovered a town with about 1,000 residents, 300 sod-roofed log cabins, several two-story buildings, twenty-eight saloons (including one with a pool table and a billiard table), eight dance halls, a free circulating library of 1,000 volumes (including a complete set of the Encyclopedia Britannica), a brewery, a log schoolhouse with a female schoolteacher, a barber shop, a local debating society, an opera house, and most of the twenty white women who lived in the entire Yukon Valley, he might well cherish the memory of the first time he saw Circle City on a spree."[28]

Circle was, in reality, a rather dismal, primitive place with outrageously high prices, inadequate supplies, no running water, electricity, or sanitary facilities, and no easy way out eight months of the year. Yet there was good money to be made—far more than in the depression-ridden world outside—and things could only get better. A bigger gold strike was coming. The old-timers who had seen prospects improve steadily for a

CIRCLE CITY
Called the "Paris of the North," this Alaska outpost was rough-hewn
with very few amenities in its early years. The population, gathered for this photo
at Jack McQuesten's trading post, was mostly male.
UW #899.

quarter of a decade were even more certain of it than the wildly optimistic
newcomers.

"No, Henry, you stay here, somebody is going to make a big strike
here soon for sure," aging trader Jack McQuesten assured a friend.[29]
Excitement bordering on hysteria was in the frozen air. Many had mortgaged their futures and risked everything, including their lives, to wager
that the big one was coming. And—gamblers all—they were right!

It seems fitting that many of those who had endured hardship and
deprivation to survive in the Far North would be there in the summer of
1896, ready to take advantage of the strike of the century in Dawson. Jack
McQuesten quickly set up shop in the budding boomtown, within walking
distance of where he had unsuccessfully established Fort Reliance in
August of 1873, and shortly thereafter retired to California with his
Athabascan wife and daughters, a wealthy man.[30]

"Swiftwater" Bill Gates, so unsuccessful at prospecting that he had no
money for a grubstake, was slinging hash in a Circle restaurant when he

overheard two customers talking about the Dawson strike. Leaving their dirty dishes in the sink, he headed upriver, where he secured rights to a claim worth more than a million.[31]

Former fruit farmer Clarence Berry, who'd prospected for years with little success, happened to be on duty as a bartender at Bill McPhee's Saloon when Antone Stander, an Austrian who had just staked on Eldorado, was refused credit at the Alaska Commercial store. By providing the needed groceries, Berry became Stander's partner and was on his way to becoming one of the most successful Klondike Kings—and one of very few who would parlay their earnings into an enduring fortune.[32]

Harry Ash, a Circle dance hall operator, hauled his piano (on which most of his girls had scratched their names with hat pins) to Dawson and averaged $3,000 per day in the profitable new location.[33] George Snow's Dramatic Company with "The Virgin," "Six Bits," and the lovely Gussie Lamore immediately headed for the new boomtown, where the talented actor/producer would make more money in gold than he did in theater.[34]

Credit for being the first white woman on the scene was claimed by Lotta (a.k.a. Lottie) Burns, a pioneering prostitute who had come to Circle from Fortymile in the first wave. Few who knew her begrudged her the honor, but most were bemused at her self-styled title, "Mother of the Klondike," for she was not exactly the motherly type.

Belying the stereotype of the hooker with a heart of gold, Lottie Burns was, by all accounts, an unabashed opportunist. She had good looks and charm enough to beguile an enamored steamboat captain out of $500 for her initial "grubstake," and was said to have delighted in ruining men.[35] In 1896, one year after her arrival in Circle, Lottie was found guilty of defrauding another prostitute, but managed to get off with a suspended sentence. Later she made big bucks purchasing mining claims at bedrock-bottom prices from men with heavy gambling debts and other hard luck sagas, which did not endear her to the Klondike's tight little fraternity of prospectors.[36] A mining camp jingle, probably composed in her honor, reflects local ambivalence:

> *Lottie went to the diggings!*
> *With Lottie we must be just*
> *If she didn't shovel tailings—*
> *Where did Lottie get her dust?*[37]

Despite her unsavory reputation—or perhaps in an attempt to repair it—Lottie gave an extraordinary interview to the *Seattle Post Intelligencer* in the fall of 1898, telling a sympathetic rags-to-riches story, a bit skewed by her omission of a few pertinent facts (like her profession) but undoubtedly laced with truth.[38]

According to this account, Lottie had a mother to support in Montreal. Tiring of the hard work she was compelled to do six days a week in a dingy factory, Lottie boldly struck out for Alaska to seek a fortune, "unmarried and alone." Without giving the trusting *P.I.* journalist any hint of how she acquired her capital, she explained that she went to Circle City to invest in town lots. "She was a shrewd woman, and by careful manipulation succeeded in getting a few thousand dollars," he reported breathlessly. "This she invested in mining property, buying mostly from owners who had gambled away their earnings and were willing to sell interests to their claims at small prices."

When the strike at Dawson was announced, Lottie immediately "bought some town lots and put money into other ventures until she had raised considerable capital," according to the article. Then she visited Montreal, where "she placed her mother in comfortable circumstances for the rest of her life."

Lottie returned to Dawson in August of 1897 with a bicycle—"the first ever in the Klondike"—which she apparently intended for her own amusement, but when miners' bids for it reached $700, she sold like the hard-headed businesswoman she had become.

During her interview, Lottie spoke with concern about the plight of the Indians "who were dying by the score on the lower Yukon" from diseases brought by the white man, particularly consumption. Then, taking full advantage of her public podium, she angrily denounced the lawlessness and confusion of mining regulations on the U.S. side of the border—perhaps remembering privately her own unhappy experiences in American miners' court.

Yet the "young mining woman," as she preferred to be called, was optimistic about the future of the Far North and savvy enough to know that the great stampede had only begun. At the time of the interview Lottie Burns was once again headed north, hell-bent on making another fortune.

2

The Great Klondike Stampede

DESTINATION: DAWSON

T he very air was electric, and the people were electric too, one hundred percent alive, whatever else ailed them. What if they had run away from wives and husbands, conventions and restrictions?" challenged Maud Parrish, who had abandoned a wealthy husband and respectable parents to become a dance hall girl during the Klondike stampede. "The call of adventure, the call of the wild, was in most of them, no matter what they were doing."[1]

The discovery that touched off this frantic excitement was made in the Klondike River valley by George Washington Carmack, a California-born ex-Marine, and his Athabascan Indian partners, brother-in-law "Skookum" Jim Mason and Jim's nephew "Tagish" Charlie. The men had prospected in Yukon Territory for nearly a decade, living off the land and earning their grubstakes by packing for miners traveling over Chilkoot Pass. Their spring cleanup in 1897 netted over $150,000, some of which they invested in other mining properties.[2] Then they went on to make a million or so more as other miners began flocking to the area.

DAWSON DANCE HALL GIRL

Her name was May Stanley and her job, dancing with miners for money,
was legal. Many such women turned to prostitution as a sideline, for dance halls were
great places for a lady of the evening to meet prospects, but simply waltzing paid well.
May's name did not appear on any playbills or on the Dawson police blotter,
so her reputation may well have been as innocent as her smile.

ASL, Wickersham Collection, PCA 277-1-183.

On July 15, 1897, twenty-five prospectors arrived in San Francisco from Dawson on the steamship *Excelsior* with more than $189,000 in gold. Two days later, the SS *Portland* docked in Seattle with sixty-eight miners carrying in excess of $1.5 million.

"A Ton of Gold!" screamed the headlines worldwide. The *Seattle Post Intelligencer* sent 212,000 copies of a special Klondike edition to other newspapers all over the country, 70,000 copies to postmasters, 6,000 to public libraries, 4,000 to city mayors, and 15,000 to the transcontinental railroads—just the beginning of publicity campaigns mounted by businessmen and politicians with a vested interest in promoting the stampede.[3]

Even better publicity resulted from the accounts of successful miners. Clarence Berry, returning on one of the first boats in, was quoted around the world as saying, "Two million dollars taken from the Klondike region in less than five months, and a hundred times that amount waiting for those who can handle a pick and shovel."[4]

In response, thousands of frenzied gold-seekers headed north. At least 200,000 people became involved, either by coming to the Klondike themselves or by backing someone else who did.[5]

Following the death of her two-month-old baby, Maud Parrish left for the Klondike without telling a soul where she was going, packing little more than a banjo. Arriving in the new boomtown of Dawson with just ten dollars, she landed a job playing in a variety show but quickly moved to the dance hall across the street, which featured "a few rooms for the amorous ones."

In her autobiography, *Nine Pounds of Luggage*, Maud Parrish proudly reported outwitting the first customer who tried to seduce her, but she obviously flirted with vice, sharing quarters with a beautiful prostitute and reveling in her newfound freedom.

"The husky, happy-go-lucky men with their gold dust gathered there, and the beautiful girls from all over the world flitted about like exotic butterflies," she wrote in later years. "Even now, I feel the *zip boom hurrah bang* of the dance hall and the 'what do we care' spirit in the air. . . . Oh, it was grand to be free and think up your own line. And up there I wasn't thought wild and headstrong and naughty."

Although Maud acknowledged the roughness of the frontier lifestyle, she found it exciting. "Toward the wee small hours, as the liquor began to take its toll of brains, usually a fight would start and likewise finish. Disputes over mining claims and the jumping of claims were often settled

THE GYPSY QUEEN

In real life this variety show entertainer was Mrs. Curly Monroe, the wife of a well-liked Dawson
bar owner. Her specialties, according to reviews, were singing and dancing.

Wickersham Collection, 1-9, courtesy of Ruth Allman.

in bars and dance halls where most of the people spent most of their time while in Dawson," she recounted. "I saw two men killed over a mining dispute the first week I was there. One was at the bar, with murder in his

"ACTRESSES" FORDING THE DYEA RIVER EN ROUTE TO THE KLONDIKE
Photographer Frank LaRouche encountered many women of the demimonde following the
gold stampede to Dawson. Most pretty young women traveling the route without husbands were
suspect, and "actress" was probably a polite cover for these determined young hikers.
UW, Photo by Frank LaRouche, #2014.

heart by the expression on his face. The other came in to kill him, and both shot each other. One died instantly, the other a few hours later."

And she found even the *legitimate* money was good. "It was two dollars a dance for a dance of a minute, dancing all night, and we got half, plus fifty cents on every drink we drank with patrons—weighed over the bar in gold dust. What a bonanza!"[6]

Grace Robinson, another entertainer, gleefully agreed. "I have worked, and worked hard, for sixteen years in the States, and it was a hand-to-mouth struggle at best, while at Dear Old Dawson, in a little over two years, I have made my fortune," she told a reporter in 1900. "The people there may be a little rough, but their hearts are in the right place, and they know how to appreciate and help a friend."

According to Grace Robinson, she "sang" her way from New York to Seattle. Her name did appear on at least one respectable Klondike theater bill, but the reporter noted that "the pretty little actress" had set out for Dawson in the summer of 1898 with Jim Donaldson, "a well-known sporting man," which would indicate broader career goals and higher earnings.

On leaving Seattle, Grace had purchased an extraordinarily fine hat, and she was determined to get that hat to Dawson or die in the attempt. She carried it strapped on her back and, when repeatedly advised to cast it aside, she would only smile and shake her head.

"The trail was so bad that it would have been impossible for me to have reached Dawson had I not received help from the outside. It was Mr. Donaldson that I owed my life to, but that is getting ahead of my story. More than once I was compelled to walk in mud and water up to my knees. Little Ruby [a sister actress who also made the trip], who has married one of the richest miners at Dawson, was the pluckiest little mortal I ever saw. No matter how hard the trail or how many difficulties we had to overcome, she never murmured or complained."

And it got worse. The party attempted to cross Lake Bennett in a thirty-two-foot boat Jim Donaldson had hammered together, and soon they were beset by a storm.

"I can remember hearing Jim say: 'It's all up, Gracie,' and then I fainted. He tied a rope around my body and subsequent events proved that my life was saved by that one act. The boat was drifting on what seemed to be a straight bluff of rocks. Just before it grounded, Jim jumped, and fortunately there was a little ledge running along at the foot of the bluff and he secured a footing upon that and pulled me through the water to him. Ruby was saved in the same manner by another gentleman of the party. The boat broke in two and sank."

While stranded on an island, Grace was overjoyed to find that her trunk with all her stage clothes, "her stock in trade," had drifted ashore. Rescue arrived three days later and she went on (with her precious Seattle-bought hat intact) to make her fortune.[7]

Basic training for the theater and saloon trade generally proved inadequate for the rigors of the overland trip to Dawson, and most pimps were less well-equipped than Jim Donaldson. The Canadian government insisted that anyone crossing its borders be equipped with 2,000 pounds of provisions, requiring many back trips if one could not afford to hire local packers. It took more than thirty miles of rugged hiking to cross the mountains from Southeastern Alaska port towns into Yukon Territory, including one brutal ascent of 1,000 feet. The steep, narrow trails over the passes were often treacherous with mud or snow and ice. Lillian Oliver, one of the few happily married women to brave the trip, described the ordeal to her ailing husband in Chicago:

"I must plead guilty of being a bit nervous, and was afraid to look back for fear I would fall to the bottom. Imagine a mountain near 4,000 feet high at an angle of 45 degrees, covered with snow to a depth of about forty feet, and which during the day gets soft, making climbing easier—but at night freezes over, making walking not only hard but fearfully dangerous. I could not get a foothold. My rubber boots caused me to slip backwards. The guide went ahead and dug holes with his heels in the ice for me to put my feet into; I took hold of his hand and with my other carried a stick, which I drove down into the snow and held onto. Every now and then I got so nervous that I had to sit down on the snow. In this way, after hard work, I finally reached the top, and though it was intensely cold, I was in a profuse perspiration. . . . "[8]

Mont Hawthorne, a former lumberjack who packed in from Dyea in 1898, recalled a dismal scene in Dead Horse Gulch. "I could see a big crowd up ahead on the trail. There must have been about seventy-five men in a bunch, all clustered around a woman and a man, oh, man was she cursing. . . . She was a saloon woman from Astoria named Tex. The fellow with her was from down there, too. He was called Jim. He was a yellow, cigarette-looking fellow," Hawthorne observed. "There he set, along the trail, puffing away on one of them six-inch holders while she cussed him out. She said he'd got her to come with him for the fun of the trip, and here she was, stuck on this mountain and he didn't care what happened to her. 'Peared like he didn't neither. He was plumb beat out and just sitting there, looking at that mountain pass, clear beyond caring about her or anything she could say to him. The freighters shoved right on through the bunch and I kept following their trails."[9]

Snowslides killed more than forty unwary travelers during the first year of the rush. Mae McKamish Melbourne Meadows, another showgirl, narrowly missed drowning in a flood and mudslide caused by the breakup of a glacial lake, despite the fact that her protector, rodeo showman "Arizona" Charlie Meadows, was six-foot-six and in terrific shape. Mae, who had a peach-like complexion and a marvelous figure, was dressing at 6:30 one morning when Charlie ran into their tent, ordering her to high ground.

"Well I wanted to stop to see the water and try to button my clothes, but Charlie kept saying to go farther up, so I had to keep on running,"

TROUSER-CLAD WOMEN DEFYING THE LAW

Yukon officials had outlawed the wearing of bloomers, and no lady wore trousers during the gold rush era. Photographer Frank LaRouche charitably labeled this shot "Actresses on the way to Happy Camp," for few of these Klondike-bound good time girls were destined for the stage.

UW, Photo by Frank LaRouche, #2049.

Mae reported in a letter to the *Santa Cruz Daily Sentinel*.[10] "If we had not got out at that moment, we would have been drowned. It was terrible. Charlie said if he had a Kadac [photograph] of me as I was running from the Sheep's Camp flood, there would not be any use of going to the Klondike, as that would be a gold mine in itself."

The flood killed three, including a cousin. The Meadowses, who were hoping to make big money with a portable bar, a restaurant, and gambling equipment, lost most of their investment but gamely started over in Dawson, where Mae (who kept her business ventures separate) was soon worth $100,000 in mining claims and Charlie made a fortune as a theater promoter.

Although Mae was an adventuress whose marriage to Charlie Meadows has never been documented, both of them came from well-heeled, respectable California families, which set them apart from many of their Chilkoot companions. J. H. E. Secretan, traveling the trail during that period, was shocked to find himself surrounded by "contraband whisky peddlers, gamblers, . . . and ladies whose briefness of skirt barely equaled the briefness of their characters."[11]

Andrew Nerland, a supplier of paint and wallpaper, while on his second trip to Dawson noted in his journal that at Lake Lindeman, "all the French women who came up from Seattle stopped there, too, and they raised regular hell."[12] Freda Maloof, an exotic dancer sometimes billed as "The Turkish Whirlwind Danseuse," was being helped over Chilkoot Pass by bartender Billie Thomas when fellow stampeders asked her to perform for them. According to the recollections of James R. Little, "Archie Burns provided performance space in his large log house at Sheep Camp. Men gathered, James Little played the fiddle, and Freda danced the hula-hula. Billie Thomas took up a collection in a gold pan that brought Freda $60 [more than double a month's salary for an ordinary working man]."[13]

The Rev. John Alexander Sinclair, who was building a Presbyterian church at Lake Bennett, often wrote to his wife about the temptations of the trail. Hungry and exhausted after a long day's portage on a trip over the pass, he stopped at the first establishment he could find, a dingy-looking barroom where the cook was off duty.

"Two fellows who had just joined us had a drink of whisky and were still leaning on the bar when in walked a brazen prostitute—rather nice-looking apart from her brass and she would get us something to eat and drink. The serpent in the woman, tempting men when we were hungry enough to be cannibals almost!"

The two men at the bar went off with the prostitute, but Rev. Sinclair stoically mushed on to the next hotel (for cold pork and beans), where he unwittingly slept with a strange woman. Waking the next morning in the stuffy loft he'd shared with twenty other men, the minister discovered that the hotel cook had discreetly placed her soft bedding in with theirs.[14]

Mrs. H. Hartshorn, traveling alone to meet her husband, found her fear of the rough, loud men on the trail compounded by the fact that she was denied lodging when hotel owners assumed she was a whore.[15] She had money and could prove she was respectable—and often money without respectability would open doors. The options of a prostitute without much cash or a male protector were decidedly more limited.

⸻

A supposedly easier alternative to the overland route was the 1,600-mile all-water route along the Pacific Coast to St. Michael, Alaska, then up the Yukon River to Dawson. Yet many vessels commissioned for the rush were unsafe, overcrowded, and vermin-infested, with rotten food. Too often they were wrecked or frozen in the river ice, but life aboard was never dull. Stampeder E. C. Trelawney-Ansell described the *Islander*, on which he embarked from Vancouver, as a floating brothel where all sorts of wild, weird, and bestial doings took place twenty-four hours a day.

"The boat was packed, jammed tight; there were Northwest Mounted Police and the crooks and riffraff of the West; there were whores, dance hall girls and gamblers; pimps, thugs and would-be gold miners; on the two decks were mules, horses, oxen, and dogs and dogs and dogs . . . " he wrote.

"The dining saloon and the so-called social hall stank of rye whisky and the cheap perfumes so favored by the 'ladies' and their awful pimps. From the cabins occupied by these prostitutes could be heard all kinds of cries from them and their men, interspersed with the clinking of glasses and popping of corks.

"Half-dressed—and often completely naked—women reeled about the passages, looking for lost cabins or for lavatories; laughing, screaming and talking in a drunken babble. Others would dance obscene dances on the dining room tables, while their bullies and pimps took the hat around for subscriptions. Heaven help the fool who watched and thought he could do so without paying."[16]

To avoid similar discomfort, the skipper of the northbound steamer *Amur*—crowded to the gunnels with fifty prostitutes among 500 passengers—put out the edict that no whore was allowed to ply her trade, much to the disgust of "Big Annie," who complained loudly.

"Indeed it's shameful, the conditions aboard this ship. But try to bear it," sympathized a fellow passenger who happened to be a preacher. "We'll be in Skagway in a little more than a week, and once there you'll see that things will be a lot better for you and the other girls."[17]

Another problem was social stigmas. Many prostitutes and actresses had the money and foresight to book staterooms early, forcing their more virtuous sisters to share accommodations or stay home. Chicago socialite Martha Black found herself quartered with a hooker and her pimp on the

Utopia, because the captain could find no other arrangement on his crowded vessel.[18] Mont Hawthorne, traveling out of Portland on the *George W. Elder* in 1898, was fascinated by this unusual social interaction.

"When the sun came out and they got on deck you could sure tell the women had been sizing each other up. The dance hall girls was dressed real fancy; I knowed a couple of them who got on with a bunch at Astoria. They were traveling with a no-account gambler from down there. It's a hard life for any girl; no matter how bold she acts you can see she ain't too comfortable around church folks. But what got me was the way them married women acted when the dance hall girls came to their end of the boat. They'd just gather their husbands up by the arm, and they'd move down to the other end of the boat, and they'd walk real straight. They were terrible skittish," Hawthorne observed.

"Only way we could have any real fun with the whole crowd together was to start running. We'd line up behind each other, and each fellow would put his hands on the shoulders of the one ahead of him. Then we'd run around and around the deck like that. . . . Even the married women that wouldn't have nothing to do with the dance hall girls when they were walking around on deck would find themselves drug into the line and all running in the same directions. Pretty soon they was laughing, too. It's a good thing for folks to learn that it takes all kinds to make a world."[19]

For those arriving by ship, the first glimpse of the brutal deprivation involved in striking it rich in the North sometimes came at St. Michael, the Pacific port on the mouth of the Yukon River. It was there that incoming stampeders on the SS *St. Paul* got a sobering view of a group of "lucky" surviving Dawson prospectors headed for the States in July of 1898 aboard the riverboat *May West.*

"Up the gangway came men in heavy winter clothes, unshaven, unwashed, with long hair and ravenous-looking faces. Then a man staggering under what looked like a huge Bologna sausage on his shoulder . . . it was gold," reported Nevill A. D. Armstrong, who was waiting to head north for the first time. "Next I saw a man without feet being carried up on another man's back. We were told that the sufferer had been on a wild gold stampede to Swede Creek, near Dawson, without taking adequate footwear. . . . Two men followed, staggering along with a square box heavily bound with strip iron; it was all they could do to carry it. This was all gold dust, over $100,000 worth.

"All the horrors of filth and physical hurt could not prevent the thrill

THE ALL-WATER ROUTE WAS POPULAR
Thousands of passengers, would-be passengers, and well-wishers crowded
Seattle docks at the start of the great Klondike strike.
UW, Wilse 531, Collection 285.

which the sight of that gold brought me," Armstrong admitted. "And there was human damage and filth aplenty aboard that tiny steamer. All the food she carried had disappeared entirely three days before. The dogs howled from hunger and the passengers were almost as primitively savage in their cravings for something to eat. There had been no opportunity for washing; the men were as dirty as the small decks—hence the atrocious odor that had spread ahead to warn us and now engulfed us suffocatingly."[20]

The last leg of the stampeder's journey was a voyage on the Yukon River, either downriver from the east or upriver from the west. Those who were strong, or persevering, or lucky, finally reached their destination: Dawson.

The town had been founded by Joe Ladue, a trader from the earliest days of Fortymile. He staked a 160-acre patch of moose pasture as a town

site near the Klondike discovery on the Yukon, imported a sawmill, and finally made his fortune. William Ogilvie, representing the Canadian government, named the town Dawson after George Dawson, a geologist who had explored the region in 1887 and predicted gold would be found there.[21]

MALE/MAIL CALL

During the early rush in Yukon Territory, it didn't take a census to determine
that the population was predominantly male. Just try to spot a female face in this
crowd surrounding the Dawson City Post Office in the summer of 1898.

NAC, Rev. Heatherington Collection, #C008396.

About 600 people mushed in over the ice during the winter of 1897, and Dawson police estimated the population at from 1,500 to 2,000, with about 5,000 in the region by the following January. In March, 7,000 would-be prospectors were camped near Lake Bennett waiting for the ice to go out,[22] and by the end of 1898 an estimated 60,000 had started for Dawson.[23] That year Dawson became the largest city in Canada west of Winnipeg.

By the time the average citizen heard about the bonanza, the best ground in the Klondike had already been staked, but determined late arrivals found good diggings nearby, in areas ignored by seasoned miners because conventional wisdom held that gold would not be found there. New discoveries—especially those by former shipping clerks, lumberjacks, and other amateurs—only fueled more Klondike dreams and enticed more newcomers.

Thomas C. Riggs, a Princeton-educated civil engineer who would later become a governor of Alaska, arrived in Dawson broke and found the town promising. "Dawson was crowded. Even at midnight the streets were hurried. The street along the waterfront was one mass of mire through which four-horse teams had been dragging their loads. . . . The wooden sidewalks were lively with men in flannel shirts. Stetsoned southerners just sitting and spitting," he recalled. "The dance halls and saloons were crowded and all we could do was look on. We had no money. Drinks were fifty cents each. Eddie [a gambling casino man from Skagway whom Riggs had fallen in with] had already gone to work for Jack Cavanaugh at the Monte Carlo. We watched him deftly dealing faro. He stood us a drink on the house.

"Mannie [Riggs's partner] found a five-dollar bill on the floor near one of the tables. We spent it on a grand meal. In the dance halls the miners were having a real time. A dance of about three minutes cost $1 here, that entitled you to a drink. . . .

"In the boxes were the Berry brothers in shirtsleeves bound with garters buying champagne at $25 per bottle. Swiftwater Bill was showing off. Charley Anderson was making up to all the women and giving them nuggets. The usual currency was gold dust at $16 to the ounce. All purchases were weighed out in the store or bar. A girl on the stage who sang a popular song was so pelted with nuggets that she had to run injured off the stage. Money meant nothing to the man who had become rich overnight. He had money and he meant to spend it in the only way he knew how.

"In the morning the streets were deserted. The men of last night were either sleeping it off or had gone back to the creeks."[24]

Nevill Armstrong, whose boat was one of the first into the "golden Mecca of the North" in 1898, painted a grimmer picture. "At first it was but a bundle of white dots on the side of a hill, but as we grew closer I began to make out myriads of cabins, huts, boats, rafts and warehouses, and then at long last we fussed up to the landing stage, there must have been a full thousand men and women of every nationality assembled there.

"All these people had spent a long and bitterly cold arctic winter in the town and the surrounding districts and were thirsting for news of the 'Outside World'; also for a chance of obtaining fresh food of some sort, as provisions became seriously short when the Yukon River froze up early in October the previous year. . . . All sorts of signs and notices were to be seen as one walked down the main muddy street or on the rickety wooden sidewalks. One sign in particular caught my eye—it was painted on a strip of white canvas stretched across the road on poles, and read as follows:

"'Charlie Brimstone—Undertaker—Bodies embalmed and shipped to the Outside.' This was not a very encouraging notice for the tenderfoot. Moreover, I found it alarmingly true that typhoid fever was rampant, the death rate being about 120 per week."[25]

Armstrong's estimate of the death rate was too high, but he was right about the threat of disease. Along the waterfront for half a mile were tiers of boats, scows, and rafts on which many people camped. Others pitched tents in ever-widening circles around the town with no regard for sanitation. Arthur Walden, a seasoned prospector visiting from Circle, won a bet with a friend by traversing the filthy main street by jumping from the carcass of one dead horse to the next. However, living conditions improved in time. The Canadian Northwest Mounted Police soon laid down strict sanitation regulations, and new arrivals included several good doctors.[26]

Overall, Nevill Armstrong's memories of the frontier settlement were bittersweet. "Wild excitements, misery, riches, debauchery, broken hearts, scurvy, frostbite, suicide; the midnight sun, the Arctic night, the Aurora Borealis, the land of gold and paradoxes—that was Dawson in '98," he wrote breathlessly.

"Entirely isolated, beyond the pale of civilization, it was entirely without one restraining influence. Vice and drunkenness became rampant. None but the staunchest characters trod the narrow path. The saloons were the only meeting places of incoming miners with their bags of gold dust; nearly everyone gathered in one or the other of the gambling saloons or dance halls by day and night—their doors were never closed.

"The saloons were always well-lighted with oil lamps. Large stoves, made out of oil drums, heated the buildings. It was the warmth, the drink and the scantily clad women that contributed to the downfall of many men."[27]

Dawson was an expensive town. The cost of living at the beginning of the Klondike rush was six dollars per day. Minimum wages for a male common laborer were eight dollars per day, but an honest, unskilled female had no chance to keep up. The average salary for housekeepers was only twelve dollars per week, plus board and room.[28] A dressmaker who put in long hours could earn about $100 a month. Cooks made about the same amount, but miners preferred to hire men for that job because they were better at cutting firewood and hauling water.[29] Clerking jobs were also generally reserved for men. Trained nurses earned only twenty-five dollars a month on a two-year contract,[30] and that profession was still looked down on as not quite respectable. Unskilled women might work in laundries at five dollars per day with board and room, or wash dishes for twenty-five dollars a week.[31]

On the other hand, a dance hall girl who did nothing more exotic than lure men to trip the light fantastic could earn forty dollars a week plus 25 percent of every drink she could hustle (at one dollar per drink). Musicians made twenty dollars a day, and girls who worked the "grand balls" after each night's vaudeville performance were paid fifty dollars per week plus commissions. Actresses, even bad ones, earned $150 a week plus 25 percent on all the drinks they could cajole customers into buying after the show. And a determined prostitute could easily make double that.[32]

Facing these economic realities, some formerly respectable women were tempted or driven into the demimonde when they reached the Klondike. Numerous accounts tell of good girls gone bad, including a dramatic letter written by the Rev. John Alexander Sinclair about his rescue from "scoundrels" of two innocent but not too bright Seattle "dining room girls" lured to Skagway with the promise of respectable jobs dancing.[33]

In his biography, *The Trail Led North*, Mont Hawthorne anguished for an honest girl from his hometown of Astoria, Oregon, who took up the trade after traveling to Dawson with her lover.

"His folks always ran him; he'd have married her before they came up there if they had let him. But she done housework, and they were uppity and made him promise not to marry her. So he sneaked her into the boat with no wedding. . . . [34]

"That was a hard winter, with the sickness and cold and running out of things. I'd lost track of them. It was just by chance I heard he was dead. . . . We [he and his friend Mac] was the only men there! But all the fancy women in town had turned out for that funeral; they seemed to be taking a real motherly interest in the girl. . . .

"I hated to see her with that crowd. But she said he'd got sick; they was out of money, and she went to work the only way she could to take care of him. The worst of it was she went into debt three thousand dollars to have him embalmed, so his worthless, pickled carcass could be sent out to his folks who was too good for her in the first place. . . . I never talked to her again, but I heard she stayed there and paid her debt." [35]

Even more heartbreaking is one report by a Dawson newspaperman. He should have been hardened by having heard a never-ending string of hard luck stories, but was moved to write sympathetically about the fall from virtue of a young German-American girl.

"Milley Lane started from Seattle last spring—we will call her Milley Lane because . . . we cannot advertise these people. She is a pretty-faced girl of German antecedents and of good reputation," he began in an account for the *Klondike Nugget*.

"The party she came in with was well fixed and had several ladies among their number. Milley was quite popular and proved herself to be adaptable and industrious. All went well as a marriage bell until Thirty Mile River was reached. A rock—a wreck—outfits all lost—a wet, shivering crowd on the bank with no provisions and hardly enough clothes on their backs to protect them from mosquitoes. Pitying passers-by bring this girl of eighteen summers to Dawson. With clothes all draggled and shabby and without a change of raiment, she sought work for three long days.

"Pocketbook and stomach empty, and employment refused, on the evening of the third day Milley found herself on the bank of the river with two courses open to her. She could either jump into the river or go to board with one of the madams in Dawson's White Chapel. Long was the matter debated in her mind, but at last the youthful love of life triumphed. Within an hour the girl was seen bathed and dressed in satins and laces, her beauty enhanced by handsome apparel and the hairdresser's art. Trail acquaintances were shocked, and when spoken to, the girl broke completely down and dissolved in tears. This is all true, happened last week and hardly forms an incident of one chapter of Dawson's history."[36]

Motherly Anna DeGraf, who sewed for theater performers, noted many innocents among them. "Hundreds of dance hall and variety show girls came in to Dawson, some for adventures, others without any idea of the temptations and hardships of that raw frontier life," she recalled. "There were among them some of the most beautiful girls I have ever seen—girls in their teens, very attractive and pleasing in their ways. In working with them, I got well acquainted with many of them and pitied and liked a number of them for they had some good qualities mixed with the bad."[37]

"Women beset the camps in the spring of '98. They were not the ordinary type of harlot but real adventuresses," recalled civil engineer Thomas Riggs. "They were strong, healthy, good-looking women. They had to be to stand the rigors of climate and trail. They were after money and they got it. There were vaudeville actresses of talent, acrobats, vocalists and just plain grafters, living in tents and advertising their wares with big posters, none of which can be quoted."[38]

Mostly, however, the country was being settled by young men, the majority of them in their prime. Lawyer John Clark remembered them as impressive. "When I first came to this camp seventeen years ago what amazed me the most was to visit the dance halls, where the people congregated, they being practically the only places where they could go to gather, and to see the great number of men, from eighteen to twenty-five years of age, physically perfect and many of them considerably in excess of six feet . . . " he recounted. "They were strong and energetic, not afraid to work and hardships meant nothing to them."[39]

Klondike newsman Elmer John "Stroller" White initially viewed this horde as less than eligible. "The majority of the single men of marriageable age—ninety years and younger—who invaded the North prior to 1900 were then and had for years been drifters," he declared.

"Many were of eastern origin and they had drifted west on attaining manhood and had then worked at many jobs and trades as they wandered from one place to another. Very few of them had much more than a spare pair of socks to show in the way of inventory at the end of any given year. With the discovery of gold in the Klondike, the farmhands, loggers, cowpunchers, clerks and others who were not permanently anchored and were able to round up the price of a ticket and a mackinaw suit headed north.

Many of them did not do any better in the Klondike than they had done elsewhere, but others struck six bits to the pan in one way or another,[40] although not necessarily at mining. And as soon as they [could, they] began to shave on Saturdays and pare their corns preparatory to engaging in the long, juicy waltz at Nigger Jim's, the Monte Carlo or another of the dance halls, these places constituting the most likely pay streak in the country when matrimony was the object."[41]

Many of these men ultimately gambled on the women who shared their Klondike adventure, and were amply rewarded, despite dire predictions from those in polite society.

"A goodly number of these women yielded to the persuasions of their favorite male customers, quit the life of the dance hall or bawdy house, and calmly settled down to a quiet home life with their husbands," Judge James Wickersham noted. "It quite frequently became my duty as judge to perform marriages for persons of that class and more often than not such marriages were successful."[42]

―――∞∞∞―――

One such match was made by the man who started it all, George Washington Carmack. The Klondike discoverer had been one of very few white men with the strength and determination to pack for hire with the Indians over Chilkoot Pass. A well-read Californian who wrote poetry for pleasure, he met his Athabascan prospecting partners while hauling 150-pound packs over the summit for his grubstake in 1885. Soon thereafter he fell in love with "Skookum" Jim Mason's older sister, who became his common-law wife. Following her death, George Carmack took up with Kate, Jim's handsome younger sister, but according to local legend it was a match more of convenience than love. Kate was given to temper-tantrums and apparently let George know when he failed to muster to the standards of her people, who were extremely well conditioned to the rugged land. They had one daughter, Graphie, born in January 1893, but their union was an uneasy one.[43]

Wealth only made things worse because George wanted to establish himself in the Seattle business community where Kate, although exceedingly handsome, was miserably uncomfortable. In her unhappiness, she developed an unfortunate fondness for alcohol, which she could not handle, and the resulting publicity proved an embarrassment. Typical is a *Seattle Times* news brief that was picked up by the Yukon papers:

DAWSON'S POLITE SOCIETY

*Parties were popular entertainment and this birthday celebration for
Mrs. Tozier and Miss O'Brien in 1900 was lavish, with properly clad waiters,
luxurious table service, and a year's supply of canned food displayed as part of the décor.
Seated next to an empty chair, left, wearing a striped tie, is George Washington Carmack,
discoverer of the Klondike lode, who was appearing in polite society for the first time
without his Native wife. Shortly thereafter, at a similar gathering, he met Marguerite Saftig,
a.k.a. Biddy McCarthy, a member of the demimonde who would become his wife.*

ASL, Wickersham Collection, PCA 277-1-199.

"Mrs. George W. Carmack, the Indian wife of the discoverer of the Klondike, who is probably the richest Indian woman in the world, was fined $3.60 by Judge Cann this morning for drunkenness. Mrs. Carmack loaded up on champagne last night, and in company with some Indian friends, made Rome howl in the Hotel Seattle. Officer Grant gathered her in, and prosecuted her this morning. She refused to tell who furnished her with champagne."[44]

In desperation, George installed Kate and their daughter at his sister's ranch in rustic Cambria, California, and traveled alone to Dawson in the spring of 1900 to dispose of his Klondike interests. Without Kate for the first time, the handsome millionaire found himself sought out for dinner parties by Dawson's elite. This group included an odd mixture of quasi-respectable women from the upper levels of the demimonde, who were well-heeled as well as "round-heeled" but not engaged in out-and-out prostitution. Among the most interesting and determined was Marguerite Saftig.

The daughter of a respectable family gone broke, Marguerite had been attracted to men early on and had married at age fourteen, but soon divorced. Under her married name of Marguerite Laimee, she had worked the mining town of Coeur d'Alene, Idaho, as an "entertainer" and then toured the camps of South Africa and Australia, where she was known as Marguerite LeGrand. She had come to Dawson under the alias of Biddy McCarthy with $2,000 in savings, hoping to win a Klondike millionaire. There Marguerite invested in a cigar store strategically located on the first floor of the Green Tree Saloon and Hotel on Dawson's main street, over which operated one of the most active whorehouses in town. Running the store positioned her to work as a madam or hustle herself on the side, as did most cigar store owners, while still keeping up a respectable front.[45]

At the time she met George Carmack, Marguerite owned prime real estate in the heart of Dawson and had accumulated far more money than could have been earned by simply selling cigars. (Later she would testify that she made $60,000 in her two years in Dawson, though that claim was probably exaggerated.) She also had been closely associated with Joseph LeGrand, a man of the underworld who made his wealth from prostitution and had followed her to Dawson.[46]

Marguerite met George in June of 1900 at a dinner party given by her respectable friends, Mr. and Mrs. Joe Collins. Then twenty-six years old, she had big brown eyes, a pretty face, an hourglass figure, and a magnificent bosom—described by one awed customer as looking like a pair of ostrich eggs under her blouse. She was dressed in high fashion, enjoyed talking business, and made herself utterly charming. If anything, Marguerite's colorful background and professional romantic skills only made her more attractive to forty-year-old George Carmack.

When he proposed that night, Marguerite knew she had found the millionaire she was looking for. She accepted without hesitation. They married four months after their first meeting—even before the settlement of a divorce suit thrown at him by his common-law wife, Kate, whose legal claims were not recognized in the States. George and Marguerite had, by all accounts, a happy and lasting union.[47]

3

Mining the Klondike Kings

NUGGETS AND NUPTIALS

⊗

F or the new millionaires of the Klondike, money had ceased to be a worry. In two hours Jim Tweed panned $4,284 worth of gold from his claim on Eldorado. Frank Dinsmore took out $24,489 in one day from Bonanza Creek. Albert Lancaster averaged $2,000 per day for eight weeks at his Gold Hill diggings. Clarence Berry netted $140,000 in his first Klondike cleanup and soon would be worth millions.[1] These men suddenly had more wealth than they'd ever dreamed of spending, with no end in sight. If a Klondike King ran out, he simply returned to his claim and dug up more gold.

Yet even for those who struck it rich, it was hard duty on the subarctic tundra, fighting isolation and loneliness in one of the coldest, darkest, and most unforgiving environments on earth. A central heating system that could cope with the bitter climate had yet to be invented. And mining was mind-numbing work, even when the end product was pay dirt.

For those with limited resources, the deprivation was even more excruciating. "The sourdoughs lay on their bunks until noon—and noon might just as well be any other time—moving painfully about only to stoke the stove or break off a chunk of rye bread, more from sheer boredom than

⊗

ONE OF THE LOVELIEST LADIES OF THE EVENING

Babe Wallace, a prostitute from Tacoma, Washington, was arrested for running a house of ill repute in Dawson in 1898 but was let off with a fine of fifty dollars. She did so well at the trade she soon purchased a piano, a nearly unheard-of luxury in the Far North. Well respected by most of the locals, she married Captain Hill Barrington, a handsome and prosperous steamboat man. Later she divorced him and left the Yukon, dying young in 1911.

Courtesy of Ruth Allman.

hunger. Many were ill with dysentery and scurvy, and worst of all, the sickening depression of futility," wrote Ellis Lucia in a telling description of winter in the gold country. "At times the men ventured into the awful bleakness to claw at the frozen ground of their claims. They returned to the drafty warmth of their cabins, holding stiffened fingers above the stove, to ask themselves aloud just why they were trapped here in this Godforsaken wilderness. . . .

"Half-crazed with cabin fever, the sourdoughs could stand it no longer. Climbing into bulky mackinaws, mukluks and fur caps, they stuffed fat buckskin pokes into their coats and headed for Dawson City. . . . It was a gay, frolicsome world, filled with fun in contrast with the awful silence of the outer wilderness. . . . Thousands in yellow gold changed hands in the gambling halls, to be lost and won again, and then to be lost once more to a pretty bit of fluff who called you honey, gave you a nice smile and a peck on the cheek, and would be your very own for the evening if you kept the champagne flowing her way. But you didn't mind, for there was plenty more of this yellow stuff where that came from. . . ."[2]

The good time girls provided welcome diversion to these lonely men, and thereby found their surest way to wealth. The two most successful legal means of acquiring a fortune in the Far North—staking claims and operating a saloon—were not open to women. Bar ownership by a female was illegal, while staking claims was not considered women's work. So many Klondike women turned to prospecting for gold in a less direct manner, noted academic researcher Bay Ryley.[3] Mining the miners became an art.

La Belle Brooks-Vincent wrote a detailed account of the techniques dance hall girls routinely used to separate men from their wealth, mainly by getting them drunk in the private boxes that surrounded every dance floor.

"She is all nerve as she enters a room and surveys the waiting crowd. . . . The dance hall girl is industrious. She is never vacillating or undecided; she is persevering. She does not flit about the room bestowing a smile here, a caress there and again a pouting neglect. When she selects her victim she stays with him. The more marked her favor, the greater his triumph. . . . He *needs* her to complete a spectacle of himself as a favored beau. . . ."[4]

These women could not have worked without the cooperation of their "victims" and the tolerance of their society. Most of the Klondike Kings had spent their lives prospecting alone in the wilds. Few had wives

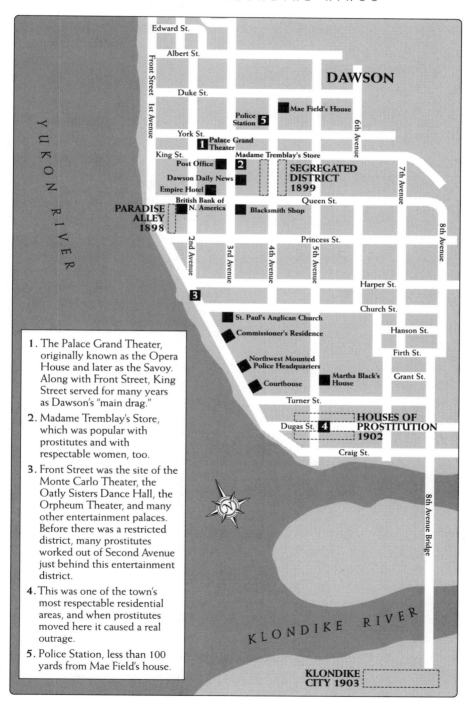

1. The Palace Grand Theater, originally known as the Opera House and later as the Savoy. Along with Front Street, King Street served for many years as Dawson's "main drag."

2. Madame Tremblay's Store, which was popular with prostitutes and with respectable women, too.

3. Front Street was the site of the Monte Carlo Theater, the Oatly Sisters Dance Hall, the Orpheum Theater, and many other entertainment palaces. Before there was a restricted district, many prostitutes worked out of Second Avenue just behind this entertainment district.

4. This was one of the town's most respectable residential areas, and when prostitutes moved here it caused a real outrage.

5. Police Station, less than 100 yards from Mae Field's house.

Thanks to Michael Gates and Mac Swaekhammer of Dawson.

or even girlfriends back home, for never before had they been considered good marriage material. Past their prime, most eagerly sought attention if not love.

"Diamond Tooth" Gertie Lovejoy, one of Dawson's most successful and outspoken showgirls, best summed up the rationale of her sister prospectors in dealing with men. "The poor ginks just gotta spend it," she observed. "They're scared they'll die before they get it out of the ground."[5]

A good case in point was Charlie "Lucky Swede" Anderson, who was duped while drunk into buying a supposedly useless claim "staked for sucker bait" that produced between $1.2 and $1.5 million. According to legend, forty-year-old Charlie became so anxious to marry a showgirl, and competition for the short, shy, balding, blue-eyed miner was so stiff, that beauteous contenders finally put him up as stakes in a poker game. The winner was actress Grace Drummond, age twenty-nine, who was living with Edgar Mizner, former manager of the Alaska Commercial Company turned gambler.[6] "Gracie," then the toast of the Monte Carlo music hall, was described as "a sophisticated and beguiling young woman with the gift of beauty and . . . the manners of a kitten and the morals of a cat." She readily agreed to dump her lover and marry the Swede if he would deposit $50,000 into her account. Charlie happily complied.

Following a big wedding officiated by Bishop Bompas of the Anglican Church on June 6, 1899, Charlie also gave his bride a tour of Europe and Mexico, $6,000 in diamonds, gold nuggets worth $1,000, a thousand pounds of gold worth $16,000, horses worth $1,500, and a home and servants in San Francisco. Then Charlie trustingly tucked $4,000 in bonds and $12,000 in gold coins into a safe deposit box for their joint use, left Gracie in California with the key, and went back to the gold fields to make more money.

The happy union did not last. When Charlie returned to his wife, she tried foisting him off on her younger sister, Maud, then locked him out of the house, according to newspaper accounts that generally favored Charlie. However, Gracie claimed that Charlie had threatened to kill her. She also complained that his idea of a good time was dropping ice-cold gold nuggets down the blouses of unsuspecting barmaids. He countered with the accusation that she had taken $63,000 from his safe deposit box—but then he moved back in with her before the divorce was final.

ST. ANDREW'S DAY BALL IN DAWSON
By 1900 Dawson was a world-class city with first-class accommodations,
where expensive ball gowns and tuxedos were a "must" for the social set, despite its
isolated location near the Arctic Circle. Although this photo was taken at 4 a.m.,
the party was still in full swing.

UAF, Bassoc Glass Plate Collection, #64-92-641.

"A very ill-suited couple," observed the Rev. George Pringle, in probably the understatement of that year. "Anderson wanted a home and children and the woman was not that kind." The court awarded Gracie $3,000 per month alimony, although it found that Anderson, who spoke broken English, did not understand the term at first.[7] Gracie moved to Los Angeles and bought a wine garden, but her alimony ceased shortly thereafter when Charlie's claim played out. She disappeared from the news, apparently returning to her hometown back east, but Charlie moved on with the stampede to Nome, where he made another fortune.

This time Charlie spent his money not on dance hall girls but on a beautiful mansion on Nob Hill, hotels, and rental property, only to lose it all in the 1906 San Francisco earthquake when his insurance company went under. Left with only five cents in his pocket, Charlie alternated between odd jobs and unsuccessful attempts at prospecting, finally ending his life as a chicken farmer. His estate totaled $1,731. Considering the downturn in his career after leaving the Far North, Charlie might well have considered Gracie one of his better investments.[8]

⸙

Grace Drummond's sister Myrtle enjoyed even more spectacular success mining miners, with less adverse publicity. The *Skagway Alaskan*, which described her as "bewitching," generously attributed her success to her dancing skills and her marriages to "Jim Hall and other noted men of sudden wealth in rapid succession."[9] Although the men in Myrtle Drummond's life were slightly more sophisticated than Charlie Anderson, most seem to have had the same desire for a "trophy" wife or mistress.

Myrtle was a trapeze performer and contortionist with a four-ring circus when she heard about the gold discoveries and headed north with the early pioneers. "She soon found that dancing in a Circle City saloon was more profitable than flying through the air and twisting herself into peculiar shapes for the amusement of young Americans," a Skagway reporter observed, "and in a short time found herself the owner of some of the best claims in the district with the entire male population and wealth at her command."

Jim Hall, a.k.a. "Arkansas Jim," struck it rich on #17 Eldorado in the first wave of Dawson millionaires, invested in the Palace Grand Theater where Myrtle performed, and gave her a $40,000 claim on Bonanza Creek as a wedding present. Following their divorce shortly thereafter, Jim remarried immediately. When his second wife died in the winter of 1899, he made headlines with his "frantic efforts" to marry yet another dance hall girl.[10] Well-meaning friends, concerned for his mental health and his future finances, briefly had Jim jailed on grounds of insanity, "forlorn and forsaken, protected by the barracks' barriers from the designing marriage offers of poke-hunting soubrettes."

At the time of this intervention, Jim was ready to exchange marriage vows with Grace "Gussie" Anderson (not Grace Drummond Anderson but the former Gussie Green, another opportunist), who also performed at his theater. "She with the trilby feet and enlarged spleen for marriage vows, it would be hard to express the depth of her chagrin and the loudness of her lamentation since others had defeated her pet plans for a profitable matrimonial alliance," the *Dawson Daily News* reported. "Her devoted Jim had done the 'grand' by not only seeking hymen at the marriage license desk, but by also making out a $10,000 check on one of the banks, drawn in her favor."

A court-appointed doctor found Jim "wanting in the virility and strength of his gray matter, and not capable of resisting the attractions of the fair sex by reason of the weakening influence caused by a protracted spree."[11] But two days later Jim was released and Gussie reclaimed him. As friends had suspected it would be, their marriage was marred by general unhappiness and hard drinking. Jim eventually committed suicide.[12]

In contrast, Myrtle Drummond, who owed her original stake to Jim Hall, was hailed by journalists in 1901 as the richest woman in the Klondike, "divorced and married many times, always getting mixed up with men of wealth." She started that year by mushing her own dog team from Whitehorse to Dawson for another stage appearance there, and it was predicted she would marry again soon.[13]

———— ∞∞∞ ————

Instead of feeling preyed upon by fortune hunters like Myrtle Drummond, most Klondike Kings viewed "poke hunting" as acceptable behavior. Since they had been driven north by the desire for wealth, they were not surprised that their female counterparts were motivated by the same goal. These men expected to pay generously for the attention of pretty women in high demand. Some bragged at great lengths about how much wealth they lavished on Klondike charmers, simply because it was one of the few ways to purchase prestige in the Far North.

Antone Stander, an Austrian who had arrived in New York City at age twenty in 1877 with just $1.75 in his pocket, paid big money to have his rags-to-riches story printed in an elegant souvenir newspaper published by "Arizona" Charlie Meadows.[14] Antone confessed frankly that actress Violet Raymond, with whom he had long been infatuated, had paid little attention to him when he was "in rough garb of the country and with few dollars in his pockets."

Violet Raymond, a prepossessing blonde, jovial in nature, with a graceful and well-developed figure,[15] had broken all attendance records at the Juneau Opera House as the "Queen of Burlesque" at age sixteen, and was paid an enormous salary to play in Dawson two years later. She was, in Antone's words, "the undisputed belle of the camp and could number her admirers by the score"[16]—and she was regarded as the personal

ILL-FATED LOVERS

*Gold king Antone Stander was so smitten with his fiancée, Miss Violet Raymond,
that he commissioned "Arizona" Charlie Meadows to announce their engagement as the
very first feature in the souvenir edition of the Klondike News, April 1, 1898. It was a real
love match, but Antone was violently jealous of his beautiful ex-burlesque queen, and his
drinking and fits of temper drove them apart. He gave most of his wealth to Violet,
dying broke while she survived in luxury to a relatively old age.*

Klondike News, April 1, 1898, courtesy of Earl Beistline.

property of Max Endleman, the aging proprietor of the Gold Hill Hotel,
who had brought her and her sister into the country.

Antone, however, had youth and good looks on his side, as well as
money. After the wash-up that made him rich in the summer of 1897, he
bought up all the diamonds in Dawson and presented them to Violet in a
flashing necklace that reached nearly to her knees. He followed up with
$20,000 in gold dust, a lard bucket full of odd-shaped nuggets, and $1,000
a month in spending money.

"They will join hearts and hands in July and spend their honeymoon in the Orient, visiting Japan and China, and will return to the little brown cot on the hill before making a trip to Paris to the Exposition," concluded the vanity newspaper piece, published on April 1, 1898.

It turned out to be a love match, but Antone's possessiveness soon drove them apart. As pocket money for their honeymoon trip, he stored one thousand pounds of gold in their stateroom of the *Humbolt*, but then he was afraid to leave his treasure to tour the ports with his new wife. "It would be hard to tell which [he] guards more jealously—his bride or his gold," a reporter for the *Examiner* wrote.[17]

Antone's solution seemed to be to give the gold to Violet bit by bit, until it was all gone, observed writer Pierre Berton, whose family knew most of the Klondike old-timers. "Antone Stander drank part of his fortune away; his wife deserted him and took the rest, including the Stander Hotel, which he had built in Seattle with profits from his claim," Berton recounted. "One cannot entirely blame her, for when Stander was drinking he was subject to crazy fits of jealousy; on one occasion he tried to cut her to pieces with a knife."

Antone Stander headed north again in search of another Klondike, working his passage by peeling potatoes, but got no farther than Southeastern Alaska. There he survived on the charity of the government Pioneer Home before being evicted for drunkenness. For Antone it was all downhill from there,[18] while Violet hung on to their money, spending her final days in luxury and comfort.

———

Two gold-mining ship captains, Sid and Hill Barrington, also became smitten with gold camp beauties. Their father, Edward J. Barrington, had pioneered shipping in the Pacific Northwest in the mid-nineteenth century, but died leaving his widow slim resources to provide for their seven youngsters. Sid, then eleven, began working on boats on Puget Sound, earning his unlimited captain's papers at age twenty-one.[19] Three years later, in 1896, he left for the Klondike, where he became the first man to take a riverboat through Miles Canyon near Whitehorse[20] and the first to bring a steamer into the trading post of Dawson.[21]

Sid soon was joined by his older brother, Eddie, who piloted the steamer *Willie Irving* on the upper Yukon, and his younger brother, Hill, who eventually became captain of *La France*. Together the Barrington

Hill.   Sid.   Harry -

The Barringtons

A FAMILY OF FIRST-CLASS CAPTAINS

Hill, Sid, and Harry Barrington, sons of a famous sea captain from Oak Harbor,
Washington, stampeded to Dawson and made a fortune, first at gold-mining and then in the
riverboat trade. Their brother Eddie, who came with them, did not survive a typhoid epidemic,
but they survived to provide several colorful chapters in Alaska/Yukon history.

Courtesy of Bill Barrington.

brothers joined the Dawson stampede of 1898, staking a claim that produced
$70,000 in just one week.[22] Their triumph was marred, however, by a
typhoid fever epidemic that hit both Hill and Eddie that summer. Hill
managed to recover, but Eddie died in August after a lingering illness.[23]

After escorting Eddie's body home to Oak Harbor, Washington, Hill
and Sid returned to Dawson determined to sample life to the fullest, and in
1900 they both married beautiful women of shady repute. Sid, always flamboyant, chose "Dirty Maude" Delisle, a circus performer from Cincinnati
whose nickname apparently had nothing to do with personal cleanliness.
She danced at the Palace, where she was known as the only woman in the
Far North who could stand flat-footed and spit over her head; she was considered an entertaining catch. But it was young Hill, the "tag-along" as his
family called him, who captured the real beauty. He wed Babe Wallace, a
much-sought-after prostitute of considerable notoriety, who had made
enough money to own a piano, an incredible luxury in Dawson.[24]

THE DELISLE SISTERS

"Dirty Maude" Delisle (top) and her sister Hazel, formerly circus performers,
made good in Dawson in song-and-dance variety shows. Each had a photo series
made showing her range of expressions, required for a vaudeville resumé in that era.
Early on, Maude wed Sid Barrington, a popular riverboat captain,
but they soon parted in an amicable divorce. Later he wed her sister,
Hazel, a union that would last almost half a century.

Courtesy of Bill Barrington.

Neither marriage lasted long. Babe Wallace died of tuberculosis, and Hill later married a ship captain's daughter and, following her death, the social-climbing daughter of a respectable railroad man.[25] Dirty Maude amicably split with Sid and next made print in 1902 by briefly marrying a well-heeled prospector/bootlegger, Ulysses "Old Joe" Crocker, in Coldfoot, the site of a new gold stampede. Later Maude followed the miners to Nome and Cordova, finally marrying a railroad man. Then Sid Barrington—who twice made and lost a million *after* his Dawson gold strike—happily wed Maude's sister, Hazel Delisle, who had teamed with her as a dancer at the Palace. Sid named the boats in his large fleet after Hazel and stayed with the match until her death nearly fifty years later.[26]

Of all the Klondike millionaires, the most celebrated fool for women was "Swiftwater" Bill Gates. He made and lost at least three fortunes, and officially married and divorced or deserted at least five beautiful girls. Not on this list is Gussie Lamore, a close friend of Myrtle Drummond, who "mined" Bill Gates in Dawson as soon as he made his first million.

Bill had grown up poor and had prospected unsuccessfully in remote regions most of his life. After discovering that his claim, Eldorado #13, was virtually knee-deep in gold, he built the grandest gambling den and dance hall in Dawson, the Monte Carlo. On opening night he announced that he was "going to have a lady and the swellest in the country."[27]

Variety actress Gussie Lamore, age twenty-two, a petite, plump, blue-eyed, flaxen-haired beauty who had just come to work for him from a stint at the Juneau Opera House, was waltzing with a big French-Canadian when she caught Bill's eye. Without approaching her, he hurried back to his hotel, filled his pockets with pokes of gold, and returned for an introduction. His approach was swift and direct: "I'll give you your weight in gold tomorrow morning if you will marry me—and I guess you'll weigh about $30,000."[28]

Although Bill was fairly handsome, he was only five-feet-five, looked a decade older than his twenty-seven years, and—despite his trademark black Prince Albert coat and black silk top hat—he lacked polish. He'd been washing dishes in Circle when Gussie was a headliner there, and even if she hadn't been quietly married to Emile Leglice,[29] she had good reason to stall. It only made the new millionaire more determined.

"I should think a man could do anything with gold! And for my part, I

SAN FRANCISCO CHRONICLE, TUESDA

MR. AND MRS. "SWIFTWATER BILL," SUED AND SUING FOR A DIVORCE

my brother told me when he came home. My sister and uncle left immediately on their arrival for their home in Santa Clara."

The law in the case is plain and severe. Section 59 of the Civil Code declares:

"SWIFTWATER'S" WIFE SUES HIM.

training last year, Corbett said that he realized then Jeffries' power. "I don't know anybody who has a cinch on licking him," Corbett remarked. He said the fights could not be well rated yet, as the fights were stopped by the police and never reached such a conclusion as to permit good judgment to be formed about him. Corbett is 31 years old, but he does not think that a pugilist always retrograd

SWIFTWATER BILL AND GRACE LAMORE
Surprisingly, no pictures are known to exist of Gussie Lamore although
she was a popular entertainer in both Circle City and Dawson.

San Francisco Chronicle, courtesy of Terrence Cole.

used to always figure that money could buy anything, even the most beautiful woman in the world for your wife," he later would tell Iola Bebee, one of his many mothers-in-law.

Throughout the winter of '97, Bill lavished money and attention on Gussie. Following a quarrel with her, Bill bought up all the eggs in Dawson at outrageous prices, because he knew she loved them and would have to deal with him if she wanted any. Gussie played along, finally leading Bill to believe she would marry him in California at the end of the summer. Instead she deserted him, and within a month she began an unrelenting series of interviews venting her contempt for the diminutive millionaire.

"He's as stupid as an owl . . . and as rich as anything," she told Alice Rix of the *San Francisco Examiner*. Bill was expected to earn $1 million that winter, "but independence is a good deal too," Gussie insisted.[30]

Bill quickly recovered his self-esteem by eloping with Gussie's lovely older sister, Grace Lamore, following a six-day courtship. When Grace grew tired of their luxurious San Francisco flat, he bought her a $25,000 home in Oakland, spent thousands on furnishings, and presented her with diamonds and sapphires. Nevertheless, Grace sued for divorce after seven weeks. "I would have loved him more had he loved me less," she said. "I lost all love for him after we had been married a few days. He squeezed and hugged me from morning until night."

Love-starved Bill still didn't get it. "I don't intend to chase her," he told the *Seattle Times*. "I have the money and she should come to me. I can shower all manner of attention on her, but I'll not run after her footsteps. I'm worth, in round figures, $1,800,000 . . . and if I don't agree to it, she can't get a cent. . . ."[31]

Bill went on to take Nell, the youngest Lamore sister, as his mistress. Although she was just eighteen, she was already a successful actress with many resources and soon she too deserted him. Then he turned his attention to girls barely into their teens who needed him more.

Later, Gussie Lamore told the press she had no regrets. "Pooh! I wouldn't have had him for a million. . . . I thought I'd get his money when he came out and then let him go. He was too easy—the easiest thing you ever saw," she said. "Why in there, all you had to do was touch him for $400 and get it. But I wouldn't have married him if he owned the Klondike."[32]

Surprisingly, Bill bore the Lamore sisters no ill will and gamely attended several of Gussie's later stage performances, where the former lovers vied to buy each other drinks to the delight of newspaper reporters.[33]

———

One of the most unusual of early Dawson matches was that of hard-partying "Diamond Tooth" Gertie Lovejoy to C. W. C. Tabor, the well-respected dean of Dawson's attorneys, and Gertie's subsequent attempt to enter Dawson's polite society.

The exquisite blond entertainer boasted a showy diamond strategically wedged between her two front teeth, contrasting with her elegant, fine-featured beauty. A formidable performer with a gift for off-color ad-libs, Gertie was a headliner at the Palace and a favorite of dozens of powerful men, including supposedly happily married dance hall owner "Arizona" Charlie Meadows and U.S. Consul James McCook. She and the fun-loving consul made headlines during a barroom spree which ended with his distributing gold nuggets and his watch to the bar girls and attaching an American flag to the seat of his trousers, inviting a good, swift kick.[34] At an afternoon baseball game, Gertie raised eyebrows by appearing resplendent in a satin ball gown.[35]

On stage Gertie would flaunt her lush figure, asking her lusting audience coyly, "Hey there, boys! Ain't it pretty? This diamond, I mean. Why, it's like real money in the bank, the family jewels!" The audience would pelt her with loose nuggets, little sacks of gold dust, and, attached to them, notes requesting after-the-show trysts that soon made her a wealthy woman.[36]

In early 1900 Gertie barely escaped a Dawson hotel fire with her life and lost $2,000 worth of personal property—an extraordinary figure for that era. But Gertie quickly recouped her finances,[37] continuing to party in style. Just why she chose to marry C. W. C. Tabor has never been explained. Competent lawyers were averaging $2,000 a month in Dawson, and he was at the very top of his field and undoubtedly earning much more. Yet Gertie had close ties with men of even greater wealth and power, so her union with the thirty-five-year-old barrister may have been a love match. She married him quietly and stayed in Dawson long after the dance halls closed, despite the "respectable" wives openly snubbing her.

Gertie was invited to a tea at Government House by Martha Black, the wife of Tabor's colleague George Black, who had been elected to head the territorial parliament. "Gertie was a demure little woman, quite pretty and very self-effacing," observed Laura Berton, who attended the event. "She had little to say but when she did speak the famous diamond could be seen glittering between her two front teeth. Tongues wagged furiously the next day."[38]

Although her husband continued as Dawson's leading lawyer, Gertie— fed up, perhaps, with the role of demure and self-effacing little woman— moved to the high rent district in San Francisco, never to return. When Tabor died in the Yukon Hotel fire in 1917, she simply sent a spray of hyacinths to the funeral.[39] Comfortable with her extraordinary memories, she lived into her nineties.[40]

Also bucking Dawson's polite society was Lulu Mae Eads, a seductive dance hall queen who, according to one legend, was the model for the vamp in Robert Service's famous poem, "The Shooting of Dan McGrew."[41] Lulu had arrived late in Dawson, coming in 1900 with a trumpet player named Lopez, and shortly thereafter married their boss, Murray Eads, the town's longest-tenured hotel and dance hall owner.[42]

Murray Eads was so well liked that in late 1901 the town and his employees gave him the largest benefit performance ever staged in Dawson. Newspapers noted that he had on his payroll "no less than sixty-eight people whose aggregate salaries amount to $2,769 a week, each of whom will contribute both his or her services and a nightly salary."[43]

Lulu apparently played a large part in managing her husband's Floradora Dance Hall. It was a marvel of opulence, hung with seven-foot-high oil paintings of nudes in tremendous gilt frames, which had been packed on men's backs over the trail in the early days. "That hotel lobby, with its enamel spittoons, its painted nudes, its black-leather Edwardian chairs and its endless poker games glimpsed through the doors in the rear, never changed in any single detail," marveled Laura Berton when it was the town's prized hostelry.[44]

The Eads managed to keep it open even after dance halls and gambling dens were outlawed, changing its name to The Alexander and courting acceptance of the citizens. But in 1907 Lulu, not Murray, was charged with allowing on the premises "women of lose, idle or suspicious character and having no honorable occupation or calling, for the purpose of keeping company with men,"[45] and Dawson society ostracized her.

Shrewdly, Mr. and Mrs. Eads diversified, investing in a brewing company and a Seattle bank, while continuing to be enthusiastic civic boosters.[46] Finally, wealthy beyond their dreams in 1918, they decided to travel to the States to visit family and friends they had not seen in two decades, despite an unnerving and well-documented premonition that the trip would cost them their lives. It did. Both drowned during the sinking of the elegant steamship, the *Princess Sophia*.

Jewelry found in a chamois bag strung around Lulu Eads's neck provides a poignant glimpse of a dance hall girl's dream come true. Inside were a lovely topaz ring with diamonds, a diamond sunburst brooch valued at $300, a $650 diamond ring, a nine-diamond pendant and chain worth $700, and the wedding ring Murray had given Lulu at the start of it all, valued at a mere three dollars but obviously worth a lot more.[47]

Marriage was not on the agenda of all high-profile Dawson showgirls. Some felt it would limit both their fun and their earnings, and instead dexterously romanced Klondike Kings who were willing to share. A surprising number of wealthy miners, perhaps restrained by marital commitments back home or simply prizing their own freedom, formed fan clubs for the most desirable of the gold-diggers. In such clubs, the men joined forces to present the women with expensive gifts and hold receptions in their honor, while competing for sexual favors.

"Gussie Lamore was the heroine of an enjoyable pink crushed high tea party given by a number of eligible bachelors at a private rendezvous last Saturday evening," the *Dawson Daily Nugget* reported without a blush on March 13, 1900. "During the height of the festivities, with the popping of champagne corks she was presented with a gold wishbone, the insignia of the club. Her health was then drunk in goblets adopted by the club, consisting of uniquely designed Cinderella glass slippers, ornamented with nuggets."

Honora Ornstein, known as "Diamond Tooth Lil" for the diamond fillings she displayed proudly in her front and eye teeth, left the territory with thousands of dollars earned not by playing favorites but by playing the field. Her dancing and singing were marginal at best. One reviewer noted she was "better at pretending to be a fleshy statue than a serpentine dancer."[48] But Lil's smile was marvelous, and her well-upholstered figure truly voluptuous. From one plump, bare shoulder to her wrist she wore a fascinating white gold snake bracelet studded with 125 real diamonds, which hypnotized some of her audience and caused the rest to howl like a pack of malamutes.[49]

A headliner for Alexander Pantages, Lil retired in the 1920s to Seattle, where she invested well in apartment houses. She briefly married a man named George Miller, whom she divorced in 1923 just one week before receiving word that she had inherited $150,000 from her mother in Los Angeles. Lil announced she would use that capital to start a dramatic stock company, but her mind began to fail. In 1935 friends committed her to the state hospital in Yakima, where she remained until 1960 when she was moved to a rest home on welfare. Her money had run out in the late '50s, after her fabulous jewelry collection and the diamonds in her teeth were sold with some difficulty because, guardians noted, some didn't want to buy jewels worn by "that woman."[50]

The most spectacularly mercenary of the good time girls was Cad Wilson, who arrived in Dawson in the fall of 1898 fresh from San

ENTERTAINING

"Diamond Tooth" Gertie Lovejoy, left, and Cad Wilson entertain Eddie Doland,
a popular comic and stage manager of the Tivoli Theater, far right, and an unidentified man,
perhaps Eddie's brother, Tommy. The waiter, known as "The Black Prince," was a Dawson
boxing champ. This photo is thought to have been taken in Cad's apartment over the Monte
Carlo Theater sometime in 1898. Gertie later married C. W. C. Tabor, one of Dawson's
most respected lawyers. Cad left the Yukon with more than $50,000 from one season's
earnings, reappeared during the Nome rush, and then disappeared from history.

ASL, Wickersham Collection, PCA 227-1-190.

Francisco. Billed as the highest-paid visiting performing artist on the
Pacific Coast, Cad was no beauty. Her figure was not outstanding and she
didn't have much of a voice, but the diminutive, brown-eyed redhead
affected a delightful air of innocence which contrasted neatly with her
risqué repertoire.

   She drew just one bad review, shortly after she arrived, from an Elks
benefit where there were "at least 100 ladies present," who "hung their
heads" at the "ginger" in Cad's suggestive act.[51] What shocked them was
apparently innuendo, for the naughtiest verse of her theme song, "Such a
Nice Girl, Too," seems laughably innocuous by today's standards:

She told me that she was a "Miss"
And scarcely had turned twenty
She said she never cared to wed
Tho' offers she had plenty.
Last week, they took her up to court,
She said, "Judge do be forgiving"
He answered, "Yes, if you can prove
You've not three husbands living."[52]

Cad's audacity only served to endear her to the enthusiastic male fans who were her only concern. She claimed to be about sixteen, from a convent near Sacramento. Her manager, comedian Eddie Doland, introduced her on stage by saying, "Her mother told her to pick nice clean friends, and I leave it to you boys if she can't pick 'em nice and clean."

Actually Cad was probably about twenty-six, but her manager was right about her picking 'em clean.[53] "She danced on the stage and she sang real pretty, but she took her time making up her mind, and she played one man against the other to get them showing off," recalled Mont Hawthorne, a young prospector from Astoria where Cad was a well-known vaudeville player. "Next thing we heard was that the fellows who called themselves Eldorado Kings were saving their biggest nuggets and having a belt made out of them for her. It was a Fourth of July present. . . .

"When Cad came out on stage that night, she was wearing that gold belt that the Eldorado Kings had ordered made special for her. They'd been arguing for months about who had found the biggest nugget. Cad ended up that night with all the big ones. That belt went clean around her once and a half and there wasn't even a medium-sized nugget in the bunch."[54]

The belt, which the proud miners allowed to be displayed to the general public by the manufacturer, L. Pound and Company, was so ornate as to be barbaric, with a miniature golden windlass and bucket, a golden brooch nearly six inches long from which were suspended intricate gold charms, and a gold pan bearing the inscription "Dawson" raised in colored letters.[55]

"That night she sure acted happy. Why, she danced so light her feet hardly touched the floor at all. The fellows went mad when she was singing 'There'll Be a Hot Time in the Old Town Tonight.' That's when they really began throwing nuggets on the stage. Cad had a little laugh that was different. She'd sing a while and then she'd look around and laugh. She used her dress for holding nuggets just like it was sort of an apron and she held it right high in front of her. Cad was smart. She'd gone up there like all the rest of us because she wanted to get all the gold she could. She done all right for herself, too."[56]

One admirer was so smitten with Cad that he paid a waiter to fill a bathtub with wine, purchased at twenty dollars a bottle, for her to bathe in. Yukon writer Pierre Berton guesses Cad did not allow him to watch or scrub her back, but probably had the stuff rebottled.[57]

In the fall of 1899, Cad focused on one fellow who spent more than $75,000 on her, but she still couldn't resist an easy mark. Too typical is her fleecing of a low-paid workman known only as "The Sawdust King" because he made his living changing the sawdust used to insulate the floors of Dawson gambling houses. He routinely lost most of his meager earnings at the gaming tables. Finally he moved up to packing water for a bar, and in an uncharacteristic streak of luck at cards parlayed his first day's wages into something over $1,800 by 3 p.m. the next day.

Ignoring former friends, the "King" went to the Tivoli Theatre and Dance Hall where Cad helped him dispose of several bottles of liquor to celebrate his luck. Then she led him to her dressing room and later installed him in a prominent theater box, "tickling his vanity by addressing remarks to him personally and throwing him countless kisses."

At two o'clock the next morning, a card dealer dropped by the dance hall expecting to find Cad with "Spitzy," her regular sugar daddy, or another sporty admirer. He was astonished to find her in the lap of the Sawdust King, who was "still dirty and ragged."

"She had one arm around his neck and caressingly stroked his unkempt hair. Each was sipping wine from the other's glass. The 'king' every now and then would look down disdainfully on the dancers below," according to a newspaper account. Wine was flowing fast and furiously. About four hours later, the Tivoli porter had to turn the Sawdust King out of the house. He had spent $800 in cash and had signed $940 worth of checks. "He still wanted to buy, but Cad mercifully refused to drink any more and left him with $60 credit in his bank."

On his departure, the Sawdust King kicked the porter, who retaliated by throwing him into the street so hard he fell and fractured his leg and didn't fully recover until summer.[58] "Cad never had a better night than the one on which the King went broke," the local paper reported.

A LEGITIMATE ACTRESS

*American Lucy Lovell came to Dawson from the London stage, and her talent so
impressed local reviewers that they focused on it instead of the usual personal gossip.
Although Lucy garnered plenty of press during her lengthy stay in 1902, her name was
not linked in print with any gold kings as was common with other actresses,
so we know little of her personal life. Unfortunately she contracted consumption
during her Far North tour and died shortly thereafter in Arizona.*

ASL, Wickersham Collection, PCA 227-1-187.

When Cad's contract expired in the fall of 1899, locals guessed that she left the territory with about $26,000 in cash. They revisited their estimate when news of an interview she had given her hometown newspaper, the *Chicago Chronicle*, got back to Dawson. "The erstwhile vaudeville star of the Klondike, who fooled the Eldorado kings about her age and palmed herself off as young and kittenish, 'such a nice girl, too,' is up to her tricks again and filled a *Chronicle* reporter in Chicago with a lot of fairy tales," the *Dawson Daily News* warned readers.[59]

According to the Chicago feature, "Miss Cad Wilson, having conquered the frozen north, melted the Pole with her warm ragtime song and sustained a variety of injuries through the carelessness of rugged miners in storming her with gold nuggets instead of bouquets, arrived in Chicago today, after a year in the Klondike. Miss Wilson comes home with something besides stories and cheerful thoughts of what might have been. She has a drayload of rough gold trinkets, drafts to the amount of $40,000 and diamonds of sufficient variety and number to light the entire Great Northern hotel, where she is stopping. She had just a brief twelve months among the Dawsonites, and sang so well and danced so prettily, suggestively and gracefully, that if her shower of gold nuggets nightly did not reach $500 in value she left the theater in a pout."

Even more interesting is the Dawson reporter's use of the words "erstwhile vaudeville star" for, despite all her newspaper hype and the fact that she was obviously a veteran performer, historians have long puzzled over who Cad Wilson really was.

The caption on her photo in Judge James Wickersham's collection claims that she was actually the East Coast stage actress Esther Lyons, who came to Alaska with her husband, theatrical producer Eugene Robinson, on vacation with photographer Veazie Wilson in 1895. The Veazie party climbed Chilkoot Pass and traveled much of Yukon Territory and Alaska before cruising down the Yukon to the Pacific Coast. Esther authored a book featuring Veazie's photos, then made a lucrative speaking tour of the United States, which may have included a private performance for President McKinley and his family and an appearance at Carnegie Hall.

Cad Wilson did look like Esther Lyons, but Esther's husband subsequently become a multimillionaire and built her a mansion at Sixth Avenue and 47th Street in New York. Nor does it seem likely that Esther would have come north to mine miners under an alias when she'd starred with the greats—Maurice Barrymore, Edwin Booth, Joseph Jefferson, and

John L. Sullivan—and her own stage name had greater drawing power.[60]

Judge Wickersham may have confused Esther Lyons with one of two other East Coast actresses: Esther Lyon, who played many of the same East Coast companies as Esther Lyons, or Essie Lyons, a popular musical comedy star in New York.[61] Both these women resembled Esther Lyons and Cad Wilson, but they were reportedly happily married, legitimate actresses.

Whoever she was, Cad Wilson returned to the Klondike for another run in the spring of 1899, still receiving good reviews but less hype and ardor from the Klondike Kings, who were fast moving out of Dawson. In the summer of 1900, Cad joined the stampede to Nome. After appearing there for several months, she quietly disappeared from the headlines and theater billings, perhaps sacrificing her Klondike notoriety for a new life as a wealthy woman under another name.

※

Even more curious is the story of Rose Blumkin who, although not an entertainer, won the hearts of the Klondike Kings and made them pay. Unfashionably slim and a bit beetle-browed, she compensated with a winsome, impish smile and outgoing personality. She may have come to Dawson to escape an unhappy marriage, and she was refined enough to seek a respectable cover when she turned to prostitution for her living. Unable to act or sing, Rose signed on at the Monte Carlo as a dance hall girl. Later she became a ticket-taker, so good at the job that one newspaper favorably reviewed her performance at the ticket window along with the show.

There is no question, however, that prostitution was Rose's main line of work. She was often referred to as a "fairy," the Dawson euphemism for a woman of the night, and she made astonishing amounts of money. Caught in the Dawson fire that destroyed the Monte Carlo in January of 1900, Rose declared the loss of $3,500 in personal property, at least $1,000 more than any of the stage stars wiped out by the blaze.[62]

When Rose saved enough to vacation in Cincinnati in 1899, one of her admirers expressed doubts she would return, so she wagered him a wine supper that she'd be back by October 20. Delayed by the wreck of the SS *Stratton* on which she had been traveling, Rose lost the bet but gamely commandeered a dog team to mush home and settle the account. "The bet will be paid off Thursday," noted Dawson columnist Stroller White, "but an ardent admirer of the comely Rose will insist on settling the tab."[63]

THE BEST TICKET-SELLER IN THE FAR NORTH

*Rose Blumkin couldn't sing or dance, but made her fame selling tickets at theaters
in Dawson and Nome. She also made a considerable fortune, which must have come from
after-hours activities, as ordinary ticket-sellers could not afford to deck
themselves in the lavish ball gowns and diamonds that she favored.*

ASL, Wickersham Collection, PCA 277-1-185.

Later the *Dawson Daily News* reported that, on her return to the Orpheum Theatre, Rose had been honored with a case of champagne and a souvenir gold ring. Just as they'd feted Cad Wilson, the miners joined forces to give the little ticket-taker a gaudy belt of gold nuggets, but she left them all behind for a married man.[64]

In 1900 she ran off with Edward Holden to Nome, where she got a job as ticket-taker for the Stander Theater and again captured the attention of local reporters. The newcomer made every purchaser feel "especially favored when he receives one of her winsome smiles," the *Nome News* reported.[65] Later she won first prize as the best-dressed lady at the Elks annual masquerade ball,[66] but did not make headlines again until Stroller White followed up on her career as a home-wrecker.

Ed Holden, the husband she had stolen, lost some of his Klondike-won wealth in a failed Nome theater venture, then squired Rose to Seattle where he entered the saloon business, White reported. Here, in addition to her nugget belt, Rose flaunted diamonds that were "the envy of the half-caste world."

"But one day the diamonds turned up missing and Edward was quick to note their absence. When questioned, Rose at first looked embarrassed and refused to tell the truth," the article continued. "Then, woman-like, she threw herself on the Holden breast and Holden mercy and told all. She had been in urgent need of money and had 'soaked' her flashers for $1,000. She was sorry, oh, so sorry for what she had done and now everybody who saw her sneered at her because she had no diamonds."

This was more than Edward's tender heart could stand, so he redeemed the diamonds, paying $1,200 for their recovery. "Now," he said, "dress up in the very best you have and we'll take a walk and show people that you can still wear the most elegant diamonds of any woman in Seattle. I will call for you in an hour." But in an hour Rose had left Seattle for Salt Lake City, White reported,[67] and his readers were not surprised.

MORNING

4

The Real Working Girls

SUICIDES AND SUCCESSES

I n August of 1902, Sergeant Frank Smith of the Dawson police testified that while working undercover he had arrested Margaret Benoit and Paulette Barge after observing them walking the streets for three weeks, accosting men.

"Did they have any explanation when you asked them what they were doing?" asked the judge.

"Yes, they said they were screwing for three dollars," Sergeant Smith answered.[1]

For every actress and dance hall girl who made a fortune romancing Klondike Kings, there were dozens who didn't have the luck, the looks, or the knack. Many came to rely on prostitution for the bulk of their earnings, using their dance hall jobs as opportunities to meet customers under a semi-respectable cover. Most of the entertainment palaces were built with saloons and gambling halls attached to the theater, with the main entrance through the saloon, so there was no embarrassment in being seen at the door.[2] Even respectable theaters used sex as an advertising draw. The Combination promised "Every Evening a Bevy of Beauties in Title Roles," while the Tivoli advertised "The Finest Formed Women in the Klondike," along with such bland classic billings as *Uncle Tom's Cabin*.[3]

"MORNING"

That is the only caption that has come down through time; no name or byline is on this photo of a Dawson beauty, indicating she was probably a lady of the evening photographed the morning after.

YA, MNJ 6070, Print #812.

Operation of a cigar store also was an excellent front, but required capital. Some enterprising prostitutes established laundries to solicit through, but such deceptions required real work. Doing enough laundry to keep up appearances was a chore, while a dance hall girl was required to spend from six to twelve hours a night on her feet, dancing and hustling drinks for the house.

The majority of Dawson prostitutes, probably between 200 and 250 at any given time during the peak years, never bothered with subterfuge because sticking to their specialty offered better money. In the same time it took a dance hall girl to make one dollar dancing, a common street-walker could turn a trick for three dollars, and a better-looking, higher-skilled woman of the demimonde could easily make twenty times that.

E. C. Trelawney-Ansell, who seems to have done considerable field research, reported that "for a very hurried entertainment—usually fifteen minutes—the 'ladies' charged four ounces ($64), but they weighed the dust on their own scales, which were crooked, with their own weights (ditto), and helped themselves from the miner's poke (bag of dust). The result was that they usually finished up with at least eight ounces."[4]

To put these figures in perspective, realize that the going wage for a male laborer was one dollar per day in the States and from five to eight dollars per day in Dawson. The cost of living in the Far North was proportionally higher, but cabin rental ranged from twenty to thirty dollars a month, giving prostitutes an excellent margin.[5]

In the beginning, of course, there were no cabins. The first prostitutes on the scene worked out of tents without fear of arrest. Women were so scarce that few citizens objected. Prospector Mont Hawthorne wrote of suffering merciless ribbing from his friends when his dog, Pedro, became attached to one girl.

"He'd gone right down by town and moved in with one of them sporting women. She had pitched her tent there on the street, with her name wrote on the front of it in big letters. When she was busy she would put him outside; and there Pedro would set in front of her tent until she let him in again," the miner recalled unhappily. "I'd go by and call him and he'd come along with me for a while. But just as soon as he could sneak away, back he'd go to visit Big Sal again. I sure got tired of the way he was doing. Every time when I went downtown the boys would say: 'Why Hawthorne, I didn't expect to see you down here. I just seen your dog waiting for you outside of Big Sal's tent.'"[6]

CIGAR STORE MADAM?

*Perhaps. Many prostitutes who had capital used cigar stores as a front to sell love.
On the other hand, the cigar trade was lucrative enough that a woman could make money
at a legitimate operation, which may be the case here, as Margie appears to be
posing willingly for the Dawson photographer in 1899.*

ASL, Larss and Duclos photograph, PCA 41-35.

Pedro probably spent more time outside the tent than in, because business was brisk. Lines of waiting customers often formed in front of the most successful operations.

⸎

When it became evident that Dawson had a major gold strike and that the boomtown was wide open, professionals flocked in from all over the world, including Colorado's Mattie Silks, probably the most famous madam in the American West. Mattie was a friend of Soapy Smith, a Denver crook who had gained control of Skagway, Alaska's gateway city to the Klondike. Originally she planned to work with him there, but she changed her mind after overhearing him and his gang members discuss their plans to rob her.[7]

DAWSON IN 1899
What had started as a tent city of a few hundred, just two years earlier,
spread far and wide with a surprising number of "permanent" buildings at the height
of the Klondike rush. The red light district, in the heart of the business district when this
photo was taken, was later moved across the river to Klondike City (also known as Lousetown).
It was accessible by a narrow bridge built at the far end of Eighth Avenue in Dawson.

YA, #3739, Larss and Duclos photograph.

Electing to go farther north, Mattie scaled Chilkoot Pass in the spring of 1898 with her handsome lover, Cortez Thompson, and eight prostitutes in her hire. From William Jenkins, proprietor of the Sourdough Saloon, she rented a good-size frame building on Second Street for $350 a month. Her girls averaged about fifty dollars per night, from which Mattie took 50 percent off the top, plus board. Her expenses were high because she ran a first-class house, but her net profit was enormous, inflated by her sale of champagne at thirty dollars per quart and of whisky made from grain alcohol at a cost of sixty dollars a gallon which sold (when colored and diluted) for $130.

Despite her success, or perhaps because of it, Mattie quit to go south that fall. Well past her prime with a face like a pug dog—looking like an army tank in the ruffled silk gowns she favored—the madam was concerned about the health of her much younger lover. Cortez Thompson had caught cold that rainy summer, playing faro in Joe Cooper's drafty Dominion Saloon. Mattie is said to have left with $38,000 in profit from her ninety-day stay *after* she paid off Cortez's heavy gambling debts.[8]

Mattie Silks's major competition was a madam named Beatrice Larnne, but big operations—although standard in most western cities—were rare in the north. In fact, the only other madam who emerged from the Klondike Rush a legend was "Diamond Lil" Davenport, who had survived basic training in the Chicago underworld to establish her own business in Skagway.

Diamond Lil's house was considered the most lavish in the region. She employed reputedly the best pianist in Skagway and several excellent singers who performed popular ditties of the day—"Swannee River," "Climbing up de Golden Stairs," and of course, "There'll Be a Hot Time in the Old Town Tonight." The major attraction, though, was Lil herself, who stood nearly six feet tall and was known not only for the astonishing diamond collection she always wore,[9] but also for her remarkably good looks.

"I remembered seeing her for the first time at dinner . . . sitting alone several tables away, aloof and silent; only talking to the waiter a few times. She was a fascinating person to watch, a young woman of unusual beauty with the bearing of a queen—tall and stately, beautifully gowned, fair skinned, velvety eyes, and a complexion like the inside petal of a lovely white lily," wrote Ella Lang Martinson in an account of a trip she made north on the SS *Rosalie*, traveling with young daughter Clemy in June 1898 to join her husband.

"After dinner I had noticed that she kept absolutely to herself and had spoken to no one. Clemy and I had sat near her while looking at magazines, but actually it was difficult to look at anything but Lady Lily. Clemy, frankly, stared at her! She was reading a book and never looked up. Suddenly I was shocked to see her fingers when she turned a page. There were rings of all shapes and sizes on every finger, and on both hands, including her thumbs. Then, I was shocked again. I could see that she was reading one of the cheapest dime novels of the day, completely taboo in refined society. The main characters were depicted in suggestive poses on the garish cover!"

On arriving in Skagway, Martinson was shocked to learn who "Lady

Lily" really was. "Certainly nature had fashioned her into a perfect beauty and at first glance she did appear to be a person of real refinement," she conceded. "But 'Diamond Lil' was a courtesan in the fullest sense of the word, only entertaining the obviously rich clients who could pay handsomely for what she had to offer. Nevertheless, she was fully entrenched in the 'world's oldest profession.'"[10]

Although a recognized member of the Chicago underworld, Lil was known to be honest in running her house of ill repute and was never arrested. She returned to her hometown with a fortune, but made the mistake of choosing as her paramour a hood named Big Joe Hopkins instead of his rival, the city detective who eventually shot him. By the time her beauty faded, she had run through her riches, but she made an honest living in her final years as a scrubwoman for a Seattle bank.[11]

The rank and file of Dawson whores had even fewer options than their elite sisters who grew rich cultivating a few well-heeled lovers. Few prostitutes could afford to be selective in their clientele; however, exceptional freedom was accorded them in the early days of the boom. Although prostitution was illegal in Canada, the Northwest Mounted Police under Inspector Charles Constantine were more concerned with controlling petty criminals and preventing crimes of violence than policing morals. Inspector Constantine did outlaw the wearing of bloomers, a forerunner to slacks which were considered scandalous. But whores were allowed to solicit on the streets and in the bars, and to work anywhere they pleased. Those with capital invested in the town's choicest lots. Others rented rooms over respectable downtown businesses, soliciting out of the upstairs windows in good weather.

Dawson newspapers initially refrained from using any form of the word "prostitute," referring delicately to the "demimonde," "the soiled doves," or "the tenderloin." They even maintained Victorian restraint when high-profile entertainer Nellie "the Pig" Lamore beat the stuffing out of the toe-dancing "Petite Sisters Pickering" after they made the mistake of snubbing her on the street.[12]

In covering a brawl at the Pavilion following the loss of $3,100 by one of the proprietors in a blackjack game, a reporter noted delicately that two dance hall girls involved called each other "names that would not be tolerated in polite society."

"DIAMOND LIL" DAVENPORT

*One of the most colorful madams of the Klondike era, Diamond Lil was based out of
Skagway, a major gateway city to Dawson. She had connections with the Chicago underworld
but was known to be completely honest in running her house of ill repute. She left the Far
North with a fortune, but soon lost it all, ending her days as a scrubwoman in Seattle.*

YA, MacBride Museum Collection, #3829.

A DRINKING BEE

Photographers Larss & Duclos did a fine series of photos in Dawson's
red light district, captioning them with whimsy. The woman at the far left is identified as
Madame Brunell, but the other happy drinkers remain nameless.

YA, MacBride Museum Collection, #3795, Larss and Duclos photograph.

"Miss Aberdeen had the misfortune to quarrel with Gracie Robinson. Evidently the fair Miss Aberdeen has the valor required of veterans, but her discretion is as poor as that of the taurus which attempted to derail an express train," he wrote tactfully. "Her temerity in precipitating a wordy altercation with Gracie is admirable, but anyone who knows Gracie would pick the latter for a winner and back her as a lead pipe cinch." Gracie Robinson did win the fight, and Miss Aberdeen was rescued by her pimp before she suffered much physical damage.

Writers were forced to resort to more straightforward coverage when, in a very public waterfront brawl, Bertha "the Adder" tore off all of "Seattle" Emily's clothes, then chased her naked victim through town, pelting her with rocks.[13]

—∞∞∞—

A number of researchers have assumed the life of a Dawson prostitute was grim. Historians Kenneth Coates and William Morrison argued that most prostitutes "led miserable lives, abused by pimps or succumbing to alcohol."[14] Charlene L. Porsild, in her thesis on the rush, flatly states that the majority of Klondike prostitutes were overwhelmingly poor, citing financial information from the 1901 census.[15]

While there were many unhappy sagas of prostitutes and dance hall girls, a few well-documented suicides, and some juicy murders, careful study shows that these had more to do with lovers' quarrels and failed personal relations than the traumas of the skin trade. Nor would the same statistics have been abnormal for a population of "respectable" shop girls and wives during the same period, when more than a few led miserable lives, were abused by their lovers, and succumbed to alcohol.

As for income, one could assume that prostitutes—most of whom worked under aliases—would not have been inclined to openly discuss their wages with government officials, especially as Dawson police began campaigns to entrap, arrest, fine, and jail them the very year the census was taken.

Given the minimum remuneration of three dollars to a low-class streetwalker for a quick trick (documented in court by the Dawson police), and the fact that the inmate of a house of ill fame there could clear twenty-five dollars a night *after* giving half her take to her madam, any working girl would have had to be pretty slow not to do better than break even, in spite of expensive tastes and Dawson's high cost of living at six dollars a day.

"It was said that some girls made as high as two hundred and fifty dollars a night, but this could only be done by 'rolling,' which meant getting a man drunk and stealing his poke," noted society matron Martha Black, who briefly considered all options when she found herself flat broke and pregnant in Dawson after deserting her wealthy husband.[16]

Resorting to crime wasn't necessary, however. "Mukluk Maud" Rouselle, an actress considered past her prime at age twenty-five, left an estate of $2,000 *exclusive of her mining property*, when she was shot in August of 1899 by Harry Davis, a jealous lover who committed suicide on the spot. True, Maud was employed as a stage comedian at the time. But her estate was well in excess of what she could have accumulated on her salary

from the Monte Carlo Theatre, and she was not given to rolling drunks.[17]

Also popular was Miss T. Ksa Yameyachi, who apparently operated independently from the usual pimp, for she amassed an unusual amount of wealth.

"The last request of Miss T. Ksa Yameyachi, the Japanese woman who died from pneumonia on Fourth Avenue Saturday [1901], was that her body be embalmed and kept here until the opening of navigation when it will be sent outside to her sister in Portland [Oregon], who will take it to a San Francisco cemetery, after which the ashes will be sent to the end of the Mikado," the *Daily Klondike Nugget* reported.

"Ksa left $9,000 in a bank in Japan besides a good-sized account in one of the Dawson banks. She also owned a claim on French Hill which was presented to her by an admirer last year."[18]

RED LIGHTS UNDER THE MIDNIGHT SUN
This photo of Dawson's restricted district is sometimes labeled "White Chapel"
after a similar institution in London, but the Klondike's White Chapel was a late development
built outside the population center. Some historians believe this is actually a picture
of the stampede's pioneering effort on Fourth Avenue in downtown Dawson.
NAC C20314, Larss and Duclos photograph.

Pearl Mitchell, another "actress," was shot dead by her lover, James Slorah, in a domestic dispute at the Green Tree Hotel, a well-known house of ill repute, a year later. She left $900 in her Dawson bank account, valuable jewelry and apparel, and another bank account in Seattle over which she and James apparently had been battling.[19] James, unsuccessful in an attempt to shoot himself, was sentenced to hang and took the verdict calmly. Later his sentence was commuted to life in prison.

———⧉———

As noted by Coates and Morrison, pimps *did* sometimes siphon off the profits from illicit love, especially from foreigners who spoke little or no English. "While many prostitutes in their isolated cabins practiced the profession quite independently, there were also some white slave girls, mostly Belgians," Martha Black noted. "These had been brought in and were managed by men known as *macques,* who not only lived 'off the avails,' but first demanded repayment of the passage money of their victims. Let it be always to the credit of the Northwest Mounted Police that they spared no efforts to bring these men of 'fancy dress and patent leather shoes' to justice. They were ruthlessly rounded up, brought to trial, and, if proven guilty, given a blue ticket, which meant shoved aboard a boat and told to 'get the hell out of the country and never come back.'"[20]

A dozen or more such cases of "white slavery" (women of any color being prostituted against their will) were documented in the Dawson papers and jail records. However, only one resulted from the complaint of a prostitute, and her motivation may have been to revenge a failed love affair rather than to escape from enslavement. In the spring of 1899, Hermine Depanw charged that Emile Rodenbach had brought her and her sister, Laura, to Dawson from Brussels in June of 1898, had virtually owned them as slaves, had often beaten them, and had taken from them all their earnings as prostitutes, an amount aggregating to over $15,000 in less than one year.[21]

At the time of his arrest, Emile Rodenbach transferred a city lot worth $6,000 to Hermine Depanw's sister. After he received a five-year sentence for "living off the avails," Hermine brought him to court again, claiming the land he transferred to Laura belonged to her. It was fraud, she explained in French, because she had given Emile the money to make the purchase for her, but he had put his own name on the title knowing she could not read English.

Emile, who claimed to be a Belgian gentleman of means, appeared at his trial wearing an expensive black suit of the latest mode accented with lavish white linen and profuse jewels, his abundant black hair and heavy mustaches adding to his charm. On his return engagement, however, the pimp fell on the "tender mercies of the police," his hair and mustaches closely clipped, his features tanned by exposure to the woodpile, and his raiment changed to a convict's garb. "The last trace of the 'Belgian gentleman' has vanished and the poor, cringing, flat-headed, slant-browed, villainous-featured man who appeared in court actually excited pity in the breast of many of those in the courtroom," the *Klondike Nugget* reporter editorialized.

Most affected was Laura Depanw, who had originally supported the testimony of her sister. On seeing Emile, she suddenly reversed her testimony and claimed that Hermine had lied. And despite her subsequent imprisonment for perjury, Laura Depanw stuck by that claim to protect her lover.[22]

———— ✺ ————

When Lucille Martin, her sister Marcelle Martin, and Louise Coragod showed no inclination to help convict their pimp, Lucien John Robert, of white slavery, they were arrested, too, for being inmates of the immoral and disorderly Bartlett House, which he apparently managed for them. The case got an unusual amount of attention because the Bartlett was described as "a notorious house of assignation giving exhibitions of a disgusting nature," offering "a species of moral depravity seldom heard of even in the lowest ranks of slum life." Unfortunately, testimony was closed to the public and the press was unable to follow up with juicy details.[23]

According to a police corporal, John Robert was dining in his shirtsleeves with his mistress, Lucille Martin, when the house was raided. As officers arrested the pimp, one of the girls abused the police in French. Marcelle Martin got mad and kicked in the panel of the door upstairs. The police entered the room to find a man under the bed, his head and feet sticking out, but the French women raised such an uproar that the man evidently escaped. After Lucille had supplied John with a necktie and handkerchief from her wardrobe, he kissed her goodbye. "He then kissed the others on the cheeks," the corporal testified soberly.

At his trial, during which the gorgeously dressed women blew him kisses, John claimed to be a former Parisian banker currently employed as a carpenter—despite a government witness's testimony that he had never seen the whorehouse manager do an honest day's work. John was described as a pale man with delicate hands and an blond mustache that turned upward. Weeping frequently, he reacted dramatically to claims that his mistress, Lucille, had sixteen other lovers. The judge dismissed John's shock as clever insincerity and sentenced him to six months of hard labor for living off the avails of prostitution.[24]

The Martin sisters and Louise Coragod pleaded guilty "to avoid the introduction of certain vile practices at the Bartlett as evidence." After serving two months in jail doing laundry for fellow prisoners, they emerged penniless. They had sold everything, including their decorated chamber pots, to raise bail for John Robert, who skipped town.[25]

⸺⸺

Even less successful was the prosecution of Sigwald Rosenfield Paulson, charged with living off money earned by Addie Mantell. Forced to testify, Addie admitted candidly that she had lived with the dapper-looking little Swede in both Seattle and Dawson and had given him about $2,000 over the past two years, all from the proceeds of prostitution. However, she insisted there was no arrangement between them regarding her money; that she had given it on her own initiative when her lover couldn't find work. Sigwald was reluctant to take her most recent donation, forty dollars for a suit of clothes, she said, and she had to press the money on him.

"I generally gave him the money with which to pay for the meals when we were out. It wouldn't look nice for a lady to go up and pay," she added demurely.

The prosecution countered with evidence that the defendant was "known as a saloon lounger" and, although Sigwald protested that he had mined and been in the saloon business, another witness testified that she had never seen him work. Sigwald was sentenced to six months in prison and fined fifty dollars, even though all suspicion of white slavery was dispelled when Addie's cashbook was introduced by the defense. On the final page, the prostitute had written in a labored hand, "Sigwald Rosenfield Paulson is my Darling sweet shugar lump and preshes darling sense 1901 feb 1. the live time long I trust to be friends and true companions and thank god if such be granted to Addie Mantell."[26]

⸺⸺

The French *macques* brought to trial in Dawson generally enjoyed an emotional as well as a financial hold over the women they lived off. While Martha Black was correct that many women (especially Americans) worked independently, most found a man's help useful in transacting business and preferable to trying to sell themselves in that near-Victorian era. Many made arrangements with bartenders or hotel keepers to supply them with customers, especially before there was a central red light district where they could display their wares.

A few enterprising charmers peddled themselves as wives for a few months, thus circumventing the problem of solicitation. Maud Parrish recalled one friend who cleared $20,000 by spending two winters with a miner on his Klondike claim,[27] and at least three dance hall girls publicly sold themselves for their weight in gold, reportedly loading their corsets with buckshot for the public weigh-in.

In the transaction that took the most brass, Mabel Larose, a prostitute known as "French Marie," auctioned herself off at the Monte Carlo on Christmas Eve, 1889. Just five-feet-two with a lovely figure, she looked far younger than her twenty-two years with her auburn hair hanging girlishly down her back in two great plaits. Neatly dressed in a decent, ankle-length frock cut low but showing no more cleavage than fashion allowed, she climbed on the bar to serve as her own auctioneer, according to E. C. Trelawne-Ansel, who happened to be there.

"Well, here I am, gentlemen. My figure is good. Most folks say that my looks are the same," she began straightforwardly. "Those you can see for yourself, my figure the buyer will see afterwards. You'll have to take that for granted, now.

"Terms. Well, I'm willing to sell myself to the highest bidder and act as his wife for six months from tonight, but I reserve the right to accept the next lowest bidder if I do not like the highest. Is that plain? Right!

"The man who buys me will find that I'll play the game with him and play it square, but the man who gets me and lifts a hand to me will get a knife in him. Pronto. Savee that. The buyer must provide a decent cabin and I'll cook him good grub, but he must have a good stock of it.

"You'll want to know, anyhow, so I may as well tell you now. I ain't exactly an iceberg. Now before we start I'll answer any questions. Shoot."

"Yes! I've been married. Next."

"A lumberjack and no darn good at that."

"Dead? I dunno. Hope so, anyhow. Should be."

"Yes! I've got a kid. The mazuma [money] is for him."

"None of your goddamned business." This to a question as to whether her parents were alive.

Bids rose quickly to $5,000 with a vile-looking Italian, the owner of two of Dawson's largest whorehouses, leading a Yankee called Sam. The Italian was a giant who in his day had gone to the mat twice with one of the best wrestlers in the States, but he had let himself go to fat and flab. The Yank was easily two inches shorter, but in splendid shape and handsome, too.

"Now, boys," said Marie walking up and down the bar, once or twice lifting her skirts to her knees and laughing. "The last bid's $5,000. Say, ain't you pikers a-goin' to bid higher than that for this?" And another flick of her skirts. "Here's a nice plump chicken awaiting for a home."

"Sure, girlie," shouted Sam. "I was only a'waiting fer the pikers to drop out, so that we can get down to real bidding. I'll make it $10,000 and that's only two days' cleanup on my claim."

The Italian bid $11,000 and when Sam again called him a "piker" upped it to $16,000.

"Twenty," countered Sam. "Oh, hell, wat's use of wasting time? Thirty."

And before the dazed Italian could answer, Marie shouted, "Going, gone at thirty."

"You're one crooked, dirty whore. You're rotten, anyhow and no decent 'house' would have you in it," the Italian raged. Then he rushed Sam, clamping his great arms around him, pinning one of Sam's arms behind him and working for a stranglehold. Sam went limp. The Italian, shifting his grip like lightening, lifted his body higher and higher.

"I break heem! I smash heem!" he shouted in rage. But suddenly Sam sprang to life, smashing the Italian's jaw just below his ear and knocking him cold. Sam gave his chit for the money to the owner of the Monte Carlo, picked up Marie, hustled her to his dog sled, and headed for home. And they were married the following summer when they learned her husband had died.[28]

———— ❈ ————

Storybook endings were, of course, rare. While strong women sometimes could triumph over the grimmer realities of prostitution and fast living, others failed spectacularly, as illustrated by the history of the dancing, singing Brocee sisters. Myrtle Brocee, at nineteen, was immortalized by the Dawson newspaper headline, "She Blew Out Her Brains," while her older sister, Florence, went on to good reviews and cash reserves for a better life.

Born and raised on a farm in Ontario, the Brocees developed a theater

PARTY, PARTY!

Many of the participants in this ballroom spree in Dawson look a bit worse for wear,
which was typical of life in the Far North's "fast lane." This event was recorded in 1902,
when the rush was beginning to slow but few had really noticed.

UAF, Bassoc Glass Plate Collection, 64-92-646.

act and won professional engagements in Chicago and Victoria. Then they
worked their way to the Klondike, arriving in Dawson with no contacts,
but quickly becoming favorites at the Tivoli. Both women apparently
traded on their respectability, but Myrtle had a weakness for men and
alcohol. She confessed to a friend that she had attempted suicide while in
Victoria and would try again "unless something turned up to rid her of the
life which she hated and which brought her the importunities of the men."[29]

In late November of 1898, a three-week bout with pneumonia weak-
ened Myrtle's spirit and demolished her finances. Then Harry Woolrich,
one of Dawson's most dashing gamblers with whom she had been living
for several weeks, unceremoniously dumped her. "She had neither money
or clothes," he explained candidly. "I told her I would not marry her." A
couple of days later, about an hour after finishing a novel titled *One Too
Many* and telling friends she identified with the heroine who committed
suicide, Myrtle put a bullet through her brain.

Wanting a respectable burial for her sister, Florence Brocee hired a lawyer to protect her from an unqualified verdict of suicide, settling for "temporary insanity" instead. James Aikman, like a dozen other suitors, testified unconvincingly that Myrtle had "occupied his bed but was absolutely virtuous."[30] And a local reporter provided a wonderful psychological autopsy.

"Tempters appeared by the score, some with wine and many of them well off; yet the girl's good name continued and continued to make her the more desirable to the eyes of admirers. The slack season came on; occasional illness caused absence from the theater with a constant diminution of revenue toward the zero point, and the girl at last found herself depressed and hopeless. Instead of wealth which was to relieve her from following a distasteful business she found hardships; instead of honorable suitors she found tempters."[31]

In contrast, Florence continued to prosper, as columnist Stroller White noted a year after her sister's suicide. "Florence Brocee is a pretty, dark-eyed variety actress at the Monte Carlo. Her youth, slender form, and coy demeanor do not evidence great experience in gilded palaces; but nevertheless, the winsome Flo cannot be classed with the spring chickens," he wrote in detailing her romance with a mercantile store clerk. The young man bought her wine in one of the theater boxes until he could no longer borrow money to court her. Straightforward about his financial straits, he declared confidence in his ability to recoup and asked Florence to marry him, according to Stroller's account.

"She evinced surprise at the sudden proposal; and, to the amazement of the lovesick youth, she proceeded to inform him that she would not consent to be his wife forever; that she was the mother of a child, and that, in monkeying with the stern realities of life she needed the assistance of an individual who possessed something more than confidence and prospects."[32]

The young man went doggedly back to his job, while considering volunteering for military service. When a fire started in her room at Monte Carlo in January of 1900, Florence declared the loss of $1,000 in savings but continued unabated in her career as a heartless charmer.

Another suicide that shocked the town was that of Stella Hill, a.k.a. Kitty Stroup of Boon's Ferry, Oregon. Also nineteen, she swallowed strychnine just four days before Christmas in 1898, shortly after Myrtle Brocee's burial. The beautiful, tall, curly-haired blonde, winner of a prize for waltzing at the Monte Carlo, had come to Dawson via Juneau and Circle with Charley Hill, a bartender at the Pioneer. Although he let her use his last name, Charley had never married Stella and appeared on the verge of dumping her for another woman. "I have lived with Charley four years and am not going to have him throw me down now," she told her friend Kitty Lawrence before touring most of the bars in town, then writing a suicide note calculated to send her lover into fits of remorse.

Apparently Stella had second thoughts, because just before the poison caused fatal spasms, she called for a doctor. Seamstress Anna DeGraf arrived at the scene with the matching blue gowns she had made for Stella and her best friend to wear to the masquerade ball that evening. She found Charley Hill standing out front and Stella's friend in tears.

"She took me into the room where her chum lay, so beautiful and fair—but now cold and still, when she had been so lively and happy. While we were looking at her, this man came in and stood and gazed at her without noticing anybody else. Then he turned on his heel, lit a cigarette and walked out of the room," DeGraf recalled with bitterness toward Stella's heartless lover.

"The other girls made up a purse and paid the funeral expenses. Another girl took her place, wore her costume that night at the ball—life went on the same, and nobody bothered about her."[33]

"Montreal" Marie Lambert, petite, pretty, and dark-eyed, who had been arrested as an inmate of the notorious Bartlett House, must have thought she was saved when H. D. Stammers, a government clerk, moved her into his cabin as his common-law wife. She bore him two children and was so grateful for their relationship that she hustled herself for money to send him home to Australia to visit his family, whom he had not seen in fifteen years.

Her lover repaid her by returning with a very young bride, a charming girl from the upper classes with large gray eyes, a pale oval face, and an expression of sweetness and innocence. Stammers got himself transferred to another district so he didn't have to deal with his past, but he did not fare well in the long run. His young wife died of blood poisoning in childbirth, and he was shot to death by a holdup man in Windsor. Marie quietly went back to her former calling, with her name clearly painted over the door, to support their children.[34]

———— ⬤ ————

These sad histories reflect the hazards of the heart, however, more than those of the skin trade. "The veteran prostitutes, who came mainly from other northern mining camps and American West Coast cities, knew what to expect," observed historian Frances Backhouse. "They faced a high possibility of dying young from venereal diseases, tuberculosis, malnutrition, or violence at the hands of pimps or clients."[35]

No permanent cure had been found for venereal disease, and the treatment with mercury, while effective, was harsh and could take up to nine months in the hospital.[36] Most women from the demimonde who later married had no children, perhaps left sterile as a result of this or the crude abortion procedures of the day.

Although Dawson's whores were less likely than most to catch venereal disease because of the isolation of the region, the sickness spread rapidly in October of 1898, and laws were passed requiring all prostitutes to have monthly medical inspections costing five dollars. This measure came too late to stem the growing epidemic, and inspections to curb it soon had to be increased to twice monthly.[37] Later, Ottawa officials would demand that the police surgeon cease issuing health certificates to "harlots" on the indisputable logic that the trade was illegal,[38] but by then the epidemic was under control and the population of Dawson was declining.

On the plus side, the bizarre sexual practices that were a threat to prostitutes in major cities were seldom a problem in the North. This was observed with relief by a Chicago prostitute who transferred to the Canadian prairies frontier during the same period. "Here there were no blasé habitués of wine-rooms and bawdy-houses, seeking a new sensation by learning a new perversion. Here were men, fine and strong, courtly gentlemen such as I have never seen anywhere else in the world," she marveled. "Their visits to the houses were a part of their playtime; they were not seeking a new sensation, those red-blooded men of the Northwest; they brought their sensations with them, and they showed a tenderness and courtesy toward women which often brought a choking into my throat."[39]

While not inclined to sexual kinkiness, Klondike miners could be brutal, especially when drunk. Seamstress Anna DeGraf, who spent much time

A GROUP OF HARD WORKERS
Another in the Larss & Duclos White Chapel series features more lingerie
than was usually seen in 1898, even on the wide open frontier.
YA #739, Larss and Duclos photograph.

with showgirls and witnessed considerable violence, recalls one talented
singer who was bedridden after a severe beating.

"She showed me on her chest the prints like a horseshoe, made by a
man's heavy boot—the nail prints of the shoe showed plainly where he'd
kicked her; and there was another large wound on the side. She told me
that he had come to her door and failing to gain admittance had kicked
down the door and acted like a wild man—drunk of course!"

DeGraf arranged for a doctor and matron at the government barracks
to nurse the girl, a stately brunette with a voice like a nightingale. She left
on the first boat in the spring, but six months later word came back she
had died from her Dawson injuries.[40]

Subtler hazards included long hours in smoke-filled rooms and the
lifestyle itself.

"There is a great deal of gambling done here. It is a common sight to
see in the saloons with gambling halls and dance halls attached, the
females (who operate in the dance rooms at $1 per dance) sitting at the
card tables, stud horse poker, blackjack or faro are the principal ones, or

standing at the roulette table cigarette in mouth and playing away for pretty high stakes," reported John McDougal, a well-traveled mining man, in an 1899 letter to a friend.

"I don't see how in the world these girls stand the racket. Take the ordinary concert hall girl. She has to go on and do her turn every night on the stage, then 'wrestle the boxes' they call it here. That is, sit in the box set aside for her or visit the private boxes occupied by any poor sucker who is an easy mark for them and get him to buy drinks for them at $1 per drink or wine at $15 per pint on which they get 25 percent after the show is over (as much as $45 or $50). Generally about twelve or one o'clock they clear the floor and dance till 5 or 6 a.m. at $1 per dance and a drink. After each dance they get a check for every drink that is bought on their behalf . . . besides their salary which is on the average of $45 per week. Well these poor devils keep this up night after night, all year round, drunk every night as they cannot help it, if they want to do business."[41]

Gussie Lamore, the famous showgirl who conned a fortune out of Swiftwater Bill Gates, apparently enjoyed life on this fast track and had a well-documented penchant for alcohol, for which she paid dearly. Her splendid good looks had already coarsened by 1902, when she played the vaudeville houses of Spokane. "She is not a bad-looking woman. She has genuine flaxen hair, a piquant expression, a pleasant smile and is neat and stylish in appearance," a reviewer conceded. "She is still young but the dissipation incidental to the consumption of champagne which the miners used to buy her has left telltale marks on her pleasing countenance." Gussie died a bloated alcoholic just five years later at age thirty-one.[42]

A few prostitutes (and bartenders, too) who had drinking problems were declared insane and shipped off to mental institutions to dry out. Estranged from her husband, Annie Gallina, "the Irish Queen," moved north in 1887 with her brother, who eventually found work with the railroad in Skagway. Initially she did well as a dance hall girl, but in 1900 she was jailed for theft and then committed to an asylum. Rumors claim that she later went respectable, marrying well, so perhaps the cure was successful.[43]

―――○∞○―――

Arrests for theft became common after Dawson matured but, surprisingly, more dance hall girls and actresses than prostitutes appeared on the police books. Typical was a complaint against Neal Buckley and legitimate actress Irene Howard, both employed at the Orpheum Dance Hall, charging they robbed S. D. Freeman of #6 Hunker Creek of two $1,000 American gold notes. According to his recollections, Freeman started drinking with the women in boxes at the M & N Saloon and later upstairs at the Orpheum. He showed them the bills, he told police, because they said they had never seen bills of that denomination before. Then he made the mistake of undressing and going to bed with Neal Buckley, while, he suspected, Irene Howard went through his pockets.

According to a follow-up by Corporal Allan A. McMillan, "I went to the room occupied by Neal Buckley; she was dressed lying asleep on the bed; she admitted that she had been drinking with S. D. Freeman and that he had spent about $100. She shewed us the amount of her percentage which amounted to $46 while with him; she also admitted that he had intercourse with her in her room; there was a bottle of wine, partly empty, and several bottles of beer, partly empty, and several broken glasses in the room. She stated that he had told her that he had two $1,000 bills but did not shew them. In the adjoining room was Irene Howard asleep in bed and a man with her."[44]

As in Irene Howard's case, there were usually no convictions because tired, hung-over victims did not make convincing witnesses. The practice of rolling drunks was common enough, however, that it would play a major part in motivating public sentiment to close the dance halls.

On the whole, surprisingly few criminal complaints were made, given the large number of showgirls and prostitutes operating during the rush, perhaps because most recognized their rare opportunity. "Dawson may have offered them a better than average life," concedes historian Backhouse. "Women of any sort were such a rare commodity that even prostitutes were tolerated and give a degree of protection by the Northwest Mounted Police."[45] And, perhaps because so many of the prostitutes were amateurs, an inordinate number were apparently trustworthy.

"Many of those girls had hearts of gold. They would give their last dollar to those who needed it. There was often a fine sportsmanship among them and a real mothering for a man who was down and out," observed Martha Black, who went on to become a social and political leader in Yukon Territory. "I have wondered since if we other women could not have been kinder to those so set apart from us. Too often many of us, secure in our legitimacy, swanked by arrogantly. I was told that the girls often laughed over this among themselves, for well they knew the double life of many of the leading citizens."[46]

Of particular note was a prostitute known as the "Rough Rider," and another called "The Angel of Hunker Creek," who brightened many lives and probably saved a few.

"Never was there a miner known to be sick, far or near on the gulches, but without hesitation she would go and see him," C. S. Hamlin, an early stampeder, wrote of the Angel. "Often have seen [her] plodding sixteen miles along a game trail with gumboots on, ankle-deep in slush, carrying a pack of something for this sick miner. . . . To all the many functions of the best society she was invited and went, with the grace of a ministering angel. None ever spoke of her as a wayward soul. They could not think of this; they knew, by that one great standard, the gold scales, she was weighted and found to be a true and living woman in the cause of suffering humanity."[47]

However, Dawson's laissez-faire attitude toward prostitution began to change in the spring of 1899, when a fire started in a whorehouse reduced about forty buildings to rubble. Helen Holden was rumored to have caused the disaster by throwing a lamp at a rival prostitute. Fines were initiated, and concerned citizens unsuccessfully attempted to exclude scarlet women from the business district.[48]

Then Sam Steele, who had replaced Constantine as the superintendent of the Mounted Police, began campaigning for a segregated district. While conceding that the prostitutes "seem to be in the eyes of the majority of the community a necessary evil," and that they were orderly, sober, "and, in fact, much less detrimental . . . than a large number of the variety actresses," Superintendent Steele insisted they be moved.[49]

Businessmen, greedily eyeing the choice downtown lots the women would be forced to abandon, readily agreed. The *Klondike Nugget* entered the fray, assuring readers that the women would not "be swept from the earth by an iron hand, but transplanted" within easy reach.[50]

"Second Avenue is now becoming one of Dawson's most prominent and important thoroughfares. Before the city had assumed its present and growing commercial importance, the *masons de joie* were located as they now are on Paradise Alley and Second Avenue. Of late the number has increased on Second Avenue until the street is prominent in its display of red curtains between First and Third Streets," the *Klondike Nugget* editor noted. "Whatever may be the opinion concerning the locations, there can certainly be no excuse for permitting the advertising so vulgarly displayed of the 'off' society of the city as may be seen today."[51]

A week after the devastating fire, the *Nugget* reported that Superintendent Steele had set aside two blocks bounded by Fourth and Fifth Avenues and First and Third Streets, just outside the business district, and ordered the prostitutes to move there by the end of May. Those who resisted were arrested and given stiff fines, and by the end of August the move was complete.[52] Who actually profited from this venture is unknown. The actual buyers used real estate agents as fronts, or "trustees," for good reason[53]—they were in position to profit nicely by collecting high rent from Dawson's demimonde.

"It was said that three well-known citizens [who] had been given the 'tip' had built the rabbit hutches in which the girls were made to live," stampeder Nevill Armstrong later recalled. "There were about fifteen of those 'hutches' on either side of a narrow roadway with a wooden sidewalk in front of each row of buildings. Each hutch had two rooms, a bed-sitting-room and kitchen and a *cache* or outhouse. Exorbitant rents were charged these women and it was told me on good authority that each of the three principals who invested in the building of Hell's Half Acre drew $800 per month as his share of the rents (averaging $26 per month), etc. . . ."

Armstrong went on to describe the prostitutes' new accommodations. "On the door of each 'hutch' was painted the Christian name or *nom de guerre* of the occupant. In some cases there were two girls in one 'hutch.' The bed-sitting-room in each case was in the room facing the sidewalk and if the occupant was not otherwise engaged, the window blind would be up and the fairy inside would be seen reclining on a bed or divan very scantily attired and using every blandishment to entice inquisitive men to enter. The miners and others would take a look at all the 'samples' and then decided on a selection. I have seen as many as eight miners waiting in a queue outside one girl's 'hutch.'"[54]

Despite the increased rent, the well-advertised central location may have been advantageous to prostitutes, who were still making far more at their trade than they would have almost anywhere else in the world. Sergeant A. Bowen Perry, the Northwest Mounted Police administrator who succeeded Steele, was alarmed to discover that most of the women in the red light district were French, with the majority having arrived in the spring and summer of 1898. Yet his report, which listed forty-three by name, concluded that "the system of segregation seemed

THE AMERICAN CONTINGENT
Although the Klondike gold stampede attracted people from all over the world,
the majority of those who came north were American. This photo, apparently of an all-American
group in the White Chapel red light district, was taken on the Fourth of July.
YA, MacBride Museum Collection, #3794, Larss and Duclos photograph.

to work well and that on the whole there was little cause for complaint."[55]

Then in January of 1900 a second fire started, this time in dance hall girl Florence Brocee's room at the Monte Carlo. It wiped out an entire block between Second and Third, causing a half-million dollars damage. But although it was proved that a faulty chimney flu caused the blaze, which was therefore not Brocee's fault,[56] the righteous citizens of Dawson began to voice their dim view of dance hall girls and other loose women.

By this time Dawson had all the advantages of a real city—telegraph service, electricity, police, banks, stores, a post office, and a school—which attracted ever-increasing numbers of wives and families. Because the entertainment business reaped huge profits, theaters, dance halls, and gambling dens multiplied at an astonishing rate, and there were soon more bars than could be visited in a single night.[57] In March of 1900 the city declared it would close dance halls, theaters, and gambling establishments that did not pay a license fee of $500 annually.[58] One year later, with prompting from the government in Ottawa, it moved to close them for good.

The building of a public school on Third Avenue and declining property values motivated several citizens to campaign for elimination of the red light district. But in May of 1901 a committee headed by Andrew Nerland—whose paint and wallpaper company recently had spent thousands on property improvements[59]—settled for the banishment of whores from within city limits.

Those prostitutes who were unsuccessful in disguising their illicit operations had the option of moving to West Dawson or across the river to Klondike City (also known affectionately as "Lousetown" because of its prior inhabitants and "White Chapel" after a similar district in London). In both areas, the available lots were rumored (but never proved) to have been bought up by the same anonymous syndicate that owned "Hell's Half Acre," from which the women had been evicted.[60]

Well-meaning citizens saw these changes as a move toward respectability and thus economic stability, but it was essentially the beginning of the end for Dawson.[61] The theaters alone employed several hundred. Already a major gold strike in Nome was drawing many entertainers and a large percentage of their audience away from the Yukon to Alaska. Closure of the dance halls, theaters, gambling dens, and red light district only hastened the exodus that would reduce the population of Dawson from 30,000 at the height of the rush to just over 4,000 two decades later.

Still, the selling of sex remained profitable enough that many prostitutes stayed. Early photos of "Lousetown" show approximately sixty cribs, four times the number built in Hell's Half Acre. Laura Beatrice Berton, who with a fellow schoolteacher spied on the red light district one summer afternoon in 1908, found it a going concern.

"At the back doors of the tiny frame houses, the whores, laughing and singing, calling out to each other and chattering like bright birds, were making their toilets for the evening. Some were washing their long hair—invariably bright gold or jet black—drying it in the sun and leisurely brushing it out," she recalled. "Others were just reclining languorously and gossiping with their neighbors. Some were singing lyrically. All were in their chemises. Our eyes stared from our heads as we gazed down on them, for these garments were quite short, scarcely down to the knees, and every woman's legs were quite bare. The chemises were also sleeveless, which seemed equally immodest, and cut with a low round neck. As they were made of colored muslin—pink, blue and yellow—the effect was indescribably gay."[62]

ONE OF THE GIRLS

5

Mae Field

TO THE POLICE BLOTTER AND BACK

In 1943, Mrs. Mae Field talked about her life in the Klondike stampede in an interview with Helen Berg, a writer for the *Alaska Sportsman*.

"I didn't care for the gold," Mrs. Field said in a voice still as clear as a bird song. "It was what the gold could buy—the pleasure it could give others, the suffering it could alleviate. The gold itself was too common, just like pebbles that were picked up and thrown around."[2]

Helen Berg was charmed by her subject, a fragile little woman "with a beautiful, sweet old face," sitting in her quaint, old-fashioned parlor. The frail pioneer said she had been barely seventeen when she wed Arthur Field and headed north from South Dakota for the gold rush. Mrs. Field said that she still pined for Arthur, even though he'd left her to make her way alone in the world as a dance hall girl. She had been so successful that she was known as the "Doll of Dawson," she added.

Had Berg checked the papers of that era or discovered Mae Field's extensive Canadian police record, she might have titled her story, "The Moll of Dawson." But Mae, who must have been over seventy at the time, had been a respected resident of Ketchikan, Alaska, for thirty years.

"Everyone knew her, and thought they knew all about her. I was to learn, however, that a capricious fate had tossed her on waves of heavenly

---

MAE FIELD

In an era when smoking was something proper women didn't do and skirts above the ankle were considered scandalous, Mae Field posed brazenly blowing smoke rings and showing her shapely legs. Few would guess that only a couple of years earlier she'd been one of Dawson's respectable young matrons.

YA #817.

joy and abysmal sadness about which even her closest friends knew nothing," Berg reported in her best purple prose. Mae, a tenacious survivor with a grand sense of humor, led her a merry chase.

———⊶⊷———

According to her account, Mae had been raised in a quiet Minnesota town. "My parents were respectable, God-fearing people of the old school. They were horrified with me, because I wanted to dance. And dance I did! I ran away from home and went to Duluth," she told Helen Berg.

The petite brunette with milk-white skin and a marvelous figure attracted the attention of promoter "Whiskey" Bartlett at the Comique Theatre, who took her career in hand until her brother fetched her home. A few months later she was off again, dancing in Hill City, South Dakota, where she fell in love with Arthur Daniel Field. He was the son of a wealthy family from Hot Springs, South Dakota, and Mae gave up her promising career for him, she said.[2]

In truth, Arthur Field, age thirty-four, seems to have had no family ties in Hot Springs but had owned or managed bars in the area since about 1890. The local government occasionally voted itself dry and when it did, Arthur was usually arrested for bootlegging. In 1894 he and his partner, W. H. Carter, were arrested for running a whorehouse, but they beat the rap. When it was again legal to sell alcohol, Arthur was the first to buy a license. He owned a lot downtown where he built a two-story hotel, then purchased additional land and invested with a partner.[3]

Mae's history during this period is murky. It is well-documented that Arthur Field was married at Hot Springs on September 10, 1897, but his bride's name was recorded as Mrs. Lavina B. Wells, age twenty-four, whose place of residence was St. Paul, Ramsy Court, Minnesota. The marriage license was signed by Clerk of Courts Thomas H. Wells, who may have been the brother of Mae's former husband.[4]

The formal wedding made the local social column.[5] Mae would later claim that her bridegroom gave her valuable property in Hot Springs as a nuptial, and land records show the couple co-owned valuable property there until 1902. A confirmed bachelor until his marriage, Arthur appears to have delighted in the match. The local newspaper extended congratulations and best wishes.

The Fields honeymooned on the Klondike Trail. Arthur had invested heavily in mining equipment, and at Lake Bennett they built scows to transport it, accompanying in a canoe numbered 2187 by the Northwest Mounted Police.[6] All went well until a horrible gale blew up while they were crossing Lake Lebarge.

"I was so frightened that I seized the bottom of the sail, and clung to it with all my might," Mae recalled. "Arthur shouted at me to let go, but in spite of his commands I hung on for all I was worth! But do you know, the wind caught that taut-held sail and blew us, bow up, high and dry on the banks without a scratch. All the other boats hit broadside, and many people were hurt."[7]

The Fields lost most of their mining equipment but arrived in Dawson on June 20, 1898, which was early in the rush. Arthur staked claims #19 and 20 on Bear Creek, just below the discovery claim on Hunker Creek. With several partners he also applied and won another liquor license back in Hot Springs, in case things didn't work out.[8]

With food shortages pending and a long winter ahead, Arthur sent Mae home to her mother. She recalled scaling Chilkoot Pass at midnight with a group of twenty-six travelers all headed Outside. "It was a frozen mountainside of ice, with stair-like steps chipped out. One slip would have meant almost certain death," she said. "But even after we'd crossed the pass at night in order to get to Skagway in time to catch the boat, it turned out to be the old, unseaworthy *Georgia*, the most feared steamer on the Skagway-Juneau run. I, alone, of the twenty-six who crossed the pass, took a chance on it. I had a safe voyage, too; but the others had to wait ten days for the next boat out of Skagway."[9]

Mae's mother was upset when her daughter arrived in Minnesota. "She said my place was with my husband, no matter where he was; so she sent me right back to him," Mae told her biographer. And it appears she managed to return to the Klondike before navigation closed.

She claimed that she was matron of honor at the Dawson wedding that December of well-known packer Mike Bartlett to her friend Mollie Walsh, another Minnesota girl, who had done well running a "grub tent" on the White Pass Trail. A newspaper account of the wedding names Mrs. J. P. Douglass as matron, but Mae still might have attended because she accurately described the event to her biographer. Mike Bartlett soon would murder his new bride, a beautiful woman with a roving eye, but the Fields' union went well during this period.[10]

"We joined the Sourdough Club that winter, and made many good friends. There was Antone Stander; Roy Lund, the well-known hockey

player; Rose and Jack Blicks; the Spencers. We had gay parties at first one home and then another."

The Fields lived eight miles out of Dawson. "Arthur bought me a pony and cart to drive to town," Mae later reminisced. As for money, Arthur and his crew of about fifty had cleaned up about $100,000 from Bear Creek Claim #19 that spring of 1899, which simplified shopping. "I just took a hammer and knocked the gold loose in the cut, caught it in a pan, and took it into town," Mae recalled.[11]

In mid-summer, she again traveled to the States, returning that fall for another harrowing trip through Chilkoot Pass. Hiking it was still required but a freight tramway had been installed. On Mae's trip, the cable broke when the tram was halfway up the mountain and it crashed down, carrying a pink parrot riding atop the luggage.

"For once the trained bird was speechless," Mae said. "Then after the bucket had landed with a thud, right beside me, the parrot screamed, 'What the hell! Cut it out!'"[12]

Mae missed the boat from Bennett to Dawson by a few hours, and it was nearly a month before she could book another, according to her account. During the wait an epidemic broke out, and because the town

FRONT STREET, DAWSON
*Mae Field was living out of town with her husband at Bear Creek Mine while
Dawson's hotel district was being built in 1900. Separating from him two years later,
she moved into the district to make her living as a good time girl.*
NAC #J6299.

was short of nurses, she went to work at the hospital. Finally, just before
freeze-up, she headed home on the *Willie Irving*, billed as the "fastest
steamer on the Yukon."

The stern-wheeler left at the same time as its rival, the *Stratton*, which
Mae noticed was in the lead when she came on deck a little after midnight
on October 24, still several hours from her destination. "Look, the *Stratton's*
going to beat us into Dawson," she remarked to Charlie Grant, a miner. They
were gazing at the lights of the *Stratton* when it disappeared in an ice jam.[13]

The *Willie Irving* began to act strangely, its doors and portholes warp-
ing out of shape. Moments later screams were heard from the *Stratton's* passengers as she sank in thirteen feet of water about 350 feet from shore.[14]
Captain S. F. Griffiths of the *Irving* realized his ship was caught in the same
disaster and quickly ordered two of his men to lay a rope across the

jammed ice for passengers to follow ashore. Mae didn't panic until she found herself a long way from land with no ice to walk on.

"There lay the rope on free water! I tried to go back, and found that the ice I was on had broken from that side, too, and was floating away down the river," she recalled. "There was nothing to do but stay on it, and pretty soon it came to rest against another ice jam a little farther down-river. . . . I jumped from floe to floe as they broke away, and managed to get ashore after a while. The next morning we had to cross all the way to the left bank on the drifting ice, to get to the Mounted Police station.

"The *Willie Irving* was a total wreck. What of it had not broken away and drifted down the river, had sunk. . . . I surely felt sorry for Charlie Grant! He had $5,000 worth of horse feed aboard the *Irving*, and he couldn't well afford to lose it. . . . We had the clothes we were wearing—nothing more."

Amazingly, no lives were lost from either vessel, but passengers had a grim time after they made land. The small detachment of Northwest Mounted Police, who had not bothered to respond to the boats' repeated distress whistles just a quarter-mile from their station at Selwyn, refused to give the survivors food and shelter. After several hours of struggling to keep warm around a beach fire, the ten women in the party were allowed to enter the station, but were given no supplies.[15]

The passengers—a troupe of theater performers with three prominent theater managers among them—cared for each other. Mae took charge of a baby while his parents, Leo and Checota Chonita, Spanish dancers and trapeze performers, recovered.

At the urging of the inhospitable police, two days later twenty-five survivors set out on foot for Dawson, making the trip in about eighteen hours. Mae negotiated a ride aboard a scow through ice-choked waters to Stewart, walked to the next Mounted Police station, and finally arrived in Dawson by dog team with the mail carrier.[16]

Her arrival that winter of 1899 was her last trip home to Bear Creek. Mae explained that their claim had worked out, and that Arthur had lost their wealth financing other failed mining ventures. She and Arthur "just drifted apart," Mae told her biographer with a "choked sob." Mae bravely signed back the Hot Springs property Arthur had given her as a wedding present. Selling it enabled him to join the Fairbanks gold stampede and

TRAVEL WAS ROUGH
In her extensive commuting between the States and Dawson,
Mae Field traveled by riverboat, dog team, and occasionally on foot,
surviving one shipwreck and numerous near-disasters.
UW #17822.

amass another fortune. Then he returned to his boyhood home a wealthy man and married a Hot Springs girl.

"Meanwhile little Mae, heavy-hearted, penniless and alone in the Far North, turned to dancing, the only thing she knew, for a livelihood," Helen Berg reported. "She became a dancing girl at the Floradora!"[17]

It wasn't quite that simple. Actually, Arthur would mine Bear Creek through 1909, but apparently most of the richest pay streak was gone, because in 1901 he got a job bartending at the Northern Annex Saloon.[18]

In February of 1900, the *Klondike Nugget* gave curious coverage to a lawsuit involving Mae Field. Until this point she had always been mentioned in the society columns as Mrs. A. D. Field, but this article made no reference to her marital status, calling her "May Fields" (and spelling her name incorrectly).

According to the newspaper, Charles Meldner, manager of the Model Steam Laundry, sued Mae Field for $18.55. Mae insisted that she owed Model Steam just eight dollars, but Meldner explained he had charged her extra because her lingerie consisted of silken materials with many frills, and that to clean it required extraordinary care. "The witness supplemented his oral testimony by the sacrilegious exhibition of numerous articles of female wearing apparel, which might create no comment strung on a clothesline, but which seemed to be incongruously out of place in the sacred temple of justice," described the *Klondike Nugget*. Meldner's case appeared to be air-tight, but the *Nugget* reporter observed that the defendant possessed uncommon resources.

"She has a pretty face and a dainty air. Her attire is rich and no doubt designed by a most expert modiste," he wrote, wondering why she would protest such a small bill. "Large diamond pendants adorned her ears, and her shapely hands were bedecked with innumerable jewels."

Mae, denying that her clothing required extra care, got good reviews on the stand, especially when she coyly submitted her silken nightgown as Exhibit A, "with many a blush and shy look." Then Andrew F. Holloway, a witness for the defense, testified that the bill should amount to no more than $12.05 . . . the amount that dignified Judge C. A. Dugas finally awarded the plaintiff.

"May pouted her pretty lips and nervously pressed the tapering forefinger of her right hand against her front teeth. She had not anticipated an adverse judgment; had not come prepared to liquidate," the newspaper concluded. "But Mr. Holloway was still in the room. She whispered a few words to him and smiled ever so sweetly as he withdrew from his pocket enough to satisfy the plaintiff's claim."[19]

Mae's bejeweled appearance came at a time when, according to her best recollections, her husband was struggling and in debt, which makes one wonder who was keeping her in the latest fashions. Numerous accounts describe her as charming, and her photograph shows her as a very attractive woman in a place where an attractive woman could name her own price.

Apparently Mae did not leave her husband for any one man but for as many of them as she could find to amuse her and keep her in diamonds. Although she asked Andrew Holloway to pay her small debt in court, there is every indication that Mae Field was living high. Her court appearance, which she easily could have avoided by paying the laundry bill, may have been calculated to embarrass Arthur, who was working for wages.

Arthur Field still had resources, however, because in November of 1902—before the Fairbanks gold strike during which Mae claimed she financed his comeback—he and William Cavanaugh bought Bodega Block in Hot Springs for $5,000 in cash, and the next summer the partners were granted a liquor license for the property.[20]

No record of divorce has been found, but in May of 1902 Arthur Field represented himself as a single man to deed two lots in Hot Springs to Anna B. Gibson for $1,200, and shortly thereafter he bought the Northern Annex where he had been working in Dawson.[21] Contrary to Mae's story about the Hot Springs girl, no records show that Arthur remarried, either in Dawson or South Dakota. Yet no doubt Mae Field was hit hard when she realized that Arthur was through with her.

On Feb. 2, 1903, the headline in the *Klondike Nugget* read:

SUICIDE
May Fields Tires of the Joy of Living
Used a Revolver Yesterday Morning
But With Poor Effect and
Now Under Arrest.

"Yesterday morning about 7 o'clock May Fields had a hunch to climb the golden stairs via the revolver route, but lacked either the determination or the opportunity, and it is hard to tell which it was, to successfully put her plans into execution. At that hour she entered the Northern Annex saloon, with a revolver in her hand and without asking permission of the bartender proceeded to cash in, and if her attempt had been successful the floor would have been covered with bright red corpuscles."

The shot went through the back of her hair and into the saloon wall. The report does not say if the bartender who wrestled the gun from her hand and called the police was Arthur, but Mae's desperate move and the trial that followed must have been traumatic for him.

Mae testified that she had not intended to do herself any harm; that "she merely wished to excite the sympathy of her husband." The court sentenced her to three months in prison, suspended pending her good behavior.[22] The *Klondike Nugget* article was headlined "ATTEMPT AT SUICIDE: Mrs. Fields Gets Three Month Sentence," but never mentioned Mr. Field. Apparently Arthur continued to operate in Dawson's tight little respectable society. Mae, however, no longer had anything to lose by defying it.

In June a woman named Eva O'Gara, a.k.a. Eva St. Clair, filed charges that Mae had assaulted her with a beer glass in the Bonanza Saloon. Eva had filed similar charges against other women, and although she appeared in court with her face badly cut and a bump on her head, bandaged in generous amounts of sticking plaster, her lawsuit against Mae was not taken too seriously.[23] There was no follow-up on the trial, so it can be assumed the judge dismissed the case. But the arrest does indicate that Mae's life had changed considerably from the carefree days when she took her pony cart into town to mix and mingle with the young married set.

And the going would get tougher. When Dawson authorities moved prostitutes out of town to a red light district called White Chapel, Mae stood her ground. While her reputation was far from unsullied, she could not be classified as a common prostitute and apparently she had friends in high places.

In May of 1904, J. W. Falconer reported to the Chief License Inspector that Mae and another woman named Ping Pong had not moved, although both had been ordered to vacate. "Mae Fields occupies a fine suite of rooms #1 and #2 at the Royal Hotel, she is a well-known notorious character about town," he wrote. "I may inform you that with the exception of the women referred to, all of the women of lewd reputation are now moved out of licensed premises in Dawson."[24]

Mae solved the problem by purchasing a small house with two cabins on Fourth Avenue between York and Duke Streets, 100 yards from the police station, and hanging out a sign reading "Furnished Rooms."

Meanwhile, Arthur Field was facing a similar challenge as proprietor of the Northern Annex. Some 8,000 people had left Dawson for the gold strike in Nome. As business slowed, the government began demanding exorbitant license fees from the establishments that stayed open. Arthur kept mining his Bear Creek claims, which continued to be profitable enough to keep on the books. If he replenished his fortune in the Fairbanks stampede, as Mae reported, it probably would have been between 1903 and 1904, but no records place him in Fairbanks. In November of 1904, the Hot Springs, South Dakota *Star* reported the former proprietor of the Bodega was visiting friends there, noting that "he is now engaged in the mining business in Dawson." Arthur was listed as proprietor of the Northern Annex through 1905 and as a resident miner and bartender in Dawson through 1910.[25]

⸻

When the dance halls closed again in January of 1908, Mae successfully continued to ply her trade as a good time girl; however, when the government licensed the Orpheum in early May 1908, she was quick to apply. Manager John K. McCrimmon refused her. He was under police pressure not to hire prostitutes and Mae was on their list, he said. Mae went to Sergeant Allan A. McMillan of the Northwest Mounted Police and bluntly accused him of sabotaging her, but he denied it. Mae had entered a steady relationship with a businessman named Harry Strong, and by mid-May she convinced John McCrimmon to hire her because she was no longer in the trade.

The Orpheum's hours were brutal—9 p.m. until 4 a.m. every day except Sunday—but Mae never missed a night. She was paid 50 percent of everything she earned at one dollar per dance (with one drink included), plus fifty cents for all extra drinks, and she quickly became one of the Orpheum's top-grossing girls.

On Monday, June 30, Mae called in sick for the first time. Joseph Anderson, a steamship waiter who had met her a couple of weeks earlier and was smitten, bicycled to her home to find out what was wrong. Mae apparently asked him to leave, but Joseph was enjoying shore leave and in a mood to party. Finally he talked her into going bicycling. They got as far as the Ogilvie Bridge out by one of the gold dredges, and then cycled to the Floradora for some beer. About 3 a.m. they headed home. Joseph, by that time pretty drunk, ran into Mae's bike, knocking her off. They got back to her house about 4 a.m. and he stayed, although Joseph later claimed Mae told him to go home.

It was the opportunity the police had been waiting for. Sergeant McMillan had kept Mae's house under surveillance for six months and had been holding a warrant for her arrest for over a month, waiting to strengthen his case. Constable James Gillis, who along with Detective George Schoenbeck had trailed her that evening, went to fetch Constable Murray and a warrant.

At 5:30 that morning they rang Mae's doorbell three times and when she failed to respond, Constable Gillis broke down her door. The couple was in bed, Joseph in pajamas and Mae in a long wrapper. She was charged with being the keeper of a bawdy house and thereby being a loose, idle, or disorderly person or vagrant.

Mae pleaded not guilty at her trial on July 4, and police were hard put to prove that she had been soliciting. Joseph Anderson testified that Mae had asked him to go away and that he knew she was sick. He insisted he had paid her nothing and that he had not had sex with her, then or ever.

Neighbors—a customs agent and a married couple—testified that Mae kept a noisy house and sounds of singing and merriment were often heard there. The wife complained that strange men knocked on her door at all hours of the day and night, looking for the dance hall girl. But no one had filed a formal complaint. Except for Sergeant McMillan, who refused to name his source, police could not find anyone to testify that Mae had ever solicited men for prostitution.

Mae spoke proudly in her own defense. "I have worked in the dance hall off and on since 1900—since I separated from my husband. I am making my own living. I have two cabins that I rent for $60 a month and I work in the dance hall. I make $8, $10, $12 to $20 every night. I live in my own house. I have two cabins in the back that I receive rent from; $40 from one and $20 from the other. . . . I have been living with Harry Strong."

Had she been with other men in the past six months? asked her lawyer, J. A. Clark.

"With no one else at all," she said.

Judge C. D. Macaulay appears to have made up his mind before hearing her testimony. "You have been a well-known character here ever since I came into the country over seven years ago and have frequently been before me and the other judges on different charges, and so far as your general reputation goes I could not live here without hearing what it was and knowing what it was," he said before pronouncing sentence.

"This is not the first time you have been up, but many times. I believe the last time you were brought before the court you were brought before my brother Dugas who at that time cautioned you that if you were found guilty again, you would be given the full benefit of the law. . . . If I sentenced you to six months it would be impossible for you to leave the country before the close of navigation. Consequently I will not impose the full sentence upon you, but I do think it absolutely necessary that some term of imprisonment should be imposed upon you as an example to yourself and others."

He sentenced her to three months of hard labor in the spartan jail of the Northwest Mounted Police at Dawson, with the understanding that she would leave the country on October 1.[26]

Mae apparently served her term and left the Yukon as ordered, but returned the next year to wrap up her affairs. She left for good on August 30, 1911, just a year after Arthur Field pulled out to join another gold stampede. Mae left the forwarding address of 151 Harris Street,

Vancouver, B.C.[27] Arthur became a resident of Iditarod, Alaska, where he was listed as a miner in the city directory.

—ೲ—

About 1912, Mae Field surfaced in Ketchikan, Alaska, bought property, and settled in. When Helen Berg interviewed her thirty years later, Mae was making her living by renting rooms in her very legitimate boardinghouse.

Biographer Berg noted that Mae was known to be generous to a fault. She had given her two largest Klondike gold nuggets to the Sisters of Mercy to care for motherless children. She had deeded a house lot to someone she knew who needed it, and helped countless other friends.[28] Mae was also generous with the time she had for Berg, though deft at sliding out of all the tough questions.

One last question Berg asked was why the dance hall queen had chosen to finish out her life in Ketchikan, a small town in Southeastern Alaska. "People didn't ask personal questions in the North," Mae gently reminded the writer. "Not in those days."[29]

That might not be the whole answer. Ketchikan was also the hometown of Henry Strong, president of the Ketchikan Steamship Company, who also had far-flung mining interests. Strong was respectable and apparently happily married, although childless. Old-timers recall he helped found the local public utility, and that the city named a wharf after him. But knowing the "Doll of Dawson," one might suspect he was the same Harry Strong with whom Mae once had lived during her wild days in the Klondike.[30]

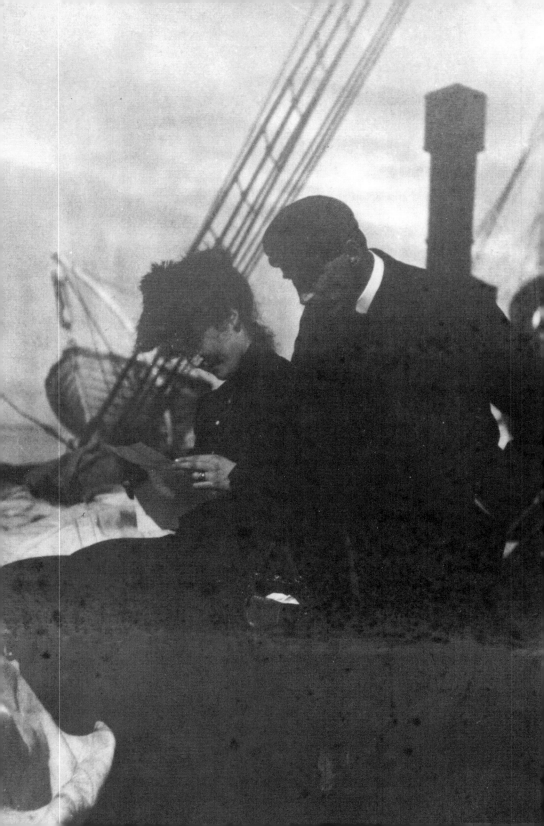

6

Corrine B. Gray

A LOST RACE WITH FORTUNE

———⟨∞⟩———

It seems strange and unfair that the body of "the little actress," Corrine B. Gray, who loved bright lights, fine champagne, and the latest Paris fashions, should lie in an unmarked grave in a nearly forgotten cemetery near the Athabascan village of Rampart, Alaska. But Corrine was a casualty of the Klondike Stampede as surely as if she'd been crushed excavating an untimbered tunnel, and most prospectors lost in that gold rush lie far afield. What makes Corrine's case intriguing is the gay abandon of her quest for riches and love, and the fact that she came very close to getting everything she wanted before her dreams slipped away.

———⟨∞⟩———

She was listed in the 1880 census as Lizzie Bissler, the six-year-old daughter of Anna and Barnhart L. Bissler of Nimishillen Township, in an Ohio farming district, but she was either a child by a previous marriage or born out of wedlock, for Anna and Barnhart had not wed until 1877. Anna Bissler was originally from England; her husband also came from England though he was German-born, a harness-maker who could afford an

———⟨∞⟩———

RESCUED

Corrine Gray was relieved to be rescued from the
Canadian Northwest Mounted Police by American William Ballou,
who smuggled her out of Dawson and over the international boundary
to Alaska via riverboat. Later he treated her to a brief trip to Seattle.
This photograph of the couple was taken en route.

UAF, William B. Ballou Collection.

apprentice.[1] Corrine's uncle, Frank Bissler, was the local barkeeper, and she and her cousin Kathleen Bissler grew up as close as sisters. Beyond that nothing is known about Corrine's early life or her subsequent marriage to a man named Gray.

A dark-haired, black-eyed beauty with an impishly sexy smile, Corrine arrived early in Juneau, moved on to Skagway and, in 1897, continued to Dawson where she easily found employment in the dance halls. She called herself an actress, but her name appears on no surviving playbills, and the press unfailingly described her as a "fairy," the only permissible one-word euphemism for "prostitute" in that post-Victorian era.

Surprisingly, Corrine did business under her real name, even including her middle initial. This was unusual for a girl from a respectable family, but she must have enjoyed her press, for she worked for it.

"Her career in Dawson has been a triumphant one, fraught with a success in social and theatrical circles that would satisfy even the average woman. She has been a star attraction in the Klondike theatrical firmament for the past two years, dimming the luster of the aurora borealis, and shading her rivalry by her luminous brilliancy," a writer for the *Bennett Sun* reported enthusiastically in November of 1899. "Her versatility has won popularity for every house wherein she has been engaged, and her magnetic charms have attracted thousands of dollars to the coffers of her manager and herself."[2]

Corrine danced at Walter Washburn's elegant Opera House, where a sign on the balcony reminded customers that "gentlemen in private boxes are expected to order refreshments" including champagne at sixty dollars per quart. She appeared at the Pavilion, built at a cost of $100,000 with ornately carved pillars, elaborate cornices, and rococo lines.[3] She also played the Palace Grand and, before it burned, the Green Tree Hotel, a favorite place for "rapid rendezvous," owned by her true friend "Arkansas" Jim Hall, one of the most flamboyant of the Eldorado gold kings.

Corrine's professional ratings were high. "Her fascinating ways have enthralled many a lovesick miner, and when she flitted about in light, gossamery accouterment at the Grand Opera or Nigger Jim's [the nickname for the Pavilion, owned by Jim Daugherty, an outstanding minstrel show performer], it brought them visions of fairyland," the *Bennett Sun* reported, tongue-in-cheek. "Even though the nights are long in Dawson, they were not long enough, for time passed quickly when in her company. There was nothing slow about times with Corrine."[4]

Unfortunately, Corrine's press coverage usually meant trouble, for which she had as strong a penchant as she did for alcohol. And teamed with A. C. Stearns, a diminutive, sixty-five-year-old former physician known as the "Gambler Ghost," she sometimes outdid herself. "Doc" Stearns had broken the bank at Monte Carlo, so he was usually treated with deference, but together they made both the *Klondike Nugget Semi-Weekly* and the Dawson police blotter on September 27, 1899.

According to that account, "'Doc' Stearns, a blasé habitué of the gambling houses and variety halls, and Corrine B. Gray, one of the airy fairies of Dawson's half-world, were ejected from the stage at the Opera House on Monday night. 'Doc' and Corrine, who was very much inebriated, were quarreling with each other behind the scenes. Their loud argument threatened to distract the attention of the audience in front, to whom the management was indebted for something more than the production of a lovers' quarrel in real life. George Hillyer, the stage manager, cautioned the noisy couple to be quiet but they refused to desist. Finally they were ejected, but not without some trouble. Corrine considered that her right of person had been violated and on Tuesday morning, she appeared at the police court somewhat the worse after a night's debauch, but, nevertheless, she was there—and swore out a complaint against Hillyer, accusing him of assault."

Stearns accompanied her, planning to offer himself as a witness for the prosecution and thus relieve the "wearisome monotony of the police court." There was no follow-up, however, perhaps because George Hillyer, who'd engaged an attorney, calmed the irate actress. But the following month, Corrine was in court again, and this time the charges were serious.

"Corrine B. Gray, the frolicsome fairy who defrauded Uncle Hoffman of $90 and then took passage on the *Sybil* for the Outside, has been intercepted by the police at Tagish," the *Klondike Nugget* reported. "She will be returned here and placed on trial in the magistrate's court."[5]

The Northwest Mounted Police, after long ignoring prostitution, were in the midst of an enthusiastic campaign to stop it, and were particularly zealous about following up on complaints of prostitutes robbing innocent miners. Corrine was charged with selling her furniture to two separate parties—one of whom was "Uncle Hoffman," who may have been pawnbroker Lewis Hoffman—then trying to leave town.[6] Four days later, the police reported that Corrine was so ill that she could not be removed from Tagish—a customs station between Whitehorse and Bennett, the terminus for the White Pass Railroad—and that she would probably be released under bond.[7]

Since she had an otherwise strong constitution, Corrine's illness may have been alcohol or drug withdrawal. She remained in the Tagish jail for a month until her friend "Arkansas" Jim Hall, the owner of #17 Eldorado, came through from a trip to Bennett and agreed to post half of the $20,000 bail the Mounties required. J. Cole, another successful miner from Hunker Creek, agreed to pay the other half, but charges were magically dropped before it was necessary.[8]

Less than a month later, Jim Hall would find himself jailed by friends who were trying to prevent him from marrying yet another dance hall girl. But Corrine did not wait around to aid her benefactor. Three days out of jail she was in Bennett, badgering the local newspaper editor to help her with an affair of the heart gone wrong.

"Am very sorry to feel myself compelled to ask your aid in my trouble which is really now more than I can bear. It being overwhelming," she wrote in a note she slipped under the editor's door when she found his office empty. "Will return in ten minutes. Please be here if your business will permit.

"Will explain to you then.

"Corrine B. Gray."

She reappeared shortly after the lunch hour, demanded a paper and pencil, and hastily wrote a letter that she wanted published. Her favored suitor would pay the bill, she said. But the editor, who knew a good yarn when he saw one, agreed to run the material for nothing if he could have editorial license in writing a story to go with it.

According to Corrine's dramatic account, two rivals for her affections had followed her from Dawson to Bennett, and the one she ultimately rejected swore revenge. It was he who had her arrested at Whitehorse Rapids, hoping that navigation would close for the winter before she could clear herself and that she would be forced to live with him in Dawson.

Corrine had turned to the rejected suitor for bail, she said, but he grew jealous and withdrew it when he discovered she had talked to his rival.

"His anger and jealousy know no bounds," she claimed. "Since he has been away from Dawson where he thinks no one knows about our affairs, he has repudiated me in full. Never-the-less he owes me $800 cash I loaned him to live on waiting to sell his claim. Now because he cannot use me as he desires he withdraws his bonds as I am an invalid."

Unbeknownst to Corrine, the "rejected one" was snugly "cached" behind the counter of the newspaper office during her interview, and the amused editor noted that he did not seem to enjoy the drama. In fact, on Corrine's departure, he declared he was as anxious to keep the account *out* of the newspaper as she was to have it in.

Omitting the names of the men involved, the editor ran the story under bold headlines:

Corrine Has More Trouble
Two of Her Favorites Clash at Bennett
ONE REJECTED SUITOR
Expresses a Desire to 'Send His Successful Rival to a Hot Climate'
Corrine's Fairy Story as to the Cause of her Arrest
She Finally Succeeds in Leaving the Country

"In her tour of the Northland Miss Gray made many friends," the *Sun* writer editorialized. "To her knowledge she never made a single or married enemy. This, she declares, is her undoing—she has too many friends. They are all friends of Corrine, but not friends of one another, and in their endeavors to harm each other they hurled boomerangs of barbed anathema, which, though they came back to the thrower to his injury, usually struck Mlle. Gray on the home stretch. When she decided to come out for the winter to spend a well-earned vacation, two of these friends braved themselves enough to come also. Miss Gray soon became aware they were not content to be on an equal footing in her affections, and that she must choose either one or the other and end the affair then and there. This she did in favor of a well-known Yukoner who has been in the country for over twelve years and owns valuable interests on Eldorado Creek. The result was that while the three were stopping in Bennett the rejected suitor expressed a desire to dispatch his successful rival to a region enjoying a milder climate than he had been accustomed to. The threat was made and was only prevented from being executed by the intervention of the bartender.

"At the direful thought of having to return to Tagish, if the 'persecuting lover' took up the $500 cash bond, the emotional Corrine sought the *Sun* to protect her spotless reputation and to throw its calcium light of publicity—not for theatrical advertising purposes—on the whole affair and thus expose to view the designs of the 'enamored' one."[9]

Corrine sailed for San Francisco, satisfied that her name had been cleared, but unwisely returned to Dawson in 1900, again provoking the police. Although newspaper accounts do not implicate her, the cause of her arrest was probably the death of Corporal M. W. Watson, age thirty-three, who "accidentally" shot himself in the stomach on March 27.

Throughout his army service, until about four weeks earlier, Corporal Watson had been a "true and noble servant of the queen," his obituary noted. "From a jovial, light-hearted companion he became a sullen and morose recluse, but never for a moment did he forget the imbued instincts of the gentleman, being at all times courteous and polite when addressed by anyone." Most were surprised to learn that Corporal Watson, an orderly room clerk, was actually the Honorable M. W. St. John Watson Beresford of Creaduff House, Athlone, Ireland, the scion of a proud and noble Irish family.

According to the police, Watson's "accident" was the result of a prolonged drinking spree. "He left his place at the barracks and devoted himself most assiduously to keeping up his drunk. The fact that his money became exhausted in no way caused him to deviate from the mad course he was pursuing, for he issued checks here and there for small amounts, usually $10, and the period of intoxication was thus elongated until, in a semi-lucid moment, the young man realized that he had not reported for twenty-one days, thereby entitling the writing of the word 'Deserter' after his name on the army roll."[10]

The jury assigned to the case came in with the verdict of accidental death, and severely chastised the Dawson papers for having reported it as suicide.[11] But some believed that the careless heart of Corrine Gray had driven Watson to his "prolonged spree," and that she was responsible for ruining a good man. That belief was why the Mounties had trumped up yet another charge against her, Corrine maintained. Again she proclaimed herself the victim of unjust persecution.

Whatever the reason, Corrine Gray found herself wanted by the Mounties in mid-September of 1901. Her longtime benefactor, Jim Hall, had outwitted his well-meaning friends to remarry, and was too busy honeymooning to help Corrine. Other Klondike Kings who had previously been interested in the pretty actress failed come to her aid. She was, in fact, facing another awful term in a Canadian jail.

Corrine's only alternative was to get out of Canada, but the Mounties closely monitored Yukon River traffic. She had all but given up when an unlikely savior appeared. An Alaskan visiting Dawson, William B. Ballou was a tall, fairly good-looking 170-pounder with a dapper mustache. The thirty-year-old bachelor—bored and horny from long isolation in Alaska's gold fields, knowing nothing about Corrine's past—decided after a brief meeting that it was his duty as a gentleman and a fellow American to rescue her.

In another life, William Ballou had worked for the Boston and Maine Railroad as a telegraph man. Happy to leave watchful neighbors who were zealous members of the Temperance League in Somerville, Massachusetts, he had departed for the gold rush in March of 1898, stopping briefly in Seattle where he toured the dance halls and red light district. Forgoing Dawson because it had little land left for staking, he hit Rampart, Alaska, at the beginning of its stampede, acquiring several moderately successful claims and purchasing a town lot at the bargain price of fifty dollars. A good liar, he had gotten most of his mining equipment through Canadian customs by posing as a lawyer and claiming his weighty boxes were law books and clothing.[12]

William's first winter in the North heightened his respect for both the country and those who managed to survive in it. Seven of his acquaintances froze to death in separate accidents. One committed suicide. His nearest neighbor crushed a foot to jelly when a jack slipped on the steamer he was trying to pry out of the ice, and two amputations later his leg was gone below the knee. Another friend froze both legs, dying during the operation to amputate. William himself suffered so badly from scurvy that his legs turned black to the knees before he could diagnose the problem and cure himself.[13] So he had a sympathetic ear for suffering.

Corrine told him that since a loved-crazed corporal had committed suicide over her, the Mounties had tried to grind her down, ruining her financially. "Anyone in Dawson who can't pay up goes behind bars," William explained in a letter to his brother Walt, an apple-grower and cider-maker back in Vermont, "therefore when I heard the case through and saw a tear glisten in that big black eye, it was all off with me and I told the little girl to trust in me and we would see her through the lines. One hour before the boat sailed in the shadow of night, the little girl was smuggled aboard and stowed in my bunk with me—with a big bottle of booze sticking from under the pillow and the little girl snuggled close in my expansive bosom and the covers well over her head we cleared the dock inspection without a jar but at Fortymile, the boundary line, two red-coated officers with a telegram searched every inch of the boat without success, even tapping me on the shoulder to ask me questions but the bottle had been too much for me and I could only answer them with a grunt.

"After getting over the line with the stars and stripes over us we came out of our hiding and had a lovely time all the way down—in fact I was perfectly willing to sail on like that for ages."

En route to Rampart, then a town of about 1,500 with several booming saloons, Corrine talked the usually thrifty William into backing her in business. "She got off here at Rampart and will start a sporting house where I am to go for a home when I wish," he reported a bit sheepishly to his brother. "The whole thing was a merry thing to do and a 'little yellow' has appeared in my pants every time I have thought about it since, but then no risk, no gain, and I console myself with the thought of 'the happy home that I have won.' It needs a little adventure like that to put the spice into life."[14]

On the same day, William wrote to his mother, "Arrived last night after a long six-day trip down the river from Dawson. The boat had freight for all stations, tying up for darkness and took on an extra supply of wood all of which seemed to delay us. Am glad to get back to the old log cabin once more after all my summer's wandering—'tis the house that I'm best fitted for after all."[15]

After traveling with Corrine to the States for a brief holiday, William set her up as promised in Rampart, and headed back to mine Claim #8 on the Little Manook. Since Corrine was new to the area, he asked Luther Durfee, a fellow miner who worked at the Northern Commercial store, to watch over her—a serious tactical mistake.

Luther Durfee, age thirty-three, looked strikingly similar to William Ballou, but was even better built. The son of a Wisconsin lumber baron, he was one of Rampart's most eligible bachelors and had much more charm than William, who was totally focused on getting rich.

When William returned to Rampart just two weeks later, he was even more angry than the town's "respectable" women to find Luther betrothed to Corrine. Momentarily he considered challenging his friend to a little pistol play, but the couple knew where the Vermonter's heart really lay and patched up their friendship.

"Although I have lost my home there for this winter I came up

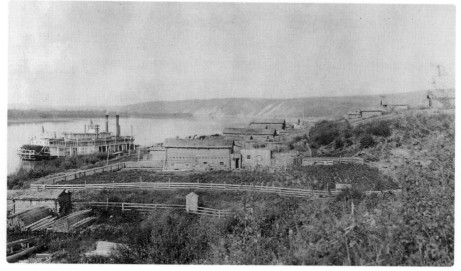

EARLY RAMPART
A way station on the Yukon River en route to Dawson, the Indian village
of Rampart experienced a minor boom when gold was discovered there in the late 1800s.
The diggings soon played out, however, and most of the white settlers moved on.
UW #18026.

promptly with my congratulations and wishes for their best happiness," William wrote his brother, "perhaps all the more so as he came down with the price of her fare from Dawson, expenses on her trunks, and two weeks board since which amounted to about a hundred which I had settled for her."[16]

Luther also purchased William's cutaway tuxedo, which William grudgingly admitted fitted the bridegroom better than himself. William also served as best man at the wedding, which was remarkable for its elegance in the rugged camp.

"The little girl came out in one of her stage dresses (a Worth from the most expensive house in Paris) and looked very sweet—so much so that I almost wished that I had capped her out myself," William reported. "Well we spliced them together and you ought to hear the talk it has made. . . .

"The newly married couple gave me a nice little supper with lots of wine and we had the big talk and I agreed not to feel abused and am to be their best friend for life—so we smoked the pipe of peace in many cigarettes."[17]

It was love. Luther, who'd been heavily into alcohol and gambling, gave both up for Corrine. And she proved remarkably content in the uncharacteristic role of sober, supportive young wife.

"My friends Mr. and Mrs. Durfee are well and very happy—they have a lovely little cabin which she has fixed all up to a queen's taste—they make me lunch with them every time I go in," William reported with mixed emotions. "She makes it a point to look very sweet in some loose kind of pink dress and I always come away with a sad feeling in my heart and kick myself thinking what might have been. The 'four hundred' in camp hasn't recovered from the sensation of their marriage and do not receive them at the pink teas."

Rampart's respectable matrons and old maids insisted that Luther was "throwing himself away," and blamed William for the match, but the jilted Vermonter came to see it as a fortunate marriage for his friend.[18] It would take the newly married couple a little longer, however, to convince Luther's family back home.

Luther Durfee was the last surviving son of William Ray Durfee, who had been born to a wealthy and politically powerful Rhode Island family and had made his way west as a fur buyer and Indian agent. In 1872 William Durfee had founded a successful mercantile business in Ashland, Wisconsin, soon to become the second-largest port on Lake Superior, and he also established a highly successful sawmill and lumber business. But his financial gains were countered by staggering personal losses, including the deaths of his first wife, Cecille, their three daughters, and Luther's older brother, Nathaniel. Three children from his second marriage, to Eugenie Prince, also died.[19]

One of William Durfee's only two surviving offspring, Luther may have been over-indulged. He apparently took to gambling and alcohol early on, and it must have been with mixed feelings that his father saw him off to the gold rush. Luther astonished the family by becoming self-sufficient and being promoted to assistant manager of the Northern Commercial store, but William Durfee was not pleased when his heir announced that he'd married an actress. However, the lumber baron was sixty-nine. His second wife, Eugenie, and her sister-in-law, Dorothy (in whom Luther confided), were liberal for that era. Just as Luther and Corrine had convinced their friend William Ballou, eventually they won over the Durfee clan.

"They are to have an increase in the family sometime all their own this time, too, and papa feels pretty smart over it," noted William Ballou, who'd replaced Corrine with the unhappy wife of a professional gambler. "His old man, the Lumber King of Wisconsin, has written them a nice long letter—forgives and forgets with his blessings and wants them to come home, so this puts an end to all my worries over them."[20]

Corrine must have felt the same relief, plus real happiness, for Luther not only adored her, but was wildly excited about becoming a father. And other Rampart wives were gradually accepting her; the Durfees began to receive invitations from respectable couples. Although "high society" in an isolated boomtown might seem a joke to the outside world, many stampeders were well-bred, well-educated, and well-heeled. Corrine's ability to move into their circle bode well for her future. Perhaps she soon would find herself living in luxury and high society with Luther's wealthy family in Ashland, Wisconsin.

<hr>

But it was not to be. In September, Luther Durfee again donned William Ballou's cutaway and Corrine her Worth gown, this time for the funeral of their newborn child. Shattered, both began drinking. Luther went so far off the deep end that he almost lost his job, but he managed to pull himself together when Corrine discovered she was pregnant again.[21]

Then, suddenly, their luck ran out. In November Luther, healthy and just three months past his thirty-fourth birthday, caught a cold that seemed harmless until it turned into pneumonia, then into consumption. Corrine, exhausted and terrified, called William Ballou to help her nurse him. After five dreadful nights during which they could do nothing to ease Luther's suffering, he slipped away.

They dressed him in William's cutaway and placed his body in a home-built coffin in an unheated cabin in the backyard; the ground was too frozen to bury him until spring. Corrine, nearly mad with grief, might have joined him had it not been for the child growing inside her, but without Luther she was lost—especially financially.[22]

Her husband had left no insurance; his illness and funeral had taken most of their savings. Struggling with their own grief, Luther's parents offered her no assistance, although she hoped they would once the baby arrived. William Ballou had been selling Luther the house on installments of twenty-five dollars a month, which Corrine could not afford to pay. In fact, she could barely afford groceries. The Rampart "four hundred" offered no support. Once again, William Ballou appeared to be Corrine's only hope, but she hesitated to approach the tight-fisted Vermonter whom she had jilted so abruptly. Instead she bided her time, and he finally came to her.

"After Durfee died I firmly and honestly resolved that there should be nothing but friendship between the widow and myself," William wrote his brother Walt in February of 1903, following a bit of soul-searching, "but one night when I was first laid up the first of Jan. I hobbled down there to her cozy house (my cabin) all fixed up with Outside furniture, carpets, lace curtains and such truck that go to make up the furnishings of a cabin when there is a woman and—and the little actress was dressed in one of those thin fleecy wrappers and was so concerned in fixing me up comfortable on the lounge by the fire and insisted on bathing my hip with liniment with her soft little hands.

"I tell you, Old Man, it isn't in the Ballou nature with a pair of big balls between his legs, to stand it and something had to happen—and, after she had shed a few stage tears and given me the old story that she had loved me all the time since I saved her from the horrid red-coated police in Dawson, we pulled the curtains closed so that poor Durfee could not look in from his coffin in the little cabin in the backyard where he lays stiff and frozen hard as a rock, and we crawls in between the white sheets (sheets are a great luxury in this country) and I truly think there is nothing better for the rheumatism in the hip than a nice plump smooth leg applied for a few hours nightly; it is this treatment which now in less than two months has put me on my feet and almost cured me for the Dr. said I should be no better till warm weather next spring same as last year.

"The little girl is with kid from Durfee and I am having the pleasure of watching the little cuss grow and the milk route swell up—we are very careful of him as he will be the only heir to all Old Man Durfee's money. I am trying to break her off from the dope but she takes it on the sly and I have put her on an allowance of booze which she consumes like a fish. She is very passionate but I keep up with her by eating lots of eggs, game and such, and sleep all day—I weigh 186# so you see I have a good chance of winning out in the contest; but it keeps me pretty busy for I have to keep in with society which generally keeps me playing cards the first part of the night until twelve or one from which I adjourn down there until six or seven then come home and to bed until breakfast at twelve."[23]

Corrine finally heard from the Durfee family in late February, when Luther's father arranged for his body to be transported to nearby Fort Gibbon for embalming, so it could be shipped home in a metallic casket the following summer.[24] Dot Prince, Luther's aunt, apparently wrote to Corrine offering her sympathy, but the rest of the family provided no assistance.

William Durfee did send money to C. R. Peck, one of Luther's close friends, to cover Luther's bills. But William Ballou convinced the lumber baron's embassy to give most of the bank draft to him as payment for Corrine's rent, leaving nothing for the widow. Corrine declared him "penurious" and kicked him out of her bed. William Ballou, who quickly moved on to a couple of grass widows in town, gave the matter only passing thought.

"There came a remittance from Old Man Durfee to my friend Peck to pay any bills and I put in my bills for rent, wood, etc., it was a mean trick on my part," William confessed to his brother, "but we are up in this country for the mighty dollar, even if we have to stint animal nature. I find that the older I get—or is it this country?—the meaner I grow."[25]

───⊱✦⊰───

For Corrine, William Ballou's casual act of greed was a monumental turning point. She reacted by going on a drunk with Mrs. White, a Rampart prostitute, wrecking Mayo's saloon and hitting bartender Frank Williams over the head with a chair when he attempted to throw them out. Then she tried (unsuccessfully) to sue Frank Williams for assault and battery.

"One of the most farcical cases ever heard in Rampart was decided by a jury in Judge Green's court Thursday afternoon," the *Rampart Forum* reported. "The jury was out about two minutes and returned a verdict of not guilty. The evidence showed that Mrs. Durfee and Mrs. Ward or White were both intoxicated and went to Williams' saloon, raised a disturbance, used foul language and were ejected. Mrs. Durfee, while on the stand, was questioned by C. J. Knapp, counsel for Williams, and asked by him if she was intoxicated at the time of the alleged assault said, 'I had only four drinks of whisky in the twenty-four hours.' Knapp said, 'I did not ask how many drinks you had, but were you intoxicated?' Mrs. Durfee answered, 'No, I was not—not at that time anyway. It would take more than four drinks to get me intoxicated, I can tell you.'

"Mrs. Durfee's counsel, C. B. Allen, in his address to the jury, persisted in bringing in outside matter, for instance, stating he had been informed that Mrs. Durfee had served nine months in the Dawson jail for selling furniture she did not own, but on investigation by him he found it to be false. After repeated warning by the judge to confine his remarks to the evidence in the case, Allen was fined $10 for contempt. He borrowed the money from a bystander, paid his fine and proceeded more regularly."[26]

Three days later, Corrine Gray Durfee filed her last will and testament with the Rampart court. Her bills and final expenses were to be paid as soon as possible after her death, and her body was to be buried beside her late husband, wherever that might be. She bequeathed half of any property that might come to her from her late husband's will or estate to go to Dot Prince of Ashland; in case of Prince's death that estate would go on to her heirs or assignees to keep it in the Durfee family.

Corrine bequeathed one-fourth of what remained to her beloved cousin, Kathleen B. Hanlay of Salem, Ohio, and another quarter to her mother, Mrs. B. L. Bissler of Canton, Ohio, to revert later to James Hopkins of East Palestine, whose relationship to the family she failed to note. She left her jewelry and personal possessions to Kathleen Hanlay and James Hopkins "to share and share alike." Her faithful lawyer, Charles B. Allen, as executor of her estate was to be rewarded with a $300 bond.[27]

Then she sent for William Ballou and asked him to buy her a supply of drugs.

"When I refused she gave me quite a stage act, as I thought at the time, and flourished the gun (which afterwards done the deed) around in a rather startling manner and threatened to take me along with her if I didn't do as she wished," the Vermonter reported to his brother Walt. "I have thought since that it is a wonder that she didn't do something of the kind, if nothing more than to make her end more dramatic—she dearly loved to do the grandstand act in real life and always spoke with pride of the Mounted Police officer in Dawson who committed suicide over her."[28]

Two days later, between noon and two o'clock on Sunday, Corrine Gray Durfee shot herself through the head with a revolver. She was found dead by two Native women at six that evening, and the coroner's inquest, held privately the next morning, established suicide as the cause.[29]

To William Ballou's immense relief, he was not called to testify. And, although he did hold himself partly responsible, he rationalized away all guilt.

"She had been mad at me for over a month since the money came in from Old Man Durfee to pay the debts and I put in my bill in full for rent for the cabin, wood and provisions," he wrote Walt. "This was my mean trick and wholly against the laws and rules of 'the underworld' but I find that this country makes one grow cold-blooded and stony hearted and, although the deed in itself is horrible and disgusting, I cannot help but feel that it was the wisest act that the little girl ever done for she was no good to herself nor anyone else—people in general think it was for love of Durfee that she done the deed but the fact of the matter was that she was out of dope and would not live without it."[30]

C. R. Peck received a telegraph from Luther's parents requesting their son be buried in Rampart, contrary to their original plan, perhaps because of the additional expense of shipping Corrine to be buried with him in Wisconsin, as stipulated in her will. So husband and wife were interred side by side with their child[31] in a beautiful clearing in the forest where the blueberries grew profusely, across from the Indian village. Mrs. Sally Hudson, who played there as a girl in the late 1930s, recalled there were no headboards (customary wooden grave markings), perhaps because a forest fire had swept the area. Today the little cemetery has been reclaimed by forest.[32]

Settlement of Corrine's estate in 1904 revealed $53 in cash and $204 from the sale of her personal property. Executor Allen paid an outstanding bill of $6 for glasses, $1.50 for watch repair, and an undisclosed sum to Louis Vallier for digging the Durfee graves. The watch went to William R. Durfee. Corrine's cousin, Kathleen, and James Hopkins each got $1.65. Her mother, who must have died in the interim, was not mentioned, and lawyer Allen settled for far less than the $300 Corrine had hoped to pay him.[33]

William Durfee died in 1915 with no male heir. His second wife outlived him, childless.

William Ballou took Luther Durfee's job at Northern Commercial and then vacationed Outside, returning in 1904 with a comely blond bride, to be re-embraced by Rampart's "four hundred." He was appointed United States Commissioner of Rampart, a political plum complete with the courtesy title of "Judge" Ballou, but that honor dimmed as the town's population dwindled from 1,500 to 150 when the gold gave out. "I have little to show for years of hard work," he wrote his brother, quite disillusioned.[34] He left Alaska for good in 1917, still searching for his fortune, but he never did get rich as he had intended.

7

Klondike Kate Rockwell

AN ENDURING CHARMER

⚬⚬⚬

Do not scorn her with words fierce and bitter
Do not laugh at her shame and downfall
For a moment just stop and consider
That a man was the cause of it all . . .

"She's More To Be Pitied Than Censured"

It was prophetic that "She's More To Be Pitied Than Censured" was the favorite number of soubrette Kate "Kitty" Rockwell Warner Matson Van Duren.[1] The "Queen of the Klondike"—as many called her—lost her heart in the Klondike rush and subsequently lost all her hard-won riches. The later prominence of her deserting lover, theater magnate Alexander Pantages, and Kate's appearance at his nationally headlined rape trial, assured her a place in history. Yet even without the hype, Kate would have been a memorable standout.

She had natural red hair, violet eyes, long black lashes, and a splendid figure. Her face was a delicate oval of innocence in marked contrast to her husky voice, her worldly experience, and her blatant sexual appeal.[2] Kate also had talent and grace—rare qualities among Dawson showgirls. Her special come-on was something she called her "pixie stare," a projection of sweet innocence and raw sex that few men could resist, but it was her

⚬⚬⚬

KLONDIKE KATE IN HER PRIME
The red-haired, violet-eyed songstress with a knack for choreography really "wowed"
the audiences of Dawson, who quickly made her their favorite performer.
Here she assumes the classic pose of the gold rush era, wrapped in fifty yards of chiffon.
YA, MacBride Museum Collection, #3880.

capacity for fun that ultimately won them. For Kate, who managed to enjoy herself even during tough times, reveled in the excitement of the great Klondike rush.

———— ⊸⊱∞⊰⊷ ————

She was born Eloisa Rockwell near Oswego, Kansas, in 1876, a birth-date she would ignore for a lifetime, preferring 1880, 1882, and—during a particularly bizarre lapse—1892. Her upbringing was surprisingly refined given the fact that her mother, Martha, was a waitress, her father, John Rockwell, was a railroad telegraph operator, and both had defied Victorian mores in divorcing their first spouses to marry each other.

After five years with John Rockwell, Martha divorced again and married her lawyer, Allison Bettis, a former legislator. He had just shed his second spouse, too, so the newlyweds moved to Spokane for a fresh start. Here Allison became a successful judge and invested in all the trappings of wealth and power: a fine house, servants, and a governess for Kate, whom he adored. Spoiled rotten, "Kitty" (as the child was known in early years) grew into an unrestrained tomboy, learning to ride horseback and camp. She also developed an unbridled enthusiasm for men, so her unnerved parents cloistered her in private Catholic girls' schools, first in Kansas, then Minnesota, then California, all with dismal results.

Kate returned to Spokane during a recession in which her stepfather lost his shirt and her mother further indebted him through real estate speculation. Divorce followed. Martha, "one of those sweet, trusting souls, who depended heavily on her husband," tried running a rooming house, then sold it for $65,000 and headed for South America with Kate to visit her son by an earlier marriage, Ralph Morris.[3] Kate was enthralled with both the eighty-seven-day cruise and the young naval officers aboard their square rigger. When she announced her engagement to one, her mother stuck her in a Catholic school in Valparaiso, Chile, and went to England on what was probably a romantic adventure of her own.

On returning to New York, Martha heard that her daughter had circumvented convent chaperones to become engaged to a young diplomatic attaché from Spain. Martha ordered Kate to take the first trustworthy vessel to New York. After a hair-raising trip around Cape Horn and ninety-seven days at sea, Kate arrived to discover that Martha had squandered all their money and was about to seek work in a shirtwaist factory.

"I was only sixteen but I knew I must help in some way," she recalled.

"I read an ad in a newspaper. It said: 'Chorus girls wanted. No experience necessary.'"

Kate was a natural. She first appeared as a page girl in a Coney Island honky-tonk, but quickly graduated to the chorus line. "I was still a virgin about life in those days," she later told a feature writer. "Mother allowed me so many minutes to get dressed after my last act and enough time to ride home from Coney Island on a streetcar."[4]

Soon she moved up to New York's legitimate vaudeville houses and on to a not-so-legitimate variety theater back in Spokane where, professing shock and distaste, she learned to work customers after each show for a commission on drinks, although she stuck to lemonade. Still working there when news of the Klondike rush broke, she decided to follow the excitement.

Settling her mother in Seattle, Kate Rockwell quit the Spokane show to start a sister act with Gertie Jackson and head north.[5] In Victoria, B.C., she became a soubrette at the Savoy, a first-class vaudeville house where she developed two new song-and-dance acts each week. Owners Jack MacDonald and Billy Jackson chaperoned her, and she became engaged long-distance to Danny Allmon, a minstrel star with a real gift for comedy whom she had met in New York. Danny, who was thirty-one and the son of a former mayor from Salem, Illinois, planned to join her but before he could make it across the country, she'd headed for Alaska. Her friend Gertie Jackson bowed out at Skagway, but Kate found work in Southeastern Alaska and stayed on.[5]

"I did the dance wearing a crown of candles for the first time in Juneau. I could have skipped rope and the men would have been just as appreciative," she confided in disgust to a reporter there years later. "The saloon was called the Louvre then, and it was the only place in town where entertainers didn't have to entertain in the upstairs rooms."[6]

Friends recalled that Kate spoke of climbing Chilkoot Pass with a man carrying a small piano. Biographer Ellis Lucia suggests Kate may have teamed with the "Sunny Sampson Sisters Sextette," a fairly respectable troupe that enlisted piano-packing "Klondike Mike" Mahoney to accompany them. The girls—turned back at the border by the Mounties, who claimed the trail was too rugged for them—retreated to Skagway, where they performed for six months in Soapy Smith's honky-tonk, yet according to the press retained their modesty and virtue.[7]

In her autobiography, Kate gave few details of this period and no account of climbing the pass, probably because the railway from Skagway to Bennett had been completed by the time she'd saved enough to make the trip. "I kept getting closer and closer to the Klondike," she wrote tersely. "I accepted an engagement to play Bennett, a gold-mad town, where the men outfitted themselves and built scows to freight into the Yukon for gold.

"It was the end of the train line—and life was high-keyed. Someone recently told me that he spent a night in an old hotel in Bennett, and there on the ceiling was my name, 'Katie Rockwell,' nailed in champagne corks. It was custom in those days."[8]

Gone were the chaperons. Her fiancé was a continent away. Bennett was a rough-and-tumble transportation center, with ill-heated, makeshift buildings, very few amenities—and no lemonade. Kate was determined to work her way out of there, whatever it took, champagne-filled evenings included. But apparently those were too few to turn much profit. Most of Kate's clientele, like herself, were working their way to the gold fields, and a dance hall show was about all they could afford.

Charles Lombard, a fine musician called the "Little Parson," who played there just before Christmas in 1899, recalls that Kate was their only entertainer and that they often played all night.[9] Sometimes she made as many as twenty appearances. Yet she didn't accumulate enough cash to move on until June of 1900, when she finally headed for Dawson.[10]

Again the Northwest Mounted Police interfered, stopping women from going down the Five Finger Rapids because it was considered too dangerous. "Well I was young and didn't give a whoop," Kate recalled. "So I put on boy's clothing, waited until the scow was about to pull out, and jumped aboard just as the lines were released from the bank.

"The Mountie saw me hit the deck—I should say hit the water—but I got a-hold and was pulled aboard. He bellowed orders 'in the name of the Queen' and he was still fuming when we hit the rapids. That Mountie didn't get his woman. I waved at him as our square boat went into the seething froth of Whitehorse and Five Finger Rapids at twelve miles an hour. My trip . . . was perhaps the most exciting trip I ever made. That man at the giant oar-rudder muscled us through with great uncanny skill."[11]

At Whitehorse a letter offered her a job with a 173-member troupe being formed back in Victoria to play the Savoy in Dawson. Kate briefly returned to Victoria to join the troupe and finally arrived in Dawson via steamship to find the town rebuilding after an disastrous fire, but lively with gold kings. She still planned to marry Danny Allmon, but she took

BENNETT

Gold stampeders headed for Dawson along the Chilkoot and White Pass Trails
usually waited out the winter at Bennett, a rough-and-tumble town where Kate Rockwell
spent several months performing because she couldn't afford transportation farther north.
By the time she finally arrived at Dawson she understood gold camp audiences
far better than performers fresh from Seattle and San Francisco.

UW #12827.

off his modest engagement ring and set to work at the Savoy. Nor did she seem distraught when Danny died of a brain hemorrhage later in November of that year, at Nanaimo en route to join her, but she saved his obituary and would treasure photos of him all her life.[12]

⸺⦿⸺

The Savoy, which had been closed by Dawson officials, re-opened to a full house and good reviews. Kate, billed as a "Soubrette Extraordinaire," was better trained than most in pleasing Klondike audiences from her grim days at Bennett. She wowed them wearing a rose-tinted, lace-trimmed gown, embellished by a Lillian Russell hat with ostrich plumes, belting out throaty renditions of old ballads that the sourdoughs loved. Showman "Arizona" Charlie Meadows was impressed, not only with her youth and talent, but what he discreetly described as her "French flair." He immediately offered her more money and the Star's Suite at his lavish Palace Grand Theater, and she took it.[13] Her new accommodations were papered in red and gold, with a red carpet, a bed, a rocking chair, a wash stand, and a window overlooking the main street and the Yukon River. Kate loved it.

FLOWERS FOR A FINE PERFORMANCE
*Klondike Kate's most famous number was her Flame Dance, in which she kept
200 yards of chiffon airborne. Dawson audiences loved it and the performer as well.*
UAF, Barrette Willoughby Collection, #72-116-336N.

Charlie Meadows recognized Kate's choreographic skills and, with his encouragement, she developed her famous Flame Dance, in which she moved gracefully to music in flashy costumes at a pace that kept about 200 yards of chiffon airborne. For this number she was paid $200 a week, and she claimed she often earned an additional $500 after each show.

"Sure I was a percentage girl. We got 50 percent on dances and 25 on drinks," she admitted to biographer Rolv Schillios in 1955. "The commission on a pint of champagne was $7.50. . . . My best night I made $750, just for talking to a lonesome miner. A good entertainer was slow if she didn't cash in at least $100 worth of percentage checks every night. Dances were short and one dollar, and the man took his girl to the bar—if not a box—and splurged."[14]

Readers may be leery of Kate's accounts of receiving huge sums for "just listening" to miners, but she had a genuinely sympathetic ear and apparently did keep a couple of depressed millionaires from suicide, for which they gratefully rewarded her.

Biographer Ellis Lucia maintained that there was sincerity in Kate's tender talk. "She felt deeply committed when told a tale of woe. It became her own personal problem and she spent many sleepless mornings wrestling with the troublesome affairs of some raw-boned sourdough who was whipped to the point of cashing in his chips. She seemed to need many men constantly about her, lavishing their attentions on her, paying her compliments and presenting her with tokens of affection," he wrote. "She soaked up this attention like a sponge, seeking more and more, almost abnormally; she yearned to feel important and needed and loved. . . . At least for the passing moment, she was tenderly loyal and sincere, and she would demonstrate her feelings by grubstaking a sourdough who was down on his luck or bringing hot soup to a stricken miner in his cabin."[15]

Ed Lung, a young miner and a happily married man, struggled to explain the impact she had on him.

"She was certainly very young! Couldn't have been more than nineteen or twenty. [Actually, she was twenty-four.] She had an appeal and winsomeness that was truly captivating. It was alluring, intangible—something, yes, difficult to describe," he began.

"She was just a bit taller than average; hair, reddish gold; eyes, blue; complexion, like peaches and cream; her voice ranged from velvety soft to musical bells; and yes, she was as sweet as honey!

"Well, impulsively, I reached into my hip pocket and drew out my small poke of nuggets. How very hard I had worked for that poke of gold!

"'Look at these yellow babies,' I said eagerly, as I spread the nuggets out in the palm of my hand, so that each shiny, gold particle could show off its best advantage in the bright sunlight.

"'They're beautiful! Real gorgeous! Why, I've never seen such rare beauties! Say, did you get them all from your claim on Dominion Creek?'

"'Sure,' I replied, 'do you like them, Miss Rockwell? Then pick one out,' I invited, 'and you can keep it.'

"'Oh, thank you, thank you,' she exclaimed. Her lovely hands grasped, fondled, and almost weighed each nugget. And then, she chose my biggest one.

"'This piece of gold will always remind me of you, Ed Lung,' she said sweetly, as she quickly opened her purse and dropped the shiny gold into a collection of many other nuggets. 'Yes, I think the one you gave me is the prettiest yet!'"[16]

Kate claimed to have accumulated more than $30,000 during her first year in Dawson, yet she insisted, "I was never a gold digger. The men threw their gold at my feet when my dances pleased them."[17] She never denied that she might have turned a trick or two to supplement those nugget showers. "We were not vestal virgins. Far from it," she said.[18] But Kate could afford to be discriminating and she was discreet, at least until she met a Greek waiter named Alexander Pantages.

His real name was Percales Pantages; he had re-christened himself after Alexander the Great. He wasn't rich and it was a stretch to call him handsome, but he lived and breathed theater, and his blinding drive to succeed was even stronger than Kate's.

Scarcely taller than she, he had a swarthy complexion, a sensuous mouth, deep-set, brooding eyes, and black hair with a patent-leather shine. His barrel-chested body, of which he was inordinately proud, was graceful and well-muscled from years of hard labor. He was at least twenty-five, but his father, a minor civil official, had altered records so his son could avoid the draft, and Alexander never knew his real birthdate. He neither drank nor smoked, and was meticulously clean and clean-shaven . . . all features that made him stand out in the frontier camp. He didn't talk much, perhaps because his English was ragged, but Kate found his accent charming. He couldn't read or write, but was fluent in several languages,

THE CAUSE OF IT ALL

Alexander Pantages, the soon-to-be-wealthy showman whom Kate Rockwell loved and lost,
embodied a prophetic line in her favorite showtune: "A man was the cause of it all."

UW #2242.

and she guessed (correctly) that she would never meet anyone smarter.[19]

Raised in punishing poverty, he had abandoned his native island of Andros at about age nine to travel to Cairo, where he worked with his father as a waiter and busboy. Escaping, he became a cabin boy on a French tramp steamer touring Mediterranean ports and then worked his way to South America. When he caught malaria, shipmates abandoned him on a Panama beach.[20] On his recovery, he headed for America, jumping ship in San Francisco. There he worked in a beer garden and as a prize-fighter (hating both jobs), and also in theater, first as an usher and handyman and later in pantomime.[21]

Catching gold fever, Alexander embarked for points north with about

$1,000 savings in 1898. How he lost his stake is unclear, but he landed in Skagway with only twenty-five cents and a pair of boots wrapped in a copy of the *Seattle Post-Intelligencer.*

"I'll give you five dollars for that paper," a man called when Alexander stepped off the boat.

"I'll give you ten!" yelled another.

"Not for sale," snapped Alexander, who that night hired a hall and a reader, selling tickets for one dollar a head to the news-starved community.[22]

In Dawson he landed a lucrative job as a bartender and also staged shows for his boss, Charlie Cole. Then he became a swamper and waiter at Charlie Meadows's Monte Carlo, where he assisted Kate in relieving drunks of their gold dust in private boxes after the show. He attracted Charlie Meadows's attention when a professional prize-fighter the club owner had booked failed to show up for a sell-out match.

"I'll save the pot for you, Charlie. I'll fight the guy myself," Alexander volunteered.

"What do you know about fighting, Pan?" Charlie asked, astonished, not realizing the sturdy Greek had fought welterweight in San Francisco.

"Not a thing—except for a few rough tumbles I've taken, but you've been a good boss, Charlie, and I'll take a licking for you right now," Alexander replied at his ingratiating best. He made short work of his opponent, kayoing him in just a few minutes. Charlie was so grateful he gave Alex a ten-percent interest in his show, and the talented Greek became his stage manager.[23] Alexander also started a stock company on the side, producing tearjerkers like *Uncle Tom's Cabin* and *East Lynne.*

Alexander Pantages had a considerable nest egg when he wooed and won Kate Rockwell. After he got her to live openly with him, he invested in a cooperative stock company with Gussie Lamore and a number of other headliners like Beatrice Lorne, "the Nightingale of the Yukon," who had a truly lovely voice.

The *Dawson Daily News* reported on January 2, 1900, that "Alex Pantages, the well-known porter at the Opera House, has been selected as the manager to look after the general supervision of the house. Alex has been thrifty in his habits and has saved quite a poke, which he is willing to chance in the Dawson show business. The salaries of the performers have been placed on the same basis as during their last engagement and any surplus is put into the general fund for contingencies."

Kate continued as a headliner at the Monte Carlo, most memorably appearing at the Christmas Cake Walk wearing a $1,500 ivory satin gown designed by Worth of Paris, with a crown miners cut from a tin can supporting fifty flaming candles. When Alex's cooperative stock company failed, she kept him in seventy-five-cent cigars and fifteen-dollar silk shirts, and spent forty-five dollars a week on meals for him. She was among his investors when he opened the Orpheum in late 1900, and she quit working for Charlie Meadows to star in her lover's show.[24]

Her friend "Diamond Tooth" Gertie Lovejoy declared publicly that Kate was "plum crazy to fall so hard for a foreign 'patent-leather kid' who will love her, take her gold and leave her." But Alexander's venture with the Orpheum paid off, grossing about $8,000 a day, and by all accounts Kate was never happier. "I began my day's work with an hour in a gymnasium to keep in trim. Then I would take my own dog team and go lashing out over the frozen snow. I had my own horse and in the summer I'd drive like wild through the strangely beautiful country," she wrote forty years later.

"Then there was gold in the streets of Dawson, gold in the hills, and gold in the Yukon. And I was named the queen of it all. . . . All my lingerie was French and handmade. My dresses were covered with rhinestones and seed pearls and spangles and sequins. . . ."

But it was Kate's lover who had become the focus of her life. "Alex Pantages and I laughed, danced and worked hard during those months at the Old Orpheum. We opened it together and it became the brightest spot north of the International Boundary Line. In the spring we'd go picking poppies together on the banks of the Klondike. And we'd make plans for the day when we would later marry."[25]

There is reason to believe Kate bore Alexander's child during this period. After a brief absence to the States, she took care of an infant, explaining that it was the child of a young tubercular girl she had befriended, who had died giving birth.[26]

Meanwhile, Alex focused on making his fortune, not only watching his audiences intently to figure out what they wanted, but after hours sweeping the floors and sifting out the gold dust. Fire gutted his theater three times. Each time he rebuilt, but when gold was discovered at Nome, business slowed in Yukon Territory.

"He was playing for high stakes and he seldom made a move without seeing dollars at the end of the trail," theater writer Eugene Elliott observed. "While he could be 'ingratiatingly servile,' according to one description, he was insolent, indifferent and taciturn to many who knew him. He rarely smiled and was seldom heard to laugh, for he lacked an open sense of humor, and often treated people coldly. . . . His mind worked in dollar signs, which was about all the reading knowledge he needed for getting ahead in this land of gold."[27]

This was a side of her lover that Kate had not observed, or perhaps had ignored because his drive was an asset in her own quest for wealth and fame. But she'd also fallen in love with the magic of the Klondike rush itself—partying and drinking on an increasingly lavish scale—and she was shocked when Alex suggested they leave in the spring of 1902.

"Leave?" she echoed. "And miss all the excitement? There isn't another place like this in the world and I love it."[28]

Alexander talked her into spending her savings on a grand tour that included New York City, a visit to her mother, and the boomtowns of Texas. While in Texas, Kate deserted him briefly for a gambler who did not treat her well. Alexander's attorney, Leroy Tozier, later congratulated him on winning back Kate, as she was a financial asset. "Sincerely, I do trust no one should ever dim the horizon that now shines in resplendent adoration in the mind's eye of your Katherine," he wrote. "Most appropriate was your conduct in going with her to the far east then carrying her safely back to the northern wilds that she might replenish the treasury."[29]

The couple took a scouting expedition to Nome, which neither found enticing. Briefly they reopened the Orpheum, but the Greek entrepreneur had set his sights on creating a national theater chain, and he soon moved to Seattle to begin working on it. Various accounts give Kate's worth at $100,000, which was probably overblown, for she stayed in Dawson to work after Alexander left. Meanwhile, he sunk everything he had and sought investors for a tacky storefront on Second Avenue in Seattle, which he named the Crystal Theater.[30]

In his letters to Kate during the winter of 1902-03, Alexander still appeared deeply in love. Dictating to friends or trusted employees because he was illiterate (although he'd just become a naturalized citizen), he begged her to write more often and also expressed frustration with her growing romance with alcohol.

"I fully expected to receive a letter from you today. I didn't and can say I felt hurt. Katie, I wonder if you will this time sincerely keep your promise and not drink any more," he pleaded just before Christmas in 1902. "I can assure you, Kate, I am sincerely sorry [for] what happened the other day. But I assure you, Katie, it's your own fault as you provoked me to it. As you know full well my disposition and you should not have done it. I think the only way to keep you away from the booze is to have you with me. . . . Warm with love, Yours Sincerely, Alex."

Her response did not survive the years, but apparently Alexander's mounting business worries and the strain of trying to finance his theater chain were lost on her. When she finally did come south, it was to play in Victoria. Then she returned to Dawson. In later years Kate would claim it was Alex who deserted her, but during this period it appears he worked hard to keep their love alive.

"It is needless for me to say that I miss you, more in fact, to speak the truth, more than any time during our past relationship," he wrote on March 4, 1903. "I have begun to realize that you are speeding on your way, separating ourselves from each other by many wiles—I can assure you, my dear, I shall ever think of you, as I know you will me, and always hold you as dear to me as at any time during our life. Write to me often and let me know how you are progressing. Always think of Papa and kiss me in your dreams. I shall ofttimes think of your dear face wishing I might kiss it to satisfy my desire."

By the following summer, Alexander seemed resigned. "Even though we are parked many thousands of miles [apart] my thoughts are ever with you," he wrote. "I'm eager to know who your correspondent is in Seattle that reports to you as to my movements. Yes, my dear, it is true I'm getting fat as a pig—You see I have no one to fight and fuss with, and I'm only waiting until your return so as to scrap in order to reduce my weight.

"Business is quite good with me, but still always bear in mind that Papa is always in need of ready cash and ever willing to put your savings alongside of his so as to make a good showing."[31]

Kate was apparently focused on the nickelodeon in Victoria she had purchased in 1902 for $350. Alexander, who was battling to raise enough credit to open the Crystal, was angered by her investment. He insisted she was "throwing money away," but shared films and vaudeville bookings with her. When her nickelodeon began to make a profit, she sold it for $1,500, returning to star billing in Dawson where she could make better money.

It wasn't until 1904 that Kate finally quit the Yukon, giving her forwarding address and that of "Lotus" Rockwell as the Alcazar Theater in

Seattle.[32] The best guess is that "Lotus" was the child Kate claimed to have adopted. Although she often declared her life an "open book," Kate dismissed this subject in just five sentences. "I took the baby. I kept him until he was three, then I found him a home and foster parents in the States," she wrote in 1944. "I sent the money for his college education and he is one of the most successful engineers in the country today. I have never disclosed his identity. He perhaps has never known of me, but I like to think of him as my son."[33]

At this point Kate apparently was reunited with Alexander, but performed at the Alcazar because he could not afford her high salary.

"People thought I was a Klondike millionaire. I didn't argue with them. I bought the picture house and spent $35,000 turning it into a cozy and beautiful place. I did it all on credit," he later recalled. "Before long we were putting on twelve to fifteen shows a day and jammed them in."[34]

Encouraged, Alexander invested in a low-class burlesque called the Strand in the Skid Row District, while Kate played in Fort Worth and Galveston, Texas, which were enjoying a black gold rush. Many months later she returned to work at the Crystal with a new specialty, the Butterfly Dance. Then, ever restless, always in search of greener pastures, she was off again to more lucrative bookings in the Pacific Northwest while Alexander negotiated for another theater.

⚬⚬⚬

In March of 1905 Kate was performing in her hometown of Spokane when a friend told her that Alex Pantages had wed a violin-playing vaudeville performer named Lois Mendenhall.[35] Kate went into shock. Before Alex met her, he'd apparently enjoyed no serious romance, and he had remained too driven by business schemes to spend much time womanizing. Nor had Kate given much heed to Lois, with whom she'd shared billings in Texas, because the girl's act was based on genuine musical talent rather than looks and sensuality. But the slender, dark-eyed violinist was just seventeen, and Kate was fast approaching thirty. Lois's prominent Oakland family could be an asset to Alexander. While Lois was a seasoned performer, her success did not depend on drinking with male customers after the show. And the innocence that attracted Alex was genuine.

"It wasn't until I met Lois that I knew anything much about good women," Alexander declared flatly in a brief statement on the nuptial. And when first contacted by a *Seattle Times* reporter, he denied even *knowing* Kate Rockwell.

Kate filed suit, seeking $25,000 damages, not for money she invested in Alexander's enterprise but for breach of his promise to marry her. She claimed she had lavished $1,700 on him when he was out of work in Dawson, and that they had traveled across the country on her savings, returning to Seattle in 1902 to live as a married couple. She showed his net worth to be about $100,000. And she claimed that the plaintiff had injured, damaged, humiliated, and disgraced her, causing her to suffer anguish of mind.[36] The case was quickly settled out of court. Kate later said the settlement was less than $5,000; other sources peg the payoff as high as $60,000.[37]

Whatever it was, the settlement was not enough to stop the pain. "For days I was despondent," Kate admitted. "Flossie [de Atley], a girl who had danced with me in Dawson [and had problems of her own with alcohol, domestic relations, and the law], wrote me a letter. She said, 'Don't throw your life away because of one man. Don't make yourself something he will always be glad he was rid of. Make yourself something he will wish he had kept.' The day I read her letter I felt better."

Briefly Kate returned to Dawson, then moved to the new Alaskan boomtown of Fairbanks where, at the suggestion of dance hall girl Edith Neile, she invested in a hotel. When the uninsured building burned in a fire that all but destroyed the city in 1906, Kate danced at the Floradora in Fairbanks to make ends meet.[38] Then she went on the circuit in the States, doing song-and-dance numbers with a performer named Arthur Searles and later with a roller-skating champion named Jimmy Ray, whom she may have married.[39] It was a rough life. She was often injured during the rigorous skating routines, and she came to rely increasingly on alcohol to dull both the physical and the mental pain.

Meanwhile, Alexander Pantages was rocketing toward success. "There is no circuit in the United States, if indeed there is in the world, of the magnate of the Pantages circuit owned by one man," the *Seattle Argus* boasted in 1910. "He owns outright or has interest in 26 theaters."[40]

Alex's good fortune ate away at Kate. "I had a nervous breakdown and the doctors ordered me to get away and try to forget everything for a year or so. I was brooding too much," she said later.[41] Martha Rockwell, who had re-established herself in the real estate business, swapped some Seattle waterfront property for a homestead site that required "proving up" near Bend, Oregon, and Kate bought it from her mother.

"I had about $3,500 in cash and $3,000 in diamonds then. I went to look at the place and found I owned a one-room shack in the middle of a 320-acre homestead. I never saw so much country in my life," she recalled. "Sagebrush as far as I could see. In ballroom gowns and high heels I started grubbing sagebrush and piling rocks. Several times I was ready to give up, and I guess if it hadn't been for the sheer beauty of the desert sunsets, I'd have quit. I found a new happiness, though, like having my soul cleaned. A perfect contentment and rest for the first time in my life. Money seemed so unimportant."[42]

To amuse herself, she flirted with the local cowboys. Finally, at age thirty-nine, she married Floyd Warner, who was handsome, rugged, over six feet tall, and just twenty years old. She made him skittish by cheating on him, ultimately pushing him to retaliation and divorce.[43] Taking a series of increasingly menial jobs, she finally ended up broke in Los Angeles, where she badgered Alexander Pantages for money. On one attempt he gave her six dollars he happened to have in his wallet.[44] On another he suggested she was "not too old to go on the street," but Kate persisted, hiring a lawyer in the early 1920s.[45]

By that time Alexander was sole owner of twenty-two vaudeville theaters and controlled interest in another twenty-eight, for which he had been offered $10 million. He was known as a man of integrity, conducting multimillion-dollar business deals on a mere handshake, and he was very much a family man, bent on protecting Lois and their two children from the bad publicity another lawsuit from Kate would bring.[46]

Biographer Lucia suggests Kate may also have had some hold over the theater magnate through the child she had in Dawson, but whatever the cause, Alexander apparently made cash deliveries to her during this period. Oregon neighbors, calling her "Aunt Kate," suggested the fading showgirl may also have supplemented her income through bootlegging and procuring prostitutes for a bawdy house.[47] Paul Hosmer, a Bend author writing about her for the *Oregonian*, observed she was "an oldish woman who had not completely grown up."

———⚬⚬⚬———

In the fall of 1929 Alexander Pantages was charged with raping a seventeen-year-old actress who sought work with his theaters. Kate, subpoenaed as a prosecution witness, was shocked at his wan appearance and burst into tears when he spoke to her civilly in a court corridor.

"It's been a long time," he said awkwardly.

"Those must have been happy days in the north," a bystander interjected.

"They were," Alexander answered, gazing at the floor. "Maybe you think I'm not game. Look what I'm going through here."

"Maybe you think I'm not going through anything myself," Kate replied.

"See you again," he said when the bailiff beckoned him back to court. But that was the end of it.

Alexander Pantages was sentenced to fifty years in San Quentin before Kate was asked to take the stand. Although he was acquitted two years later, the ordeal caused him a heart attack and considerable financial loss, from which he never really recovered.[48] His wife, charged with drunken driving and manslaughter during his imprisonment, was later cleared but paid $78,500 to the family of the man whom she'd killed with her car.[49] Alexander lived only five years after he was released from prison.

Buoyed by what she may have considered retribution—and some heady national publicity generated by her trial appearance—Kate's spirits rose. After several unsuccessful attempts to land another husband, she suddenly had a choice of two. First on the scene was William L. Van Duren, formerly a successful Oregon accountant, whose wife had left him when cataracts destroyed his eyesight and he could no longer support her. Still bent on rescuing underdogs, Kate cared for him and negotiated expensive eye surgery which proved successful. And William, head over heels in love, purchased a sizable diamond to seal the match.[50]

He was edged out, however, by Johnny Matson, a hopelessly shy Norwegian miner who had worshipped the dance hall queen from afar during the Klondike rush, without the funds or the command of English to press his suit. After reading about the Pantages trial a year or so after the fact, Johnny decided Kate might need help and wrote to her. Kate was intrigued, not only because she remembered his awkward shyness, but because he was soon enclosing money orders with his carefully penned letters.[51]

Their marriage on July 14, 1933, generated another welcome round of national publicity. He was about seventy, but in great shape from a lifetime of rugged outdoor living. Kate, silver-haired at fifty-seven, still had a fine figure, gorgeous legs, and a penchant for rolling her own smokes with Bull Durham. Columbia acquired her movie rights for an undisclosed sum,[52] and she later made *Esquire* magazine. Despite the fact that Kate lived mainly in Oregon while Johnny remained in the Yukon—or perhaps because of it—the match lasted until his death in the wilds in 1946.[53]

A HAPPY SURVIVOR

*Despite the ravages of a broken heart and the loss of the great fortune
she had amassed in Dawson, showgirl Kate Rockwell survived to marry at least
three times and enjoy life no matter what fate handed her.*

YA, Robert Ward Collection, #8775.

Two years later, Kate Rockwell and William L. Van Duren applied for a marriage license in Vancouver, Washington, requesting a waiver of the three-day waiting period.

"Time is of the essence," William, age seventy-one, assured the judge, hoping to outwit reporters.

"I was the flower of the North, but the petals are falling awfully fast, honey," Kate quipped.[54]

─────

In 1956, less than a year before her peaceful death, Kate told Rolv Schillios, who was writing her memoirs, that she had no regrets. The biographer said that Kate reminded him of Cherry Malotte, the heroine of Rex Beach's *Silver Horde*, and that he suspected the author, who had known Kate well, had used her as his model for the character. Schillios read Kate some passages from the book, including "Cherry's" introductory dialogue:

"You must know who I am . . . you know I had followed the mining camps, you know I had lived by the wits. . . . You must have known what people thought of me. I cast my lot with the people of this country, and had to match my wits with those of every man I met. You know the North. . . . I have made mistakes—what girl doesn't who has to fight her way alone? But my past is my own; it concerns nobody but me. . . ."

Rex Beach also had written that Cherry Malotte was a "thoroughbred" and that any man who captured her heart won his derby.[55]

Kate never claimed to be Beach's model, but the comparison pleased her. And her biographer was not alone in admiring her strong points, while ignoring the mistakes even thoroughbreds sometimes make.

In 1931, more than one thousand Alaska-Yukon Pioneers from the Klondike era had toasted Kate Rockwell at their annual stampede in Portland. "To us she was laughter and beauty and song," the master of ceremonies began. "She was forgetfulness of hardship and homesickness. But she was more than that, she was our friend—a square shooter."

Kate's face was lined, her complexion coarsened by too much Bull Durham, champagne, weather, and time. But her violet eyes still shone brightly as she rose to accept their tribute. She was dressed in the lovely ivory satin Worth gown with lavish silk fringes that she'd purchased from Paris for $1,500 to please Alex Pantages three decades earlier, and she still wore it well.

"Comrades, it is my honor and pleasure to present her again tonight," the emcee continued, "not Aunt Kate of Oregon, but our Kate, the Belle of the Yukon, Klondike Kate, the sweetheart of the sourdoughs."[56]

And—one thousand strong—they gave her a standing ovation, spirited enough that even doubters would understand it came from the heart.

8

Nome's Crooked Gold Rush

A SECOND CHANCE

❧

Actress Blanche Lamonte was a seductive nineteen-year-old when she arrived in Dawson from San Francisco in 1898. She had taken her stage name from the young victim of San Francisco's notorious belfry murderer,[1] and inadvertently had made lurid headlines of her own when Maude Roselle, another actress, ran to Blanche's room at the Monte Carlo for protection from her rejected lover, Harry Davis. Tiny Blanche stood by helplessly as Harry shot Maude dead, then committed suicide.[2]

Blanche was one of Dawson's most popular soubrettes. It was rumored that Bob Ensley offered her weight in gold if she would marry him, that the scales were set up in the M & N Saloon and the transaction completed.[3] Klondike King Charlie Anderson was said to have made her a similar offer.[4] But although Blanche "vamped" with the best of them, like Cad Wilson and Klondike Kate, and earned good money, she was far short of the fortune she had envisioned, and she'd had more than her fill of Dawson when word arrived of a new gold strike in Nome. "She gave her

❧

JOSEPHINE EARP
Although she came from a well-heeled California family, Josephine Earp
was a showgirl before her marriage to Wyatt Earp, the famous gunman.
Biographer Glen Boyer believes this to be a photo of her in her early years, although
he notes that it has also been identified as that of a close friend.
Josephine was, by all accounts, a real beauty, even though she was a
decade or so older when she arrived in Nome.

Courtesy of Glen Boyer.

'macs' the malamute laugh as the steamer pulled away from the dock on Saturday last," the *Dawson Daily News* reported.[5]

———

The discovery of gold on Cape Nome, Alaska, during the Indian summer of 1898 marked the beginning of America's last big placer gold stampede. Justifiably ballyhooed as a match for the great Klondike discoveries which were made by seasoned prospectors, Nome's gold was found by greenhorns who had been in the Far North less than a year.

Eric Lindblom, a forty-one-year-old Swedish tailor, had made his way to Alaska as a deckhand on a whaler, jumping ship at Grantley Harbor. Jafet Lindberg, a twenty-four-year-old Norwegian, had conned his ticket to Alaska by pretending to be an experienced reindeer herder. John Brynteson, a twenty-seven-year-old Swede and the only miner among them, had worked only iron and coal. Although they were headed for the Klondike, the three Scandinavians were so late in acquiring passage that all the land was taken, which is why they ended up 1,000 miles west of Yukon Territory in the bleak and barren lands of the American Arctic.[6]

Their discovery would yield $3.5 million in gold by 1900 and $80 million during the next two decades. It was a latecomers' gold rush, a rare opportunity for amateurs, and a second chance for pros who had failed in Dawson.[7]

On one of the first boats in was Tex Rickard, professional gambler and fight promoter who had lost everything in a Dawson faro game, including his immensely profitable Monte Carlo Saloon. In Nome he teamed with Pat Murphy, who already had opened the Northern Saloon. Tex went on to make a second fortune, which he later parlayed into a prime investment in New York City called Madison Square Gardens.

Tex Rickard's friend, "Klondike Mike" Mahoney, had made $120,000 off a Klondike claim and lost it trying to develop ground on Jack Wade Creek that proved worthless. Going on to Nome, Big Mike worked longshore, ran mail, and also beat the world's heavyweight champ, Tommy Burns. Later he would successfully invest his Nome profits in stampedes in Alaska's Interior, retiring as a millionaire to his native Canada.[8]

On arriving in Nome, Blanche Lamonte and her lover, C. B. Heath, alias the "Hobo Kid," invested in a gambling house and saloon called the Kid's Club.[9] Blanche was so determined to make her fortune that when a no-good named Flory Wynkoop attempted to steal her poke, she trashed

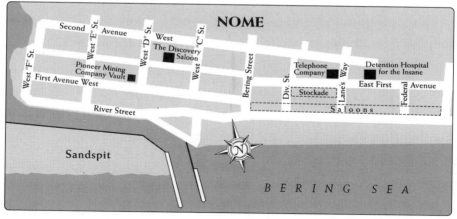

NOME

For nearly four years Nome's many prostitutes worked throughout the city,
but eventually they were rounded up into a fenced district called the "Stockade,"
neighboring the home of the federal judge and handy to city hall. The town was replatted
in 1934, changing the location of a number of lots, but the red light district
remained just outside the heart of town until after World War II.

Thanks to James Walsh of Nome and Seattle.

him severely enough to make newspaper headlines. She remained single
and apparently did well in Nome.[10]

———————

In 1899, 8,000 people left Dawson, some for the Outside but many
more for Nome, giving Canada's Northwest Mounted Police reason to
rejoice. For every beauty like Blanche Lamonte who headed over the border, so did at least a dozen hardened criminals. Thoughtfully, the
Mounties forwarded an all-male list of "the worst criminals known on this
continent" to U.S. Army personnel in the area. Blanche's Hobo Kid was, of
course, among them: "C. B. Heath—alias Hobo Kid; general cook, clever
poker player, will most likely be found living with a dance hall girl."[11]

With such a strong criminal element, Nome's gold rush got off to a
horrible start. Although American mining law clearly stated that mineral
content had to be proved before ground could be staked, most Nome
prospectors blithely ignored the requirement, claiming everything in sight
in their own names or those of friends, relatives, and casual acquaintances.[12]
Latecomers, frustrated by their greed and egged on by talk that the

CROWDED STREETS

*Thousands of fortune hunters crowded Nome's muddy streets at the height of the gold
rush there in 1901. The relatively cheap and easy transportation from the States (when compared
with the difficulties of getting to the Klondike) attracted great hordes of opportunists.*

UAF #88-231-05N.

original discoverers were not American and therefore did not deserve title
(although American mining law clearly allowed aliens to file), began staking lands already taken. Three weeks after navigation opened in June of
1899, almost every potentially valuable claim in the Nome district had
been jumped at least twice and some had half a dozen claimants.[13]

Meanwhile, almost nobody was making any money. Of an estimated
3,000 people in Nome in July 1899, 1,000 were destitute.[14] Unrest and a
lack of any civil government brought Nome under military law, gingerly
enforced by the small detachment of American soldiers sent up from St.
Michael. But what ultimately brought a truce, if not peace, to the camp
was a discovery on the beach. A soldier from the barracks and an old
Idaho prospector, too sick to leave the coast, found out that Nome's beach
sands were rich with gold. Since tidelands were public property, anyone

could work without the legal hassle of staking and recording.[15] The subsequent stampede was billed as the "Poor Man's Gold Rush," and newcomers came north by the thousands to pan an average of twenty to one hundred dollars a day in gold dust.

Nome's census in June of 1900 counted 12,488, but by midsummer about 20,000 were in residence.[16] The town, hastily established on an unsheltered shore, was the busiest seaport in the world without a harbor. Usually at least forty-five ships were anchored in the roadstead. Nome's post office employed twenty-three clerks who handled 546,000 letters between June and August; the "B" names alone took seventy boxes.[17]

"The beach from high-water mark was one solid rampart of piled goods; while longshoremen, earning from fifty to one hundred dollars each day, landed more and more freight every hour of the twenty-four," reported E. C. Trelawney-Ansell, by then a veteran stampeder.

"The front street was filled with a yelling, shouting, struggling, drunken, cursing throng, through which pushed teams and wagons, or the pack-trains, owned by Sam Heron, splashed their way through belly-high mud.

"Traders, gamblers, saloon-keepers and the women—dance hall girls, stage girls, and whores, black, white, or yellow—coined money. From the first, Nome differed from the Yukon camps; it was easy of access and cost little to get there either in effort or money.

"Nome was different, it was a place where the creeks and the town itself filled with thousands of cheechacos who had never known the hardship of the trail and few if any other hardships. Worse still, the camp and surrounding country was filled with gamblers, cutthroats and murderers of the worst kind. . . . The other northern camps had all contained a very large percentage of old sourdoughs, men whose word once given was worth all they owned and was never broken, be the man a poor miner or a millionaire claim owner. The say-so of these men on a bet of any size from ten dollars to ten thousand was taken by one and all. This was not the case in Nome."[18]

"Nome was a city of many diverse elements thrown together, all with only one idea in common," observed John B. Wallace. "That was to get rich as soon as possible and go back Outside."[19]

With such high transient turnover, little camaraderie, and no American equivalent to Canada's Northwest Mounted Police, the crime rate was extraordinary. Trelawney-Ansell reported eighty murders by the end of 1900, a figure so high it appears ridiculous. But so was the official count

of only five murders and four suicides![20] Nome was, by all accounts, a "wide open city," a problem city fathers had combated in 1899 by exporting all known criminals to Seattle on the revenue cutter *Bear* without legal authority.[21] By 1900, however, the gold encampment had more than sixty saloons where shoot-outs and muggings were routine. Miner William Ballou, down from Rampart to check out the rush, stayed only three days, each one of which included a murder. "We had a dead man for breakfast every morning," he wrote home.[22] Even Alfred Brooks, the generally unflappable geologist, found Nome exceptionally violent.

"A number of robberies occurred on the city streets. During my many years of Alaskan journeys, beginning with the Klondike rush and including visits to every important mining camp, I found Nome in 1900 the only spot in which I had the slightest apprehension of being robbed," he wrote. "At Nome, since I carried a large sum of money, I went armed, as did many others. The reasons for this lawlessness were two: 1) Nome had attracted many of the criminal class who found no difficulty in reaching it, and 2) those federal agencies which were above suspicion were engaged in other work than the handling of the rougher criminals."[23]

Law enforcement focused on combating murder and major thefts, but even those crimes sometimes went unpunished, for most of Nome's officials were crooked. Historian William Hunt suspects Nome's Deputy Marshall William M. Eddy, fired in 1905, was an early robbery suspect in Colorado and had escaped charges of burglary and disturbing the peace in Utah.[24] The postmaster, Joseph Wright, soon would be charged with embezzlement.[25] U.S. District Attorney Joseph Wood, Republican

BIRD'S-EYE VIEW OF NOME

Despite its precarious location on an unsheltered shore, Nome produced enough gold to warrant permanent settlement and by 1902 it was a formidable town.

UAF, Seiffert Family Collection, #85-122-25N.

National Committee man Alexander McKenzie (who was appointed receiver in Nome's claims litigation), and Nome's city tax assessor all would serve time in federal prison later for illicit financial dealings in Nome.[26] Nome's federal judge, Arthur Noyes, would be fired and fined $1,000 for making crooked rulings, although his strong political connections saved him from a prison term. And Nome's "crusading" newspaper editor, J. F. A. Strong, who allied himself with the crooked judge and district attorney, was later fired as governor of Alaska because he had lied about his Canadian birth and was never naturalized.[27]

⸺⟨∞⟩⸺

Also attracted to Nome's lawlessness were a few hundred prostitutes, who lived in shacks, hutches, and some ordinary houses behind the saloons at the back of the main street. And here, as in Dawson, female entertainers and dance hall girls were given to "prospecting" beyond the limits of the law.

"There were more of these in Nome than in any mining camp I was ever in," E. C. Trelawney-Ansell reported flatly. "Nothing in the worst days of Montmartre in Paris, or on State Street, Chicago, ever paralleled the shows given here. When they finished, the floor was cleaned and the dancers swarmed on it. The dance hall girls in Nome were younger and fresher than any that had been seen in the North up till then."[28]

Yet unlike Dawson, where good time girls were at the center of social life, the women of Nome's demimonde were low-profile, seldom mentioned in the early press. Even flamboyant showgirls like Cad Wilson, Diamond Tooth Gertie, and Klondike Kate gleaned only brief, formal theater reviews, with no coverage of their romances which had made such good reading in Dawson.

One reason was the lack of high-spending Klondike Kings to court them. Nome's discoverers were too busy battling claim jumpers and crooked judges to flaunt wealth they weren't sure they could keep. And most successful Nome miners were not weathered loners who had spent years prospecting remote regions, but newcomers who already had wives and sweethearts—some of whom journeyed to the gold fields with them.

Nome attracted many more "respectable" women than had early stampedes, and also had a much faster turnover of actresses, dance hall girls, and prostitutes. In Dawson, where rivers froze up early and mountain passes were threatened with snowslides, many "wintered over," but Nome was an open port easily accessible by ship from West Coast cities until the Bering Sea froze (from November to May).

"In fact, Nome men became so accustomed to a rapid turnover of pretty new faces, that the remark could be heard: 'W'at d'ye mean, that Dame Mabel? She's been in here six months or more,'" Trelawney-Ansell observed.[29]

Because of this, and because the living conditions were rough, the goal of most good time girls was to make a quick fortune and leave. And, although prostitution was illegal, law enforcement agents left members of the demimonde pretty much to their own devices.

Maud Parrish, just seventeen on arrival, found Nome a real comedown from Dawson, where she had done well on the fast track. "It was like coming into a calm pool after shooting the rapids," she wrote. "Nome was a bad town, wild and crooked, full of thieves and murderers and real lawlessness; while in Dawson people could leave their gold dust in bags outside a door and it would be safe. You couldn't do anything like that in Nome. . . . Everybody—every kind—that had the price of a ticket, dumped themselves in Nome to live off the hardier ones. But opportunities were less."[30]

Another good time girl, a prostitute known only as "Japanese Mary," prospered when she bet $1,000 on the prowess of Jujiro Wada, a fellow Japanese immigrant, who won a winter marathon on Nome's enclosed track. She invested her winnings in grubstaking prospectors and when one made a rich strike, threw a lavish party at a Nome roadhouse that was talked about for years.[31]

According to one account, Mary used her money to return to her family and respectability, but her good fortune did not last. Back in business in Iditarod's restricted district, she was strangled with a shoelace and a towel. "A gold nugget chain and a cross, which she usually wore around her neck, was missing," reported one newspaper. "She was believed by many to have had a great deal of money but none of it was found in the cabin." And the mystery of her murder was never solved.[32]

The less publicity the better for the good time girls, who realized its glare would hasten government regulation, limiting their earning potential. With virtually no press and no arrests of prostitutes through 1900, it is difficult to gain a clear picture of how they operated in those first, lawless days. There is reason to believe, however, that many did well. Despite the misnomer of "Poor Man's Gold Rush" and the increased availability of respectable women, Nome proved lucrative for big speculators of the demimonde—as made evident by the opulence of its dance halls and saloons, and the power held by the men who ran them.

The first city council was dominated by Charles Hoxie, who owned the Dexter Saloon with Wyatt Earp, Northern Saloon owner Tex Rickard, and Bill Tierney and Bill McPhee, also gamblers and saloon-keepers from Dawson's early days. When Tex Rickard declined the honor of becoming mayor, the job fell to Julius F. Geise, who'd made his fortune crafting sheet iron and stovepipes. Geise was well respected as one of Nome's leading merchants and hotel-keepers, but his formal education was so limited that he generally let the well-spoken saloon man call the shots.[33]

Since Nome had no tax base, one of the city council's first accomplishments was to get permission from Congress to use liquor license fees to support the local government. By charging $1,000 per license, the councilmen conveniently eliminated the small operators, leaving the field to major players like themselves.[34] And they played for high stakes.

"A description of the Bering Sea saloon might not be amiss. It was the most lavish, spectacular and elaborate of its kind in the North or in any mining camp I was ever in," testified E. C. Trelawney-Ansell. "The owner of the Bering Sea knew nothing about running such a place, but he had the

A FAMOUS GUNMAN

Wyatt Earp, center, was down on his luck when he joined the great Klondike gold rush
and failed to get to Dawson before all the good claims were staked. After turning down
a law enforcement job at Wrangell, wintering at Rampart, and briefly running a saloon at
St. Michael, he recouped his fortunes as part owner of the Dexter Saloon at Nome.

UAF, Wyatt Earp Photo Collection, #75-140-1N.

money and the organizing ability; his manager knew all that there was to know about such joints and ran it on a percentage basis.

"The bar fixtures . . . had been specially made in Chicago, and the owner told me that they had set him back £30,000 (about $100,000). . . . Across from the bar were the gambling tables, while at the rear of the saloon was a hall and stage where shows were given until midnight, this part being turned into a dance hall."[35]

E. J. "Lucky" Baldwin, an eccentric San Francisco millionaire down on his luck and short of finances (after several former wives tried to murder him and his swank $3.5 million San Francisco hotel burned to the ground), re-established himself on Front Street with "one of the finest drinking and gambling saloons in Nome." It had mahogany wainscoting, mirrors, stained-glass windows, and the best piano in town, and it quickly helped Baldwin regain his lost fortune.[36]

Charles Hoxie and Wyatt Earp's Dexter Saloon was the first two-story building in town and also the largest, with twelve "clubrooms" upstairs furnished with thick carpets, fine mirrors, carved sideboards, and draperies.[37] "It was the most fashionable saloon in town and would have been a standout even in San Francisco. The crowds thronged to it; the money Tex Rickard had forecast began to roll in," noted Wyatt Earp's wife, Josie, who helped decorate.

The Dexter made so much money that Josie, a former showgirl who was still a knockout at age thirty-seven, began gambling wildly until her husband cut her off and asked other gambling house owners to do the same. Angrily, Josie went out on her own, and her autobiography does not discuss how she survived. A woman as beautiful as Josie could easily find rich men to indulge her in Nome, but Wyatt was patient with her, for she'd recently lost a child at birth. He himself was on the edge; nearly broke when he arrived in Nome at age fifty-two despite his ready employment in his gun-slinging days, he was ripe for a mid-life crisis. Twice he was arrested in nasty bar fights, but within a year the Earps recouped their fortune and left the territory together.[38]

———— ⌘ ————

The gold in Nome's beach sands eventually played out. In August of 1900 a price war between the steamship companies reduced fares from Nome to the States from seventy dollars to fifteen; two thousand people left town in two weeks. A month later, a fierce storm with winds topping seventy-five miles per hour sent towering waves into Nome, destroying much of the business section and all beach operations. Plenty of gold was still to be unearthed on inland placer claims, but the "Poor Man's Gold Rush" was over.[39]

About 15,000 people went south, but the criminal element in Nome remained strong. C. A. S. Frost, a special examiner for the attorney general's office in Washington, D.C., reported "the largest number of vicious men and women that ever infected a pioneer mining camp." He warned, "There is great danger of their ranks being further augmented this fall by people who are stranded here lacking the means of livelihood, and without sufficient money to get out of the country."[40]

Earlier that summer, two cases of arson had been reported in Nome, one in a compound occupied by Belgian prostitutes behind the Second Class Saloon. As reported in the *Nome Daily News*, the blaze was quickly extinguished, but it was all too reminiscent of the fires in Dawson's red light district that destroyed sections of the town.

Also reported that evening was an altercation in a theater between "a lady of evil repute," Daisy Straws, and an unidentified man whom she hit over the head with a hammer. According to the account, "The man picked himself up, drew a large-sized gun and stooping down behind Sam Donnenbaum's cigar store, waited for the fair Daisy to reappear, so that he might bag her when she should emerge. Unfortunately for the sportsman's hopes, Daisy came out just as a soldier appeared and pulled both of them before any further damage could be done."[41]

U. S. Marshal C. L. Vawter, one of Nome's few honest officials, had enlisted as his deputy Albert J. Cody, a former Portland police officer with a quick mind and almost superhuman strength. Cody, who was doing well at mining, accepted the assignment only on the condition that those he arrested be jailed without visiting privileges, and that no writs of habeas corpus would allow prisoners to complain before the court—thus freeing himself from having to answer to the justice system.[42]

With local newspapers suddenly showing interest, and public sentiment shifting toward law and order, federal lawmen moved to clean up the town. Their first major effort was a raid on houses of ill fame in back of the Front Street saloons to arrest seven or eight whores who refused to pay a fine of ten dollars. "Little publicity was given the matter and the deputy marshals took great pains to conduct their prisoners through Lane's Alley, which runs from Front Street back of Second Avenue," the *Nome Daily Chronicle* reported. "When the news of [Deputy Marshal] Mercer's raid became noised around this morning, none of the attachés of the marshal's office could give any details, and inquiry at Judge Stevens's courtroom disclosed the fact that none of the women appeared there for trial this morning nor were their names registered upon his docket."

Investigation showed that one Ivena Henrietta had been fined ten dollars without being taken into custody; Jessie Dale, a black prostitute, was fined ten dollars without arrest; and Camille Bountaine was fined eighteen dollars "because it was after midnight."[43]

But the case that brought real public outrage was that of Gladys Shores and her pimp, Joseph Myers, who drugged and robbed George Nelson, nearly killing him in the process. Their arrest provoked a rousing editorial from the *Nome Daily Chronicle* asking local judges to teach the criminals a lesson.

RUGGED WATERFRONT

Open to the fierce weather and waves of the shallow Bering Sea, Nome's waterfront
was a precarious landing place, made even more dangerous by criminals who hung out
there looking for easy marks. Eventually high seas would wipe out half the town.
UW, Hegg #1247.

"There are any number of loose women in town who do not steal and
who depend alone on their charms for their income," the editorial writer
noted. "If this robbing and drugging continues, the number of arrested
criminals will become altogether too large to be properly cared for here,
and it is not beyond the bounds of possibility that a general deportation to
some outside penitentiary will be the result. It will be hard to segregate
the bad from the very bad and consequently many who have committed
no felony will be obliged to move on with the rest. Therefore it behooves
those sporting women who are not crooked to stand together and aid the
authorities in the efforts that will be made to cleanse the city of those vermin,
who by their operations are jeopardizing both the pure and impure."[44]

Anna Woods, a titian-haired, freckle-faced "amazon," was apparently
not a newspaper reader, for just one week later she enticed George Burnett
to enter her brothel, picked his pocket of eighty dollars while he slept,
and then kicked him out. George was quite drunk but still convincing
when he appeared in court to testify against Anna. She was released on

bond, but she had laughed at the proceedings, something the local paper was careful to note.[45]

During this era polite society maintained that a woman's place should be in the home, and the Nome Grand Jury, meeting a couple of weeks later with Albert J. Cody at its helm, observed that in saloons "lewd and dissolute women are permitted to resort and congregate and there demean themselves like men." It recommended that females be excluded from saloons, and that the district attorney move on all "dissolute persons who have no lawful occupation or profession."[46]

Not surprisingly, Cody—switching hats to act as a law enforcement official—followed up swiftly on the grand jury's recommendation. Not only were women barred from the saloons (except for performers, who were forbidden to consort with men at the bar or gamble), but two days after the jury adjourned, Nome police made their first arrest of a pimp, one Luddovich Dallagiodanni, for keeping a house of prostitution.[47]

Then Louise Vannes and a woman called Victoria made headlines by staging an exciting hair-pulling match on Second Avenue. "The women quarreled, so they say, over a man, but whatever the bone of contention was, they certainly must have held it in high esteem, for they put up a bout that would make a championship battle look like a walking match," the *Nome Daily Chronicle* reported. "Victoria was the first to land. She accosted the Vannes woman on the street and, without the usual verbal ceremony, she sent a left hook to the other woman's head, and her fingers accidentally caught in her hair and, as there was no referee present to award her opponent the battle on a foul, she followed up her advantage and held on.

"Louise began to get groggy, but when she got her second wind she, too, found the hair of her assailant a vulnerable spot, and they fell to the sidewalk, each using the other's glossy locks for a ground mop.

"The spectacle of two women fighting so viciously drew a large crowd, but none were able to part the warring contestants."

Both women were arrested, and the incident helped place Nome's demimonde under further scrutiny.[48]

"On Second Avenue, not far from the post office, there is a colony of painted French women who hang out of their windows and shout across the street to one another in strident tones that can be heard a block away," the *Nome Gold Digger* noted the same week. "Even passersby, who have no knowledge of French, are scarcely likely to imagine that the women are

MEN ONLY

Trying to cut down on muggings, the Nome City Council passed a law making it
illegal for women to enter bars. Enforcement was difficult at best, and female entertainers were
allowed on stage, but this establishment definitely appears to be within the law.

UAF, Lynn Denny Nome Album, #95-224-45N.

discussing the management of well-regulated households or singing odes
to the moon. The brazen effrontery of their manager speaks for itself."[49]

The closure of all theaters and gambling houses in Dawson in the
spring of 1901 sent a new flood of "sporting people" to Nome. Despite a
brief show of public sympathy for law and order, Marshal Vawter and
Deputy Cody got little backing from their bar-owning council members,
and most Nome citizens showed little concern over the wildness of their
town. Robberies, thefts, and frauds continued to plague the dance halls,
but they operated boldly. "Forty of the Prettiest Girls in Camp—40, come
on, Boys!!!" read an ad for the Columbia Dance Hall in the *Nome Gold Digger*
late that summer.[50] When Judge James Wickersham, backed by the grand
jury, asked that Charles Snyder's license for the Gold Belt Dance Hall be
immediately canceled because of reports that Charles's wife, Belle, and
dance hall girl Helen Wagner were robbing and "frisking" customers, the
regular court returned a verdict of not guilty.[51]

GOLDEN SANDS

When gold was discovered in the beach sands of Nome, even respectable
women took up mining, although dressed in the cumbersome feminine fashion
of the era which included long skirts and three or four petticoats.

UAF, Ralph MacKay Collection, #70-58-507N.

Judge Wickersham himself was fascinated by the demimonde but cautious. Early in his career, he had been convicted of seducing a client and escaped prosecution only after a second trial which revealed that his "victim" did not have an unsullied reputation.[52] When Mrs. Emma Downing, a "dangerous woman," visited him in his hotel room, he told her to leave, congratulating himself three weeks later when he learned she had had a "delicate operation" (probably an abortion). He sentenced one prostitute to three years in the federal penitentiary when it was proved that she robbed a man in the Gold Belt Saloon. Still, the judge was intrigued by "Russian Rosa," an adventuress attached to Magnus Kjelsberg, one of the millionaire partners of the Pioneer Mining Company.

"She is really a remarkable woman. She has tact, taste and great talents. Her power with men is astonishing," he observed in his diary. "Highly educated—a linguist—a woman of great physical charms and strength—strong in her natural mental endowments and skilled in the game of the world—she is such a woman as has in times gone by overturned thrones—Cleopatra—Sara Bernhardt—Delilah—these are the ingredients that enter into the composition of this Russian Adventuress, who made a fortune in San Francisco as a keeper of an assignation house— and in a year as the wife of one of the magnates of Anvil Creek, gets Nome society by the ears."[53]

Actually, Rosa had neglected to wed Magnus Kjelsberg, an oversight she soon corrected by cajoling Judge Wickersham into performing a quiet ceremony, which attests to the growing strength of Nome's "respectable" society.

Wickersham, whom the federal government had sent to clean up Nome after the firing of Judge Noyes, was in tune with the frontier philosophy that held both gambling and prostitution to be necessary evils. He did not believe in prosecuting gamblers, and he routinely fined prostitutes and bawdy house keepers just "a reasonable amount each quarter in vindication of the laws and as an aid to the fund to maintain the police."[54] In fact, Nome city fathers were so protective of their demimonde that District Attorney Joseph Wood tried to coerce them by threatening to "close down every gambling game in town and drive out every woman of ill repute" if they didn't cooperate with him and fire a certain part-time city attorney. (The testimony of that city attorney later would help send D.A. Wood to federal prison.)[55]

Overall, the demimonde co-existed quite well with polite society during Wickersham's judgeship, despite the town's growing refinements.[56] Klondy Dufresne, who was five when she and her mother came to Nome in 1902, recalls befriending a good-looking woman called "Toodles" on the boat trip north. "She was almost as beautiful as mother but in a different way," Klondy recalled in later years. "She had a long ostrich feather boa around her neck, and her cheeks were bright pink but the color wouldn't come and go like the delicate blush from mother's cheeks. I asked Toodles if she was going to Nome to meet her husband, but she said she didn't have a husband."

"Toodles" was given a grand reception on the beach by several men, while Klondy and her mother were left to their own devices by Klondy's father, who had not come in from the creeks to greet them. Later, while exploring Nome's main street, Klondy became intrigued by the lovely nude paintings she glimpsed through the doorway of the Northern Saloon and, catching sight of Toodles, followed her inside.

"A quiet man in a wide-brimmed Stetson hat and gray chamois vest with a nugget chain walked over and asked me what I wanted. He said he was the owner, his name was Tex Rickard, and I was probably the youngest customer he'd ever had," Klondy recalled. "I told him I was looking for my friend Toodles. Just then she rushed toward me and grabbed my arm. She didn't say hello or anything. She yanked me out through the swinging doors, knelt beside me and hugged me, saying in a low voice, 'Listen, young lady, I never want to see you in there again.'"[57]

News coverage of local prostitutes did increase as Nome matured. On July 9, 1901 the *Nome Nugget* reported that George Carey had been robbed of forty dollars by Maggie Dixon and May Goodwin. Two weeks later it noted that Nellie Waters, "who is known as a vaudeville actress," had attempted suicide and lay at death's door from an overdose of morphine or opium.[58]

Cigar store owner Augustine Dubois of Queen Street received brief mention in the *Nome Nugget* on April 16, 1902 when convicted of being an inmate of a house of prostitution. Eugenia Starr, a dance hall performer at the Columbia, made print by appearing with a revolver and threatening to blow holes through her boyfriend and a female rival who had moved her trunk into his room. Mr. Kennedy, one of the owners of the Columbia, struck the gun from Eugenia's hand, causing it to fire accidentally, but no one was hurt, the *Nome News* reported on October 3, 1903. Eugenia was arrested and bail was set.

But it was prostitute Lottie Wilson, taken advantage of by police deputy Sam James, who garnered the most publicity that year when Deputy James was shot dead on Nome's main street by Police Chief John J. Jolley. The editor of the *Nome Gold Digger*, S. H. Stevens, had witnessed the shooting and called it a falling-out among thieves. Certain classes paid protection money to Jolly and James to avoid prosecution, he speculated, and James either wanted a bigger share of the graft or threatened to expose his chief.

Chief Jolley denied the charge that he and his deputy were taking protection money. He testified that the trouble had started when Lottie Wilson summoned him to her lodging, demanding seventy-five dollars for services she performed for Officer James. It appears that Deputy James considered his romantic dalliance with Lottie a "freebie" while she had assumed it was a business transaction.

"I says to her, 'why, my dear lady, I cannot help that,'" Chief Jolley testified.

"'Well,' she says, 'I can send him to McNeil Island [Federal Penitentiary], and I will if he doesn't pay me this $75.'

"I says, 'Why do you want to send this man to McNeil Island? What has he done?'"

Lottie told of many crimes. Sam James had stolen coal from the Northern Commercial company, coal oil from the city, and pistols from someone, she said.

"I says, 'That's kind of funny you should keep tabs on him like that.' She flew at me then. I ought to pay $75. I told her to go and do her best. I goes to James' room immediately. I says, 'James, this woman Lottie sent for me this morning and accuses you of stealing coal.' . . . I say, 'God knows what you haven't stolen.' I says, 'James, I am going to lay you off and investigate these charges. . . . Jim, you have been drinking a good deal lately, you have been gambling a good deal lately, and I am afraid you have been neglecting your duty as a policeman.'"

According to Chief Jolley, one week later Sam James came to his house drunk and threatened to kill the police chief unless he was given his job back. Shortly thereafter, James stopped Jolley in front of the Hunter Saloon and threatened to blow his belly away. Chief Jolley edged away, but when James took aim with his derringer, Jolley shot him dead. Over protests of the grand jury, the local court acquitted Jolley, but he lost his police job.[59]

The Jolley case was not alone in raising questions of government corruption. Earlier, U.S. Attorney Joseph Wood had been embarrassed during his prosecution of R. J. Parks for gambling, when Tex Rickard and other saloon men testified in Park's defense that the attorney had demanded $3,000 a month not to close them down. Tex Rickard later would tell Judge Wickersham that he'd made payoffs totaling 15 percent of the take to stay open in Nome.[60]

———— ⬥ ————

By 1904 the citizens of Nome were getting tired of lawlessness and payoffs. Judge Wickersham moved on to Fairbanks and was replaced by Judge Alfred Moore, an easterner who quickly expressed his moral indignation at the condoning of vice. Early that May, Nome's usually benign police department began frenzied activity to clean up the town. Three pimps—Emille Leroux, Tom Greoire, and Louis Doe—were indicted on vagrancy charges. When Louis Doe (actually Louis Doumaine, later a big player in Fairbanks) skipped out, two deputy marshals actually tracked him to the Penny River and brought him back to the federal prison. Marie and

Alise Elsie, alleged white slaves of the men, were also arrested for vagrancy but released on bond.[61]

Louise Burley, a.k.a. "Boney," was found guilty of keeping a house of ill repute, was fined $500, and had her cigar store license revoked.[62] Sybilla Sackhart and E. E. Spring were found guilty of cohabiting in adultery and fined $200.[63] Vivian Carlyle, Jennie Stanley, B. H. Smith, Frank J. Higgins, and H. Sullivan were charged with frequenting an opium den, for which Smith and Higgins were sentenced to six months at McNeil Island Federal Penitentiary in Washington State.[64]

Bar owners and gamblers no longer ran the city council. In June of 1904, council members passed stronger ordinances forbidding women to frequent or be employed in barrooms and saloons, and prohibiting gambling within the city.[65]

One of the first arrested for gambling was former councilman Charles Hoxie, owner of the Dexter Saloon. Tex Rickard saw the move to respectability coming, sold out his share in the Northern, and left Nome for good. Others posted guards along the street and outside their card rooms, hoping to hide their operations during the crackdown, but this time there was no let-up.

Law and order had come to Nome to stay. Mabel Dixon, known to her customers as "Australian Mabel," committed suicide by swallowing carbolic acid. Friends and business associates noted she had been drinking and was despondent. The note she'd pinned to her dress said simply, "Goodbye, girls, I am tired of it all."[66]

The rest—"Hoo Hoo" Henderson, "Japanese" Kitty, and "Pile Driver" Kate among them—were quietly moved to a restricted district. Judge Moore favored total elimination of prostitution, but the idea was not popular and he was up for reappointment, so he allowed the red light district to be created. Surrounded by a twelve-foot board fence between Front Street and First Avenue, bounded by Hunter Way on the Wild Goose mining property,[67] the district was fittingly called the Stockade. Despite its grim-sounding name, the restricted district had its own phone system, messenger service, and eventually a new sewer system and electric lights. The girls lived in small but comfortable two- and three-room houses, some luxuriously furnished. Most had sweethearts in town, many of whom were prominent merchants and saloon owners. One cigar store owner shocked the community by marrying his Stockade-bound mistress so she would not be deported as an alien.[68]

Then a major fire started either in the back room of the Alaska Saloon or in a nearby cabin in the red light district. The blaze took out two blocks in the center of Nome, destroying fifty businesses including several saloons and twenty cabins in the Stockade; damage was estimated at $250,000. Five of the burned saloons opened for business within three days, but Nome would never be the same.[69] A number of saloon and casino operators had already pulled out because of the legal crackdowns. Nome's population was in steady decline, and many businesses never bothered to rebuild.

Meanwhile Judge Alfred Moore, once reappointed, boldly pushed the city council to do away with the Stockade, ostensibly because it was a health hazard and a fire risk.[70] His real motive, according to rumor, was that he and his daughter had to pass the Stockade on their way to and from court and wanted it gone.

Judge Moore's success in having the segregated district torn down in June of 1908[71] brought an angry backlash he had not anticipated. Thrown out of the Stockade, the prostitutes dispersed through town, doing business next to the homes of respectable citizens who were less than pleased with their new neighbors. As "Doc" Hill phrased it, "They have taken a boil and scattered it, and now the body politic, instead of having one big boil that can be lanced when necessary, has fifty small boils to be treated."[72]

Compounding the problem was the fact that Police Chief Larson, who was also the mayor's brother-in-law, appeared to be planning to force the ladies of the night to rent housing he was constructing on a sand spit near the Eskimo village. So embarrassing was the exposé in the *Nome Gold Digger* that the mayor tried to defend his honor by doing combat with the editor who broke the story, S. H. Stevens, also known as "Big Mitt." The fistfight was a draw, and the girls continued to work without regulation for several years before a second Stockade was established for them.[73]

By then Nome's working conditions had ceased to be an issue for most of the golden girls. When the last boats left Nome for the season in 1910, over 4,000 passengers departed, dropping the town's population to just 2,000.[74] For many the destination was Fairbanks, which had just supplanted Nome as Alaska's largest city and the best place in the Far North for a working girl to get ahead.

9

Fairbanks
Battling the Odds

ESTABLISHING THE BEST LINE IN THE WEST

⟨∞⟩

I n 1904 Fairbanks boasted dozens of saloons and gambling dens—
thirty-three of them in four blocks along First Avenue—all with no locks
because they never closed. And city fathers were downright delighted
when a Dawson prostitute, "Cheechaco Lil," established herself on Second
Avenue, indicating her staunch faith in the future of the camp. Her arrival
brought to four the number of "working girls" in Fairbanks—not nearly
enough to meet local demand, but more girls were arriving daily.[1]

⟨∞⟩

The founders of Fairbanks could not have picked a less likely place for
a city. While other gold rush towns were accessible by ocean trade routes
and the mighty Yukon River, this camp was in the Tanana Valley, deep in
Alaska's Interior on the Chena (which had been given an Indian name that
meant "Rock River" because of its shallowness in the dry season). The
Chena was a remote tributary of the Tanana River, which was a major but

⟨∞⟩

SHE LOOKED LIKE THE GIRL NEXT DOOR
But she worked in the Fairbanks red light district in 1906 during a mining
boom that may have made her fortune. Her photograph and those of a dozen or so
of her co-workers were commissioned by an ambitious bartender named George Akimoto,
who was trying to get the backing of an outside syndicate to purchase more property
on the lucrative Line. The unusual photos were saved from oblivion by the late
Fabian Carey of Fairbanks and are now in the safekeeping of his son.

Michael Carey Collection.

remote tributary of the Yukon, in an unmapped area surrounded by mountains on three sides.[2]

Italian discoverer Felix Pedro, a.k.a. Felice Pedroni, a veteran prospector, was ill, disillusioned, and in debt when he staked his claim in the Tanana Valley. A year earlier, in 1901, Pedro had made his first major find here, but mapped it so poorly that he could not relocate it after a 130-mile trip to Circle to resupply.[3] And he might have misplaced his second strike had not trader E. T. Barnette been dumped conveniently on a nearby riverbank with a year's supply of trading goods.

Barnette, a convicted felon who recreated himself as a respectable businessman, had chartered the stern-wheeler *Lavelle Young* after his own supply boat sank at the Yukon's mouth off St. Michael. He planned to establish a trading post about 400 miles up the Tanana River at Tanana Crossing, a telegraph site falsely rumored to be a future railhead.[4] At Barnette's urging, his charter captain, Charles Adams, detoured to the Chena trying to get around Bates Rapids, commonly thought to block navigation on the Tanana, but the stern-wheeler went aground about seven miles above the mouth of the Chena. This was more than 200 miles down-river from Barnette's destination, but Captain Adams refused to continue.

It was late August 1901, and Barnette was beside himself until Felix Pedro and his partner, Tom Gilmore, came down from the hills to purchase their winter outfits, assuring him that a gold strike was imminent and more customers would follow.[5] But it took a year for that to happen, and even after Felix had successfully staked Pedro Dome on July 28, 1902, the usual stampede did not ensue.

Anxious for business, Barnette ordered his cook, an outstanding athlete named Jujiro Wada, to run to Dawson in the dead of winter to announce the strike. Wada's arrival in Yukon Territory made headlines.[6] However, the plan backfired when a Dawson contingent arrived that spring to find most of the Tanana Valley illegally staked (one man alone had tied up almost 3,000 acres) and no one making money yet. Dawson bartender James "Curly" Monroe, who'd brought $10,000 to invest, returned to the Klondike with his bankroll intact, predicting that perhaps in six months or two years the Tanana camp might become worthwhile.[7] "Ham Grease" Jimmie O'Connor, another veteran, reported the diggings were so poor they would not support one dance hall.[8]

Indeed, the area's 500 or so miners appeared to be living on hope. Gold in the Tanana Valley lay more deeply underground than in previously

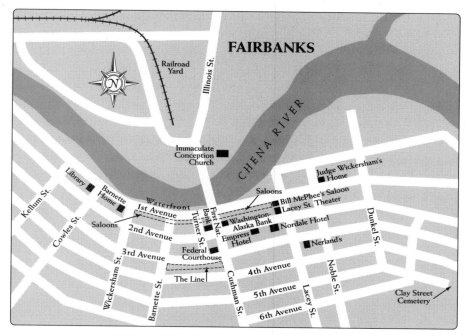

Thanks to Pat Cook and Olga Steger of Fairbanks.

mined locations. It wasn't until late in 1903 that the undercapitalized Fairbanks miners—mostly old pros working with primitive hand tools—established that they had a major strike. By then, Felix Pedro had discovered a second, richer gold deposit on Cleary Creek, and "Two Step" Louis Schmidt, Dennis O'Shea, Jesse Noble, Tom Gilmore, James Dodson, and a few others also had struck it rich.[9]

Fairbanks's first dance hall opened April 20, 1903, and closed shortly thereafter.[10] When Sarah Gibson came to town hoping to start a hotel in May, she wrote her son Tom in Dawson that there were lots of buildings going up and one dance hall but no girls yet. Her arrival brought the number of women in Fairbanks to six.[11]

By Christmas from 1,500 to 1,800 men were in the area, most of them seasoned miners. Judge James Wickersham, who talked E. T. Barnette into naming the town after soon-to-be U.S. Vice President Charles W. Fairbanks, included it in his 300,000-square-mile judicial district. After treeless, wind-strafed Nome, Judge Wickersham was quite taken by the valley's rolling forests and its farming potential. When Barnette presented him with a prime house lot and offered land for a courthouse as well, Wickersham made the town his headquarters, pronouncing it an "American Dawson."[12]

One year later, gold production increased from $40,000 to $600,000 and Fairbanks outdid its predecessor. "To walk down Front Street here one would think that one had been asleep and awakened in Dawson, so far as faces were concerned, for nine-tenths of the people here have been in Dawson," an old-timer reported.[13]

But Fairbanks was much wilder than Dawson, where the "yellow legs" (Northwest Mounted Police) were strict in law enforcement, observed George Preston, who worked at Northern Commercial. The American camp's reputation for violence was established when Alexander Coutts, an unpopular bear of a man, expressed a grievance over a building lot and was shot through the lungs by mining recorder William Duenkel.[14] Coutts recovered, and Judge Wickersham allowed Duenkel to walk on $1,000 bond.

When angry Dawson miners threatened to lynch Jujiro Wada for luring them to Fairbanks for a "fake" stampede, the judge dispatched his brother Edgar to the site as a federal deputy marshal.[15] Edgar Wickersham was subsequently fired as the result of a drinking problem, but maintaining order in that frontier town was a thankless task, even for the sober.[16]

───── ⊷∞⊶ ─────

Yet almost from its beginnings, Fairbanks provided surprising amenities: electricity, telegraph service, a telephone system, mail service, seasonal steamboat transport, and a government-pioneered trail to the deep water port of Valdez to the south. All these made women feel more comfortable in Fairbanks than in the rough-and-tumble settings of earlier camps. E. T. Barnette's wife, Isabelle, accompanied him on his first trip and stayed on. Judge Wickersham settled his family, and others followed suit. "Many of the earlier Fairbanks miners had been in the north for many years and were looking for a permanency and stability that the other communities of Dawson and Nome lacked," noted historian Gary Stephens. "There was a strong conservative element in the community."[17]

But because gold-mining in the Tanana Valley was labor-intensive, it also attracted a large number of virile young men. When gold production reached nearly $4 million in 1905, prostitutes and their pimps began flocking there.

The city of Fairbanks—well-organized from its inception and guided by Judge Wickersham's policy of moderately taxing vice for civic betterment—established a system of monthly fines that served as "license fees"

SEASONED PROSPECTORS

Fairbanks, in the heart of Interior Alaska, was settled by veteran prospectors who
used riverboats as their main mode of transportation. Town founder E. T. Barnette arrived
with his wife, but otherwise women were slow to move to the isolated region.

UAF, Ralph MacKay Collection, #70-58-238N.

for illicit operations, and welcomed the influx. "Are you a lady or a whore?" the city attorney would ask, meeting females off each incoming boat. "If you are a lady, pass on; if you are a whore, seventeen dollars and a half."[18]

The take averaged $1,200 a month, according to an informant for the *Valdez News*, and moralists in the rival settlement were scandalized.[19]

"Fairbanks papers are going into ecstasies over the fact that the town has been conducted for the last year without levying a property tax. Why the people should be proud of the condition of affairs there is incomprehensible," the *Alaskan Prospector* editorialized.

"The money, apart from licenses, used for running expenses of the town has been collected entirely from the sporting class by a system of fines. Every game in operation has to pay a monthly tax and the sporting element are assessed a heavy per capita tax. The town is supported by licenses collected from prostitutes and gamblers. This method of raising

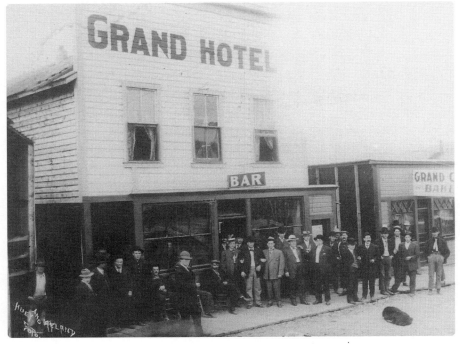

FAIRBANKS FOUNDERS

*Early Fairbanks residents worried that women might never settle in the gold
rush community, and it took some time to attract them. This early town portrait includes
Charles L. Thompson, owner of the prestigious Tanana Club (eleventh from the left with tipped-
back hat and a grey double-breasted suit), and Leroy Tozier, a lawyer who had
made a fine name for himself in Dawson (to Thompson's right in the white hat).*

Courtesy of A. Christopher, Blanche Cascaden, Pioneer Museum, Alaska.

money is so obnoxious to the average person that one would think the
people of Fairbanks would say as little as possible about it."[20]

Nome's crackdown on prostitutes and gamblers in 1904 and closure of
dance halls and gambling dens in Dawson left Fairbanks as the only major
gold camp where the demimonde could operate comfortably. "This means
that the population of our town will be largely increased by that element,
which is headed this way," noted the *Fairbanks Daily Times* in 1906, unfazed.
"Our community has always had a fair proportion of its population who
were identified with the class referred to but the community being small
and these characters well-known a limited field for operation has
been offered."[21]

In the same editorial, the *Times* editor boasted about the superiority of the Fairbanks Police Department, but its track record did not inspire confidence. Police Chief Tom Harker had just left town to avoid an investigation for "taking money from fallen women,"[22] and James Hagen, appointed to replace him, had questionable associations with the underworld.

Suspicions were aroused when one T. E. Nordness committed suicide by cutting his wrists and then driving a bullet through his forehead after Police Chief Hagen had ignored for three days his complaints that he had been held at gunpoint and "cajoled" out of his entire life savings by a Floradora dance hall girl.[23] Chief Hagen also failed to discover who had fired a five-gallon keg of gasoline "set for spite" at the Tanana Bottling Works, owned by two of the town's most flamboyant businessmen.[24] Nor had he been much help when Gabrielle Mitchell, a.k.a. Louise Vassiaux (a prostitute well-connected with the Fairbanks underworld), beat Irene Wallace, a competitor, so badly that a doctor had to repair the victim's face. Gabrielle, who proudly demonstrated her prizefighting techniques to the court by "punching holes in the air to show how different blows could be delivered with force," was fined only fifty dollars. Irene, fearing for her life, fled on the next boat.[25]

Even tolerant Fairbanksans began to wonder about their law enforcement when Annie Fields, a.k.a. "Woodpile Annie," was reported to have shot herself in the head with Chief Hagen's .44. The suicide attempt allegedly took place at 8 a.m. on a Sunday at the cabin James Hagen shared with Tom Sites, a bookkeeper for the Tanana Bar. In fact Annie, "very much under the influence of drink or drugs," had tried to dispatch herself at the home of one of the town's most prominent citizens, and Chief Hagen apparently had been pressured into concocting a story for the press involving himself.[26] The career lawman was fired about a month later on a vote of four to three by the Fairbanks City Council.[27]

Alaska's Episcopal Archdeacon Hudson Stuck, although hardened by the Texas cowboy towns where he had begun his career as a priest, was awed by Fairbanks violence.[28] Later described by one biographer as a latent homosexual, Archdeacon Stuck had an inordinate fondness and sympathy for young men and was appalled at how frequently they were mugged, robbed, or brutally beaten by Fairbanks pimps and their women.[29] But he was also a well-educated free thinker who realized that outlawing prostitution was no solution in a rough frontier setting. It was not lost on Stuck that the first grand ball of the Fairbanks Arctic

Brotherhood, held shortly after his arrival in the fall of 1904, attracted only seventeen women to sixty-six men.[30] Or that the fast-growing city depended on vice for the majority of its revenues.

The solution—quasi-legal prostitution in a carefully supervised restricted district—may have been suggested to Archdeacon Stuck by Luther Hess, who was the assistant U.S. district attorney under Judge Wickersham and who knew from personal experience how well it could work.

Born of a wealthy family in Milton, Illinois, Luther Hess had stampeded to Dawson via Dyea, then passed the Alaska Bar and moved to Fairbanks. When he returned to visit his hometown, flush from trading in mining claims and other northern business ventures, he urged friends to come North to make their fortunes. He found a protégé in Georgia Lee, the beautiful, fun-loving daughter of a poor neighbor, and agreed to back her career as a prostitute in the Far North. To help her polish her trade before coming to Fairbanks, Luther arranged for Georgia to apprentice in the red light district of St. Louis.[31]

The first city in America to regulate vice, from 1870 to 1874 St. Louis had openly operated a red light district with over 700 prostitutes, under the "Social Evil Ordinance." It provided police protection for both management and clients, medical inspections, and even free hospitalization for prostitutes with venereal disease. Had the St. Louis system not become a political football, it might have become a national model, and the city remained progressive in dealing with its demimonde.[32] The plan Archdeacon Stuck urged Fairbanks city fathers to adopt in 1906—the same year Georgia Lee arrived fresh from training in St. Louis—was almost identical to St. Louis's Social Evil Ordinance.

The archdeacon's timing could not have been better. Fairbanks's annual gold revenues had exceeded $9 million that year, and the town was just starting to rebuild after devastating bouts with fire and flood. Block 48, a long stretch slated for rebuilding on the even-numbered side of Fourth Avenue between Cushman and Barnette Streets, just beyond the heart of town, was selected for the district. With the backing of the town council, Stuck convinced Andrew Nerland to help with land title transfers and other business arrangements.[33]

Though a staunch Presbyterian and a family man, Andrew Nerland was the perfect choice for the project. A Norwegian-born paint and wallpaper supplier, he had moved from Dawson to become one of Fairbanks's leading businessmen. Much of the town's demimonde traded at his shop. Earlier Nerland had chaired the committee that moved the red light district out of Dawson's city limits, so he understood the economics of prostitution better than most.[34] And his wife, Annie, had just moved south for the sake of their small son's health,[35] which would spare her the embarrassment of her husband's delicate assignment.

In Dawson, prostitutes had been forced to rent from unscrupulous landowners whose real names were cleverly concealed. To Andrew Nerland's credit, the Fairbanks women were given the opportunity to purchase lots in their district, and rents were kept fairly reasonable by city fathers who invested openly.

While Nerland arranged the land transactions, Archdeacon Stuck briefed the police chief and wrote the regulations. Prostitutes could no longer solicit in bars or dance halls, but must confine all business activities to their special district, which would be carefully patrolled. They were to limit movie-going to special, after-hours shows especially for them, and were not to mix and mingle in respectable society. They also must agree to regular health inspections and continue to pay the monthly fines on which the city subsisted. In return, they would be allowed to operate without fear of legal reprisals, with the backing of that well-heeled community. Many prostitutes, long the target of unscrupulous lawmen and politicians, saw it as the chance of a lifetime.

Opposed to the plan were a number of moralists, who found themselves strangely allied with rent-gouging landlords and saloon-keepers who had depended on wild women to lure male customers. "Archdeacon Stuck was burned in effigy as the man who was responsible for establishing a regular district for prostitutes," recalled Albert N. Jones, an Episcopal priest later assigned to Stuck's Fairbanks post. "The dance hall girls, some saloon-keepers, etc. found this decision bad for business and so the Archdeacon was symbolically 'worked over.'"[36]

Although no official ordinances were passed, the city backed Stuck's plan. On September 8, 1906, the *Fairbanks Evening News* reported an emphatic grand jury protest against "licensed women" (Fairbanks prostitutes who paid their fines) being permitted to live wherever they choose. The council took heed, for just five days later the *Fairbanks Daily News Miner* referred for the first time to a "woman of the restricted district."

The paper was reporting the case of Willey Hooper, "a colored girl on Fourth Avenue" who was robbed by Ike Moses, a tailor. Ike had beaten

Willey in an attempt to steal her diamond earrings, valued at $500. Police officer Jack Hayes arrested the man within a half-hour, and Willey assured the judge that her attacker—broke and desperate to raise money for his family Outside—was crazy.[37]

Once the restricted district (also referred to as "The Line" and "The Row") was well established, complaints of muggings and robberies ceased. In fact, miners began leaving their gold dust and paychecks with girls in the district for safekeeping if the banks were closed when they got to town.[38] "Respectable women" were spared having to deal with annoying propositions from sex-starved miners who could not always tell wanton women from those of stout moral fiber.

Initially the Line had about fifty inmates living in small log houses built side by side, some no bigger than six by nine feet. The "cribs," as they were called, were smartly painted, boasting bright awnings and leaded glass windows. Each had a tiny kitchen with an entrance on Fourth Avenue that was seldom used.[39] Business was solicited from a living room at the back of each house, accessible via boardwalk through an alley. Every living room had a picture window through which men "shopping" for love could see the occupants.

"These women were not the noisy type of hooker pictured in the dance halls," recalled Robert Redding, who delivered water to the Line before it was plumbed. "They were quiet, neatly dressed, and quite often were reading the current bestseller. They didn't need to be noisy. They knew why they were there and so did the customers."

A potential client entered through the back door and might visit in the living room a while before heading for the snug little bedroom sandwiched between it and the kitchen.[40] Not all visitors had romance in mind, either. One of the girls owned the best library in the Far North and attracted an odd following of miners who just came for a good read. And the Line also became a popular after-hours drinking spot.[41]

Although town founder E. T. Barnette did not speculate in red light real estate, most of the city council did, including bar owners Charles Thompson and Dave Petree, and teamster Dan Callahan. Barnette did try to force the girls to vote his party line, but that attracted such embarrassing press coverage he apparently gave up on the idea.[42]

Of even greater concern was a rash of suicides by Fairbanks prostitutes which began during the holiday season in 1906. Following a long period when she appeared to be in good spirits, well-liked Kate Ambler, who was

THE FAIRBANKS LINE IN OPERATION

*This is the only known photo of would-be patrons "window-shopping" in the
red light district. If a prostitute's window was uncurtained, it usually meant she was
open for business and could be viewed by prospective customers before they negotiated.
While many of the girls posed willingly for photographers, patrons were usually
less willing, which may explain the shaky quality of this photo.*

Michael Carey Collection.

working to support her child in Tacoma, baffled friends by downing
strychnine and refusing the aid of a doctor.[43]

Nine days later "French Alice," whose true name was unknown even to
close friends, swallowed patent antiseptic tablets, her second suicide
attempt in six weeks. "Unrequited love, on the part of one of the men who
prey upon the earnings of fallen women for their livelihood, is said to be
the cause of the woman's attempt to commit suicide," the *Fairbanks Evening
News* speculated.

Then Frankie Polson succeeded with strychnine. Annie Fields followed
with her bizarre shooting attempt, supposedly out of dislike for the police
chief but more likely prompted by the departure of her pimp.[44] Katzu
Okabazashi cured her longing for a heartless Japanese bartender by taking
mercury-bichloride.[45]

However, it took the tragic death of Marie LaFontaine, a well-
respected prostitute who worked under the name of LaFlame, to move
Fairbanks officials to action. One of the most orderly women in the district, Marie never had been known to drink, but the day before her death
she went on a terrible bender, causing a disturbance at the dance hall and

breaking a windowpane with her fist. Concerned friends got her into police custody, but after being released she continued to drink and finished off the evening by downing a two-ounce bottle of carbolic acid, which she did not survive.[46] Apparently her pimp, Emille Leroux, who earlier had been run out of Nome on charges of white slavery, had gambled away the savings she had planned to use to visit her aging mother and sister in Montreal.[47] Perhaps Marie had hoped to start over.

Outraged, some of the town's most respected citizens served as Marie's pall bearers. Their floral tribute was extraordinary. The ladies of St. Matthew's choir sang at her service. And within twenty-four hours, the Fairbanks City Council passed a harsh ordinance that made it impossible for pimps to function.[48]

According to the ordinance, a prostitute could answer to a lover or business manager, but that was her choice. Pimps (also called "macques") were forbidden to reside on the Line, and since prostitution was quasi-legal, pimps could not control women by threatening to turn them in to the authorities. If a girl was mistreated by a pimp, she could easily get rid of him by having him arrested. Plenty of customers found their own way to the restricted district without pimps luring them there; local bartenders would refer more customers for a reasonable commission, a service performed by taxi drivers in later years. So for the first time, perhaps in the history of the United States, it was possible for a common prostitute to survive on her own, with a real chance of building a better life.

While the city council was liberal, attuned to its frontier public, federal officials were horrified by quasi-legal prostitution, as was the Fairbanks grand jury. In April of 1908, on the jury's recommendation, District Judge Silas H. Reid ordered immediate closure of the dance halls in the Third Judicial District, and they never reopened. Judge Reid ignored the jury's recommendation to cancel liquor permits of any business permitting women on its premises, but he did order licenses taken from those who allowed women of ill repute to live or loiter upon the premises or allowed them to solicit drinks for a percentage.[49] When the Tammany Dance Hall tried to circumvent the order by staying open but selling only soft drinks, Judge Reid ordered it closed anyway.[50]

Following Judge Reid's lead and his own righteous bent, newly appointed District Attorney James Crossley, a former state senator for Iowa, saw reform as a quick way to make a name for himself. On the job less than a month, he engineered raids on a dozen or so of the town's most

prominent citizens who bedded women of the demimonde. D. A. Crossley
had them arrested on charges ranging from adultery and unlawful cohabitation to conducting a bawdy house.

Among those jailed was Charles L. Thompson, owner of Fairbanks's
most prestigious bar, the Tanana Club. Although connected with the
underworld, Charles Thompson was well loved as the town's fairest baseball umpire and the only citizen with both the money to finance public
fireworks displays and the courage to set them off. The bar owner was
astonished to be charged with adultery for sleeping with his mistress, prostitute Georgia Lee, because neither of them was married and everyone in
town knew it. At the urging of his astute attorney, Thompson pleaded
guilty and paid the fifty-dollar fine anyway, making the whole proceeding
a bit of a farce.

Worse yet, Crossley laid the same charge on Thomas Marquam, the
town's cleverest defense lawyer, who proceeded to defeat the district attorney in court. Others simply shrugged and paid their fines because unlawful
cohabitation wasn't a big deal on the frontier.[51] Somewhat deflated, D. A.
Crossley lay low for a while. As their concession to moral decency, the
city fathers enclosed the Line with a twelve-foot-high board fence.[52]

Nationally, Americans had become concerned about "white slave"
traffic, and in 1908 the U.S. signed an international treaty aimed at stopping
the enslavement of girls and women of any color for prostitution. The
media, led by the august *New York Times* and early movie-makers, convinced
citizens that international rings of white slavers were kidnapping as many as
60,000 women a year. Hysteria ensued, but crime sweeps across the nation
uncovered no evidence to prove the problem existed. The *New York Times* and
other reputable media quickly dropped the subject, which within five years
would be referred to as the "myth of an international and interstate 'syndicate' trafficking in women" and a "figment of imaginative fly-gobblers." But
while white slavery briefly remained a cause celebre, a number of public
officials used it to build their careers and fight prostitution in general.[53]

Among the most zealous was Kazis Krauczunas, an immigration
inspector for the U.S. Department of Commerce and Labor based in
Ketchikan, Alaska, who decided after a preliminary investigation that
Fairbanks was a hotbed for the trade. In June of 1909, Krauczunas's excited
superiors dispatched him to Fairbanks to arrest white slavers and deport

HOUSES OF PROSTITUTION, FAI

the women they had corrupted. He was forearmed with a list of names provided by Captain T. A. Wroughton of the Northwest Mounted Police, which earlier had driven many of the suspects out of Dawson.[54]

Two of the worst offenders, Inspector Krauczunas decided, were Felix Duplan,[55] who had skipped bail in Canada, and his wife, Lily DeVarley, who had been convicted of running a disorderly house in South Dawson and asked to leave town. Lily, beautiful and well-liked, had worked quietly on the Fairbanks Line with two sisters since its inception.[56] Neither she nor Felix had recruited inexperienced, unconsenting young women, nor did they have Fairbanks police records. However, Krauczunas knew that on June 17 of that year they would complete three years of U.S. residency, making it all but impossible to deport them. Realizing he would not come north before then, Krauczunas wired Fairbanks's U.S. marshal, requesting that he arrest the couple. On his arrival five days later, Krauczunas was relieved to find that his request had been honored.

NKS, ALASKA, JUNE, 1909

CRIMINAL EVIDENCE
Federal immigration inspector Kazis Krauczunas journeyed to Interior Alaska in
1909 hoping to arrest and export foreign pimps and prostitutes for white slavery operations.
In the process he photographed red light districts wherever he could find them.
He described Fairbanks as a hotbed of activity, but was astonished to find not a
single citizen who would testify against residents of the restricted district.
NA, File #52484-28, RG85 with grateful thanks to Claus Naske who discovered the photos.

It was, however, the last cooperation he would get in Fairbanks (except from District Attorney James Crossley, whose backing proved a hindrance because his politics were so unpopular). Krauczunas proceeded as he had in other Alaskan towns, handing out cigars and buying meals for potential informants, but he had not one shred of success. Fairbanks citizens were "extremely friendly" toward prostitution "to such an extent that the majority of the permanent residents know the prostitutes by their first and second names," he wrote his boss in despair, "even the schoolchildren know the prostitutes by names and reputations."

Nor was the three-man police force much better. One officer was rumored to be "on very intimate terms with one of the prostitutes" while the other had been "a bartender and a gambler of note in the early days of Dawson," Krauczunas reported. And the police chief lived "with a woman in an unmarried state."

Desperate for help, the immigration agent wired the Northwest Mounted Police in Dawson, who responded with names and police records of likely slavers. But someone at the telegraph office leaked a warning to the suspects before Krauczunas got the dispatches.

Some of the alleged slavers took to the woods, while others hit the trail to Valdez, drifted down the Chena River, or high-tailed it for the mining camps that surrounded the town. Unaware of the exodus, Krauczunas got a warrant to search the quarters of suspected pimps along Fifth Avenue but found them empty except for hastily left personal possessions, supplies of wine and whisky, and paraphernalia belonging to the prostitutes.

Determined, Krauczunas visited several of the surrounding mining camps, most of which were connected to Fairbanks by telephone and thus forewarned of his arrival. In Fox he found twenty shanties, of which nine were houses of prostitution, four saloons, and two churches, he reported in disgust to his home office. The ratio was about the same at Chatanika, Ester Creek, Dome Creek, and the other camps. Fairbanks, with a population of about 4,000, had approximately 150 prostitutes to half a dozen churches.

Krauczunas was even more unnerved when a "pimp" named Francois Berrinet attempted to bribe him for the release of Marie Ruhlmann, one of the few prostitutes he had managed to arrest. And the immigration agent was shocked to learn that a year earlier the same man had offered John Cameron, deputy collector of Internal Revenue, $6,000 to keep the woman from being deported. Cameron had not taken the bribe, but he had not reported it either, and Krauczunas forced him to make an affidavit in the U.S. Attorney's office acknowledging the incident.

A determined and dedicated bureaucrat, Krauczunas put in twelve- to eighteen-hour days, finally managing to arrest twelve prostitutes and five procurers. Included was an innovative woman named Camille Leonard, a.k.a. "French Camille," who paid a local barber $2,000 to marry her, instantly becoming an American citizen. Previously the owner of a cigar

KIDNAPPED

Foreign-born Fairbanks prostitute Clemence Ponnelle, far right, escaped arrest by immigration officials in 1909 when she declared she had been kidnapped by a pimp a year or two earlier. Immigration inspector Kazis Krauczunas committed the seventeen-year-old to a Catholic orphanage in the remote Eskimo village of Holy Cross on the Yukon River, and no account of what became of her after that can be found.

NA, File #52484-28, RC85 with grateful thanks to Claus Naske who discovered the photo.

store in Dawson, Camille had invested in a half-dozen profitable lots on the Fairbanks Line, and she was not anxious to return to Paris. Uncertain of the law, Krauczunas checked with District Attorney Crossley, who incorrectly assured him the marriage would not change Camille's status. The relieved inspector headed south on a river steamer with his prisoners. One, Clemence Ponnelle, traveling under the name of Mrs. E. Beretzi, claimed to have been kidnapped from Quebec by Ernest Beretzi, a.k.a. Emil Chaillet, whom Krauczunas also had under arrest. Since Clemence proved to be only seventeen, Krauczunas left her in the care of nuns at the Holy Cross Mission on the Lower Yukon, where she quickly disappeared from record.

When he presented his "white slavers" for prosecution in Seattle, the immigration agent was roundly congratulated by his home office, but matters did not turn out as he had hoped. The federal judge who heard the first case insisted the prisoners could be prosecuted only in Fairbanks, and

JAPANESE PROSTITUTES

*It was unusual for early gold camps to attract Japanese prostitutes, but Fairbanks
had at least three. One pictured here is believed to be Mary Akimoto, wife of bartender
George Akimoto, who died mysteriously shortly after this photo was taken in 1906.
Another is probably Katzu Okabazashi, who committed suicide by swallowing
mercury-bichloride when the widowed George spurned her less than a year later.*

Courtesy of Paul Solka.

when the government declined to undertake the vast expense of returning them, they were all simply deported.[57]

All, that is, except Camille Leonard, the newly married American citizen. Camille returned to Fairbanks to ply her former trade with no further brushes with the law and live quite independently. Her "husband," the barber, having gone through her generous "dowry," prudently hit the trail for Valdez, paying someone to return with the "sad news" that he had died near the summit of Thompson Pass, where he was supposedly buried under a cross. The relieved "widow" went on to become one of Fairbanks's major property holders and was still enjoying residing there in the mid-1920s.[58]

———— ∞∞∞ ————

Kazis Krauczunas was not alone in his preoccupation with white slavery. Public concern over the issue grew into international hysteria during this era. Although it proved not a major problem for American females, it was a real threat to Asian women, especially if they had left their homelands illegally.

Early on, Fairbanks proved a mecca for Japanese immigrants. E. T. Barnette's cook, Jujiro Ingero Wada, recruited many of his fellow countrymen from other gold camps to come to Fairbanks. The town's first banquet, hosted by Judge James Wickersham to honor Felix Pedro, was catered in a tent by Japanese owners of the Tokyo Restaurant. A laundry was established by Henry Saito.[59] Magosaburto Sakamoot and his partners, Fujitani and Tanaka from Yamagata Prefecture, prospected the area.[60] And Japanese prostitutes were imported to work the Fairbanks red light district. Whether or not the women had been kidnapped for the assignment is not known, but none fared well.

Mary Akimoto, presumed to be an inmate of the Line as well as the wife of bartender George Akimoto, died under circumstances that warranted an inquest in September 1906. No follow-up charges can be found, so George must have been cleared.[61] Less than a year later, prostitute Katzu Okabazashi committed suicide by taking mercury-bichloride. Evidence was introduced to show the cause was unrequited love for a Japanese bartender, and George Akimoto was the only man in town who fit the discription. Other prostitutes, however, testifed that Okabazashi had been grieving over her father's death, and the jury entered a verdict of suicide, discreetly omitting George's name from its press release.[62]

A photo taken about that time shows three well-dressed Japanese women outside a string of Fairbanks cribs. Episcopal churchman Albert N. Jones, who served in Fairbanks in the 1940s, recalled that a Japanese man imported them from his homeland through some syndicate. "Some of these women were killed and the venture proved unsuccessful," he noted.[63] The importer may well have been George Akimoto, but if so, he was to shift his focus.

Shortly thereafter, in a bold attempt to interest investors in backing his takeover of the red light district, George commissioned photographs of Fairbanks's white prostitutes in their natural habitat. Few of these lovely portraits were even moderately risqué, but they showed the ladies of the night as they liked to think of themselves, finely dressed amidst the late-Victorian elegance of their small but well-furnished cribs. These photos are particularly astonishing because Fairbanks was then very much a raw frontier, where bear attacks and freezing to death were both real dangers—which is probably why George had the photos taken. He must have needed to convince backers that his was a high-class enterprise, and apparently he succeeded.[64]

By 1911 George appears to have found backing, either from a Japanese syndicate or through the underworld connections of his ally, bar owner Charles Thompson. Deeds to more than 30 percent of Fairbanks's houses of ill repute were in George's name by 1917, while Charles and prostitutes associated with him controlled about one-fourth. Together they fulfilled George Akimoto's dream of monopolizing the red light district, and rents there soon increased.[65]

In 1913 an ambitious district attorney in Nome wrote the U.S. attorney general suggesting that the inspector in charge of immigration again be dispatched to Alaska for a repeat performance, but the request was denied on the grounds that such a sweep would be too expensive.[66] Undeterred, Fairbanks District Attorney Crossley, still fixated on stamping out vice, finally mustered the political backing to do away with the restricted district. In September of 1914, he ordered the Fairbanks City Council to open up the line or he threatened to do it himself and prosecute the prostitutes who failed leave it.[67]

The fence was torn down, and local newspapers marked the passing of the red light district with nostalgia. "In the world's second-greatest gold camp, where close to $70,000,000 in dust has been taken since the year 1903, Fourth Avenue played no small part," the *Fairbanks Daily News Miner* noted. "The millions of dollars that have been poured into and out of that short, fenced-in street, with a row of small cabins on each side including two or three famous dance halls, would build a city."[68]

Indeed it had, and it would again, for D. A. Crossley's triumph was short-lived. Members of the demimonde dispersed through town, of course, so that it became difficult for well-meaning lawmen to monitor their activities. Disoriented customers in search of love often made the

GEORGE AKIMOTO

He's hiding under an oversize hat, but the middle man is believed to be bartender
George Akimoto, who commissioned photographs of the women of the Fairbanks
red light district and ultimately owned many of its houses of ill repute.

Michael Carey Collection.

mistake of propositioning respectable women they met on the streets, infuriating their husbands.[69] But it was the gruesome murder of a fairhaired prostitute named Alice Astor that caused city fathers to reassess the value of a restricted district.

Born Eugenie Russey in a small town about forty miles from Paris, the woman later called Alice Astor had fallen into the hands of a confidence man known under various aliases including George Fairbanks. When she was little more than a child, he brought her to America, placing her in a house of ill fame in New York and taking the major portion of her earnings. Nevertheless, she remained infatuated with him. Coming to Alaska, she continued to send him large sums of money and longed for him even after her marriage to William Harp, a respectable miner prospecting in Ruby.

INDECENT EXPOSURE
Of the extraordinary set of photographs of Fairbanks prostitutes commissioned
by bartender George Akimoto, most were elegant portraits that showed the women exquisitely
dressed in elegant surroundings. Just two could be classed as indecent by the standards
of the day, which did not even allow ladies to expose their ankles.

Michael Carey Collection.

In 1913, according to a close friend, Alice traveled to London to see George Fairbanks, taking with her about $1,000 and some valuable diamonds. After staying with her for several days in a large hotel, George was rumored to have drugged her and vanished, stealing everything including her clothes.

Alice returned to Fairbanks and separated from her husband. According to her friend, she went hungry for several days because she did not wish to continue the life of a prostitute. In vain she begged a charitable married woman to find her some honorable occupation. Then, resigned, she returned to her trade.

On April 7, 1915, Alice was found dead, her throat cut, in the house she had rented on Fifth Avenue. According to the autopsy report (which should not be read on a full stomach), the murderer had cut the jugular, severed her spinal cord, trachea, and esophagus, and taken cartilage from the lower third cervical vertebra. He also had taken muscular tissue off the fourth and sixth cervical vertebrae, and surgically removed the right ovary and tube.

At the time of her death, Alice had been wearing a pink chemise, a pink silk scarf, and red silk stockings. There was no sign of a struggle, and all her jewelry—a gold comb, gold wristwatch, gold bracelet, four diamond rings, diamond earrings, and the gold nugget chain with a cross that she was wearing—was left untouched.[70]

Believing the murderer must have taken the keys to Alice's safe deposit box, police advertised for them, and they were quickly located by A. J. Day, the pound master. Inside the box was found $4,120 in twenty-dollar gold pieces, $2,195 in currency, some gold nuggets and dust, jewelry valued at $250, and a marriage license to William Harp, dated three years earlier.

George Fairbanks was not found, and the mystery of Alice's bizarre murder—the most gruesome in Fairbanks's history up to that time—was never unraveled. It was, however, a crime that never could have happened in the restricted district, with its neighborhood watch and a police station just a stone's throw away.[71]

Shortly thereafter, Fairbanks prostitutes quietly returned to their cribs on Fourth Avenue, and the city fathers erected another fence. The Alaska Territorial Legislature had just made prostitution illegal, so nothing went on the official town record, but it was business as usual again for the good time girls.[72]

10

Georgia Lee

FAIRBANKS'S MOST SUCCESSFUL PROSTITUTE

L uther Hess had come home to Milton, Illinois, for a visit. Georgia Anna spotted him on the stern-wheeler up from St. Louis, dressed like a prince, sporting a watch fob with gold nuggets as big as robins' eggs. He noticed her, too—who wouldn't! At age twenty-six she was lovely: five-feet-two and with huge gray eyes, thick, straight dark hair, and a perfectly proportioned figure. She hoped he would introduce himself, but she was in the company of one of her traveling salesmen and Luther kept his distance.

Later, her patron—a wealthy businessman with important political connections from Detroit, Illinois,[1] so prominent that Georgia was forbidden to tell anyone (especially his wife) that she knew him—decided to show her off to Luther Hess. That was his mistake.

The Hess family was about the richest for miles around. Now Luther was making money of his own at some new Alaska gold camp called Fairbanks, the Detroit businessman told Georgia. Actually, Luther was a lawyer and a competent one, but he'd done even better in mining. Georgia Anna's patron said Luther Hess had a good eye for investments, and he was right. What he didn't know was that Luther soon would decide to invest in Georgia Anna.

GEORGIA LEE

Usually in the company of good-looking men, Georgia Lee was one of the most successful and enduring ladies of the evening in Fairbanks. She arrived in 1906 and when business slowed in that gold camp moved on to the new boomtown of Livengood where this photo was taken. When railroad construction revived the Fairbanks economy, she returned to make it her permanent home. On her death in 1954 at age seventy-seven, she left an estate of over $100,000.

Blanche Cascaden photograph, courtesy of Orea and Cliff Hayden.

Georgia didn't need to be told that the Hess family was wealthy. Since her childhood she'd gazed with envy at their seventeen-room white house, crowned by its stately cupola. It was still a farm, but nothing like the miserable, patch-together farms where she'd grown up.

Georgia's mother, Sarah Callender, was from a family almost as well-heeled as Luther Hess's, but they gave her no help in 1865 when at age seventeen she bore William Eldredge a daughter, Nancy.[2] Eighteen months later, William ran off to marry Harriet Daniels, and when Sarah saw the match would stick, she wed Aaron Harrison because it was tough supporting a baby on her own.[3] Harriet died in 1874, leaving William Eldredge with two young children, Margaret, age eight, and John, age two. William knew that Sarah still had a weakness for him and talked her into marrying him that same year.[4]

Their second child, Georgia Anna, was born in 1877. She was unusually beautiful and the Eldredges would have been pleased except that William was not strong and was having trouble holding a job. The family drifted between the small farming communities of Milton, Detroit, Pearl Station, Florence, and the county seat of Pittsfield, trying to make a living.[5]

When Nancy was fourteen and Georgia Anna only three, their father died of pneumonia,[6] leaving Sarah alone to provide for them and their step-siblings, John, seven, and Margaret, thirteen. One year later Sarah wed Thomas Crossman in what might have been a match of desperation,[7] for she could not support four children working as a cleaning woman or a cook, the only positions open to her. Nor did Thomas have many resources, so even after she married him Sarah hired out to the Daniels family, often bringing her children to help.

At age seventeen Nancy escaped her family's bitter poverty by marrying Wilbur Daniels, a son of the farm owners, and moving to Florence. Margaret married John Couch from neighboring Nebo.[8] The obvious replacement for her older sisters, Georgia Anna was taken out of school, where she had been doing well, to supplement the family income by serving as a household drudge.

She hated it! Life as a "hired girl" in that farm community meant working ceaseless twelve-hour days, cleaning, ironing, toiling over hot stoves in the devastating heat of summer, and mopping floors and doing laundry in winter when it was so cold the wash water froze.

Georgia Anna had watched her mother, locked in a loveless marriage, grow prematurely old in her grueling struggle to raise her children. Marriage hadn't gotten her sister Nancy much either, except two howling babies to look after, with another on the way. But Georgia Anna had a way out. Men, she quickly discovered, would give her almost anything she wanted. Her beauty, her astonishingly deep, husky voice, and her penchant for having fun made her a standout in their community of plain, overworked farm women. Men really liked her, and she really liked men.

She recruited the help of James "Ben" Daniels, her sister Nancy's brother-in-law, who worked as a bartender on the Eagle Packet Line. He was five years younger than Georgia Anna, but he was sweet on her and would do whatever she told him. With his help, she began to slip away from the farm to visit Nancy in the nearby port town of Florence. It gave her a chance to check out the Yellow Dog Saloon across the river, where the prostitutes worked, and to ride the packet boats to St. Louis.

Horrified, her mother turned to the church, insisting Georgia Anna be baptized with her brother, John Owen, in 1892. But Georgia Anna saw no future in religion and soon made her base of operations with Nancy and Wilbur Daniels in Florence.[9]

Word got around. "It was common and general knowledge in the vicinity of Milton, Detroit, and Florence, Pike County, Illinois, that Georgia Anna Eldredge was a 'wild woman.' She was always with a man and was used for immoral purposes frequently, both on the boats and during her stay in St. Louis," Captain Harry Lyle of the Eagle Packet Line reported. "Boatmen would tell you that she would get a man when the boat docked in St. Louis."[10]

Ben Daniels continued to be useful to Georgia Anna. He wasn't her pimp, exactly, but did help her get transportation on the river. He also kept an eye on her dealings with the riverboat men and drummers who stopped at the Finny Hotel, in case she got into trouble.

It was during one of Georgia Anna's stern-wheeler rides that she was noticed by Luther Hess, and he later told her about the high demand for love in the Far North. A clever girl could easily make $100 a night, he said, and he was certain she'd do well. However, Luther insisted that she learn the trade before she came north. He knew someone in St. Louis's red light district who would show her all the tricks. Of course, she would earn while she learned.

Excited, Georgia told the news to Ben Daniels. He was skeptical.

"Shoot," he said, "Ol' Lu's been telling anyone who will listen they can make a fortune in Alaska. But why would you go? You're making a fortune right here."[11]

Granted, she was doing better than Ben, but the townsfolk held a low opinion of her and so did most of her kin.[12] She didn't want to spend the rest of her life working backwater farmers and packet boat men because they never had much cash. She could probably sweet-talk her prominent patron into setting her up. But Georgia Anna suspected she could do better, especially if Luther Hess thought so.

Georgia Anna's last confrontation with her mother—probably about 1903—could not have been pleasant. Sarah was humiliated by the gossip and unimpressed with her daughter's newfound earning power. Georgia Anna left without mentioning her plans, and Ben Daniels, faithful and discreet as usual, drove her to Florence to catch the boat for St. Louis. To his astonishment, Luther Hess was waiting for her.

"Well, I'll see you someday, Ben," Luther said awkwardly as Ben saw the couple off. Georgia Anna kept her peace. She knew she would never see Ben or any of her family again. She also knew they'd feel more relief than pain when they discovered she had run away. Most of them hated what she had become.

Ben decided to tell no one that Georgia Anna had gone off with Luther. He kept the secret, but word spread quickly that she had become an inmate in a "red light house." Her Detroit patron began finding excuses to visit St. Louis, and he wasn't the only Pike County resident following her career. Ben's fellow crew members boasted of seeing her in the "house" on various occasions, and so did local farmhands.

"All the boys used to wait eagerly to fatten a hog enough to take it to market in St. Louis so they could see Georgia," Ben Daniels later recalled with a wistful smile. "Luther Hess came back to visit Milton many times but he never mentioned Georgia Anna Eldredge and I never asked. I figured it was none of my business."[13]

By 1906 Georgia Anna was established in a fine brick duplex at 4753 Michigan Avenue, a quiet, brick-paved street near Carondelet Park. Her residence was west of the red light district, yet conveniently near the docks. Listed in the city directory under the name Georgia Lee, she could afford a telephone[14] and succeeded at her calling without once getting arrested. She had developed a taste for fine furniture, high fashion, and good whisky. She could curse like a stevedore, but could also pass for a lady

LUTHER HESS (left)
A well-educated lawyer from a wealthy family in Illinois,
Luther was among Fairbanks's first settlers and soon became city attorney.
Later he became the wealthiest man in town, investing in banking,
gold-mining, and Georgia Lee, who came from his hometown.

UAF, V.F. Addendum Historical Photograph #89-02-56N.

CHARLES L. THOMPSON (right)
Also pioneering Fairbanks was bar owner Charles L. Thompson,
who made a fortune, partly due to his underworld connections. An avid sportsman
and gold camp booster, Charles was highly popular with both Fairbanks citizens
and numerous ladies of the red light district. Georgia Lee was the first to capture
his heart, but she lost him to a French prostitute called "Mignon" Miller.

From Alaska Probate Records, Juneau.

when she cared to. The rough edges of her rural upbringing were gone.

Luther Hess had reason to be proud of his prodigy, and that summer she moved to Fairbanks where he quietly backed her business. Luther had just resigned his position as assistant district attorney to help organize the First National Bank of Fairbanks. The venture was successful. He became the bank's director and began pumping his personal earnings into mining property. And Georgia Lee proved one of his most useful early assets.[15]

—∞∞∞—

The raw boomtown of Fairbanks must have been a comedown for Georgia Lee after the elegance of St. Louis, but Luther Hess had predicted correctly that the Fairbanks stampede would be worth getting in on. Over 8,000 stampeders were in town. Gold production had topped $9 million, and Georgia Lee discovered the money was even better than Luther had promised. She worked out of a tiny cabin in the new restricted district, where bartenders at the Floradora Dance Hall, the Fast Track, and the Seattle Saloon would send her customers on commission. A nearby downtown area called the Great White Way had several blocks of bars and gambling dens that never closed.[16] Most of her clientele were mining men, tough but clean-cut, fun to be with, and free spenders.

Georgia quickly repaid her debt to Luther, but continued to help when he had cash flow problems. In return he advised her on investments, but otherwise she saw little of him. As the former assistant district attorney and now a respectable banker, Luther had a reputation to maintain, and Georgia's attention was elsewhere.[17]

She'd fallen in love for the first time in her life. Her man was bar owner Charles Thompson, not quite thirty, not quite six feet tall, but extremely handsome with blue eyes and wavy brown hair. He was a flashy but careful dresser with a ready wad of big bills always in his pocket, and his hands flashed with real diamond rings. He loved sports, especially baseball, and had an affable charm that endeared him to the general citizenry, even though most suspected that he had ties to the underworld.

Charles Thompson also had more sex appeal than Georgia had ever encountered. The attraction was instant and mutual. Charles had played the field for years, but he fell hard for elegant little Georgia Lee. For the first time in Fairbanks he asked a woman to live with him, and Georgia agreed—although she continued to ply her trade.[18]

There were repercussions. No sooner had Georgia hung her silk negligee in Charles's closet than the marshal busted in to charge them with adultery. At first they thought it was a joke, but it turned out the hotshot new federal district attorney, James Crossley, was trying to make a name for himself by staging raids all over town. Charles's attorney, Leroy Tozier, said the list read like a who's who of Fairbanks, and it would have been embarrassing if Charles *hadn't* been on it. Everybody knew the charges were ridiculous, because neither Charlie nor Georgia was married. However, they could have been convicted of "cohabiting in a state of fornication," so at Tozier's suggestion Charles paid the adultery fine of only fifty dollars.[19]

Otherwise, life was good. Charles gave Georgia diamonds and pretty clothes, and they moved into a fine apartment he built over the Tanana Club, his elegant new bar. His goal was to become rich, and watching him parlay his small holdings into the finest drinking establishment in town was not only exciting but an education for Georgia. Charles also began accumulating property on the Line, and moved toward gaining control of the town's gambling and bootlegging operations.

Charlie said little about his past, although he did share his dream of returning to Bay City, Michigan, to dazzle his parents and three sisters with his affluence—once he acquired some. He had not been in touch with them since he left home at age seventeen in 1895. He had connections with major underworld figures in the "Syndicate," who apparently backed some of his Fairbanks investments. But Charles was respected locally, and Georgia Lee found him a square shooter. His real name, she discovered, was Leo Kaiser, but that didn't seem strange because she'd also changed her name. His world became hers, and she could not imagine life without him.[20]

However, Georgia had always been independent, and she took Charlie for granted, which was a mistake. She failed to notice when he started spending time with a leggy French prostitute who had an evil temper and an impressive police record. Her real name was Josephine "Louise" Therese Vassiaux, but she'd made a reputation for herself as "Mignon" Miller, Gabrielle Mitchelle, and a few other aliases.[21]

Arriving in Fairbanks from Dawson about 1905, Mignon had attracted attention when a dog from Deputy Marshal A. H. Hansen's team, detouring through the red light district, snapped up her small poodle from the sidewalk and tossed it over its head at Hansen, where it dropped dead at his feet. Mignon, garbed in a kimono and red satin slippers, cursed the driver in heavily accented English for more than ten minutes, never using the same vile name twice. When a crowd gathered, she threatened to kill the offending animal, the team, and Hansen himself.

Later, Hansen gave Mignon's business manager the money to buy her another dog, but no one doubted that Hansen was a marked man. "She'll kill you sure as hell," the manager warned him.[22]

Georgia had never considered the French whore a rival because she was not beautiful and may have been older than Charles. Yet in the spring of 1910, Charlie moved Georgia out and Mignon in.

Devastated, Georgia downed a handful of antiseptic tablets, but friends countered with prompt applications of olive oil and a stomach pump. Two weeks later, recovered physically but not mentally, Georgia invaded Charles's Tanana Club early one morning armed with a Colt automatic, looking for Mignon. Thwarted, she began smashing Charlie's fine furniture. It took the marshal and four deputies to carry her, spread-eagle, off to jail, where she was charged with disorderly conduct. On her release Georgia swore out a warrant against Charlie for abuse, but she soon dropped charges and made peace, both with her former lover and with Mignon.[23]

Then Georgia Lee began to focus on getting rich. Mignon had been arrested that fall for selling liquor without a license and escaped prison only because the federal witness against her had vanished before the trial.[24] No doubt Charlie Thompson's underworld connections had helped on that one, but Georgia wanted to make good on her own.

Easy pickings in Fairbanks were a thing of the past. Gold production had slumped but a new discovery had been made in Livengood, a rough camp one day's journey north. Few Fairbanks girls cared to give up their comforts for it, but several hundred prospectors were in residence and Georgia Lee decided to pioneer the area.

Since the camp had few women and no restricted district, Georgia set up shop next door to her friend Blanche Cascaden, the rough-and-tumble owner of a fair-sized mining operation. After a couple of failed marriages, Blanche had come to Alaska from Dawson with two young children to support, and made a happy match with John Cascaden, who subsequently staked profitable mining ground in Livengood. When he died unexpectedly, claim-jumpers tried to take the property, but Blanche had fought them off with her shotgun from a hill of pay dirt. She became known as one widow it did not pay to mess with.[25]

Another neighbor was a blond, blue-eyed French "housewife" known as Mrs. Belle, who had been imported from San Francisco's red light district by "Two Step" Louis Schmidt, a veteran prospector. "Two Step," who got his nickname because of his limited dancing repertoire, had made and lost several fortunes. He was considerably older than Mrs. Belle and when he got up in years, he suggested she divorce him and find someone younger. She complied, marrying a well-paid timekeeper for the Fairbanks Exploration Company, and keeping a boyfriend on the side. Like Blanche Cascaden, Mrs. Belle had a keen mind for finances in an era when the "weaker sex" seldom considered business ventures of their own. Both Blanche and Mrs. Belle had taken firm control of their resources, and Georgia Lee quickly followed their example.[26]

After making good money in Livengood, Georgia moved on to Nenana, where she invested with foresight. The federal government was building a railroad from the coast to Fairbanks, hoping to bring down the cost of living and save the town. The railroad line's completion was a few years off, but Nenana, sixty miles south of Fairbanks, would be a major construction site from which hundreds of men would be deployed. Georgia got in on the ground floor, not only as a prostitute but as the owner of a fine home, a dress shop, and a legitimate hotel called the Flower.[27]

In 1923 the Fairbanks Exploration Co., attracted by the new railroad link to the coast, established a big mining operation in Fairbanks, hiring a thousand or more men to run its great dredges. Fairbanks thrived again and Georgia, who had sold out near the peak of the Nenana boom, had money to invest. What she didn't have was a business education, but her all-too-brief experience in the one-room schools of Pike's County had gone well enough that she thought she'd profit from college instruction.

Georgia turned to the new Agricultural College and School of Mines, which had just hired a bright young woman to teach business courses.[28] College President Charles E. Bunnell, a straight arrow with little sense of humor, had served six years as Fairbanks's federal judge. Rumor had it he was so desperate to attract students to the fledgling university that he'd stooped to recruiting them from jail.

Still, he was thunderstruck when Georgia Lee arrived in his office, tuition in hand. She had dressed with restraint for the interview. Her police record was minor. But Georgia Lee was one of the best-known whores in the Far North, and President Bunnell refused to allow her to enter his college.[29]

Resigned, Georgia Lee returned to the source of her early training, Charles Thompson. By 1917, the height of Fairbanks's depression, he had accumulated enough wealth to seek out his mother in Bay City, Michigan,

LIVING IT UP IN LIVENGOOD
Georgia Lee made good money selling love in Livengood, a gold camp that
boomed as Fairbanks failed. Here she is pictured, center, with her friend,
mine owner Blanche Cascaden (in the hat), and bush pilot Joe Crossen, far right.
Blanche Cascaden photograph, courtesy of Orea and Cliff Hayden.

for his long-fantasized reunion, bragging to her that he owned the Tanana Club, a Fairbanks showcase. A year later fire destroyed the building, but Charles never looked back.

In Fairbanks's early years, Charles had befriended a bartender named George Akimoto who, as the front for a Japanese syndicate, had purchased considerable property on the Line. When Akimoto left town around 1913, Charlie moved to buy him out, investing with Georgia Lee to broaden his control, knowing she remained loyal to him.

In 1922, federal authorities attempted to eliminate the Line, forcing the women out of houses they owned and confiscating their property. Georgia hired Tom Marquam, the best criminal lawyer in town, to defend her. Working with Charlie Thompson to organize her colleagues, Georgia and Tom mustered enough opposition to defeat the unconstitutional action.[30]

Charlie and Mignon were still an item, but that no longer bothered Georgia. The French woman proved well suited for the domineering Charles, and Georgia Lee finally had found a true love of her own.

Tom McKinnen was a well-respected, well-heeled mining man whom she had met in Livengood. He was married to a woman known in Fairbanks as "Ma" McKinnen, who had been wild in her youth but settled into respectability to raise her two sons by another husband. The boys were grown now and one of them, Tommy Carr, had married Kitty O'Brien, who had worked with Georgia on the Line before successfully investing in a taxi cab company. In a town as small as Fairbanks, Tom McKinnen's family must have known of his romance, but the lovers pursued their relationship with a discretion uncharacteristic for Georgia Lee. In later years she would call it the happiest event in her life.[31]

Tom McKinnen may have helped Georgia with her financial planning, for she branched out from the restricted district to buy in respectable areas, soon making a good living on rents alone. She also purchased a small house for herself on Sixth Avenue, furnishing it lavishly. There Georgia cultivated friendships with her neighbors: city councilman John Butrovich, his wife Grace, and Ruth McCoy, the self-reliant wife of an iron worker, who occasionally cleaned houses on the Line for pin money.

Tom asked Georgia Lee to quit selling herself, and she promised she would. But she loved a good party and lots of her old customers still depended on her, so she quietly pursued her trade when her lover was out of town. Tom always sent for taxi driver Jim McClung when he was coming in from the mine, and Georgia arranged for Jim to warn her so she could return home from the Line in time to present a picture of domestic tranquillity.[32] Actually, she was edging into it, increasingly occupied with her lovely garden and doing charity work when she thought no one would notice. With Ruth McCoy she helped organize a Fairbanks branch of the Humane Society, and she also had a soft spot for her young renters.[33]

In contrast, Georgia's former lover, Charlie Thompson, was going the opposite direction. He had made part of his fortune bootlegging after Alaska passed a "Bone Dry" prohibition law in 1916, and when a nation-wide ban on alcohol went into effect he moved to take advantage of it through his underworld connections outside the territory. Without liquidating any Fairbanks holdings, Charlie departed for the States in November of 1930 with Mignon Miller on his arm and $110,000 in cash on his person. The couple, presenting themselves as married, settled in Chule Vista, California, not far from Tijuana, Mexico, where Charles bought the Red Top Distillery. Their affluence in the face of a national depression readily bought them a place in San Diego society. Alaskans who occasionally read clippings from California society pages, sent north by friends, were bemused to see photos of "Mr. and Mrs. Thompson" dressed in their finery, usually with luxury cars in the background.[34]

But Charlie's business was risky. Sometime in 1930, Mignon confided to friends that a distillery employee told her he had been offered money to murder her and Charlie and dispose of their bodies. Although that man had refused, the couple did receive extortion notes threatening Charles's life and demanding $5,000. Later that year Charlie had a noisy confrontation with his distillery manager, Hugh McClemmy. On January 12, 1931, McClemmy pleaded not guilty to federal bootlegging charges and was released on $10,000 bond.[35]

Charlie Thompson and Mignon Miller were last seen on December 5, 1931. A few casual friends received Christmas cards from them postmarked Tijuana, but police investigating the disappearance said many close friends received no cards and the signatures on those sent appeared to be forgeries.

The disappearance made California headlines for several weeks and, although the Federal Bureau of Investigation was called in, no trace of the couple was ever found. Nor was there an explanation for the disappearance at the same time of J. L. Summers, an engineer at their distillery who had worked with Charlie in Fairbanks. George Smith, an early Fairbanks mayor and a friend of twenty-two years who was Charlie's neighbor in California, appeared to have no clues.[36]

The search was called off in February of 1933. One month later, Charles Thompson's mother, Margaret Kaiser, opened his safe deposit box in a border bank near San Diego to find only $1,100 and some insignificant jewelry.[37] No other large amounts of cash or valuables turned up. Hugh McClemmy, Charlie's partner at the Red Cap Distillery, served three years at McNeil Island Federal Penitentiary on the bootlegging charge without throwing any light on the mystery.[38]

When Charles and Mignon were declared legally dead five years later, their combined estate was worth only $33,611, of which $18,500 was

Objects of Wide Search

Police in France, Alaska, the United States and Mexico we
asked to aid last night in the search for Mr. and Mrs. Charl
Thompson. They have been missing from Tijuana since Dec. 5.

DISAPPEARED

Charlie Thompson and Mignon Miller disappeared in 1931 while living in San Diego and "rum running" from a distillery he owned in Mexico. Rumor had it they were murdered, but friends suspected they might have used their considerable assets to start a new life elsewhere.

San Diego Union, February 3, 1933.

from Fairbanks real estate holdings.[39] Rumor had it that they had been robbed and murdered, reduced to ashes in the furnace of their Mexican distillery. But friends wondered whether, under threat of federal investigation or mob reprisals or both, the couple might have fled with their bankroll to build another life.

———⊗≈⊗———

Georgia Lee, meanwhile, had parlayed her earnings into assets valued at about $100,000. She narrowly escaped charges of federal tax evasion because an Internal Revenue Service agent tricked her into paying. Warned in advance that she would be hard to deal with, the tax collector saved her for last when he interviewed all the inmates of the Line about their earnings. As expected, Georgia insisted she had no income to declare; operating costs for clothes, refreshments, etc., had eaten up her profits, she said.

"Gee, Panama Hattie has declared $10,000," the agent said, giving the still-handsome hooker an appraising look. "I would think you'd probably do at least as well."

"Why that old has-been!" Georgia exploded. "Put me down for *twice* that much."[40]

Georgia's world dimmed when Tom McKinnen died, but his portrait remained prominently displayed in her home and she often spoke of him as "her man." Now in her fifties, she was courted by a number of much younger men, one of whom begged her to marry him. When she refused, citing their age difference, he phoned her friend, Blanche Cascaden, asking her to intervene. Blanche, who knew Georgia would never consider marriage because of her childhood memories, tried to break it to him gently. Calmly the suitor stated that he could not live without Georgia Lee. He asked Blanche to tell Georgia that he loved her. He had a gun at his head, he said. Then he pulled the trigger, leaving Blanche with the sound of the explosion echoing in her ear and the sad task of informing Georgia Lee and the police.[41]

———⊗≈⊗———

In 1947 Albert Zucchini, a young entrepreneur from St. Louis, rented a building from Georgia Lee for his business in surplus war material, which he called the Auction. Scarcely taller than herself, Albert was one of the few men Georgia could look right in the eye, and she liked him right

STILL WORKING

*Georgia Lee promised her lover she would quit the Line, but quietly
continued to work at her trade out of consideration for old and faithful customers.
She also took interest in Fairbanks civic affairs and became co-founder
of the Fairbanks branch of the Humane Society.*

Courtesy of Rozena Stonefield.

away. She also liked his partner, a good-looking World War II veteran named Johnny Williams.[42]

Raised in upstate New York and an electrician by trade, Johnny had come to Fairbanks to operate a second-hand store after serving in the South Pacific. The venture was successful enough that he purchased a nice home. Only after it burned did he discover that he had no insurance coverage—his insurance payments had been pocketed by the disbarred lawyer who was his agent.[43] Bereft of capital, he began working as a laborer and Georgia, who hired him as a handyman, found him handy indeed. He still owned a small house in North Pole, but quickly moved to a little cabin on Georgia's property. She became the focus of his life, having faith in his ability to recuperate from his losses when nobody else did, and loaning him $2,000 to make a new start.

In October of 1954, Georgia Lee embarked on a trip down the Alcan Highway to the States with her neighbors, Ruth and Louis McCoy. She had been suffering from chronic bronchitis and hoped to get sophisticated medical help in Seattle, but this was also a pleasure trip. Ruth McCoy had become one of Georgia's best friends. Like Georgia, Ruth had come up hard, helping raise six younger brothers and sisters after her father died. And, although Ruth wasn't in the trade herself, she did not look down on Georgia's profession. Ruth looked like a taller, younger version of Georgia Lee, and the two women had grown so close folks often mistook them for mother and daughter. The dusty auto trip was to be a real vacation for them. Instead, at Beaver Creek just over the border, Georgia Lee died quietly in her sleep from heart failure.[44]

Johnny Williams did not take the news well. He called several of their friends, including Blanche Cascaden, to break the news and inform them that he did not intend to go on without Georgia Lee. Few took him seriously, but within a few hours he shot his big black dog and then turned his .30-30 rifle on himself, dying instantly. He was fifty years old.[45] Georgia Lee was seventy-seven.

———— ✺ ————

Blanche Cascaden had wonderful fun with Georgia Lee's funeral notice, lopping five years off her birthdate and reporting that she had been employed as a cook in Fairbanks and Nenana after coming to Valdez. However, Blanche did give correct information about Georgia's hometown, which Ruth McCoy followed up on administering the estate. Apparently Georgia had told them she had no relatives, but they suspected differently.

Late in 1954, young Derald McGlauchen, a grandson of Georgia's sister Nancy, was loafing around the Milton, Illinois, filling station when the town mayor arrived with a letter, which he read aloud to everyone. It was

NEIGHBORS

*Ruth McCoy, one of Georgia Lee's neighbors, was so close to her
and so resembled her that many thought they were mother and daughter.
Ruth had never worked on the Line but was tolerant of those who had.*

Courtesy of Rozena Stonefield.

from an attorney in Fairbanks, Alaska, seeking anyone related to Georgia Lee Eldredge. Derald went home to ask his mother, Ethel McGlauchen, if they didn't have someone named Eldredge in the family. Ethel contacted her sister, Viola Harris, and word got around.[46]

The headline in the local paper read, "Local People Think They May Be Heirs to $100,000 Fortune," and the article outlined the family's dilemma. "Georgia Ann Eldredge left Milton when a young woman—'ran away from home'—and because of circumstances surrounding her going, it was considered more or less a disgrace and was never discussed in the family very much," stated the *Milton Democrat*. "However, it was learned that she eventually went to Alaska and was reported to be doing well. . . . There is a family of seven brothers and sisters who think they are nieces and nephews of this woman, although there is a slight difference in the spelling of the name."[47]

The only survivor from Georgia Anna's era was Nancy's brother-in-law, James "Ben" Daniels, who had helped her start her illustrious career. Ben was not an heir, but he was happy to testify on the qualifications of his nephew William Willis and his six brothers and sisters. And he was even happier to hear—after fifty years of wondering—that Georgia Anna had turned out well enough to force the rest of the family to admit they were related.

11

Richard Henry Geoghegan

THE LINGUIST WHO
LOVED THE LADIES OF THE LINE

A favorite in Richard Geoghegan's old age—his indulgence—was a young, part-Athabascan whore named Josephine Finger, whom he called "Lovely One" because she was. But actually he adored them all, all the girls on the Fairbanks Line who brightened those hardscrabble last years. Eagerly they scooped up his meager income, but they also looked after him and amused him when nothing else could. To the end he delighted in their impromptu parties, even when they appeared at his door uninvited at outlandish hours as they did one June morning in 1942.

"At 6:30 a.m. Lovely One with Myrtle and Dolly, all in party dresses with rhubarb leaves and pink bows for hats, burst in all feeling pretty gay and happy in the delightful sunshine," he wrote in his diary in Pitman shorthand with a scattering of foreign languages, to protect his secrets. "I gave them the few drinks [and everything] I had to one dollar in money— my entire wealth and received a kiss from each and we chatted and laughed until 7:15 when whisky being exhausted they left and went to the Tamale House."[1]

Richard Henry Geoghegan was one of the world's leading experts on Esperanto, an international language which many at the turn of the

---

RICHARD HENRY GEOGHEGAN
Crippled shortly after birth, Richard struggled to lead a normal life after graduating with honors from Oxford. A brilliant linguist, in 1903 he moved to Valdez and then Fairbanks to work for Alaska's federal judge, James Wickersham, and finally found his niche. Attracted to the red lights of the restricted district, he eventually married in.

UAF, Geoghegan Collection.

century hoped would help bring world peace. A brilliant Oxford graduate, he had worked as a stenographer for Judge James Wickersham, in 1904 the most powerful man in the region. Richard was well-respected, both in Alaska and abroad, but because of a sad twist his life had taken early on, his private world was the demimonde, and it would be for a lifetime.

———— ∞∞ ————

Richard was born in Liverpool, England, in 1866 of wealthy Irish parents. One source claims that before he reached the age of four a needle was accidentally lodged in his leg. According to his biographer, David Richardson, he was dropped down a flight of stairs by his nurse, who fell heavily on top of him, severely injuring his left leg or hip. Whatever the cause, the leg was too severely damaged to heal well, nor did it grow properly, despite the best efforts of Richard's father, Richard Taylor Geoghegan, a prominent physician. Although the boy grew tall from the waist up, he was forced to walk in a semi-crouch with the aid of two crutches, eyes on the ground, looking smaller and frailer than he actually was.[2]

Despite his deformity, Richard set his sights on Oxford, daring to dream that his natural bent as a linguist might allow him to live a normal life. This hope was crushed following his graduation when a representative of the Chinese Consulate refused to hire him, explaining cruelly that it didn't take cripples. Instead, the disappointed young scholar moved to London to eke out a living tutoring private students.

In 1886, Richard's youngest brother, Jim, just seventeen, was offered a job with a telegraph company in Africa. The thought horrified his recently widowed mother, Bessie, who packed up her whole family (Jim, Richard, two other sons, and two daughters) to immigrate to Canada. From there they moved to the farming community of Eastsound on Orcas Island in northwest Washington State, where both Richard and Jim were bored to distraction.

Jim solved the problem by joining the gold rush in 1897, heading first for the Klondike, then on to Alaska. Richard yearned to follow but doubted that he'd have much success climbing Chilkoot Pass on crutches. Instead he found work as a secretary and bookkeeper in Tacoma. When the University of Washington turned him down for the position of Chinese professor, he got an assignment to fill in for the absent British Consul and also worked for the Japanese consulate.[3]

At the turn of the century James Wickersham, then attorney for the

City of Tacoma, went beach-combing and found a foreign coin he could not identify even though he was a formidable amateur linguist. Puzzled, he placed a classified ad in the local paper. Richard replied by postcard that he might be able to identify the coin. The two men—both roundly educated freethinkers—began a lively correspondence that turned into fast friendship. When Wickersham was appointed to a judgeship in Alaska, Richard expressed envy. On New Year's Day, 1903, Wickersham telegraphed Richard, offering him a job as his secretary at a "good salary." Seven days later Richard Henry Geoghegan was on the SS *City of Nome* bound for Alaska.[4]

Wickersham's judicial district covered thousands of square miles, from Valdez to the Aleutian Chain to Eagle, then his home base. The judge and his staff traveled constantly, but initially Richard was hired to help Wickersham with a book on Alaska legal reports, so the linguist was sent to Valdez.

He found the raw young port city booming but expensive, quickly discovering that $170 a month wasn't as generous a salary as he had been led to believe. Some of the young lawyers with whom he toured the dance halls and whorehouses were making $1,500 a month, yet were often short of funds themselves. However, money didn't mean much to Richard. His habit was to lavish whatever he had on some dance hall girl, usually spending most of it within twenty-four hours of payday, depending on loans from friends to tide him over to the next one.

Then he met a blond dance hall girl named Bessie Simpson, whose husband, Percy, didn't mind her dating other men as long as they paid her well. Richard had been deeply in love with an auburn-haired schoolteacher, Lillian Wright, whom he'd met in Seattle, but he suspected she would never marry him, and he spent considerable time and money on Mrs. Simpson.[5]

In August of 1903 Judge Wickersham fired his law clerk, George Jeffries, an affable young lawyer from Tacoma, and hired Richard to replace him in Eagle. It meant better pay and more interesting work, but Richard reluctantly parted with Bessie to take the winter stage north.

The new assignment, with its constant travel over rough trails to primitive frontier settlements—often in temperatures below minus 40 Fahrenheit—must have been a challenge to the crippled, city-bred linguist. Surprisingly, he thrived. Soon he began walking with just one crutch. Later he substituted a cane for the crutch, and ultimately walked unassisted, although always with a rolling limp.[6]

In April of 1904, the "Federal Brigade" (as local papers referred to the

traveling court) arrived by horse sled in the new mining town of Fairbanks. There Richard was reunited with his brother Jim, who was working as a professional meat hunter after several unsuccessful mining ventures.[7] The town was booming. New saloons were being built and a dance hall had just opened. The Geoghegan brothers liked the pace and so did Judge Wickersham, who permanently moved his headquarters there from Eagle. But the following February, court funding ran out, along with (briefly) Wickersham's political clout. Jobless, Richard returned to Seattle.

There he made decent money as a freelance court reporter, but after Alaska, Seattle seemed as tame as Eastsound had after London. Richard's heart was in the North and, amazingly, he managed to save enough money for a return ticket. In February of 1906 he traveled to Valdez, where he was appointed clerk to U. S. Attorney Nathan Harlan, father of Ed Harlan, who was a shorthand expert and one of Richard's drinking cronies. In March, the linguist was appointed court clerk in Fairbanks, which he would call home for the rest of his life.

It was the most exciting city in the territory, growing every day! Dozens of bars and gambling dens perched shoulder-to-shoulder along the waterfront—the Tanana, the Seattle, the Senate, the Horseshoe, the Pioneer, Tammany Hall, the Eagle, the Fairbanks, the Northern, the Fraction, the California—with more being built. One street over, joined to the Third Avenue Hotel, was the Floradora Dance Hall, which never closed.

True, the winter weather was horrible, but Richard made even that sound interesting in the long letters he wrote his little niece, Marjorie Woods.

OPEN TWENTY-FOUR HOURS A DAY

The bars along the Fairbanks waterfront had no locks because they
never closed during the great gold stampede. It was here that Richard Geoghegan
spent most of his meager paycheck on dance hall girls.

UAF, Ralph MacKay Collection, #70-55-349.

"It is very cool here now, and when you go forth on the streets your ears hurt you, just as if somebody had poured hot water on them. Most of the children are now wearing the hides of wild beasts on their heads and their noses are red. There is not much snow on the ground, but it is very hard and makes a noise when you walk on it, like new shoes, only a great deal louder. . . .

"When you take hold of your ax handle or door handle it makes you weep, because the cold makes them sticky, and when you try to let go, your skin falls off therewith. . . .

"Two skating rinks have been made on the river. They have got a great enormous tent over one and a stove in it, and the youths and maidens have been having a glorious time skating; but today it is 50 degrees below zero, and when you talk your words fall from your mouth frozen solid, and your teeth make you scream whenever you open your mouth; so they have quit skating till the sun shineth once more."

As for amenities, there was electricity, which he could afford, and telephone service, which he could not. Other basics were hard to come by.

"Water is a precious thing here; they have to go many miles to get it, because what they get in the river is evil and people cannot live on it; to tell the truth, it is mostly mud and dead dogs. . . ."

And he was entertained by the oddities of frontier living.

"It is also very pleasing to watch the battles of the hounds; when they are not practicing singing opera, they spend their time in warfare; they sing mostly by night, so people won't make them feel bashful by telling they don't know how to do it. . . . Everyday when the noon whistle blows, all the dogs of the place sing their songs of praise; it lasts about four minutes and it is a very touching piece of poetry; they have another song that they sing at five minutes to nine in the morning and twenty-five minutes past three in the afternoon, and the signal for that is the train whistle warbleth, going to Gilmore and coming back."[8]

Richard's brother Jim was still in Fairbanks, dabbling unsuccessfully at mining, and so—to the linguist's great joy—was the beauteous Bessie Simpson.[9] Her husband had reduced his role in her life to cameo appearances after which she sported bruises and reddened eyelids. She replaced him with a low-profile pimp who encouraged Richard's suit. The bachelor needed little encouragement, however, even though he was aware that his "naughty sweetheart's" interest in him peaked around payday. Lillian Wright, the Seattle schoolteacher with whom he'd fallen in love, wed in January of 1907. Although Richard continued to write lovingly of Lillian in his diary for years, he soon became blindly infatuated with young Bessie, so much so that he took her profession in stride.

" . . . At 10 p.m. went to Bessie's where found the Swede lover who had just arrived in town from the creeks. Stayed at her cabin until 11 when we all went to dance hall," he wrote cryptically in his diary, January 27. "Took me out and kissed me, said she unfortunately had to earn her living while she could and promised to see me tomorrow night for sure if the hated rival left by that time." When Bessie avoided Richard, he bided his time with a pretty substitute, but Bessie came first and the next payday found him cruising the bars in search of her.

"In the evening went with Oldham and George Jeffries [whom Wickersham had fired] to Northern where Fanny [Hall] came but Bessie was out with her Swede. Drank wine there and adjourned to dance hall where got pretty full. . . . I also lost every cent I had on me, $35. I stayed with pleasant black-haired girl, Leona, but too full to make success of it.

Police came up and searched girls. Bessie came up when I was in bed with Leona. Got home at 6 a.m. after taking Bessie to her cabin. The little girl looking very weary says she is still sick. Asked me to go to her cabin for supper tomorrow, Sunday night."[10]

Although she was prone to standing him up, Bessie followed through with this supper because she needed the court clerk's political clout. "She was a nervous wreck and looked very tough," he noted. "Didn't have any supper. Was crying and I came away soon."

The reason, she later confided, was her arrest during the raid of the Floradora. "Says Dillon city attorney is trying to graft the little girl for $200 to square matters. Afterward talked with Charlie Dreibilbis [office deputy of the federal Justice Department] about it and he said he would do what he could," Richard wrote, and apparently Dreibilbis resolved the problem. Bessie soon left her job at the dance hall, but only because her husband came back to town and insisted. Percy Simpson did not stay long, and Richard quickly renewed his suit.

"Received note from Bessie asking for $20 and for me to come and see her this evening. Sent her $10 and at 9:30 went to her house where stayed until 1 a.m.," read a typical entry April 5. "Delightful time. She is looking very well and pretty. Says she has been 'at home' ever since I last saw her. Gave me some fine plum cake and beer and showed me little hat with roses. I contributed $5 towards it for a kiss and then $5 for a bottle of whisky for which we sent. . . . She says was at the Borthel's drinking last night with two macs who want her to do the lesbian act with the French girls on the Row. Treated it as a great joke. While we were talking they called her up and asked her to keep the appointment. Laughingly she told them she was better employed. Says she can't understand a girl doing such things. Supposed it must be result of excessive passion."

Three days later she phoned Richard at work, inviting him to the Northern. "Went there and had a drink in her box with her and she confessed that she had leukorrhea so going to the hospital tomorrow for curing," he calmly recorded. "Naughty child. Thence went to California and in back got box where had drinks and she became very confident and told me several interesting scientific facts about female sexual vassalage. Says she had no curse for one year without any pleasure at all. That she had pleasure and 'went off' for a year before she had her curse. That at the moment of going off there is a sensation as she expressed it like an electric shock and a 'top spinning around' for about three seconds then that the pleasure lasts for four or five minutes with her. That she prefers to go off a little ahead of the lover whose passion much increases her pleasure after she has gone off. Swears she has never 'jacked off.' That there is no visible difference in the pudenda at the time of erection and a very sensible contraction of the parts which she expressed by squeezing her hand together and a pleasant thrill. Says she ejaculates no liquid so far as she knows but has 'heard' that girls only give out a single drop.

"Promised to give me a dinner at her cabin next Sunday and to show me the 'whole works' some of these days. Was very sweet and rather lewd this night. A little full I expect. The charming little darling was looking extraordinarily pretty. Says she may go to work at Jake's? Peter's? place. Asked my influence with the new authorities. Took my beer with me and went to cabin at 11:30 after giving the little girl $5. $30 in all this week."

Things went well between them until Bessie announced she was following her husband to the Innoko rush in June. When that plan fell through, she decided to visit Boise, Idaho, and then go on to Katalla, the scene of another new gold discovery. Richard buried himself in Korean and Aleut translations when he wasn't working at court and agonizing over her impending departure.

The first of July, again payday, he found her out on the town with her Swede. "She quit him and came to me and we had numerous drinks with various girls then upstairs where I gave her $40 for a new dress," he wrote victoriously. "She was looking very bright but rather capricious however and allowed me to take a cursory "look" [at her wares?]. Afterwards downstairs and in box more wine until 4 a.m. when she said she would go home with me if I would give her $10. Gave it to her but when we got outside she saw messenger boy on bicycle and insisted on trying to ride. Spent 3/4 of an hour and then she refused to go with me but said she would call me up by telephone tomorrow afternoon. . . . Spent $120 on this performance. It is a fright how I love this bad little child!"

Bessie avoided Richard for a couple of weeks until her close friend, Fannie Hall, appeared with some two thousand dollars worth of diamonds given her by Dan McCarty, one of the original Fairbanks gold kings. Despite Bessie's recent sickness, this display fired her with ambition. "She was up and after a while insisted on going to Fanny's and latter displayed diamonds," Richard reported, "and of course my little girl had thought her friends would do as much by her and immediately began to try to graft, so returned with her to her own cabin where she said was feeling rather ill and we had a pleasant time talking until 11 p.m. I took her a lot of magazines and some candied fruits. She was not looking so well tonight and said she felt despondent. Poor little child."

Bessie lingered in Fairbanks throughout the summer of 1907, threatening to leave every other week, playing Richard against her Swede, getting him to sign for a couple of fifty-dollar dresses at Gordon's Store, and seldom missing a payday. Yet the young prostitute also could be generous when Richard was broke, and at times seemed genuinely fond of him. A diary entry of late August shows how she intrigued him.

"At 6 p.m. went to Bessie's cabin and found the little girl busy in kitchen in little white frock with big spots, very pretty and homelike. She was looking very tired and said she had been up all night till then, and was going out again tonight but denied she made any money. Could not quite understand why mood was very nice but refused to be touched or kissed. Gave me delicious boiled dinner with five or six kinds of vegetables and then told me I must find some cash for her, which I said would probably be impossible."

Three days later, the law clerk used much of his monthly salary voucher of $166.66 to pay old debts and Bessie took the rest. "At 6 p.m. called up Bessie and asked if I could come out broke," he noted. "She said for me to come and take her to the new dance hall at 9 p.m. Went at 8:30 and gave her $35 towards waist at Mrs. Andersen's and $20 towards new red traveling suit. She was very affectionate and lay back on me and allowed me to feel her legs right up, which she has never done before. . . . She promised to come to cabin and let me do 'whatever you want to' tomorrow night if I would call at the new dance hall at 10 p.m. for her."

But it was not to be. When Richard arrived to escort her from the new dance hall, she confided she'd gotten the clap from her Swede and asked him to visit her the next night at her cabin. There he found her "looking extraordinarily pretty but very feverish, lying on bed feeling blue. Afraid she is going to be thrown out by her mac." And she was!

After hitting up Richard for money to buy medicine, and charging one more expensive outfit to his account at Gordon's, Bessie was off to Katalla and then Idaho without so much as a private goodbye. Richard sent a telegram to her at Rampart and a letter to Idaho, confiding in his diary that "she has certainly been a dear little wife to me." From Tanana she wrote him a brief note saying she had failed at farewells because she had "fallen by the roadside" and didn't get back to her cabin until 8 a.m., just an hour before catching the boat. "Wonder who she was with!" he anguished. But he had lost her, with $100 yet to pay on her Gordon's bill.

After Bessie Simpson's departure, Richard buried himself in his work. He succeeded in mastering more than one hundred languages including Aleut, Tibetan, Swahili, Khmer, Papiamento, and hieroglyphics, receiving worldwide recognition. His friendship with Judge Wickersham continued; they were so close that townsfolk referred to them in one breath as "Wick and Dick."[11] Because of this, Richard was easily accepted in Fairbanks's respectable social circles, but his personal life now centered on casual relationships in the red light district. Reticent, perhaps because the Seattle schoolteacher's rejection had heightened his embarrassment about his crippled leg, Richard Geoghegan never again paid court to a respectable woman. His next love would be, like Bessie, an unconventional lady of the demimonde.

Ella Joseph-de-Saccrist, a.k.a. Lola Belmont, a.k.a. Portuguese Annie, was an exotic prostitute of a highly independent nature, even by Alaskan standards, and an unlikely match for a brilliant but shy and retiring linguist. On returning from a trip to Japan with his niece, financed by a small inheritance from his mother, Richard read about Ella on the front page of the *Fairbanks Daily Times* on February 11, 1915—"SHOOTING AFFRAY CIRCLE CITY: MAN IS WOUNDED. Lola Belmont, a mulatto woman, shot Joe Lagoux, a Chilean."

Joe Lagoux claimed he was outside Ella's place, hoping to reclaim mittens he had left there earlier that evening, when she opened the door and shot him. Ella, whose testimony was corroborated by a French co-worker, claimed that Joe, very drunk, had forced his way into their house at 1 a.m. and started abusing them; that he had struck the French woman on the breast and punched Ella in the eye. Ella said she retreated to the kitchen but Joe followed with a knife, so she nailed him in the left shoulder with her "single-barrel, break action, 45-gauge shotgun [sic], designed for small game." Ella's story checked out with Deputy U.S. Marshal Chester T. Spincer. When Joe Lagoux survived, Ella prudently moved to Fairbanks.[12]

A strikingly beautiful woman, Ella Joseph-de-Saccrist was welcome on the Line because it was thought good luck to have one black woman in a red light district—although Ella had only a small fraction of Negro blood and her heritage was French. She had been born in Nashville, but her

THE LOVE OF HIS LIFE

Ella Joseph-de-Saccrist, age thirty-two when Richard met her, was a
well-spoken, honey-skinned woman of West Indian descent. She took up residence
on the Fairbanks Line and may well have been the center of this unusual pageant photo.
To escape "blue laws" that forbade rowdy stage shows on Sundays,
enterprising club owners often enlisted performers from the demimonde to pose in
tableaux reproducing famous paintings, and Ella was known to be cooperative for a fee.
This photo was probably taken by Fairbanks photographer Charlie Cann,
who also photographed the Pioneers and church groups.

UAF, Griffin Photo Collection, #59-85-2104.

father was thought to have come from the West Indian colony of Martinique, perhaps from a well-heeled family, for Ella had a rare grace, refined speech, and fine manners that set her apart from other prostitutes.

When Richard met her, she was thirty-two, slim, fine-boned, with fine dark hair she wore piled in an updo to add to her five-foot stature. Her lovely, burnished complexion prompted him to call her "Honey Girl." She had run her house of prostitution in Circle successfully and was as prudent with her money as Richard was spendthrift. Not only did she purchase two houses on the Line, but she also invested in the respectable sections of Fairbanks.

Ella was less than impressed with the pudgy, balding linguist, with his short leg and awkward limp. Still, he made a decent salary as a clerk for the territorial government and often supplemented his income with lucrative stints as a court reporter and as a language tutor. He was gentle, easy to please, and pathetically eager to help when he heard her transparent sob stories. Hardened by years in the skin trade, the veteran prostitute played on his sympathies and his need for affection even more brutally than had Bessie Simpson, repaying his kindness with snide remarks to others about his physical deformity and naiveté.[13]

But Richard, then fifty, was genuinely in love. Because of his long experience with women on the Line, he understood Ella's emotional makeup and limitations perhaps better than she herself did. Concerned friends were quick to report that she mocked him, but he kept his own counsel and bided his time. When he first suggested marriage, she laughed. She was worth much more than he was, and what was the point of marrying a gullible, paying customer? Yet Richard possessed a trusting, childlike charm, and the fact that he really cared for her finally sank in.

Richard's friends were appalled, not only because Ella was a prostitute with no intention of quitting the trade, but because she was black. Marrying her would ruin him with the social set on whom he depended for tutoring and translation work. Nor were Ella's friends pleased, especially her lawyer and business partner Charles Williams, although she insisted her marriage would make no difference in their relationship (which may have been personal).

So no well-wishers accompanied them when, on a sluggishly cold day, May 16, 1915, the betrothed couple quietly left town and drove thirty miles north to the small mining community of Livengood to repeat their vows before Commissioner Charles H. "Alabam" LaBoyteaux. Garbed in his usual bib overalls and open-necked wool shirt, a chaw of tobacco socked tightly in one cheek, LaBoyteaux could not have added much romance to the occasion.[14] Nor did his paperwork for the ceremony ever appear on public record. Yet the bride and groom were very much in earnest, and time would prove their union one of Fairbanks's better matches, enduring for more than two decades.

Happily, the marriage apparently did not lessen Richard's ability to get freelance assignments, probably because the living arrangements of the couple were discreet. Richard returned to his book-lined log cabin on Sixth Avenue and Ella to her white-painted crib on the Line, where she continued to sell her favors. But they constantly exchanged affectionate correspondence by messenger service. They met for beer at the Fast Track, next to Ella's house, and spent off hours and weekends together, finding more joy in each other's company than either had dreamed possible.[15] Richard wrote from the heart:

For most men find in marriage
A stumbling block, they say
They can't do this, they can't do that,
All things are in their way.

I find you an anchor,
With a steady, welded chain;
It makes no difference how the pull,
The links have stood the strain.[16]

Ella, too, welcomed an anchor, increasingly as her life began a downward spiral. In May of 1921 she again made headlines when she shot Louis Doumain, a well-known pimp who earlier had been run out of Nome and had a record of minor criminal convictions.[17]

According to the newspaper account, Louis Doumaine entered Ella's house in a frenzy of anger and attempted to beat her. A black woman known as Big Minnie forced her way between them, allowing Ella sufficient time to reach into a bureau drawer for a revolver. Unlike her first experience, this time Ella aimed to kill, "the bullet hitting his ear and following the skull, describing a complete turn and lodging below the cheek bone. The lead pellet, which was found to be of 32 caliber, was completely flattened out." Louis remained unconscious throughout the night and the following morning was reported in critical condition, mumbling and not in his rational mind.[18]

The report noted that Louis was known to be troublesome, and was currently free on bonds on two separate indictments, one for robbery and the other a federal charge for bootlegging. Ella, taken before the district attorney that morning, "told a very straight story." However, a search of her house turned up a considerable amount of whisky and other intoxicating concoctions.

Ella—who had turned to bootlegging to supplement her income— owned seven pieces of property, either on her own or in partnership with other members of the demimonde. Her properties were valued at $3,600, but a year later, perhaps because of legal expenses and a loss of business due to police scrutiny, they were all listed for delinquent taxes.[19]

Then in March of 1922 Ella and her partner, Charles Williams, were indicted for perjury in connection with bootlegging charges. Thomas Marquam, the best criminal lawyer in the territory, got the case dismissed, but his services did not come cheaply.[20]

Through it all, Richard and Ella pulled tighter together. Perhaps with her encouragement, he purchased his own cabin on Sixth and a smaller one on Fourth Avenue for which he received modest rent. They delighted in owning a car, piling in with their dogs, Bug and Blackie, to tour the countryside on weekends. It was the happiest time of Richard's life. Unbelievably, he loved a woman who loved him. And, no longer a stateless person, he became an American citizen.[21]

As a linguist Richard continued to make his mark, focusing in later years on Alaska's beautiful Aleut language, which had never received attention from Americans. His translations of Russian material for Wickersham one day would help Alaska Natives win a land claim settlement of $1 billion and 40 million acres from the federal government, and his Russian translations for the weather service helped Alaskan meteorologists untangle northern mysteries. He corresponded with hundreds of foreign linguists on everything from errors in translations of the classics to his beloved Esperanto.[22] Eventually he gave up his government service to pursue his scholarship.

This tranquil period ended in 1932 when Ella, forty-nine, began a heartbreaking battle with pulmonary tuberculosis. By October of 1935 she was bedridden and Richard lived openly with her, not caring what anyone thought. Spasms of coughing kept her from sleeping and toward the end, when she coughed up blood almost daily, she was unable to eat. Yet she never complained.[23]

Then came a wonderful day in the last week of February that new year when she awoke hungry. "She was nibbling on coconuts, pineapple, macaroons, pickled beets, asparagus, chicken and a whole lot of things that took her fancy and that she had not been able to even look at for a year or eighteen months," he wrote his friend Wickersham, marveling at the hope the day had brought them. Suddenly peppy and gay, she had risen from her sick bed to dance with her delighted lover—an awkward pair, she skeleton-thin and he with one shortened, withered leg.

"I feel like a fighting cock," she declared, pretending to box with him. But hours later her cough got worse and her strength disappeared as quickly as it had materialized. Richard called the doctor, who gave her a drug that "made her wonderfully happy."

Richard hoped she would pick up again. He invested his meager savings in a day or two of hospital rest, then again cared for her at home. But time ran out. She went peacefully, pressing the first finger of her left hand to her lips, as if to blow her husband a kiss.[24]

How Richard managed to have her buried in the all-white "pioneer" section of Fairbanks's Clay Street Cemetery is unknown, but the most elegant tombstone there belongs to Ella Joseph-de-Saccrist Geoghegan, "Entered into rest: 3rd March AD 1936."

It was the height of the Depression. Richard still owned his small, unplumbed cabin and his little rental, but Ella's long illness had taken the rest of his money and he lived in merciless poverty, often without heat or food. His eyesight was failing and his fingers became so paralyzed he could no longer correspond without difficulty, yet his spirit never faltered.[25] Finally George Loudoun, a friend and welfare worker, enabled him to get a modest monthly dole from the territory, which helped, but it was the girls on the Line who looked after him.[26]

Surprisingly, Richard's diary written in 1942 at age seventy-six does not read too differently from the one he kept on his voyage of exploration in Fairbanks thirty-five years earlier. Josephine Finger, the beautiful, twenty-seven-year-old, part-Athabascan girl who became his tenant, took the place of the scheming Bessie Simpson, although Josephine was kinder. Others—Josephine's friend Laura and old pros like hard-driving Lena Ferguson, black prostitute Cleo Wadell, and illiterate Anna White who depended on Richard to correspond with her family—also watched over the old man when their own lives were not out of hand.

Early diary entries set the scene:

"Jan. 26—Josephine gave me a chicken dinner and peach cobbler and a couple of delicious kisses.

"Jan. 27—Josephine came over in evening, gave me two delicious kisses. Said she would move into 4th Ave. cabin. Some of Laura's and pimp's clothes there. Josephine very sweet and dear. Told her would give her twenty dollars the first of February. Laura invisible.

"Jan. 28—Laura called in afternoon. Told her I had rented house. Got post office key from her. Josephine brought rice pudding in evening and gave me two kisses. I tried to get another but she refused.

"Feb. 1—Carrie [Josephine's friend] looked in at five and told me the day was Sunday. No signs of Josephine. Hear that her husband has, returned. Probably trouble for the unfortunate beauty.

"Feb. 2—Carrie reports Josephine celebrating. Poor little fellow. Lena and Landass brought paper in evening. Josephine brought chicken dinner at 10:30 p.m. and said she would move into 4th St. cabin tomorrow. Gave me two of the most exquisite soft warm kisses I ever had from her, the darling."[27]

Lena reported that Josephine was in the hospital with a cut arm. Josephine's pimp claimed she was at the Pioneer Hotel, but eventually Richard located her back at his Fourth Avenue cabin.

"Josephine in bed looking very sweet but pimp present so I was very discreet and didn't stay long. Josephine said would be over later in the day," he wrote hopefully. "Had cut left arm badly." Later he learned her pimp had been convicted of passing a bad check but got off with a suspended sentence.

Richard's preoccupation with the soap opera of Josephine's life was occasionally broken by bouts of nostalgia . . .

"March 3—I took a walk to old cabin next door to [prostitute] Kitty O'Brien. Sad and happy memories of long ago.

"March 7—Passed all abodes of my darling wife, re-entering my cabin felt urge to play her favorite 'Carry Me Back.'

"March 13—Flowers for wife's grave and clean up and weed lot."

But stubbornly he refused to linger in the past. Anna White brought him back to reality when she arrived with half a bottle of whisky as thanks for writing a letter for her. And he devoted time to trying to understand Lovely One and catching up on gossip.

"[Josephine] said she was seventeen when married in 1935 to Finger who was thirty-seven. Consequently has now been married seven years. Was born 1915 on 26 of March," he noted shortly after her birthday. "Later she writes her brother downriver. He refers to her as if Native. Suppers with Sam Sampson when not with pimp."

Richard was seldom alone for long. His lively family of whores kept coming to borrow his typewriter, books, magazines, food and drink, or to sleep on his couch (and occasionally in his bed) when they were at odds with their pimps or lovers.

In September of 1942, after nine months of keeping him company, Lovely One dashed his hopes by moving out, but Richard carried on with remarkable spirit, considering he was seventy-six years old.

"Oct. 4—Got taxi and went with Dutch and Lena and had bath at old Palace Bath House, sad memories of old times with my darling. Apparently Lovely One has left town. Guess the romance with Lovely One is over, alas. It is cruel to be aged. If only I had been forty years younger."

"Oct. 5—Went to Cleo's where spent two dollars for port wine. Rather pleasant little time then went to Roe's but she was apparently busy so took couple of turns up and down and finally landed in Sweet Crab Crib near old Fast Track and bought couple of drinks but many soldiers around and fights going on so went to Lena's who was seemingly asleep intoxicated."

Then life took a turn for the better.

"Oct. 9—Lovely back. Said they had a glorious time and had got a moose. They had gone fifteen miles beyond Livengood where she had shot beaver. Had been drinking at Charlie Phillips' place."

On Oct. 10 Josephine was arrested and jailed for rolling a soldier, and Richard hastened to her when she was released four days later.[28]

"She had terrible time without blankets, water or matron in city jail. . . . Her eyes look as if she had been taking dope, too bright," he observed. "I wrote a letter to J. G. Rivers, municipal magistrate, about police searching Jo's cabin."

One night in early December, Josephine actually slept with him in his bed, apparently because she temporarily had no place to stay. To his amazement, in her sleepy haze she mistook him for her lover, "kissing me passionately, unbuttoning my pants and endeavoring to excite me," he reported. "Most delirious joy if only, if only. Sweetest episode of my life. I experience for the first time what the real love of a woman for her true love can be. Although, alas, it was not intended for me."

Lovely One soon moved on, leaving Richard in the care of Lena Ferguson, a tough veteran from a respected Jewish family in New Jersey, who guarded him jealously and resented anyone else attending him, even when she was too drunk to walk as far as his cabin. Yet in the end, he remained true to Ella Joseph-de-Saccrist, his beautiful "Honey Girl."

At his request, on his death, October 27, 1943, he was buried beside her beneath a simple tombstone of his own creation. "LAIMH LE RUININ A CHROIDHE" it read in his beloved native Gaelic, with an English translation so there would be no doubt:

"BESIDE THE DARLING OF HIS HEART."

12

The Callahans

THE TERRORIZING TEAMSTER AND
THE WOMAN WHO BESTED HIM

A listing of early land transactions for the Fairbanks red light district pro- vides a provocative introduction to the boomtown demimonde, but it is perplexing to find Irinia "Ellen" Pavloff Cherosky Callahan's name there alongside well-known whores. Ellen was a Native Alaskan, born with the status of a princess, whom the Athabascan people revered as an elder in her final years. Yet through intriguing circumstances, Ellen did own prop- erty in the Fairbanks restricted district during an era of frontier bigotry when Indian women were not even allowed to work there.

As a young woman, Ellen was as exotically beautiful as any lady of the evening. She was a Creole, however, one of those whose mixed Russian and Native parentage had made them the elite class during the last of Russia's Alaskan occupation in the nineteenth century, and she had no need to consider prostitution. Her father, Evan Pavloff, a half-Russian born at Sitka, was an influential Athabascan chief. Her mother, Malanka, came from Nulato, where Ellen was born about the time Russia sold Alaska to the United States in 1867. Before she was sixteen, Ellen wed Sergei Cherosky, the respected Creole interpreter for white traders who, with her brother Pitka Pavloff, discovered gold at Circle. Another brother, John

IRINIA "ELLEN" PAVLOFF CHEROSKY CALLAHAN
The daughter of Creole parents, Ellen caught the eye of
teamster Dan Callahan, who wed her in Circle and adopted her two
daughters by a former marriage. It was a love match, but Dan's
fiery temper ultimately drove his wife to drastic measures.
UAF, Helen Roselle Lindberg Collection, #93-151-402N.

THE CALLAHAN FAMILY IN HAPPY DAYS
*From the left are Axinia, Helen, Dan, Ellen, and their adopted son, Dick, with an
unidentified man in the background. When Fairbanks boomed, the family prospered there and Dan
began a long political career that would eventually take him to the Alaska Territorial Legislature.*
UAF, Helen Roselle Lindberg Collection, #93-151-443N.

Minook, made the major gold strike at Rampart and was the only Native allowed to file claims there.[1]

Ellen was present at the Circle discovery that had been grubstaked by veteran trader Jack McQuesten. Her husband, while blind drunk celebrating their triumph, made the mistake of telling a number of white men about the find. And although Ellen and her brother Pitka made it back to build cabins, their claims were taken by outsiders. The Creoles, who lost their status and most of their rights as citizens after the United States purchased Alaska, never profited from the discovery.[2]

Ellen subsequently left her husband, taking their two children, twelve-year-old Helen and sixteen-year-old Axinia, to Circle, by then a lively boomtown. It was there "Big Dan" Callahan, a charismatic Irish teamster with a political bent, proposed that she become his wife. Mixed marriages were frowned on in frontier society, but Ellen and her parents were respected by many in Circle and Dan cared little for the conventions of "polite society."[3]

Born in Fort Dodge, Iowa, in 1865, Dan Callahan had worked his way west as a logger, a miner, and a freighter, arriving at the gold fields of British Columbia in 1892, then following various stampedes to Dawson and Alaska.[4] He was a huge man, six-foot-two, weighing well over 200 pounds, as strong as a horse, known as a bully, and used to taking what he wanted. Many were afraid of him, but Ellen—although well under five feet tall— was not among them. Dan Callahan could be utterly charming. It was obvious that he loved her, and she wanted him.

In August of 1901, before their marriage, Dan was tried for raping a Circle miner's wife, a white woman named Ida Green. She charged that Dan had committed the crime after delivering letters from her husband and her cousin, who kept a roadhouse near Quartz Creek.

"Thinking him to be an honest and safe person, because of my husband's apparently knowing him, I did not hesitate to converse with him," she testified. "At the time he was in no manner rude or insulting. He came again during the evening and I did not hesitate to go riding with him the following evening." But once the outing was over, Mrs. Green claimed, Dan returned from putting his horses up and demanded a kiss. When she refused, he persisted, "threatening me with violence repeatedly, and succeeded in criminally assaulting me."[5]

In spite of her testimony, Dan Callahan was acquitted. The Irish teamster was so personable that few gave the rape charges much thought.[6] Ida Green appeared in public as if nothing had happened. And Dan's wedding to Ellen Cherosky two months later was, according to the local paper, "the biggest time ever had in this camp."[7]

The newspaper referred to the teamster as "Dan'l 'King' Calahan," noting that he got the name by marrying the chief's daughter at Circle. "She is a squaw and has two daughters sixteen and twelve years old. She is also a sister of Minook of Rampart. The family are good workers, making the best parkies and mitts on the river. The 'King' sits with his feet on the table and smiles when he thinks of all the tons of flour and other things in the cache which go with the squaw."[8]

Despite that era's general disdain of interracial relationships, Dan entered enthusiastically into the match, apparently his first and only excursion into matrimony. Ellen's oldest daughter, Axinia, wed Nels Rasmussen, one of Dan's fellow teamsters. Dan quickly adopted Helen, Ellen's younger daughter, and the couple also took in Richard Funchion, a homeless, part-Athabascan boy from Nenana, about 200 miles southwest of Circle. About twelve years old, he legally changed his name to Dick Callahan and fit into the family comfortably.

The ambitious teamster moved his family to Fairbanks in 1904 when it showed signs of becoming a bigger gold camp than Circle. By 1906 he had acquired property in downtown Fairbanks, which was mostly bars, gambling dens, and dance halls. And because he had a knack for organizing voters, he was readily accepted as a spokesman by the owners, employees, and patrons of these establishments. At that time Fairbanks had no property taxes, so city operations were supported solely by license fees from such businesses and by the monthly "fines" collected from the quasi-legal prostitution operations. Naturally, the men involved in these businesses wanted control of the city they were supporting, so to make sure that they got it they elected Callahan and a slate of his choosing to Fairbanks's first city council. It was rumored that Dan Callahan controlled all the pimps in town, and apparently he united the vote of the demimonde in the classic manner of an Irish ward politician.[9]

Dan was also extremely popular with the general public and the press, for he was colorful, fun-loving, and larger than life. Who else, on St. Patrick's Day, would don a green felt suit to "glad hand" jovially around town? He had a wonderful way with kids; few of them could resist when "Big Dan" Callahan invited them to come drive his horses or try to catch his fighting roosters. And in the wild frontier setting, a large percentage of the population shared his strong dislike for law and order.[10] There was general rejoicing when, in December of 1906, Dan culminated his longstanding battle with pompous Judge G. B. Erwin by getting the city council to cut the judge's salary of $200 a month by 50 percent. "If Judge Erwin is not satisfied, an equally well-fitted man could be obtained," he gleefully told the *Fairbanks Daily Times*.[11]

One month later, Dan nimbly escaped charges of assault and battery after he publicly beat Patrolman Jack Hayes in the Seattle Saloon. Jack Hayes had been following the teamster, and Dan told the jury that he hated the cop so much he could not drink when Jack was present.

When the patrolman entered the Seattle Saloon, Dan began cursing him and Jack threatened arrest. Dan struck out with his fist, hitting the officer in the head and disorienting him so badly he couldn't wield his billy club. They clinched and rolled on the floor with Dan on top. Then Dan got possession of the club, handing it to a bystander, and the patrolman's only other weapon, his gun, dropped from his pocket to the floor. No one intervened as Dan pummeled Jack until he conceded he'd had enough.

TWO OF ALASKA'S MOST RESPECTED CITIZENS

The daughters Dan Callahan adopted when he married Ellen, Axinia and Helen Cherosky,
would later become well-respected citizens. Axinia married Nels Rasmussen, a Circle-based
teamster like her stepfather, and raised a large family there. Helen, who remained single, became a
schoolteacher and the first Native woman in Alaska to own an automobile. She also was the
first member of the Doyon Corporation under the Alaska Native Land Claims Act.

UAF, Helen Roselle Lindberg Collection, #93-151-442N.

The eye patch which Jack wore in court did not begin to cover the damage. Yet to the consternation of Judge Erwin, who presided, Dan had enough friends on the jury to hang it.[12]

When the city council quietly created a restricted district for prostitutes on Fourth Avenue in 1906, Dan added property there to his numerous real-estate holdings. He was purposely absent, however, when the council voted to outlaw pimps in December of 1907.[13] He knew he couldn't buy the votes to stop the popular move, nor did he care to vote against it because Fairbanks was suddenly in the grip of rabble-rousers campaigning for law and order. The political climate was such that he did not run for council again until 1910, when he found himself the third-highest vote-getter.[14]

⸺⸺⸺

While Dan Callahan was popular, his wife, Ellen, had become genuinely loved. As gracious as she was beautiful, she had a fine sense of humor that allowed her to poke fun at herself. She showed a penchant for helping people in trouble and taking on strays of any race. Yet she easily made friends in the white community, even with people who generally had little to do with Native Alaskans. She worked hard at skin sewing, a craft at which she was a master, and she did her best to help her husband. But about 1910 the tiny woman—who stood only as tall as his elbow and was not fluent in English—did what none of Dan Callahan's political opponents had been able to accomplish: she stopped the big Irishman cold.

Although Dan still loved his wife, he was in the habit of beating her up when he came home in a bad mood after making his round of the bars. When he sobered he became so remorseful that she put up with it for a while, but she came to resent the punishment. Finally she issued an ultimatum: if it happened again, she would get a divorce.

The idea struck Dan as hilariously funny. No Indian woman would ever succeed in divorcing a white man, he told her, laughing, especially not a popular politician like himself. He repeated the story to numerous cronies, and then forgot it.

The next time he beat Ellen, raising a lump like an egg, she waited until he was sleeping off his drunk, then dressed in her best and went straight to the court. Judge Erwin, who was the leader of the opposition party and whose salary Dan had halved, proved anxious to help. Because Dan had told everyone about Ellen's threat and the cause of it, she had an excellent case. Judge Erwin realized that getting divorced by an Indian woman would certainly damage his rival's political prestige, and he helped her file for it.

Dan failed to take the pending court action seriously until he came home one evening, determined to turn Ellen from their house, only to discover that he no longer owned it or anything else. A year or so earlier, when he had feared a lawsuit, the Irishman had transferred everything—

his townhouse, mining claims, several fine teams of horses, numerous sleds and wagons, *and* property in the red light district—to his wife's name to limit his personal liability. In the presence of supportive family and neighboring white men, Ellen now reminded him that he had no legal title to any of it. As an act of generosity, she would give him a cabin at the other end of town and one good team with full equipment with which to continue his trade as a teamster. Nothing else! And she made it stick.[15]

She also withdrew from his bed. "A white woman is good enough for him!" she declared to her well-respected little Creole family.[16]

Thus did Ellen Callahan become the owner of two houses of ill repute in Fairbanks. They were small but there was such a demand for space in the red light district that they rented for double the average rate. A year or so later, Ellen sold the property to a couple of local prostitutes. She invested the returns in a highly successful fur-sewing enterprise that made her a financially independent businesswoman.

Meanwhile, Dan Callahan's power was waning, for the city no longer depended solely on license fees and fines from vice, but was also supported by property taxes. In the wake of a crippling miners' strike and a decline in gold production, a number of bars and gambling operations faltered or folded. Reformers rushed to replace representatives of the demimonde in the city's power structure, and when Dan ran for city council in 1911, he lost by a heavy margin. Following an unsuccessful (and unpopular) attempt by reformers to close the Line, he regained his council seat in 1913 and held it the following year. But after sitting out the next election, Dan was roundly defeated in 1916, perhaps because voters realized that he was finally on his way to jail.[17]

On January 7, 1916, May Williams charged him with felonious assault, testifying that he had choked her, twisted her wrists, and thrown her violently against the door of her house. Dan, who had been unarmed, quickly got out of jail on $1,000 bond and stayed out. In part because May was a veteran prostitute known from Dawson to Seattle, Dan was found not guilty.[18]

By mid-February, however, Dan was back in federal jail on charges of statutory rape, this time without the option of bail. He had been arrested with W. H. Wooldridge, a wood contractor, and Robert Jones, a cab driver, apparently following a barroom party and a murky interlude at the Rose Machine Repair Shop.

Dan hired Leroy Tozier, a crack criminal lawyer who had worked for Alexander Pantages in Dawson before passing the Alaska Bar. Ellen, with

DAN CALLAHAN

*Surviving a conviction and imprisonment for rape, the veteran politician returned
to his hometown of Fairbanks, where he successfully ran for the Territorial Legislature.
Old-timers prefer to remember his Irish charm instead of his brushes with the law.*

Courtesy of Candace Waugaman. UAF, Dorothy Loftus Collection, #80-84-105N.

her usual generosity, testified in court that the defendant was impotent. His adopted son, Dick, appeared as a character witness. But this time the affable politician did not have enough friends on the jury to hang it, and the charges were serious. Unlike the earlier trials involving women of questionable repute, whose testimony was paid little respect, his accusers were two local girls not employed on the Line. They were both young, and one had a well-respected mother who lent credibility to her testimony.

Dan was the last of those accused to be tried. Robert Jones, defended by Tom Marquam, Dan's political rival, was found not guilty after his jury deliberated eight and a half hours.[19] W. H. Wooldridge was acquitted on the rape charge but, in a decision that surprised the community, he was found guilty of attempting the crime and sentenced to from eighteen months to ten years in federal prison. [20]

Dan sweated out his jury for twenty hours as rumors flew. One was that the count stood eleven to one for acquittal; another account had one vote for acquittal and eleven for conviction—which turned out to be closer to the truth.[21] On April 11, 1916, Dan Callahan was sentenced to twelve years at the federal prison on McNeil Island.

Released for good behavior, Dan returned to Fairbanks in time to run for city council in 1921 and, although he lost by a considerable margin, he did not appear discouraged. On the contrary, he changed his political affiliation from Democrat to Independent and ran for the Alaska Territorial House of Representatives, campaigning for full citizenship for women, their right to sit on juries and hold public office, and also for good roads. Dan won with 561 votes, 117 more than his competitor, Hosea Ross, the local undertaker,[22] who failed to overcome Big Dan's unique campaign slogan, "Vote for Hosea and bury the town."[23]

During her ex-husband's 1922 campaign, Ellen Callahan vacationed from her business in Fairbanks to visit her daughter Axinia, son-in-law Nels, and their eight children in Circle. She could afford the break. She had, in fact, become the most successful independent Native businesswoman in the region, and she'd invested her profits so widely in charities that she was considered a one-woman welfare agency. Ellen's success was not exactly what Dan Callahan had envisioned when he invested in the whorehouse lots that staked her enterprise, but few ill-gotten gains were ever put to better use, and he was pleased with her success.

13

Tom Marquam

THE LAWYER WHO FLOUTED CONVENTION AND ALMOST GOT AWAY WITH IT

Tom Marquam, scion of a wealthy and politically powerful Oregon family, came north during the Klondike rush to make his own way in the world, turning his back on the restraints of conventional society to revel in the permissive freedom of the frontier. A brilliant lawyer, handsome and affable, he thought he could have it all—wealth, social standing, and political success while still enjoying the company of saloon-owners, gamblers, and prostitutes. He came as close as anybody, but time, which eventually tamed the Last Frontier, was not on his side.

Few had more reason for optimism than young Tom Marquam. Articulate and tall, he was extremely handsome with striking blue eyes and a peachy complexion. His father, Judge Philip A. Marquam, was the largest landholder in Multnomah County, Oregon. Marquam Hill, crowning 298 acres that the judge owned in Portland, was named in his honor, as was the magnificent Marquam Theater downtown.[1]

Tom, the youngest of the judge's four sons and seven daughters, became a barkeeper in 1881,[2] but he aspired to emulate his father's career

TOM MARQUAM

Son of a wealthy and politically prominent Oregon family, Tom Marquam came north during the Klondike rush to make good on his own. Many considered him Alaska's cleverest criminal lawyer, and he almost made it to the U.S. Congress, but his fascination with the demimonde ultimately cost him dearly.

Courtesy of Candace Waugaman, Photo Album #1. UAF #96-198.

and soon enrolled at the University of Oregon, from which he graduated with high marks, and Stanford, where he excelled in Spanish, theater, and sports.[3] His classmates included Julius L. Meier, destined to become governor of Oregon, and Herbert Hoover, later president of the United States. Tom was also well-connected in Portland, where he apprenticed as a lawyer and became a commissioned officer in the National Guard.[4]

But his father had gotten his start by going west for the California gold rush of 1849, and Tom was excited by news of the Klondike stampede. Half a dozen young Portland lawyers also contracted "gold fever," and in the spring of 1897 they headed north together to pioneer jurisprudence. Leroy Tozier, who like Marquam would later become a prominent lawyer, decided to practice in Dawson, but Tom valued his American ties and liked the look of Alaska.[5]

Former Oregon lawyer Lytton Taylor was U.S. Attorney in Southeastern and may have helped Tom secure a job as a customs agent, but Taylor's performance was so erratic that Alaska Governor James Sheakley reported him insane to President Grover Cleveland. Taylor resigned, and shortly thereafter, a Juneau grand jury indicted Tom and six of his fellow officers for trafficking in smuggled liquor. Their boss, Collector of Customs Joseph Ivey, denounced the move as a political plot. The case fell apart when a key witness and a defendant disappeared, and the indictment did not hinder the law practice Tom subsequently established in Skagway and Haines.[6]

At age twenty-six, Tom enthusiastically welcomed the start of the twentieth century with a group of fast friends.

"As the clock struck the last hour of the old year, the town of Haines was flooded with a burst of melody that echoed and re-echoed from the surrounding hills and floated down Lynn Canal on the freshening breeze," a local paper reported. "A deafening report followed that roused the laggard from his sleep and ushered in the first hour of the year 1900. In the immediate neighborhood of where the music originated was found W. A. Biglow, T. Marquam, Ed. Grygla, H. Brie, Mike the Sloop Man and P. R. McGuire, up to their necks in snow singing, 'we won't go home until morning,' and they didn't. Those who were serenaded responded so generously that some of the boys went home with snowshoes on their hands as well as their feet."[7]

Nicknamed "Fighting Tom," he was elected to represent Republicans from Skagway and Haines at the 1900 territorial Republican convention in Juneau.[8] Two years later he beat a personal rap for contempt of court apparently engineered by a political opponent.[9] He lost his bid to become Alaska's delegate to the National Republican Convention,[10] but represented Haines as a witness before a U.S. Senate subcommittee investigating conditions in Alaska in the summer of 1903.[11]

Somewhere along the way—probably in Skagway at the start of the new century—he met Iowa Allman, a handsome brunette with social grace and a perfect hourglass figure. She had a seven-year-old son, Stanford "Jack" Allman, whom Tom came to love even more than Iowa, but he feared marriage would damage his political future and she was not insistent. Although she came from a respected Iowa family, much of her past was murky, and it was rumored that she had been a sporting woman before becoming Tom's mistress.[12]

For both, Fairbanks seemed a perfect place to make a fresh start. Tom had gone there in the summer of 1906 to campaign for Judge Cornelius Murane, a Nome attorney then running for congressional delegate. Murane was soundly beaten by Tom Cale of Fairbanks, who was later discovered to have worked as a private investigator for Pinkerton, America's most famous detective agency, and to have been on the lam for murdering his brother's killer in Oregon.[13] Tom not only accepted the defeat gracefully, "becoming a Cale man," but decided the rapidly growing mining camp would be a better political base than Southeastern with its dwindling population and sluggish economy. Lawyer Leroy Tozier had recently relocated there and was doing very well. On August 31 the *Fairbanks Daily News* reported Tom's decision enthusiastically: "He will practice independently, despite the fact that several flattering offers have been made to enter into partnership with members of the local bar."[14]

Tom quickly established himself as the most popular criminal lawyer in the territory, becoming the first choice for prostitutes, gamblers, and bar owners, not only because he ran with that crowd, but because he usually won. When he defended a major case, businessmen closed their offices to attend.[15] His enviable success record did not endear the articulate attorney to self-righteous citizens, however, and Tom made additional enemies by becoming the editor of the *Fairbanks Times* in 1908 and using the newspaper to badger his opponents.

———❦———

Revenge came swiftly when District Attorney James Crossley, an ambitious political opponent, engineered an arrest to publicly embarrass Tom. In a broad police sweep on May 8, Joseph LeGrand, a Parisian boot-legger who also handled business for some women in the red light district, was arrested for keeping a bawdy house. Tom was arrested as a patron of the house, along with Charlie Thompson, an underworld kingpin and one of the town's wealthiest landowners; James "Ham Grease" O'Connor, a dance hall operator from Dawson; Jake Marks, a pimp who used a tailor shop as his cover; and nearly a dozen other prominent citizens who were not given to church-going. The majority, charged with cohabiting in a state of fornication, quickly pleaded guilty and paid the fifty-dollar fine, but Crossley had singled out Tom to indict for adultery with his mistress. The crusading D.A. had discovered that Iowa had previously married a local man and failed to divorce him before moving in with Tom. The mar-riage was on the books in Washington State, but Tom decided to fight the charge on a technicality.[16]

He hired as his defense attorney "Judge" Louis K. Pratt, a former district judge from Kansas, who had begun practicing law in Skagway in 1897, the year Tom joined the Customs Service, and had moved to Fairbanks in 1904. Pratt was colorful, imbibed freely, and made a ritual out of tobacco-chewing, but he had a reputation for effective if unconven-tional courtroom behavior.[17]

Crossley, his adversary, was a strong "law and order man" with consid-erable ambition and ego, justified perhaps because he was a Yale graduate who before coming north had served nine years as a state senator in Iowa (ironically, the home state of Iowa Allman). Crossley's able clerk, Cecil Clegg, played local Democratic politics, frequented the local saloons, and hated Tom Marquam.[18]

J. S. Harding, a deputy marshal as well as the "wronged husband," introduced a certificate of marriage issued to himself and Iowa Allman on March 2, 1903, signed by the commissioner of the superior court of Chelan County, Washington State. To counter, Pratt submitted the code of Washington, which said that only ministers, supreme and superior court judges, and justices of the peace could perform marriage services, making Harding's marriage invalid. The prosecution attempted to block this move on the grounds that the legislation was not proved to be the Washington code, but presiding judge Silas Reid allowed Tom's attorney to argue that the marriage had never been legal.

Spectators (just about everyone in Fairbanks) found the debate riveting. The *Fairbanks Times* reviewed performances of the protagonists as it might have a theater event, with astonishing fairness considering that Tom had just resigned as the newspaper's editor. "Attorney Crossley justified the opinion of those who have been watching the conduct of cases by the new district attorney, and he has demonstrated that he will be well-equipped for the work that he will have to do in the future," the reporter wrote. Assistant Clegg, who made the opening argument for the prosecution, stated the case with clearness and force, according to the *Fairbanks Times*. "His style is always positive and his sentences roll out with the abruptness of a shot from a catapult. He is the prosecutor pure and simple, and he is merciless toward the man whom he thinks is deserving of punishment."

Defense attorney Pratt was "just what those who have heard him on other occasions expected. He never appears to better advantage than when he fully and thoroughly believes he is right, and what appears to be an arrogant and overbearing manner at times is but a vocal and physical expression of the promptings of his heart."

The debate was so evenly balanced that no one had the faintest idea where they stood when the jury retired.[19] "Speculation became rife. It was a generally accepted belief that they would not reach an agreement and there would be a hung jury," the *Fairbanks Daily News* reported breathlessly. "When court convened at ten o'clock this morning, they filed into the courtroom a tired and sleepy looking lot of men [after nineteen hours of deliberation]. There was much coughing and sneezing, and it didn't require very close scrutiny to discern the fact they had put in a bad night of it.

"As soon as the roll was called, the court asked them if they had reached a verdict. 'No sir, we have not,' said Dick Wood." And out they went again.

Finally, at 2 p.m. they returned looking relieved, each with an overcoat over his arm. "Marquam, who showed the signs of a night of suspense, listened carefully and as the court pronounced the words that meant his clearance it was evident that he was thoroughly alive to what that meant," the *News Miner* reported. "He stands cleared on a bad charge and his friends congratulate him on the outcome of the trial."[20]

Two years later Thomas Marquam married Mrs. Iowa V. Allman in a quiet ceremony performed at the Marquam residence at Ninth and Lacey, with the Rev. J. J. Condit of the Presbyterian Church officiating. Judge Louis K. Pratt and John W. Troy, who would one day become governor of Alaska, witnessed the event along with Mrs. E. A. Herring, a friend of the bride.[21]

Sending Iowa's son, Jack, Outside to college to become an engineer, the Marquams settled down with surprising tranquillity, hosting well-known Klondike old-timers like Captain Al Mayo and bar-owner William McPhee. When A. H. Hansen, a popular marshal from Iowa, wed Elizabeth Sullivan, a nurse from Portland, the Marquams were the first named in the wedding party. Together Tom and Iowa journeyed to Portland to attend the huge funeral of Judge Philip Marquam, who had suffered financial ruin shortly after Tom settled in Alaska.[22]

Although Tom was holding his own in polite society, he remained combative. At a trial in November of 1911, he caught opposing witness Walter King apparently giving signals to Eric Overstad, whom Tom had under cross-examination. When Commissioner George Jeffries ignored Tom's request that the communication be stopped, Tom hit King in the face, drawing blood.[23] He was then fined for striking an opposing witness.

Later, in a local saloon, Tom knocked down Cecil Clegg, the assistant district attorney who had prosecuted him in the adultery case. Clegg, who had angered Tom with drunken political taunts, later insisted he'd had little to drink, that he had been drugged and then "brutally and wantonly attacked." "His purpose was to deprive me of office and strengthen enemies of the D.A.'s office and embarrass Crossley through me," Clegg declared in his affidavit. The case certainly did embarrass Attorney General Crossley, and Clegg lost his job in 1913, which must have tickled Tom.[24]

Yet apparently Tom realized that brawling with his enemies was damaging his reputation, and in the decade that followed he stayed clear of trouble and politics. He might have been biding his time, but more likely he was preoccupied with his family. His adopted son, Jack, returned to Alaska for the Chisana gold stampede in 1913 and then lived with Tom and Iowa until he enlisted in the U.S. Army Engineers during World War I to serve in France. Iowa moved to Seattle in 1916 to seek medical

RESPECTABILITY
Political enemies had Tom arrested and tried for adultery because of his affair with
Iowa Allman, a woman who spoke little about her past. He beat the rap and later married her.
Fellow attorney A. H. Hansen and his bride helped the Marquams (center)
celebrate, and Iowa became accepted in Fairbanks society.
UAF, A. H. Hansen Collection, #85-090-226N.

attention for a severe illness, leaving Tom alone. Rumors circulated that he had divorced her, but her death in February of 1917 apparently came as a shock, and he listed her as "the beloved wife of Thomas A. Marquam" in her funeral announcement.[25]

Tom sought solace in Fairbanks's red light district, which increasingly became the focus of his private life and his law practice. "There are dozens of lawyers in town but every time there is a hooker, I get to defend them," he told a family member, bemused. But in truth, he still found the demimonde more exciting than straight-laced society.

Surprisingly, this was not a stigma when Tom reentered politics in 1920 as a candidate for city council. A top vote-getter, Tom was subsequently elected mayor, which proved how desperate Fairbanks was for leadership. Tough times had come to the former boomtown. Gold production had dropped drastically as easy-to-mine placer deposits played out. The cost of living soared. Wood supplies needed for both mining and heating homes were dwindling. In ten years the population of Fairbanks had dropped from 9,320 to 1,100.

Salvation lay in cheap transportation which would make it possible to import coal from Healy. Putting their political differences on hold, city fathers pulled together, successfully lobbying congress to build a railroad to Fairbanks from the port of Seward. As an unexpected side effect, the Fairbanks Exploration Company undertook an extensive exploration and drilling project, buying out small mining companies to launch large-scale operations that ultimately put the town back on its feet.[26]

With prosperity in sight and the election of Warren G. Harding as U.S. president, Tom's star ascended, for he had solid political ties to the Republicans. City fathers decided to invite the new president to Fairbanks to drive the final golden spike in the railroad, and Tom persuaded Harding to make the long, difficult trip.

The only problem was that, for a year or so, Tom had been enjoying an affair with a prostitute named Ray Alderman, and everyone in town knew it. Iowa Allman may have had a shady past, but Ray was still actively selling her favors on the Line. A delegation of irate matrons demanded that, as presidential host, Tom abandon his illicit union.[27] But Tom wasn't about to give Ray up. Outgoing, thoroughly amusing, a wonderful piano player, and a neat housekeeper, she filled a gap in his life. Since the respectable women of the town had clout, he promised to end the clandestine relationship. They were less than pleased when they discovered he'd quietly married Ray before Judge Charles E. Bunnell in February of 1920.[28]

Also angered was James Wickersham, then in his sixth term as Alaska's delegate to Congress. "Am preparing a strong case against Marquam," he wrote in his diary. "Both Marquam and [Hawley] Sterling brought their long association in such houses [of prostitution] in Fairbanks and Nenana to a close by each marrying a notorious prostitute out of such houses for a wife. Am also getting court records on Marquam's criminal record at Dyea in 1898-9."[29]

Early in his political career, James Wickersham had been convicted of adultery. His wife, Debbie, stuck with him and the conviction was later overturned when the woman with whom he was sinning proved to have a bad name.[30] In the years that followed, the judge was often forced to live apart from his wife, who was dying slowly of tuberculosis. Although he had the inclinations of a great womanizer, enjoyed the company of "dangerous women" when he met them in public, and avidly collected pictures

MRS. MARQUAM ENTERTAINS PRESIDENT HARDING
Some Fairbanks residents were scandalized when Tom Marquam, their
elected mayor, married Ray Alderman from the red light district—and even more so
to discover she would serve as hostess when President Harding visited their town.
But Ray charmed the president, as well as her husband.
Courtesy of Candace Waugaman, Photo Album #1. UAF #96-198.

of dance hall girls and prostitutes along with other historical memorabilia, he dared not step over the line again. To see other men—especially hated political rivals—flaunt their illicit relationships galled him. He could not figure out how to damage Hawley Sterling, a highway engineer with no political ambitions, but Tom Marquam was a prime target. In 1905 Wickersham had lost his appointment as a federal judge, and he strongly believed Tom was among those who had worked against him. Now Wickersham wasted no time in launching an attack on his fellow Republican.[31]

Tom's cherished dream was to become a judge as his father had been, and in 1921 the Fairbanks Republican Club nominated him for the federal post. Unaware of Wickersham's vendetta, Tom was surprised when the appointment failed. Cecil Clegg, Tom's old adversary whom he had beaten both in the courtroom and in the saloon, was appointed federal judge instead.

Tom took consolation in an appointment to the board of regents of the new Alaska Agricultural College (later the University of Alaska Fairbanks). He easily won reelection as mayor, and, unbeknownst to his Fairbanks constituents, he had a tentative promise of a South American ambassadorship from Warren Harding.

When it became obvious that Dan Sutherland, Alaska's delegate to Congress, was at odds with the president and would not escort Harding on his Alaska visit, Tom happily volunteered to do it himself, with his bride by his side. It is not recorded how Fairbanks's movers and shakers reacted to the prospect of one of the town's most notorious prostitutes being the presidential hostess, but apparently all went well. Harding, a man of the world with a mistress of his own, appreciated the mayor's pretty wife. He invited the Marquams to accompany him in his private railroad car, and Tom's appointment as ambassador seemed assured until Harding died less than three weeks later.[32]

Undaunted, Tom quietly began laying the foundations for a congressional campaign by hosting a dinner for Alaska Governor Scott Bone and his wife. Also in attendance were Fairbanks newspaper publisher W. F. Thompson and his wife, Assistant District Attorney Collings, and Tom's former adversary, Judge Cecil Clegg.[33]

At the time Tom was defending about half of the Fairbanks prostitutes against flimsy federal charges calculated to close down the Line, which must have put a social strain on the evening. But prostitution had been quasi-legal in Fairbanks for almost two decades. Most residents, especially in the business community, still considered it a necessary evil, and Tom used the dinner party to his advantage. Judge Clegg subsequently came out in favor of retaining the restricted district, and the prostitutes were back in business. Governor Bone appointed Tom to the board of the Governor's National Aeronautical Association, and Tom soon became Fairbanks's delegate to the Republican National Convention.[34]

In 1925, amidst grateful tributes, Tom Marquam retired as mayor and announced he would run as an independent candidate for Congress. He had not only brought Fairbanks out of debt but left it with a substantial

CLOSE TO POWER

*President Harding had promised Tom Marquam (smiling, right)
an ambassadorship to South America. The deal was apparently sealed by
Harding's visit to Alaska, but fell apart when he died shortly thereafter.*

UAF, Joseph Romig Collection, #90-43-349.

cash balance,[35] and he easily found support from the voters of Interior Alaska. Democratic opposition was weak, and many Alaskans had grown disenchanted with Republican incumbent Dan Sutherland.

Tom enjoyed his campaign tour, confessing he "sort of forgot about politics" in his pleasure at meeting and visiting with old-timers he had known for two decades. He got great press, in part because he bribed editors[36]—which was standard for that era—but also because he had genuine charisma. In Juneau, upward of 1,000 voters turned out for a torchlight procession in his honor, led by the Juneau City Band.

"The sidewalks were crowded and the torch-carriers were lustily cheered from the sidelines. By eight o'clock all the more than 700 seats on the main floor of the theater were filled, the balcony was crowded to capacity and more than 200 were standing in the entrance doors off the corridor," the *Stroller's Weekly* reported. "Marquam's address required two hours. He had nothing to say against his opponent as a man, but as a delegate to Congress he showed him up to the extent of making him appear ridiculous."[37]

Dan Sutherland, however, had the backing of Judge James Wickersham and others of Tom's enemies who deftly moved to make an issue of Tom's private life. They used a personal letter from Presbyterian elder S. Hall Young to Rev. O. A. Stillman to attack the character of the Marquams. Rev. Stillman, angered by the use of his name, declined to take sides, and most newspapers downplayed the couple's past. But the letter-writing, word-of-mouth smear campaign was so effective that Tom lost, 6,960 to 4,242.[38]

That wasn't enough for Tom's enemies. In the fall of 1928 a federal grand jury in Washington, D.C., indicted him on four counts of election fraud on the technicality that he had failed to file returns on his election expenditures, and a bench warrant was issued for his arrest.[39] When Tom waived a hearing in Fairbanks District Court, Judge Cecil Clegg fixed bail at $5,000 and ordered his removal to Washington, D.C., for the trial.[40]

Ray stayed in Fairbanks, spending most of her time chain-smoking and playing cards with fellow graduates from Line.[41] Tom pleaded not guilty, and although there was not enough evidence to convict him, the case dragged on for a couple of years. In March of 1928 Tom moved to New York City, apparently for medical treatment and to be closer to his adopted son, Jack, who had returned from an assignment as a foreign correspondent in Paris to write radio scripts for a national network.

Despite the fact that Tom Marquam had been battling health problems, his death on November 23, 1931, at age fifty-seven was not well-explained. One newspaper reported that he had died of a heart attack; another referred to several operations and a long illness. One reporter referred to the attorney's "sudden" death. There were rumors that he had been murdered by fellow politicians who feared he would turn state's evidence, implicating them in the election fraud to gain leniency for himself. It was also suggested that he had committed suicide in a fit of depression over the still-unsettled charges against him.

Jack Allman held a memorial service in New York for the only father he had ever acknowledged, and the Marquam family in Oregon—from whom Tom had been estranged in later years—held a quiet funeral. His body was cremated, and no mention is made of a burial.[42]

Tom's widow, Ray, short of funds, mortgaged their home and entered a short, combative relationship with a Fairbanks carpenter who eventually walked out. In 1935, she sold out, disappearing from Alaska record.[43]

James Wickersham died four years later, smug in the knowledge that he had rid Alaska of the wicked Marquam influence. Yet it is interesting to note that, in 1949, Tom's handsome and beloved stepson Jack Allman wed pretty Ruth Coffin, Wickersham's equally beloved niece.[44] While not exactly what the vindictive judge or the disappointed attorney would have hoped for, it proved to be a strong marriage.

14

Sin in Southern Alaska

BARGAINING FOR LOVE

⸎

W hile Dawson had the most colorful red light district, and the well-run Fairbanks Line offered the most lucrative opportunity for good time girls, quasi-legal prostitution was also a given throughout southern Alaska's port towns, which served as gateways into the gold country. In one instance, the trade there helped improve Alaska's territorial standing.

In October of 1902, Mrs. Fred Rassmussen was busted for running a whorehouse in Juneau. The place was licensed to well-known bartender George Kyrage, but Fred Rassmussen actually owned the Peerless Saloon, where the prostitution arrest took place. City fathers had been trying to nail him for some time, so they arrested Fred instead of his wife.

At first the Rassmussen case did not seem precedent-setting. A Dawson veteran who'd moved to Juneau, Fred had been arrested before, recently with other prominent citizens on gambling charges that would not hold up in court.[1] This time the indictment was for keeping a house of ill fame for the purpose of prostitution, fornication, and lewdness. Even though Fred Rassmussen could prove he wasn't on the property at the time, U.S. Attorney John J. Boyce and Judge Melville Brown were on a moral crusade and determined to make an example out of him. Fred hired attorney W. E. Crews, an original thinker, to take them on.

⸎

DOLLY ARTHUR
The most famous whore in Southeastern, Dolly came to the North from Idaho via British Columbia. Arriving after the gold stampedes had slowed, she instead did business with the fishing fleets of Wrangell and Ketchikan. "I like it here because the men come in bunches..."she explained.

Courtesy of Don Dawson. THS #90.1.10.5.

His trial, held December 9, 1902, resulted in a hung jury. Because the prosecutors had trouble scraping up twelve more recruits in the small town, they retried Fred's case before a "petit jury" of only six men, which federal law allowed in unorganized territories. W. E. Crews objected that his client was an American citizen and deserved a full jury of his peers, but Judge Brown was anxious to get on with it. Crews was overruled.[2]

No one was surprised when Fred Rassmussen was found guilty as charged, but even cynical news reporters were shocked that he was given the maximum sentence. While John Penglase and Sam Gius of the Douglas Opera House were ordered to serve six months in jail on the same charges, Judge Brown gave Fred a full year, saddled him with a $2,500 bond, and topped off these indignities with a lecture.

"Mr. Rassmussen, I have always made it a practice to advise men who have been found guilty to lead a better life in the future, but owing to the brags and boasts you have made, I have nothing to say to you," he chastised. "I do hope, however, that you may become a better man and live better. I sentence you to the common jail at Sitka . . . and to pay all costs of this action."[3]

Crews appealed, right on up to the U.S. Supreme Court—not on the grounds that Fred was innocent, but that he had been unjustly denied a twelve-man jury. In 1905 Judge Brown lost big time. The high court declared that Alaska, though unorganized, was incorporated into the United States, and therefore its citizens did have full constitutional rights. So Fred Rassmussen (or anyone else) was entitled to a trial by a twelve-man jury.[4]

The Rassmussen decision changed Alaska's official designation from "district" to "territory," setting in motion a measure which gave it a delegate to Congress . . . something Alaskans had fought for without success for many years.[5] Fred Rassmussen did not face another trial, which would have put him in double jeopardy. Relieved to have his bail bond back, he came out of exile in Dawson to follow the latest gold rush to Tanana, Alaska, perhaps unaware of the service he and the whores of his Peerless Saloon had done for their fellow Alaskans.[6]

—————⌘—————

Although Juneau was no more subject to moral reforms than anywhere else in the Far North, it was known as a tough place for prostitutes, as was the rest of Southeastern in the early mining days. Most ladies of the evening, forced to work out of tiny, stifling cribs over saloons and dance halls, were at the mercy of landlords, pimps, and customers. There survives from a century past an elegant invitation, printed in gold script on red velvet finished paper, that reads, "Yourself and Friends are cordially invited to be present at the Opening of the Red Light, by Miss Gertie Joseph on Saturday Evening, February 15, 1896. Main Street between Front and Second, Juneau." Historian R. N. DeArmond, who discovered the post-Valentine's Day treasure, speculated that Miss Joseph may have attempted to expand her operation beyond the restricted area, but if so, she failed. While Juneau did not fence in prostitutes as did Nome and Fairbanks, ultimately it did confine them to Lower Front Street, where they worked the saloons despite an ordinance that prohibited them from "loitering" there.[7]

Juneau's best-known case of the sale of love gone wrong was that of Kitty O'Brien, a.k.a. Kate Dulaney, and Robert Stroud, who may have been pimping for her. Robert was only eighteen at the time. Known as the "Peanut Kid" even though he looked older than his years and was six feet tall, Robert had run away from home in Seattle several years earlier and taken to the hobo trail, living by his wits. Coming north, he had met Kate Dulaney in 1908 while he was looking for railroad construction work in Cordova, where she was working as a "box hustler" pushing drinks in a dance hall.[8]

According to biographer Jolene Babyak and later prison records, Robert was aggressively homosexual and always had been,[9] but he certainly developed emotional ties to Kate, and perhaps a physical relationship as well. Although she was thirty-six, "Irish Kate" was still a charmer with a magnificent figure, deep blue eyes, and a good, open face. And she could be equally open with her heart. When Robert caught pneumonia, she nursed him back to health and helped him rent a popcorn machine which he worked to recover his finances.

Things went well until they ran into F. K. Von Dahmer, one of Kate's former clients. Despite his German heritage and the fact that he'd been raised in Russia, he was known as Charlie Dahmer and he affected the dress and style of a riverboat gambler. Only three years older than Robert, Charlie was also quite taken by Kate Dulaney's mature charms. Craftily he suggested the couple might profit by following him to Juneau, where he was taking a job tending bar.

When business fell off in Cordova the next winter, Robert and Kate took Charlie's advice, moving into cramped quarters in the Clark Building in downtown Juneau. Kate was hired by a cabaret, but Robert had trouble finding work. According to both, Charlie Dahmer owed them money and when he offered to treat them to beer on the night of January 18, 1909, they decided that might be the only way they'd ever collect. They made the rounds of some bars, then retired to Charlie's cottage. Robert went to pick up some fish for supper, leaving Katie in the company of Charlie and his roommate. The cottage was empty when he returned shortly thereafter, and there were signs of a struggle. He found Kate back at their room at the Clark, hysterical, with two black eyes and a red mark around her neck where her gold chain and locket previously had been displayed.[10]

According to one account, Kate told Robert that Charlie had demanded she live with him and ripped off her locket—which he knew contained a treasured picture of her daughter—threatening to keep it until she moved in. A second version was that Charlie refused to pay the full ten dollars usually charged for Kate's services.[11] But no one disputed the fact that Kate asked Robert to kill the bastard. Or that Robert—who could not tolerate violence against women because he'd seen his mother abused too often—shot Charlie Dahmer immediately after he learned Kate had been beaten.

Charlie's body was quickly discovered by neighbors who had seen both Kate and Robert at the scene, and the couple was immediately booked for manslaughter. Kate admitted in court that she had asked Robert to kill Charlie, but insisted that she had been "unconscious and hysterical and incapable of understanding what was said at the time."[12] Charges against her were quickly dropped with no objection from Robert. Tried for manslaughter with a clean record, he expected to be sentenced to a couple of years in federal prison. Instead the judge put the teenager away for twelve years.

Kate corresponded faithfully, but when she finally worked her passage to Seattle two years later to visit Robert in prison, she had grown fat and matronly, showing signs of too much alcohol. Still, Robert said her letters meant a lot to him and asked her to stay in touch. However, Robert's mother, who blamed Kate for his imprisonment, managed to cut off the woman's correspondence. Kate Dulaney disappeared, from both Robert's life and the record.[13]

Robert Stroud, who was short-tempered, killed a fellow prisoner about a year later, and the harsh prison system ultimately condemned him to almost thirty-eight years in solitary confinement. To keep from cracking up, he spent his time studying the birds that chanced by his lonely cell. Ultimately he produced some brilliant scientific works on birds and bird diseases that brought him public attention. A best-selling book was written about him by Thomas E. Gaddis, titled *Birdman of Alcatraz*, and the subsequent movie made him the world's most famous prisoner.

Juneau also may deserve credit for having been the site of the shooting of Dan McGrew, the subject of Robert Service's most famous poem. Although most people associate the poem with Dawson, an account of the events taking place in Juneau was supplied by Dr. Leonard S. Sugden of New York, a "surgeon, mining engineer, and motion picture man," in an interview he gave the *Seattle Post Intelligencer* while visiting Juneau in 1923.

"I happened into one of the leading saloons and gambling joints in Juneau in 1897 at the beginning of the Klondike rush. Dan McGrew, one of the most prominent gamblers of the camp, was dealing faro, while Lou watched the game as his 'capper,' [someone who helps players mark their bets with a coin-like copper cap]," Dr. Sugden recalled. "The door opened and a tall stranger with matted beard and bare at the throat came in the door. He was a striking figure of a man."

Dr. Sugden's version much resembles Robert Service's. The stranger ordered a couple of rounds of drinks and noted the "Rag Time Kid" was at the bar, so he sat down on the Kid's piano stool and gave a wonderful concert. "The rattle of chips ceased and he held the crowd spellbound," Dr. Sugden recounted. "He ran the gamut from the classics to rag and ended with a wild and crashing Russian overture."

Then, true to Robert Service, the stranger sprang from his stool and faced the crowd. "There's a dirty hound from hell in this crowd and I came here tonight to kill him," he declared, looking squarely in the eyes of Dan McGrew, who quietly drew his revolver. The bartender, accustomed to gunplay, turned out the lights to ruin the aim of the combatants. Both McGrew and the stranger died in the shoot-out that followed, and Dr. Sugden recalled seeing "the lady that was known as Lou" take a poke of gold dust from the pocket of the stranger, just as the lights flashed on.

Carlton Fichett, reporting the doctor's recollections, assured readers that both Dan McGrew and the man who shot him were members of "prominent Back Bay families in Boston before they became bad men of the north." And he also insisted that "Lou" married and became a respectable housewife shortly thereafter.[14]

It's hard to judge the authenticity of Dr. Sugden's story. A conflicting version claims that Lou was actually Lulu Eads, a gorgeous good time girl (but *never* a housewife) who married Murray Eads, one of Dawson's most enduring dance hall owners.[15] Dan McGrew owned no mining property in Yukon Territory and is not listed in the city directories, but that would be in keeping with his mysterious past. No accounts of the shooting have been found in Juneau or Dawson papers. While the omission would have been strange in Dawson, where rival journalists were thorough in their coverage, it wouldn't have been surprising for Juneau's press, which usually ignored the demimonde. So there may have been merit in Dr. Sugden's account.

Despite Juneau's bad reputation, at times it paled in comparison to those of Wrangell and Skagway. Sam Steele of the Canadian Northwest Mounted Police, who stopped in Wrangell at the beginning of the Klondike rush in February of 1898, when about 5,000 stampeders camped there, called it a "mean, squalid spot, with the usual number of gambling dens and other low dives frequented by tough-looking characters."[16]

"Woe to the stampeder who paused at Wrangell!" wrote Klondike historian Pierre Berton, who interviewed many of the survivors. "Robberies were frequent, and guns popped in the streets at night. Women cavorted nude for high fees in the dance halls, and even the sanctity of the courtroom was not immune to gunplay. In February a whisky dealer on trial for illicit sales took umbrage at the evidence of a prosecution witness, drew his revolver, and shot him as he testified."[17]

Wyatt Earp, the famed Arizona gunman, called it a "Hell on Wheels," and his wife, Josie, sized it up as another "Tombstone" when they stopped there briefly. The U.S. marshal for Alaska offered Wyatt the job of deputy, which he declined, although he did fill in for a few days until another gunman could be found.[18]

Part of the problem was that Wrangell had been invaded by the gang of Jefferson Davis "Soapy" Smith, a promising criminal from the days of the Colorado gold rush who had matured into a master organizer. However, for his real base of operations Soapy wisely picked Skagway, at the mouth of the White Pass. The most prosperous of the American boomtowns during the Klondike excitement, it had 15,000 stampeders,

JEFFERSON DAVIS "SOAPY" SMITH
At the height of his power he controlled Skagway, the booming gateway to the Klondike.
Eventually his reputation as a thief and murderer caught up with him, but not before he had his
mistress murdered and made a fortune from stampeders unaware of his frightful reputation.
ASL, Early Prints of Alaska Collection, Larss & Duclos photograph, #01-1976.

sixty-one saloons, as many gambling dens, and more than a hundred prostitutes. Famous performers like Lilly Langtree, John L. Sullivan, Little Egypt, and Calamity Jane played in its theaters. In the winter of 1898-90, city fathers collected $90,000 in saloon license fees alone, but they didn't reinvest in honest law enforcement. Sam Steele, on a brief visit, was astonished when bullets from a gunfight whizzed through the thin boards of his cabin, but "the circumstance was such a common event that we did not even rise from our beds," he noted.[19]

"Soapy" Smith and his gang of about one hundred worked out of a modest bar called Smith's Parlor, rigging gambling tables, running crooked shell games, and operating a phony telegraph station and a guide service designed to relieve wealthy stampeders of their pokes. They had no qualms whatsoever about adding murder to the list.[20]

One of Smith's coldest executions was the strangulation of his mistress, Ella Wilson, age twenty-eight, a beautiful mulatto singer-turned-prostitute of whom the gang leader had tired. Although her robbery-murder caused

LITTLE EGYPT
Fahruda Manzar, famed "Little Egypt" of the Chicago World's Fair,
was among the well-known performers attracted to Skagway during the gold rush.
Later she appeared in Dawson, where local police made her wear a less
revealing costume than her theater posters displayed.

YA, National Museum of Canada Collection, #816.

little stir at the time, visiting Denver madam Mattie Silks overheard through the thin walls of her hotel room an argument between Soapy and his gang about how to divide the $3,800 they had taken from Ella. Mattie was herself a member of the underworld and had few qualms about murder and robbery, but when she heard her name come up as possibly the gang's next victim, the madam fled.[21] Although Ella Wilson had been murdered on May 28, 1898, an inquest was not held until after Soapy Smith was gunned down by Frank Reid in a shoot-out that killed them both the following July.[22]

—⚬⚬⚬—

Replacing Soapy was a more conservative community leader, Frank Keelar, who dealt in loans and investments and was a powerful member of the city council. The colorful businessman referred to himself as "Colonel Keelar, the Money King of Alaska," and boasted in his pawnshop advertisements that he owned a steam yacht, a mine, and a $3,000 sled dog team. He had come from Oakland, California, in 1898, and established his family in a plush suite of the Hotel Mondamin, one of Skagway's finest hostelries. With them he brought a well-educated adopted son, J. Kuta Sangi, age sixteen, who called himself a civil engineer but also served as Frank's servant. Just what other ties the "Money King" had with Japan remains uncertain, but an unusually large number of Japanese prostitutes worked in Skagway—enough so they had their own district called "Jap Alley" or "Yokohama Row." Frank Keelar was quick to defend them.[23]

"Several Japanese women arrived in the city lately. This is not stated as a YMCA note," the local paper observed. "Skagway should be entitled to a mark on the credit side of the column if every Jap woman in town was shipped out. To fill out a cargo, there are several dozen other females that should be sent out with them. Prostitution and mangy dogs are too common in this particular section of the broad white north. Let us have less of both social evils."[24]

One of these women was probably Yamada Waka, who had come from farm country near Yokohama to America to escape a wretched marriage and earn money to support her parents.[25] An illegal immigrant speaking no English, Waka was kidnapped, forced to work in brothels in Seattle, and briefly brought north through a Japanese syndicate that specialized in providing fresh faces for Southeastern Alaska.[26]

Eventually the beautiful, doe-eyed girl escaped to a Presbyterian mission in San Francisco, where she was sent to school and married her teacher.[27] Returning to Japan, Waka became one of its leading feminists. Bright and charming, she was later sent on a goodwill tour of the United States where she met First Lady Eleanor Roosevelt and other luminaries.[28]

However, most respectable Skagway residents were too unnerved by the foreign red light district to evaluate its tenants on an individual basis, or even notice their suffering. Yokohama Row was on the route their children took to school, and the city council was called upon to investigate the "social evil." Frank Keelar argued eloquently and without a trace of logic that moving the girls to a restricted district "would hurt the town." He complained that the Japanese row had been specifically targeted even though Skagway had prostitutes of many races, and made it clear he personally was a "friend of the fallen women, the drunks, the poor, etc."[29]

Despite Frank Keelar's resistence, the Japanese women were given fifteen days to find a better location or leave town. They settled on Seventh Avenue, where white prostitutes also resided, and that seems to have ended the racial tension. By 1908 Skagway had more than thirty Japanese residents, including six wives, two of whom were college graduates.[30]

Neighboring Dyea, at the mouth of famed Chilkoot Pass, was a lively transit point for about 13,000 stampeders. "Dance halls and saloons were going full blast," noted Ed Lung in his memoirs of his 1898 visit. "Yes, Dyea was a typical gold rush town . . . even to its prostitutes, gamblers, and 'sure thing' men! But it didn't have the sinister atmosphere of Skagway. . . .

"I was hoping for a restful sleep that night of the 23rd [of May], as I was leaving the following morning to tackle the big climb up Chilkoot. But, great Scott! It did not turn out that way! There was too much commotion going on in the next room and the thin partitions were like sounding boards. How many visitors that 'daughter of joy' had during the night, I lost count! But, at close intervals, the squeaky door would open, there would be stealthy footsteps going down the hall and, in a moment, more stealthy footsteps creaking up the hall and a woman's hoarse, grating voice called, 'next!'"[31]

Prospectors from remote Klondike mines seeking a quiet place to spend the winter sometimes chose Tenakee, an out-of-the-way resort by lovely hot springs. In its best years the little Southeastern settlement boasted only one dance hall, so it was the custom for bachelor miners to hire a prostitute for the season, discreetly referred to as a "winter bride." This worked well as long as the girls did not attempt to mix with respectable women, but when two of the pros sneaked into a high-society masked ball, the town was scandalized.[32]

Valdez was a busy gold rush gateway in Southcentral Alaska, but its population was so transient that the names of its good time girls were seldom recorded. One exception was Tessie LeRoy, a.k.a. Tillie LeRoi, who ran a lively house there, backed a number of miners, and was involved in several robberies and lawsuits. Testimony to her enduring charms is said to have been engraved on her tombstone: "Tessie LeRoy, the Mucker's Dream."[33]

Cordova, also on the coast, saw even more action as a transportation center for the prosperous, copper-rich region. "At one point there were over 30,000 miners in the area, so there was definite need for sexual activity on a large scale . . . the largest group of whores ever in Alaska was when the Kennecott Copper mining operation was in full bore just north," recalled Homer S. Thompson, whose family was based there. "The houses of prostitution were many to house the 3,000 prostitutes that made their home in Cordova. Most of the houses were three-story buildings, ranging from one level on the main street to the third level at the street above and north of the main drag. . . . Many of the town's leading citizens in the 1960s were descendants of the miners and prostitutes coupling."

Thompson's figures may sound overblown, but James Wickersham noted with concern in 1921 that the largest houses of prostitution in Alaska were in Cordova, believing at least one to be the investment of George Cheever Hazelet, one of the most respected city fathers.[34]

———— ⬥⬥⬥ ————

By the 1910s, gold production in Alaska's interior was declining, eliminating the usefulness of southern ports as gateways for the stampeders. But by then Alaska's fishing fleets had grown until they merited red light districts, the most famous of which was in Ketchikan.

Called Creek Street, "the only place in the world where both the fish and the fishermen go upstream to spawn," the red light district was built on pilings edging Ketchikan Creek. Its "sporting women" were required to screen their windows to prevent drunken revelers from putting their fists through the glass, or falling out and becoming "floaters," thus catching the attention of the marshal. Since Ketchikan was the first American port of

call north of Canada, and a major supply point, there were usually plenty of revelers . . . enough to support twelve two-story whorehouses by 1917 and expansion in later years.[35]

KGBU, Ketchikan's first radio station, was established by Roy R. Thornton from one of these houses to inform listeners when the rumrunners were due in town.[36] Other public services of the restricted district are not recorded, but by 1925 it was so notorious that James Wickersham referred to it as "Alaska's Tenderloin" and "the Barbary Coast of the North."[37]

There was little or no gambling, but everything else. Some girls advertised by posing nude in the windows behind lace curtains, while

CREEK STREET

The red light district of Ketchikan was built on pilings out over the bay.
Old-timers used to joke that it was where the fishermen and the salmon both went to spawn.

Courtesy of David Nichols, THS #90.1.10.5.

others loitered semi-clad in doorways, calling, "Come on in, daddy!" to customers who showed interest.[38]

The most famous tenant was Dolly Arthur, a.k.a. Thelma Dolly Copland, a buxom blonde with an impish smile, who left McCall, Idaho, at age thirteen in 1901 and entered the trade five years later in Vancouver,

YAMADA WAKA WITH HER HUSBAND
*A Japanese woman trapped in the trade by unscrupulous brothel owners in Seattle,
apparently she was sent briefly to Southeastern on a routine red light circuit. Finally she escaped to
San Francisco, finding haven at a Presbyterian mission. After being educated in America
and marrying her teacher, Yamada Kakichi, she returned to Japan, where she
became one of the leading feminists of her day, but she never forgot her roots.*

Courtesy of Yaheiji Yamada.

B. C. In 1914 she moved to Juneau but left after only two weeks because she didn't care for its cramped cribs. After brief tenure at the Star, a major whorehouse in Petersburg, Dolly was flush enough to build her own house in Ketchikan and two years later she bought a better one, #24 Creek Street, from a schoolteacher who had drifted into the trade and later ended up in the madhouse.[39]

The money was so good, Dolly decided to stay. "I like it here because the men come in bunches . . . crews of five to fifteen men off the fishing boats," she explained.[40] And she remained until her death in 1956, working steadily through the '30s and the '40s and intermittently thereafter.

Also popular was "Black Mary," the woman for whom Dolly had worked in Petersburg, who later operated the Black Pearl in Ketchikan. Mary was known for running a good house, usually with six or seven girls, but it was during a big Petersburg fire that she won the undying gratitude of its citizens. When firemen discovered that the local stream was too low for pumping, Mary—a mountain of a woman—shed her clothes on the spot and sat in the creek, damming it so that firefighters could extinguish the blaze.[41] Like Dolly, Mary retired only late in life. She died peacefully, sitting in a chair near her window, with a roll of greenbacks in her hands, still counting.[42]

15

Tough Times in Fairbanks

MARRIAGES AND MIGRATIONS

⊸∞⊷

In 1909 E. T. Barnette quietly decided to leave Fairbanks for good, which did not bode well for the town he had founded. Had the news been public, few would have thought much of it, however. After all, it was a peak year. The mining camp had survived crippling labor disputes in 1908 to top all records in gold production—$10.5 million that season. With its population at about 9,320, also an all-time high, Fairbanks was easily the biggest and most important city in Alaska Territory. The town boasted 400 telephones, a good library, two hospitals, five churches, twelve hotels, and fifteen saloons.[1] Property values were soaring, especially in the red light district.[2]

But Barnette realized the boom could not last. New gold discoveries had become rare, and that year's record production marked the end of most easy-to-mine reserves. The bulk of what remained—and no miner knew how much that was—would require modern equipment and vast capital to extract it from depths of eighty to ninety feet.

Barnette also had personal reasons for leaving. A lawsuit brought by an early backer he had neglected to repay compromised him not only financially but socially, for testimony exposed that Barnette had been jailed in

⊸∞⊷

THE "GIRLS"

Although not all of the prostitutes in the Fairbanks red light district were . . .
especially in later years, when the average age was over forty and some were into their sixties.
This shot, taken on Fourth Avenue, shows the fence (behind the women) that
surrounded the restricted district. The uncaptioned picture was found attached
to the back of a photo of Fairbanks gold discoverer Felix Pedro.

Courtesy of Bill Williams, Gold Rush Saloon.

Oregon for stealing $2,300 from a partner. Secretly Barnette submitted his resignation as president of the Washington-Alaska Bank, a near-monopoly he had created by allegedly purchasing the Washington-Alaska with its own money and merging it with his faltering Fairbanks Banking Company. Later it would be charged that Barnette had withdrawn at least $731,000 from it to invest in California and Mexican properties.[3]

The failure of Barnette's bank in January of 1911 caused losses of about $1 million for Fairbanks citizens. Some miners were so unnerved by the event that they ceased to trust any bank and preferred to leave their gold in the safekeeping of prostitutes they trusted, but that was just the beginning of hard times. Gold production dropped more than 50 percent to $4.5 million, while the cost of living skyrocketed. Fairbanks depended on firewood to heat its homes, run its stern-wheelers, and produce steam for thawing frozen mining grounds. Once the easily accessible timber was gone, wood prices increased rapidly.[4] So did rentals and the cost of property in the red light district.

World War I cost Alaska 20 percent of its population, but 75 percent of those who served were from Fairbanks.[5] By 1920 the town had only 1,155 residents and, although still the largest settlement in the territory, Fairbanks suffered a major economic slump.[6]

⸻

A surprising number of prostitutes overcame these bad economic odds by retiring to married life, although love also was often a major factor in their deserting the demimonde. One of the most successful matches was that of Delia Dunham, a doll of a woman with a flawless, porcelain-hued complexion who had performed with a legitimate theater company in Dawson before moving to a more lucrative industry. Apparently she worked the Fairbanks Line only briefly before marrying Frank Dunham, the local druggist, whom she utterly adored and treated like a prince. And the devotion was mutual.

Frank set Delia up in a lovely little house surrounded by a white picket fence and, when their fortunes improved, presented her with a new Buick which she named "the Duchess." Delia proved a remarkable housekeeper, mopping the garage floor and installing bath mats to protect the floor of her Buick. She was also a meticulous gardener, volunteering to keep the grounds at the public library as well as her own fine flowerbeds. Delia's lovely voice made her a favorite to sing at weddings and funerals, even

A FLORADORA GIRL

Delia, who worked in Dawson as a Floradora girl and briefly on the Fairbanks Line,
married Frank Dunham, a much-respected local druggist, and settled in to become an excellent
wife and housekeeper. She also kept the gardens at the public library next door (background)
and was in demand to sing at weddings and funerals when she was well up in years.

UAF, Albert Johnson Collection, #89-166-223.

when she was in her eighties, and everybody knew her through her work at Frank's Red Cross Drug Store.[7]

Lillian Liehman, another pioneering good time girl who owned property in the restricted district, married Otto Liehman, a respected banker.[8] Kitty O'Brien, one of the Line's most adored tenants, quit to marry Tommy Carr, who worked for the Highway Commission. She later established the Far North Taxi Service, the town's one and only, which proved highly successful.[9] And the mayor, the highway commissioner, and numerous other prominent citizens also married graduates of the red light district.

Not all Line matches were successful, of course. Saddest was the story of Rose Tiffany. The San Francisco press had nicknamed her the "Sweet Pea Girl" because, while attending the trial of murderer Theodore Durrant, she always wore a cluster of sweet peas. She had arrived in Fairbanks with a slightly tarnished reputation from Nome, and while working out of a dance hall had fallen in love with Charley Bechtol, a wealthy young miner.

After their marriage, Charley's father, John "Bishop" Bechtol—a well-known bartender from Dawson who had struck it rich with his son—succeeded in breaking up the couple. The Bechtols' strike on Cleary Creek was one of the biggest in the region, and he was determined to buy the family's way into polite society in Los Angeles. Rose tried to sue "the Bishop" for $40,000 for alienating her husband's affections, but the dance hall girl never had a chance against the staid millionaire.

Years rolled by, and people forgot about the Sweet Pea Girl. Then, while in Juneau, a former Fairbanks resident noticed a strange, quiet woman making daily pilgrimages to inquire for mail, wearing a robe apparently made of curtain material. Although she was old beyond her years, he recognized Rose Tiffany Bechtol and tried to help her. Unfortunately, the Sweet Pea Girl's mind had played out, and she was sent to Morningside, the territorial mental institution.[10]

The suicide of Lola Downing, about age thirty-five, following the death of her husband of one year, was covered dramatically by the *Fairbanks Sunday Times* in the spring of 1913. "When found by her neighbor, Rose, who heard the report of the shot and investigated, the girl was stretched on her couch, garbed in a flowing gown of her kind, with blood trickling from the corner of her mouth down her cheek to stain in crimson the linen of the pillow. A revolver was grasped in her right hand with the grip of death, the weapon resting on a lifeless bosom." Lola had married just before coming north and apparently had worked on the Fairbanks Line to improve the family fortunes. Earlier that week she had complained about the lack of business, and the news of her husband's death in Los Angeles must have destroyed any hope she might have harbored.[11]

Presbyterian preacher S. Hall Young recalled helping many prostitutes go respectable, but he was also tolerant of those who tried and failed, because he knew how tough the transition could be. "I had a dog team given me by a woman of not unspotted reputation for whom I performed a wedding service in Fairbanks, but who had left that husband, and what Christ said of the woman of Samaria was true of her: 'He whom thou has is not thy husband,'" Rev. Young noted in his autobiography. "But she had a dog team, five puppies of one litter, which she had brought up from 'puppyhood,' trained to be a fine team and could no longer take care of them so she decided to give them to me saying, 'As I am not good myself, I wish my dogs to be of some good.'"[12]

Hulda Ford, the wealthiest woman in Fairbanks, was wrongly rumored to have been a graduate of its Line, but she had been a prostitute in Dawson and her story is also one of failed respectability. Old-timers recall first seeing Hulda as an outstandingly beautiful member of the Dawson demimonde, with a fine-boned face and a fabulous wardrobe. Later she joined the Nome stampede, taking time out to visit Spokane, where she fell in love with Sheldon Ford, who deserted her shortly after their wedding. Returning to Nome, Hulda opened a respectable hotel with a sign old-timers still chuckle over: "Horses and dogs boarded here."

Toward the end of the Nome stampede, Hulda became engaged to a young man who agreed to check out the new gold camp of Fairbanks, where she hoped to build another hotel. In 1906 she gave him money, closed her business in Nome, and arrived in Fairbanks to discover that her intended had squandered her capital and done nothing about building the hotel. From then on Hulda would have nothing to do with him—or any other human being—on a personal basis.

Hulda had a gift for finances and, investing in Fairbanks property, she became quite wealthy. In later years she dressed in rags, rifled garbage pails, and lived as a reclusive pack rat with hordes of cats which she fed better than herself.[13] But she was still well-spoken and astute, and she hammered out a successful working relationship with Austin "Cap" Lathrop, the town's only millionaire, who always spoke well of her and sometimes partnered with her to finance property.

Not that Hulda needed mollycoddling. When one of Fairbanks's leading matrons asked why she stooped to going through garbage pails, Hulda answered, "For the money . . . and I can remember when you had a price tag on your butt!"[14]

Margaret Murie, who moved to Fairbanks during its pioneer days, described it as two towns "with the 'proper' and the 'improper' lives constantly mingling." However, girls who went respectable were seldom allowed to forget their origins.[15]

One exception was well-brought-up Anna May Eisenberg, who was forced into the demimonde through a nasty twist of fate. She was rumored to have come from a large Eastern European family with five daughters, which sent one girl to America each year as they could afford the fare, hoping to give them better lives. All the daughters married well except Anna, whose care, unbeknownst to her parents, fell to unscrupulous Seattle people who forced her to work under unsavory circumstances.[16]

ANNA MAY GIBSON

Her unusual beauty caught the eye of Tom Gibson, a confirmed Fairbanks bachelor, and he rescued her from the bright lights of Seattle and an unfortunate past. Her charm and basic innocence were such that she was completely accepted in Fairbanks society.

UAF, Thomas Gibson Collection, #78-76-41N.

Shortly thereafter, Anna met handsome Tom Gibson, who earned his living as a professional hunter for the gold camps and had traveled to Seattle to care for his dying mother.

Tom, age twenty-seven, was a confirmed bachelor. In 1908, a year before he met Anna May, an aunt had inquired if he ever intended to marry. "Well! I had not thought of such a thing, and have no *idea* of such a *terrible* thing at present. No! No!" he replied with astonishment. "Lots of young married ladies have had experience and therefore know how to entertain a friend, so no wedding bells for me."[17]

But tiny Anna May was as bright as she was beautiful, with huge dark eyes, curly dark hair, and hourglass figure with much of the sand at the top. Despite the rotten lot life had handed her, she was fun. Tom went home to Alaska but, unable to forget her, returned for her the next year, making one of Fairbanks's most envied marriages. Anna May encouraged him in his new business, the Gibson Auto Stage Line; at racing his Gibson-improved automobiles; and at riverboating, a hobby he loved.[18] The marriage lasted until Tom's death more than fifty years later, and because of it the town and its most respectable organizations, including the Rebecca Lodge and the Pioneers, completely accepted her.[19]

Women who decided to stay in the trade during the fifteen years that followed Barnette's bank failure found it tough going in Fairbanks. The number of occupied houses on the Line dwindled from fifty in its glory days to fifteen by 1920.[20] George Akimoto, the district's major land owner, had sold out gradually as backing for an anti-Japanese immigration law increased in the States. His name appeared for the final time in the Fairbanks Polk Directory of 1915-1916. In 1919 he sold the last of his property and disappeared from Alaska record as quietly as he had materialized, leaving a small box of possessions—including the marvelous photos of the Line he had commissioned in 1906—with his friend Charles Thompson.[21] Many of the "sporting women" joined the miners on new gold rushes to Ruby, Iditarod, Innoko, Livengood, Wiseman, and Flat. These secondary mining stampedes in the Interior, however, were small and short-lived, as were the resulting red light districts.

In his book on Wiseman, naturalist Robert Marshall noted an interesting correlation between gold production and the number of prostitutes in camp. When Wiseman produced $200,000 in 1902, ten prostitutes were in residence, but the number dropped to seven at the camp's early peak of $301,000 in 1903 and to zero the next year when mining proceeds totaled $200,000. Nine girls moved into camp in 1913 when production took an upswing to $216,000, but their number dropped to eight a year later when production reached an all-time high of $368,000. One might guess that once the men hit pay dirt they were too busy "cleaning up" to party.

Mining veterans estimated that at least half the money taken out of the ground went for booze and prostitutes. Two miners spent $1,500 in one night on champagne. John Bowman squandered between $10,000 and $11,000 on a single prostitute in a two-week period—which took some doing when the going price for one night was twenty dollars.[22]

"It's this way. When a fellow gets out on the creeks, he's so busy and has so much to be thinking about all the time that he doesn't have much chance to worry about women, especially with all the hard physical labor involved," an old-timer told Marshall. "It's only when a man's mind hasn't got anything to occupy it and his body's got nothing to get it tired that he can't get along without women. Of course, when you see them all the time and have a dance to flirt with them, that's different."[23]

Surprisingly, this remote camp produced the most grisly murders in the region's history, those of John Holmberg and "Dutch" Marie Schmidt. John had come to the Klondike in 1897, prospecting without much success until he hit Hammond River in the Wiseman area.[24] Marie had pioneered in Rampart and was well-known in Fairbanks and Circle Hot Springs, where she had twice made the papers when someone beat her up and stole from her.[25] By 1914, however, she was a wealthy woman a bit past her prime for the trade, and when John suggested they marry, she agreed.[26]

They left Wiseman in the late fall of 1914 on a small boat called the *Sea Pup*, owned by Thomas Johnson, a.k.a. the "Blueberry Kid." After they stopped in Bettles, the couple simply disappeared. This was no small feat, for John, though only five-foot-five, weighed 200 pounds, and Marie was an attractive white woman in a country where they were rare.[27] In August of that year, Natives found a badly decomposed body believed to be Dutch Marie's.[28] The following July, investigating lawmen located human bones and spectacles thought to have belonged to John, along with a woman's wig, hair rat, veil, and overshoes that could have been Marie's. The Blueberry Kid had arrived in Seattle with more money than usual, but he, too, disappeared. The mystery was never solved.[29]

For the most part, the remote camps were relatively safe and often

A JEWEL OF A WHOREHOUSE

*Ester Duffy, a veteran madam from Dawson, shown (left) with one of her girls, went broke
in Fort Gibbon, then moved to the new boomtown of Berry outside Fairbanks where
she established a successful hotel. What else she established is not known, but eventually
the town was renamed in her honor and is still very much on the map.*

ASL, Wickersham Collection, PCA 277-1-198.

became tight little communities where working girls found considerable
acceptance. The Pretzel Dance, thrown annually by prostitutes in Iditarod,
became a tradition enjoyed by the whole town.[30] And when that stampede
died, most of the community relocated to nearby Flat, where they carried
on much the same.

"Tootsie," a black woman whose real name was Mattie Crosby, began
her Alaskan career running a whorehouse "disguised" as a bathhouse and
laundry at Iditarod. She and most of the community later moved to Flat,
where she became a valued citizen as a restaurant owner and bootlegger.
She had come to the country as a personal maid, but did very well on her
own, eventually retiring to the Pioneer Home in Sitka to write an autobiography (since lost) titled *Everybody Knows Tootsie!*[31]

Ester City, outside Fairbanks, was named in honor of prostitute Ester
Duffy,[32] who was long famous for charming high-rollers. She had accompanied pioneers to Circle City, where she established a reputation for
good-heartedness and generosity.[33] Billy Chappell, one of Dawson's most
successful miners (who eventually made millions by investing in Seattle's

red light district), gave her a piano for the opening of a whorehouse called the Jewel, which she started near the American Army post of Fort Gibbon. Somehow Ester went broke there, but she sold the piano to prostitute Babe Wallace for $1,000 for another stake,[34] following Clarence and Frank Berry to a new camp. Clarence Berry, perhaps the Klondike's most successful miner, was happily married but his brother, Frank, may have been the reason Ester established her California Hotel there. The town, originally named Berry, was re-christened in Ester's honor for reasons better left unresearched.

Livengood, the last of the gold-mining stampedes, was too small to support a restricted district, but lives in legend thanks to several of its unique citizens. Dan McCarty, who had helped E. T. Barnette found Fairbanks and eventually struck pay dirt there, married a prostitute in Livengood whom he later angered to the point that she shot him fatally. Known as "Gentleman Dan," he battled the wounds for some time, which gave him a chance to think over the assault. Knowing well his wife's notorious temper, Dan came to the conclusion that he'd simply committed suicide by angering her, so he made sure all charges against her were dropped before he breathed his last.[35]

But the favorite Livengood legend is about Grace Lowe, a tall, slender, good-looking woman—but tough as nails—who ran a large-scale mining operation. Once, when no prostitutes were in camp, her workmen announced that they wished to go into Fairbanks to visit the Line. It was an all-day trip and Grace, not wanting to stop production, agreed to take them on herself, in a most professional manner. Grace often drove heavy equipment topless during hot weather and, although she was by no means an experienced prostitute, her crew did not hold her amateur standing against her. Everyone was happy until the following payday, when each miner who had enjoyed her services discovered that fifty dollars had been deducted from his wages.[36]

—⧉—

When the mining stampedes gave out, the demimonde focused on other industries, following the railroad builders to Cordova and Tiekel, about forty miles northeast of Valdez. Now a ghost town, Tiekel originally boomed as a Signal Corps station in 1902 and became even more lucrative in 1908 as 3,000 men were moved there to build the Copper River line.[37]

Once the Copper River boom was over, attention turned to Anchorage, established as the headquarters for the Alaska Railroad in 1913. Prostitutes were not permitted to bid on land within the new town site, so they "squatted," first at the mouth of Ship's Creek, then on both sides of a dead-end thoroughfare near Ninth and C Streets.

City planners were appalled. The town site had been withdrawn from the Chugach National Forest and was controlled by a board made up of Lieutenant Fred Mears of the Alaska Engineering Commission, A. Christensen of the U.S. General Land Office, and T. M. Hunt, Supervisor of the U.S. Forest Service. These three argued fiercely about how to dispose of the girls. Supervisor Hunt was emphatic that *under no circumstances* should the prostitutes be allowed to occupy national forest lands, but while he was "absent in another part of the forest," Christensen quietly contacted the marshal and moved the whores over the city border into virgin timberland.

Hunt was outraged. Now he was required by law to issue "camping permits" to each woman, and he complained to his boss that this made the Forest Service look bad. Eventually he talked the planners into offering a free camping area within the town, and the prostitutes happily returned to Ninth and C. Then Hunt discovered to his horror that even though the prostitutes were back within the city, the Forest Service was still responsible for them under its administrative rules. And—worse yet—the women appeared to be settling permanently in the "camping area."

On January 6, 1917, Assistant District Forester Charles Flory wrote a desperate letter marked "Strictly Confidential" to his boss, the district forester. Whorehouses costing as much as $3,000 were being built in the new Anchorage red light district on lots distributed to the prostitutes through a quietly held drawing. "Practically all the women have their own individual house, or crib, located on a lot specifically assigned to her. The houses are all small one-story frame two- or three-room affairs, with the exception of one large two-story log house . . ." he reported.

"Who its present sponsors are I was unable to learn. I did observe, however, that it is a lucrative source of income to a number of the principal merchants of the town. The items of fuel, groceries, laundry, restaurant meals, jitney hire, clothing, furniture is no doubt very large. The women are notoriously good buyers and spend their money freely."[38]

Flory recommended that the Forest Service relinquish all administrative power over Anchorage. Bureaucrats in D.C. were hesitant, but eventually

CAMPING PERMITS REQUIRED

The early red light district for Anchorage was located in the Chugach National Forest,
and its tenants were required to obtain camping permits from the Forest Service. Later the women
set up camp in town and the Forest Service bowed out of its responsibilities to them.

NAPA, RB 95 Box 46 Alaska Region Tongass, Stikine and Chugach National Forests, Special Use Permits.

the embarrassment of running a red light district was too much for them and they relinquished their seat on the town's governing board. Thus Anchorage city fathers had the good time girls to thank for their freedom from federal meddling, and continued to treat them with respect.[39]

If any reminders were needed, they probably came from a talented black prostitute named Zula Swanson, who arrived from Portland, Oregon, about a decade later to make the Anchorage red light district her own. Born in Jackson Gap, Alabama, in 1891, the graceful, fresh-looking beauty had done well enough in the skin trade to bring north considerable capital. Her pimp had been jailed in Washington State for bootlegging and, although she still sent him money, she had no plans to return, for she had narrowly escaped drunk-driving charges there involving the death of another woman.

Investing wisely, perhaps with the help of one of the town's most respectable financiers who became her lover, Zula soon owned more property than any other woman in town. Eventually, through her heavy holdings in the red light district and her lover's political clout, she amassed considerable power. Although his death in the 1950s was devastating to her, Zula continued to do well.[40] She also became respected locally, becoming a member of the Northern Lights Civic and Social Club and the

ZULA SWANSON

The most famous madam in Anchorage, Zula embarked on a lasting affair with one of
Alaska's most prominent businessmen. With his help and political clout, she managed to avoid
most brushes with the law and survived him to make a fortune on her own. In later years
she was as civic-minded as she was charming and became well-respected in her community.

AMHA #B77.104.1.

#95.

TEIKHELL ROADHOUSE

Daughters of the Elks, and helping organize the Anchorage chapter of the National Association for the Advancement of Colored People. In 1971 she wed a man named Bill Wester, a few decades her junior, and went into semi-retirement as a housewife at the age of eighty.[41]

⁂

Soon after the federal government decided to leave Anchorage alone, moralists in Fairbanks—waiting since 1914, when their plans to do away with the restricted district failed—found it a perfect time to strike again. The Women's Christian Temperance League, on the verge of gaining

TIEKEL ROADHOUSE

Working girls flocked to the Tiekel area near Valdez along with several thousand men who were
stationed there to build a railroad. Much has been said about the romance of Alaska roadhouses,
but living conditions were not exactly plush and prostitutes there really earned their money.

AMHA #B93.18.94.

federal ratification for prohibition, had gained enormous strength nationally and even more in Alaska, where it pushed through a "Bone Dry" law in 1916. With the backing of this group and many other citizens, the federal government moved on the Line. The zealous Cecil H. Clegg—previously fired as assistant district attorney—was back as a newly appointed federal judge. He and a tenderfoot district attorney, Julien Hurley, initiated "abatement action" in 1922. This time simple arrest wasn't enough. Federal prosecutors confiscated the prostitutes' homes and furniture without any regard for their constitutional rights.

At first the only protest came from W. F. Thompson, the liberal editor of the *Fairbanks Daily News-Miner*, who had been in Fairbanks almost since its founding and believed in its original "live and let live" philosophy.

"At its last meeting the City Council, urged thereto by the Federal Bunch . . . the City Dads solemnly ordered the Scarlet Women of Our Town (who are of every color and shade other than scarlet) to go right away from where they are and squat somewhere else again in our town, and 'The Girls' are much perturbed," he reported at the beginning of a series of sarcastic editorials. ". . . We would advise them to purchase interests in bathhouses, rooming houses, cigar stores, cabarets and laundries, as they do in Anchorage and other Alaskan towns, thereby gaining better locations, advertise and go into business wholesale-like, or buy a cabin next door to YOU or ME, raise their prices to suit their needs and 'live private.'"[42]

Many prostitutes took his advice, setting up shop in respectable residential neighborhoods. Some escaped to Anchorage or Seward, where the new government railroad was being built. Two sought sanctuary in the insane asylum, and two moved to Juneau.[43] Mrs. Evelyn Courtney committed suicide, leaving a sad but conscientious little note.

"I have given life a fair trial and I want no more of it. To think that one has lived for twenty-eight years and has made no better showing than I have," she lamented. "I am sure the world is better off to be rid of such failures. It seems to me that if people can't make a success of life before that age it is too late to start again.

"I have lost that which is all that a woman has, and that is the respect of people, and whenever that is gone, how can one ever redeem oneself? Many people err in life and I am sorry that this will reflect on one of my best friends—the person who loaned me this gun, and I wish it understood that I lied to obtain possession of it . . . I ask that this person be absolved from all blame. If people were more tolerant of others' shortcomings there would be more happiness in this world.

"Signed EVELYN COURTNEY."[44]

The battle over the restricted district became so bitter and the town's indignation so strong that in September of that year, moralists sabotaged Thompson's press, causing him such a financial loss that he was forced to reorganize and seek new capital.[45] Still he editorialized, noting that the prostitutes had scattered so that it was difficult to police them and reminding readers of the grisly murder of Alice Astor, which had caused the Line to be reorganized in 1914.[46]

Finally, following hearings in February of 1923 during which seventy witnesses were examined, public opinion began to turn. It became obvious, even to those morally opposed to prostitution, that taking private property without compensation was unconstitutional, and that it was difficult to control red light operations when houses were scattered throughout the town. The grand jury recommended that Fairbanks prostitutes be "kept together under police protection and observation."[47] But federal officials continued to prosecute, oblivious to the fact that they were playing a losing game.

Federal funding for a railroad from Fairbanks to the coast was not only boosting the economy with a temporary building boom, but promised to cut the high cost of living by drastically reducing shipping and transportation costs. Again men heavily outnumbered women, and the argument that prostitution was a "necessary evil" became more valid. The "abatement" suits dragged on for three years as convictions were stalled by clever defense lawyers.[48]

By 1926 citizens had grown so disgusted with the proceedings that Charles Thompson, the Line's heaviest financial backer, actually ran for city council and won. And W. F. Thompson, not related to Charles Thompson but a close friend, continued his strong editorials favoring the restricted district, even though he was dying by inches from cancer.

A few months earlier city council members had met with Attorney General Hurley, who assured them he intended to go through with each individual abatement case and also pursue any luckless prostitute who moved to another location in Fairbanks.[49] Most of the women he'd originally charged were found guilty, were fined five dollars, and their homes were closed for a year. But public opinion grew so strong against Hurley that he finally abandoned his campaign to prosecute prostitutes.

On January 4, 1926, W. F. Thompson wrote his final editorial and checked himself into St. Joseph's Hospital to die a few hours later, not knowing that he had won the last round.[50] The Fairbanks Line was soon in operation again.

16

Edith Neile

THERE WALKED A WOMAN

⟨⟨⟩⟩

Of all those who plied the trade in the Far North, one woman best typified their pioneering gold rush spirit. She was called the "Oregon Mare," often outrageous, always an enigma. She began her career in Yukon Territory at the turn of the century and endured to the very end of the era, becoming Alaska's most famous and admired good time girl.

Nevill Armstrong, shanghaied to a party in the hotel room of a Northwest Mounted Police inspector who was celebrating his son's birth in Dawson, described his first astonishing encounter with her.

". . . I was greeted by 'The Oregon Mare,' a nickname applied to a very handsome woman who was a well-known Dawson demimondaine. 'The Oregon' was wearing a pink silk nightdress over which she had on the scarlet tunic of my friend, his Stetson hat, gauntlet gloves and she held his riding whip in her hand," the gold stampeder later recalled. "She was standing up in the middle of the bed and I must say presented a very striking picture."[1]

The Mare, a.k.a. Edith Radford Neile, lived for the moment and had little if any concern for social conventions. The deep-voiced, magnificently proportioned brunette—close to six feet tall and age twenty at the height of the Klondike rush—left a trail of outlandish legends.

"This woman, when working in the Monte Carlo, had for a bet made

⟨⟨⟩⟩

EDITH NEILE IN DAWSON
Known as the Oregon Mare, Edith Neile came to the Klondike as a well-paid stage performer but gave up that career for a more lucrative lifestyle. Old-timers revered her, for she was genuinely entertaining, was generous to a fault, and put her life on the line to help in times of trouble.

Courtesy of Ruth Allman.

in the dance hall before all present, undertaken to accommodate a certain number of men during one evening, hence her name," miner E. C. Trelawney-Ansell recollected.[2] His account is suspect because he confused the Mare's given name with that of Belinda Mulrooney, who owned the Fairview Hotel out of which Edith often worked, but similar reports are given of Edith's stamina as a sexual athlete and her pride in her prowess.

"The most printable explanation of the Oregon Mare's nickname was that she whistled and squealed like a horse when she was dancing, but it was said that she had other equine talents as well. She was one of the best-known girls in town—a big, handsome woman who made men get off the sidewalk when she walked by," recalled Klondike writer Pierre Berton, drawing on stories he'd heard from old-timers. "Seldom short of funds, she would, when in an expansive mood, stand up at the bar and cry: 'Here, boys—there's my poke. Have a drink with me all of you.'"[3]

C. S. Hamlin began his Dawson reminiscences of Edith with a whinny.

"Up jumps a fellow from the gambling table near the rear of the saloon. . . . 'Hell, do they allow them to ride horses into the saloons?'

"'You darn fool, that isn't a horse. Why, that's the whinny of the Oregon Mare.'"

According to Hamlin's account, the Mare told a miner she expected a Christmas present the next day and maybe she'd go with him the day after. He presented her with a pair of garters, "one with a bangle with a nugget as large as a sugar cube." Edith was pleased, but as she donned the garter with the nugget, five boys came in carrying a huge bale of hay from Mac's Livery Stable.

"We hope you will appreciate our little gift," they told her. New cuss words "coined purposely for them" were her angry reaction.[4]

Ex-senator from California Jeremiah Lynch reported watching Edith spend $1,000 in one hour at the roulette table. It is also legend that the Mare kicked customers who refused to dance with her, that she had been an Oregon cowgirl, that she drank as wildly as she gambled, and that she was estranged from her kin.

Edith's family, from whom she was definitely *not* estranged, found many of these legends painful, for they never knew her to drink, gamble, swear, or become physically violent. Edith was raised on a small chicken ranch on the San Francisco Peninsula, not in Oregon, they pointed out, and she had little to do with horses.[5]

Edith herself did nothing to separate fact from fiction. Unlike her

FAMILY MEANT A LOT

*According to rumor, Edith Neile had little to do with her family, but in fact she
adored her younger sister, Edna, and worked hard to give her mother a good life. Here, Edith
(left) vacations in style with Edna (center) and a stepsister from the Denny clan.*

Courtesy of Joseph Sterling.

close friend, the self-promoting "Klondike Kate" Rockwell, who delighted in holding press conferences and cooperating with biographers, Edith was not known to have given a single interview in her eighty-three years. Nor was she prone to discussing her private life, not even with lovers, close friends, or family.

Only two legends about the famed dance hall girl are indisputable. Edith Neile, no matter how high-spirited and outrageous, was as well-liked as she was well-loved. And she was openhanded to a fault.

<hr />

She was born in Yreka, California, in 1878, the first child of Marie and William Radford. Her Spanish-born mother, a schoolteacher and better educated than most women of her day, had come from the East Coast via covered wagon at the age of three, landing in Oklahoma. Marie had married a prominent man named Denny, who left her widowed with four children. Her second marriage, to Englishman William Radford, was a happy one. They welcomed Edith's birth and that of their second daughter, Edna, ten years later.

William Radford had first appeared in Siskiou, the county seat for Yreka, as a miner about 1872, but he soon found work as a lawman, earning a good reputation. In 1895, when a lynch mob of 250 men invaded the jail where he was guarding four accused murderers, William refused to hand over the keys. He kept the angry men at bay until they adjourned to a neighboring blacksmith shop and hammered out a tool with which to pick the locks.[6]

Two years later William was killed, reportedly while attempting to arrest stagecoach robber William Harrall. "He was never known to flinch from duty, no matter what the risks were in store for him," the official report noted.[7] The family account is that William Radford had previously hung an Indian and that the dead man's brother went to the lawman's home and shot him as he was returning from the creek, balancing a yoke with two full buckets of water. Widowed, Marie was left to support Edna, who was then only eight.[8]

Edith came home for her father's funeral, apparently already married to a man named Neile in Tacoma, about whom little is known except that his relationship with Edith failed. Given Edith's nature, she undoubtedly felt obliged to help support her mother and sister, and about a year later she was en route to the Klondike as a well-paid performer for a legitimate vaudeville company.

The real origin of her nickname, "The Mare," is made clear by an enthusiastic review of Edith's stagecraft, written by Ed Lung. Then a young miner, he met her when she was traveling with a theatrical troupe from the Palace Grand Theater to Hunker Creek, a rugged mining camp about eighteen miles from Dawson.

"And there was the handsome 'Oregon Mare,' the fourth girl in the troupe. She's the talk of Dawson and wherever she goes," he wrote. "Some say she's a cowgirl from Oregon, others say Montana. Anyway, she surely knows horses. And she must be a ventriloquist, too, the way she throws her voice.

"Sometimes she wears a horse mask. She hoofs it, kicks, cavorts and horseplays all over the stage. Sometimes even gallops like mad around the audience. Her imitations of a pony are a rollicking scream!

"Often, she stops in her wild antics to give those long, drawn-out horse laughs which you would swear are real. Then, back to the stage she gallops. There are imaginary horse-races, horse-fights and silly, moon-eyed lovemaking accompanied by lots of significant whinnying, neighing and kicking.

"Well, to tell about it seems nothing at all, but to see her is something special! Anyway, she surely makes a hit with the fellows. Just seems to tickle their funny bones!

"They throw nuggets at the 'Oregon Mare.' And as she romps off the stage they slap their sides and exclaim between fits of laughter, 'By George! She's earned 'em! By George! Haven't had so much fun in a coon's age!'"[9]

Obviously Edith had a future in the theater, and why she tossed it away to pursue prostitution will probably never be known. The money a popular girl could make selling love was spectacular, but Edith would later prove that money itself meant very little to her.

In 1903 Edith Neile took her little sister on a vacation in Mexico, perhaps at their mother's urging. The girls were unusually close, and Edna—who was, if anything, more willful than Edith—was becoming too much for Marie to manage. Edith did prove an inspiring role model for the fun-loving fourteen-year-old, but not in the way their mother had hoped. When Edith returned to the dance halls, Mrs. Radford grew even more concerned about her wild younger daughter and committed her to a convent in Spokane.

Edna soon climbed the convent wall and ran away, finding work as a nurse's aid in Spokane's Sacred Heart Hospital at age fifteen.[10] Shortly thereafter she made her way to Dawson, where Edith tried to help her break into the dance hall trade—without ringing success. The "Colt" or the "Little Filly," as Edna was called, was almost as tall as her sister, with thick black hair and a pretty, fresh face, but she wasn't cut out for the job. Her gracious manners got in the way, and she soon departed for points south where she embarked on a string of unsuccessful marriages.[11]

———

When gold was discovered in Nome and Fairbanks, Dawson became a virtual ghost town and the Oregon Mare followed the stampedes to Alaska. Nome was not to her liking but Fairbanks offered many amenities and rich pickings, so she settled in, importing the first record player the town had ever seen and a radio, a $3,000 Stromberg Carlson, which attracted as much business as her personal charms.[12]

Edith did so well she invited her friend Klondike Kate Rockwell to join her, and Kate, who had just been publicly jilted by her lover, Alexander Pantages, came north from Seattle hoping for a change of luck.

Unfortunately, Kate was in the middle of a losing streak. Although she had departed Dawson with thousands of dollars only three years earlier, little was left. That she invested in a Fairbanks hotel which burned to the ground in 1906, and she was reduced to dancing at the Floradora for return fare to Seattle.[13]

Edith, meanwhile, accumulated enough cash for a real vacation. Since Edna was between marriages, the sisters decided to visit their mother, who had moved to San Francisco. Their timing could not have been worse; they were caught in the Great San Francisco Earthquake. Somehow, in the chaos, Marie managed to hire a rowboat for two dollars and they rowed to safety in Oakland. Much later, in 1918, the sisters would transfer from the *Princess Sophia* to another boat just before the *Sophia* sank off Juneau, taking 353 lives.

Returning to Fairbanks still flush, Edith purchased a small house in the center of the new red light district. Things continued to go well until she tried to work out of the Senate Saloon, where she was arrested for keeping a bawdy house along with the building's owners, H. C. Kelly and Ronnie Hoyt, and two other prostitutes, Runy Vernon and Myrtle Clark. Both Runy and Myrtle told the arresting officer their last names were "Doe." Edith, straightforward as usual, made sure "Neile" was spelled correctly. Some of her customers were subpoenaed to testify, which discouraged business from those who demanded discretion.[14] So after paying her fine, the Mare rented out her Fairbanks house and moved to Circle City about 160 miles north. In 1910 she stampeded to Flat, with about 400 miners, and then on to Iditarod.[15]

Edna, meanwhile, having divorced her first and second husbands, married a doctor named Palmer in San Francisco. When that match also ended in disaster, she turned once again to Edith, who suggested they pioneer Nenana, a three-hour boat trip from Fairbanks on the Tanana River. The village had a population of less than 200 until about 1915, when the government made it a major construction site for the Alaska Railroad. Both Edith and Edna successfully set up shop in its new red light district.

Sometime in 1917, Edna Radford Palmer went to a movie and found herself sitting next to Margaret Young Sterling, about her own age, whose husband, Hawley, headed the Nenana construction camp. Margaret was pregnant with her first child and Edna, who seldom met pregnant women

THE MAN WHO WON EDITH NEILE'S HEART
She refused to wed but was tempted when Hawley Sterling proposed that
she help him raise his young son, Joey, whom she adored.
Courtesy of Joseph Sterling.

on the fast track she'd been traveling, was intrigued. When the baby began to kick, Margaret let her feel the motion. Edna thought enough of the incident to mention it to Edith, although she didn't know how it would change both their lives.[16]

In October of the following year, Margaret Sterling left her newborn son, Joe, in Nenana to travel to Fairbanks to visit her father, whom she thought to be dying. The fastest transport was the Hungry Kid's Launch, owned by George Vernon. Except for the windshield, it was wrapped in heavy canvas to protect passengers from the wintry weather. Later that day, the launch was found mostly submerged near the Tanana turn-off to Fairbanks. All eight passengers and George Vernon were declared dead, but Margaret's body was not found. A champion swimmer, she had escaped the wreck, but there was no hope that she had survived the cold waters.[17]

Margaret's father recovered nicely, but her widower nearly went mad with grief, and he would not rest until he reclaimed his wife's body from the silt-laden Tanana. It did not appear before freezeup, so the next spring he again patrolled the river, finally locating her just two and a half miles from their home in Nenana. The body was still buttoned into a heavy fur

YOUNG HAWLEY STERLING (left)

Defying family tradition, Hawley Sterling turned his back on politics and Ivy League colleges, graduating as an engineer from the University of Denver. After working on the Los Angeles sewer system, he came north to become one of Alaska's most successful road and railroad builders.

Courtesy of Joseph Sterling.

SISTER EDNA (right)

Edith's sister Edna fell in love with Hawley Sterling after Edith gave him up. Edna proved to be a fine mother for Joe Sterling, despite doubts and a lawsuit from his maternal grandparents. She also was a devoted wife, a gracious hostess, and an excellent teacher when the Sterlings were too far into the wilderness to find schools for their son.

Courtesy of Joseph Sterling.

coat, which explained why Margaret never made it to shore. She had been just twenty-three.[18]

Bitterly unhappy, Hawley frequented Nenana's red light district, for few other single women were available. Eventually he decided he was in love with Edith Neile and asked her to marry him. His son, Joe, then almost two years old, was boarding with Margaret's parents in Fairbanks, and Hawley was anxious to establish a home for him.

Hawley, the black sheep of a prominent Pennsylvania family, had been slated to follow in his father's footsteps by going to Stanford and becoming a lawyer. Instead he had majored in civil engineering at the University of Denver and taken a job working on the Los Angeles sewer system before becoming a guard at a coal mine. Finally, in 1910, he landed a good engineering assignment with the Treadwell mine in Juneau, and then became a construction engineer for the Alaska Railroad. In 1913 he had led a party of climbers up Mount St. Elias, and he had displayed similar physical prowess on the Alaska-Canadian Boundary survey crew.

Exceedingly handsome and strong, the young widower was easy to love, and Edith adored his son, Joey. But Edith had entertained many offers of marriage. She knew she would not be a suitable wife for Hawley (or anyone else), and she told him so. When Edith would not change her mind, Hawley began an affair with Edna which turned into a real love match. The "Colt" was as anxious to retire from the red light district as Hawley was to have her. She'd been intrigued with little Joe since she first felt him kicking in his mother's belly, and was thrilled by the idea of helping raise him.

Pleased with the match, Edith discreetly returned to Fairbanks where she reestablished herself, making no further attempts to bend the rules by working outside the restricted district. Actually, there was no need to. Railroad construction had given the Fairbanks economy a real boost, and the girls on the Line had all the business they could handle.

Edith enjoyed being back in Fairbanks after nearly a decade of camping in frontier boomtowns. Many Fairbanks old-timers had first met her in Dawson and other frontier outposts, and she quietly helped them out if they ran low on luck. In fact, she spent every extra dime she made contributing to the pioneer fund or buying meal tickets on the sly for those who needed them. Openhandedness was a tradition of the gold camps she'd come up in, and why not? Another strike would always be somewhere down the road.[19]

In early 1920 Fairbanks received a desperate call for help from Nenana. The "Spanish Grippe," a violent flu virus that had been epidemic around the world a year earlier, had finally caught up with the small railroad town and paralyzed it. Several residents were dead, few were left on their feet, and volunteers were needed. The lack of immunization made it a dangerous assignment, but Edith Neile was among the first of twenty volunteers who stepped forward. Her sister and Hawley were not among the victims, but she knew most of the families in Nenana and they had been kind to her.

Those who went described it as a pest hole. ". . . Fifty percent of those who were taken in, were taken out dead," reported one newspaper. "Edith worked all the time, without taking her clothes off for twenty-four hours."[20]

"There's one fine woman. . . . She was right in there with her sleeves rolled up nursing the sick," wrote Ernest Patty, later president of the University of Alaska. "The doctor told her she was the best damn nurse he'd had and she'd better get some rest before she took sick too.

"'Don't worry about me, Doc,' she told him. 'I'm not afraid of any flu bug.'

"Sporting girl, hell. She was an angel during that nightmare."[21]

The death toll was forty-six, about one third of Nenana's population. When her help was no longer needed, Edith herself nearly succumbed to the virus. She recovered to receive grateful thanks from dozens of people who owed her their lives, but the sickness permanently destroyed her hearing, shutting her off in a silent world at age forty-two.[22]

———— ∞ ————

On September 26, 1920, Edna Radford Palmer and Hawley Sterling said their vows before R. S. McDonald, the U.S. Commissioner in Nenana, embarking on a highly successful lifelong marriage. The only problem was that Hawley's former in-laws, Frank Young Sr. and his wife, refused him custody of his son on the grounds that Edna would be an unfit mother. The Sterlings went to court, a brave move because it made their private lives public. But Edna wanted little Joe as much as Hawley did, and they waged an unflinching campaign to win him.

The Youngs spared them no pain. Hawley testified that the Youngs already had so turned his son against him that the four-year-old was afraid to go for a walk with his father. The Youngs argued that the child should remain in their custody because "the home provided, and the surroundings created by the said re-marriage of said Hawley Sterling are altogether unfit for the bringing up of a child under tender and impressionable years."[23]

The Youngs maintained that Edna had been a prostitute right up to the very day of her marriage. She had been intoxicated, used profane language, and continued to associate with women of ill-repute, they said. Also, they charged Hawley with intemperate and immoral habits. Their daughter had wanted them to have her boy because she was concerned about Hawley's lifestyle, they added. And they claimed Hawley had not paid them adequate child support.

It was widely known that Margaret Young Sterling had adored her husband, and Hawley quietly said so. He proved to the court's satisfaction that he had attempted to pay child support but that the Youngs often refused it. Then, surprisingly, he dealt head-on with the issue of his past and that of his wife. He conceded that Edna had at one time been a prostitute in Nenana and Fairbanks and that his own past was not unblemished, but he insisted that "for a considerable period of time prior to the marriage of the petitioner and his said wife, she had ceased to live an immoral life, and since the marriage . . . [she] has led an absolutely clean and moral life, and has severed all associations with other residents of the restricted district," except for one woman who had cared for her when she was ill.

Hawley also had the foresight to investigate the Youngs, and countered their charges by pointing out that one of their most frequent former callers was in the government penitentiary on charges of incest, while another was doing time for burglary. Hawley concluded his testimony by reminding the court that he was the superintendent of the Alaska Road Commission at Fairbanks, and able and willing to provide a fit and proper home for his child. The judge agreed,[24] and the Sterlings proved him right.

Years later Joe Sterling would recall his childhood as a normal and happy one. He loved Edna, and he also loved his Aunt Edith, who was delighted to have a bright young nephew. She had cared about Joe even before Edna met Hawley, and her look of joy holding him in an early baby photo says it all.

Little Joey was the bright spot in Edith Neile's life at a time when she didn't have many.[25] She continued to make good money in her trade, teaming with Edna and Hawley to buy Marie Radford a nice house on 66th Avenue in Oakland, where they all enjoyed family reunions. "Grandma Radford" was still going strong at seventy, once astonishing her family by playing football with neighborhood youngsters. But there was too little time with family for Edith, who spent most of hers working in Fairbanks.

In 1928 the Sterlings moved to South America, where Hawley was a chief engineer for South American Gulf Oil. Edna took over Joe's schooling for a year and was pleased when he skipped from fifth to seventh grade under her tutorship. Bigger and better engineering jobs came Hawley's way and Edna, with her perfect manners and easy charm, proved as fine a hostess as she was a mother.

But while the Sterlings were moving up, Edith Neile began a painful decline. Hampered by deafness and age, she finally quit the Line to purchase a bathhouse, still a good business in Fairbanks because even in the early 1940s few homes had running water. However, Edith continued to give away most of her earnings. After she sold the bathhouse sometime in the mid-'40s, she worked a discouraging series of low-paying menial jobs because she had no retirement savings. The cost of living was high in Alaska, and eventually she moved to Seattle, which was more reasonable. Edna, who was widowed in 1948, purchased a nice apartment hoping Edith would share it with her, but Edith stayed less than a week. The willful Mare was used to living on her own and the very thought of taking charity angered her.

When Edna died of cancer in 1953, Joe Sterling, then doing well in the lumber business, tried to help Edith, but he was rebuffed as his mother had been. In the end, Edith moved to a dreary rest home after refusing to accept any help, including a sizable inheritance left by a former lover.

But her friends in Fairbanks had not forgotten her. They made her an honorary member of Alaska's Pioneer Auxiliary 8, and were taking up a collection to bring her home to Alaska when she died quietly of heart disease in February of 1962.[26]

Edith Radford Neile had given away about $300,000 in her lifetime, "mostly to old guys with dreams of mining in Alaska who never made it," her nephew recalled. The whore with a heart of gold is a cliché, of course, but Edith Neile actually was one, and she was not alone. She was a prostitute without pretensions and she was not alone there, either, for her generation of good time girls had no need to misrepresent themselves in the Far North.

"I personally hate the words 'whore' and 'prostitute,'" her nephew Joe Sterling wrote in considering this book. "Mainly because in today's world and to this generation they bring to mind a young girl in short-shorts standing and soliciting sex on Sunset Blvd., Hollywood, CA, mainly for drug money, etc. These are not the 'sporting girls' as I knew them. I believe that most of the pioneers in Alaska will or would have agreed with me. . . . They were a breed unto themselves."[27]

The tribute that the *Fairbanks Daily News-Miner* paid Edith Neile on her death echoed this thought, and held true as well for many of Edith's working sisters who contributed so much to the Last Frontier. It was not the usual brief but instead a heart-felt eulogy, published not with the obituaries but on the editorial page, written by an editor who understood the code of the Far North:

" . . . Once in a while along comes a person who has stood far above the crowd in acts of kindness and charity for her fellow person. One such was Edith Neile, an eighty-three-year-old woman who died Thursday in a rest home in Seattle, and who was cremated today.

"Miss Neile, who wouldn't be classed as one of our 'Blue Bloods' in the sense of the word as it is used today, left her mark on Alaska—and for that matter, was responsible for many an Alaskan being here today.

"It was Edith Neile who nursed untold families and individuals back to health during the great flu epidemic after World War I in Nenana. She put in hundreds of hours at this chore and no one will probably ever know how many lives she actually saved.

"Then there were the acts of kindness she performed anonymously for down-and-out old-timers in the late 1930s and early 1940s.

"One restaurant owner said she couldn't count the times that Miss Neile walked into her restaurant, laid down twenty dollars for a meal ticket for some old-timer who was down on his luck, and left orders, 'just call me when that money is gone, but don't tell anyone where it came from. . . . '

"Possibly as a parting but belated tribute, her ashes could be scattered over the Tanana Valley where she is remembered fondly by so many people, or at least returned to Alaska for burial as this is where her heart has always been.

"You can pay tributes to people in hundreds of different ways but of Edith Neile you can always say, 'There walked a woman!'"[28]

Epilogue

THE END OF THE LINE

During the late 1920s, the gold rush town of Fairbanks made a surprising comeback. Construction of the Alaska Railroad had produced an unexpected bonus in the creation of the Fairbanks Exploration Co. Norman Stines, later its general manager, bought up hundreds of small, ill-paying, or defunct placer operations, raising capital to attract dredging operations big enough to make them pay. He also promoted the building of the Davidson Ditch, a seemingly impossible engineering feat which transported water ninety miles to run the operation. FE hired some 1,000 men and its annual payroll averaged between $1 and $2 million.[1] There were no new gold kings, but with so many men in town on steady wages, the Fairbanks Line once again became a major economic force, one the community relied on more and more.

"The ladies of the church and the home could not speak to the ladies of the Row, but when there was an emergency of any kind, a drive to raise funds for a hospital or a library, or relief for a destitute or 'burnt-out' family, they gladly accepted donations from the Row," recalled Margaret Murie, "and if one of the cabins on the Row burned down, the respectable ladies would contribute clothing and funds to the unfortunate one. There was a good deal of live-and-let-live, a good deal of gossip, but of a rather

THE LAST OF THE RESTRICTED DISTRICTS
The Fairbanks red light district was among the last in Alaska to close,
and did so not due to local sentiment but because of threats from federal officials.
Owners had failed to maintain it well because of its uncertain future, but it still generated
at least $100,000 a year in revenues right up until its closure in the mid-1950s.

Courtesy of Pat Cook.

humorous, casual, unmalicious kind. We were all far away from the rest of the world; we had to depend on one another."[2]

One prostitute operated what was the forerunner of a beauty parlor, patronized by many respectable matrons including Mrs. LaDessa Nordale, who later became a judge.[3] Once each year, high and low society mingled when the inmates of the Line threw a ball at the Moose Hall, inviting the mayor and everyone else in town. "One of the mayor's duties was to be available to dance with any one of the ladies of the evening," recalled Bob Casey, who drove taxi for girls on the Line. "You can imagine every lady in town wanted to see what they were like."[4]

Millionaire developer Austin Lathrop, who offered a special, after-hours movie showing for prostitutes, was quick to grasp their economic importance. "She might be a whore on Fourth Avenue, but by God on Fifth Avenue she better be treated like a lady," he told employees.[5]

At a time when the average woman expected to pay from six to eleven dollars for a dress, Fairbanks clothing stores featured $110 dresses. Prostitutes were such favored customers that store owners gave them after-hours showings or even took merchandise to their cribs if a special occasion was coming up.[6] The Line was the most sought-after route in town for paper boys because residents tipped so well.[7] Nor did mothers worry when their sons delivered, for Fairbanks prostitutes were very careful in dealing with youngsters.

Chuck Herbert remembered being young, broke, and pretty green, coming into town from gold camp at Christmastime with a friend who suggested they visit Patsy Berke. "She was in her late forties. Nice looking. Busy entertaining a group of coal miners but she let us have some drinks with them and we both got stewed," he recalled with a chuckle. "I woke up the next morning in a nice bed [alone] and found a five-dollar bill in my pocket."[8]

The Fairbanks population rose to 2,101 in 1930 and to 3,455 in 1939 as residents weathered the Depression in style. While other cities across the nation were sponsoring bread lines, Fairbanks paved its streets, and the town's financial institutions stayed open during the National Bank Holiday. "Well, we didn't hear about that vacation until it was too late," Ed Stroecker of First National Bank explained.[9]

—⊷∞⊶—

Early in 1940, Lawrence Bayer and Wayne Drayton, two University of Alaska students, researched the Fairbanks red light district for a paper for a class in contemporary society. Prostitution ranked high among the top ten of the city's industries, they discovered, grossing in excess of $100,000 annually. The Line had grown dilapidated, but twenty-six cribs were in operation, valued at between $1,500 and $3,500 each. One informant said only six of the cribs were owner-occupied; another put the total at seventeen. Rents ranged from forty-five to sixty dollars a month. A girl could make from $3,500 to $15,000 in a season, and many went Outside in the winter. Income was generated by the sale of alcohol at fifty cents per drink and coitus: three dollars for a single act and twenty for an evening.[10]

The students estimated between fifty and sixty professional prostitutes were in town. They were required to register with the police, to turn up for a medical exam once every two weeks, and to submit blood for testing every three months.

"No figures but opinions coincided in the belief a 'good number' of the girls owned fine cases of tertiary and secondary syphilis," they reported. "Gonorrhea is more rare and promptly stepped on by city authorities, as are primary cases of syphilis."[11]

Bayer and Drayton found the Fairbanks Line different from the average red light district in two respects. "Restrictions . . . have eliminated many of the problems occurring in older, vastly larger and perhaps more respectable communities," they observed. "The vocation of pimping, for instance, has been blitzkrieged into a pastime by the cooperative city fathers. Gang rule, protection payments, and other customary sources of overhead do not annoy the prostitutes of Fairbanks."[12]

More unusual was the fact that very few of the prostitutes were below the age of forty; most were between forty-five and fifty-five, and several were in their sixties. Bayer and Drayton tactfully described "Texas Rose" as "a lady of damaged appearance believed to be sixty-eight."

Some of the older women had been widowed by early sourdoughs, the researchers noted. Many had as customers single miners with whom they'd had relationships for decades, much like long-established marriages.

—⟊⟊⟊—

For some of these women, any thought of retirement vanished with the October 1943 robbery of ninety safe deposit boxes at the Fairbanks Agency, an insurance company many women on the Line used instead of a bank. Whores dealt in cash and most were not anxious to have anyone, especially local bankers and the Internal Revenue Service, know their worth. Realizing this, thieves moved into the basement of a building adjoining the Fairbanks Agency and over a weekend tunneled through, taking time to explore the boxes. Their take was estimated at $57,000 in cash and $7,500 in jewelry, but the real total was probably much higher.[13]

The only item ever recovered was one woman's $400 Russian-dyed ermine coat, found in the possession of Louise Allred, the agency's office manager. Allred was subsequently indicted on eight counts of embezzlement and four counts of larceny, and served time in federal prison without mentioning accomplices.[14] Some believed the robbery was an inside job involving at least one high-ranking police official, but no evidence ever materialized.[15]

Fortunately for the good time girls with heavy losses, the robbery coincided with the biggest boom yet. At the start of World War II, the U.S. government had begun building two large military bases in Fairbanks, another in neighboring Delta, and a major highway south to Dawson Creek, B.C. Gold-mining was officially shut down, but suddenly thousands of construction men and soldiers were in town.

Every available whore was needed and appreciated, *even those who were pushing sixty!* Newspaper boys of that era recall fifty or sixty men waiting patiently in a queue extending out of the Line on paydays, and as more men arrived, the queue extended to the post office, more than a block away.[16] Crib rents soared to $200 a month when the going rate in town was $35, but even when they later escalated to $600 a month, there were no vacancies. Business was just too good.[17]

Carol "Tex" Erwin, a veteran madam who moved in from Kodiak, recalled there were 40,000 soldiers in town. "Every house on the Line did a rushing business of course," she recalled in her unusual autobiography, *The Orderly Disorderly House.* "All the madams had agreed that we'd accept only enlisted men, no officers. Officers were only trouble—they'd think they rated special treatment, and they pulled rank on the enlisted men, and they got drunk and disorderly. . . . The privates and corporals and sergeants were nice fellows and we had no trouble with them at all.

"And they were getting a good deal too. They'd never seen a Line run like this one in Fairbanks. They weren't rolled, they could leave their paycheck with the madam when they got drunk and be sure it was safe and returned to them when they sobered up. And they never got any venereal diseases. Of course, some of the girls on the Line were sixty years old. But they didn't seem to mind that."[18]

The good times lasted long after the end of World War II, because Fairbanks military establishments were enlarged to serve as Cold War bases. Iris Woodcock, a photographer who drove north promoting a motor home in 1948, discovered prostitutes could average $3,000 a month while paying $700 for rent and equally high rates for utilities.[19]

Ambitious girls supplemented this income by flying on the "Connie," a regularly scheduled Constellation, to Seward when the Navy docked there; although the little port had its own Line, it was not nearly big enough to handle the massive shore leave. Realtor Earl Cook, noticing that a prostitute named Lillian looked unusually wan after one of these lucrative coastal excursions, inquired after her well-being. Lillian was one of his better clients, investing every dime she could save in property, which she would later use to escape the trade, and she was used to confiding in Cook.

"Oh, Earl," she said earnestly. "It was so busy in Seward yesterday, I said, 'Guys, if you're not ready, don't stand in line!'"[20]

The bonanza began to self-destruct when federal law enforcement agencies at last focused on the Far North. In 1952, Wrangell's compact red light district, housed in half of a large apartment building next to the Elks Club and the local movie theater, burned along with half the town. It was never rebuilt, for word was out that the government was moving to shut down prostitution throughout the territory.[21]

"Every year they'd send someone from Washington, D. C., who said, 'You'd better close down the Line,'" recalled Bernie Hulk, who headed the Juneau police force during this period. "He'd come again the next year and say the same thing and it went on and on. But finally [in 1956] he said 'I'm here again and this time you're going to close the Line before I leave and if you don't you're headed for McNeil Federal Prison.'"

Hulk went to see the local district attorney, who told him not to worry about it, but Hulk's freedom was at stake and he followed the federal official's orders. When the mayor reversed the action, reopening the Line, Hulk's resignation made headlines. And soon most Juneau prostitutes left town or entered other fields.[22]

The pattern was repeated throughout the territory. Towns that resisted, like Ketchikan, found themselves facing messy federal investigations and charges of police corruption. Like it or not, it was the end of an era . . . ended not by Alaskans but by the federal government, which many Alaskans thought was pretty far removed from the realities of the frontier.

The situation was perhaps best handled in Seward, where the good time girls were still a large percentage of the small population, and were loved well beyond the physical sense of the word. When it became clear a federal vendetta against prostitution was inevitable, the local marshal shrewdly arrested all the girls, fined each of them one dollar, and sent them on their way—thus protecting them from serious federal prosecution on the grounds of double jeopardy.[23]

Fairbanks residents ignored federal warnings until, doomed by its own success, the Line became even more crowded. Evelyn Benson, a perennial known as "Panama Hattie," ran the largest and roughest house on the Line, working about nine girls instead of going solo as was general practice. Old-timers claim she was "grandfathered" in by the city council. She had arrived about 1910 from Panama after her lover had been killed,[24] and she considered herself different from the other women, perhaps a bit of an outcast.[25] Her prices were higher than others' and her reputation was such that some cab drivers refused to recommend her house to would-be customers.[26] When a military man was found murdered on the Line, it was rumored to have been at Hattie's place, despite a very hush-hush investigation that resulted in no arrests.[27]

But the problem wasn't just Hattie. Newcomers had arrived, including prostitutes who had worked at Mamie Stover's in Hawaii. The new girls were out to make a fast buck, ignoring the rules. Customers grew less inclined to leave their pokes and their paychecks with the girls, and seldom did a customer spend the night.[28] From a window near his office in the Federal Building, the marshal could look right down on the Line, making surveillance with field glasses quite simple. But trying to control outsiders who refused to register with the city and worked out of bars was a much bigger job than the office was staffed for. Robbery became common and, worst of all, the outsiders brought venereal disease to the Line.[29]

"The new girls let their pimps move right into the houses with them and that created an awful situation. A lot of the pimps were dopeheads and they began to peddle the stuff to soldiers," Tex Erwin recalled. "There were several unsolved murders, all related to dope. So finally the army just had to declare the whole Line off limits."[3]

The town fought it, for the Line was almost as big an economic boon to the community as military spending, and the idea of trying to cope with so many servicemen without it made old-timers shudder. But in January of 1952 undercover investigators for the American Social Hygiene Association, billed as a thirty-five-year-old organization devoted to "promoting the highest ideals of American family life," moved into Fairbanks. According to its report, aired before the city council and Brigadier General Donald B. Smith, commanding officer of Ladd Air Force Base, Fairbanks had fifteen houses of prostitution, plus a large number of prostitutes plying their trade openly at local bars. C.O. Smith reminded city officials of the very sharp increase in venereal disease among servicemen and also the increase in robberies and burglaries.[31]

The credentials of the American Social Hygiene Association were never publicly established, nor would Fairbanks ever hear of the organization again. Off the record, however, military commanders told city fathers they would place the whole town of Fairbanks off limits if the Line was not closed down.[32] Not only did a territorial law prohibit prostitution, but the newly passed Truman Anti-Crib Act also made it illegal. Ultimately city officials had no choice but to comply.

Those women who wanted to stay in business dispersed throughout town, facing zealous federal marshals, the underworld's demands of protection payoffs, and a 300 percent increase in venereal disease.[33] Some prostitutes tried working out of their cars, forcing Judge LaDessa Nordale to rule on whether or not a Cadillac could be classed as a whorehouse. Drawing on a precedent-setting case in Wisconsin in which a judge had ruled that a horse and buggy could be a whorehouse, Judge Nordale ruled that the Cadillac could be one, too—weathering a lot of kidding because she drove one herself.[34]

A friend of Bob Redding, homesteading at Tok Cutoff, came to town unaware that the Line had been closed and wondered why folks were grinning at him as he knocked on doors without success.[35] A well-founded rumor claimed that a Safeway food market was to be built on the site. Redding and his friends preferred things the way they had been, but the idea gave a chuckle to those "who knew there was never a real safe way."[36]

Transient prostitutes quickly abandoned the Fourth Avenue district, but the Line had been home for several decades to old-timers who had "bought in." The federal government offered to purchase their houses for a fraction of their former value, and some of these women could not afford to move.

"I gotta put a padlock on the door," a deputy told Carol Erwin.

"You put it on the front door if you want to, but not on this side door to my apartment. You can close the joint, but you can't dispossess me out of my home, by God," she told him.[37]

One seasoned veteran, mustering the courage that had brought her north in pioneering days, stood defiantly in the path of a bulldozer dispatched by the city for "urban renewal." Eventually the women fought closure in federal court, won a slightly higher sale price for their houses, but ultimately were forced to vacate. A softhearted state trooper allowed a couple of the older "girls" to move their cribs to his homestead just outside of town, for they literally had no place to go and no money to purchase land.[38]

The dozen or so little houses that remained—long bare of paint, with shingles flapping in the wind—were bulldozed under to build a new shopping plaza that included not only a Safeway but also an ultra-modern J.C. Penney's store.

The closing of quasi-legal red light districts did not end prostitution in the Far North. In fact, the industry peaked during the construction of the trans-Alaska pipeline in the 1970s, but it was an entirely different game by then, clandestine and set apart from mainstream society.

In the golden era, the good time girls had been a recognized part of the community and had contributed to it. "A blind man could have sensed their constant presence and their influence," noted a physician who lived through the early stampedes.[39] They were condoned as a "necessary evil" and, indeed, were as necessary as females are in any civilization. As for their being evil, it is wise not to be too quick to condemn those whores of yore, for they were a breed apart from ordinary prostitutes—and at least one cut above them.

Geologist Alfred Brooks, who covered every major gold rush in the region, argued convincingly that life in the Klondike was a great winnowing process, and that those who succeeded there were something special. "A small percentage failed through lack of moral stamina, for there was ample opportunity to go to the dogs in the northern gold camps," he observed. "On the other hand, many a man who had not developed beyond mediocrity in his own community, tightly bound by tradition and custom, found in Alaska his opportunity and rose to his true level. This last of our frontiers, therefore, has played a part in developing breadth of view and character among our people."[40]

The only recorded view from a working girl came from a conversation Carol Erwin had with a veteran Nome madam near the end of the era.

"When you talk about holding a tight rein on your girls, these hustlers aren't girls—some of them are forty and fifty years old, and every bit as popular as younger ones," the Nome madam noted. "A lot of them marry and settle down. Why, I could name you dozens of social leaders, club and churchwomen in Fairbanks and Anchorage who were once hustlers. Everybody knows it; nobody minds."[41]

Today they are all gone, of course, and it is doubtful that their ghosts linger comfortably among the urban renewal projects that displaced them. Nor will you find much trace of them in official histories of this last frontier.

But memories of their golden age can still bring a smile: Violet Raymond with Antone Stander's necklace of diamonds sparkling right down to her knees . . . plucky Grace Robinson packing her fancy Seattle hat over Chilkoot Pass and rescuing it from the wild waters of Lake Bennett . . . Mae Field wickedly flaunting her lingerie and her laundry bill in Dawson court . . . and Corrine B. Gray donning a satin gown by Worth of Paris to wed the son of a merchant prince in the tiny outpost of Rampart.

It is difficult for old-timers to walk down Fourth Avenue in Fairbanks without thinking of the good time girls who made that Line the very best in the West. Girls like little Georgia Lee, who escaped the brutal poverty of her farm via the St. Louis red light district for what she knew could only be a better life in Alaska. Edith Neile, so tall, beautiful, independent, and openhanded. Gracious prostitute Ray Alderman, who became Alaska's first first lady to host a U.S. president. "Lovely One" and Myrtle and Dolly—all in party dresses with rhubarb leaves and pink bows for hats—bursting in on their old neighbor at 6 a.m. Klondike Kate Rockwell and her lilting theme song, "Do not scorn her with words fierce and bitter. . . ."

These unique women and their sisters brought to the Far North the gifts of warmth, laughter, and the lightness of a woman's touch, commodities that were all too scarce before the good time girls gambled their futures to brave our rugged trails.

Notes

PREFACE
1 Woolston, Howard B. *Prostitution in the United States Prior to the Entrance of the United States in World War.* (Originally published by Century Press, 1921.) Reprinted in Publication No. 29, Patterson Smith Reprint Series in Criminology, Law Enforcement and Social Problems. Montclair, N.J.: Patterson Smith, 1969, pp 19-20.

INTRODUCTION
1 Warren, Father William. Interview with the author, Fairbanks Episcopal Church, spring 1972. For the genesis of the Fairbanks Line, see the Grand Jury Report, *Fairbanks Evening News,* September 8, 1906.
2 Fairbanks Ordinance 177, December 13, 1912.
3 Frey, Richard C. Jr. "A.M. & Company: A Klondike Venture," *Call Number,* Vol. 24 #1, p 4. Portland: University of Oregon. This source offers a good estimate of how many stampeders came north.
4 Rosen, Ruth. *The Lost Sisterhood: Prostitution in America 1900-1981.* Baltimore: The John Hopkins University Press. Introduction, p. xi.
5 O'Connor, Richard. *High Jinks on the Klondike.* Indianapolis, New York: The Bobbs-Merrill Company, Inc., 1935, pp. 12-16.
6 Brooks-Vincent, Mrs. La Belle. *The Scarlet Life of Dawson and the Roseate Dawn of Nome.* Copyrighted by M. R. Mayor, A. D. in the United States, in England, and all Foreign Countries, 1900, p.72. This book is not available in libraries or archives in the western United States. I owe Candice Waugaman of Fairbanks a debt of gratitude for loaning me a copy from her wonderful private collection.
7 Rosen, *The Lost Sisterhood,* p. xi.
8 Alberts, Laurie. "Petticoats and Pickaxes," *Alaska Journal,* Summer 1977, p. 146.
9 O'Connor, *High Jinks,* p. 14.
10 Backhouse, Frances H. "Women of the Klondike," *The Beaver,* December 1988-Jan. 1989, pp. 30-32.
11 Guest, Hal J. *A History of the City of Dawson, Yukon Territory, 1896-1920.* Microfiche Reporter Series No. 7, Canadian Parks Service, 1981. Guest cites La Belle Brooks-Vincent on the high number, and articles in the *Klondike Nugget,* Sept. 14 and 17, 1898, p. 1. for stories on the arrest of ladies of the evening. Police records also bear him out.
12 Lynch, Jeremiah. *Three Years in the Klondike.* Chicago: R. R. Donnelley & Sons, 1967, p. 58.

13 Langum, David J. *Crossing Over the Line: Legislating Morality and the Mann Act.* Chicago and London: The University of Chicago Press, 1994, pp. 5, 15-47.
14 Rosen, *The Lost Sisterhood,* p. xvii.
15 Mulrooney got a lovely puff piece in the *Klondike News,* April 1, 1898. Martha Black tells her own story in *My Seventy Years* (London, Edinburgh, Paris, Melbourne, Toronto, and New York: Thomas Nelson and Sons Ltd., 1938). Francis Backhouse offers a "laundry list" of successful scrub women in *Women of the Klondike,* p. 78-82.
16 Brooks, Alfred H. *Blazing Alaska's Trails.* (Second Edition) Fairbanks, Alaska: University of Alaska Press, 1953, p. 363.
17 Berton, Laura B. *I Married the Klondike.* Toronto: McClelland & Stewart Inc., 1967, pp. 28-29.
18 DeGraf, Anna. *Pioneering on the Yukon: 1892-1917.* Edited by Roger S. Brown. Hamden, Connecticut: The Shoestring Press, Inc., Archon Books, 1992, p. 6. Census figures that back DeGraf are offered in Barbara Kensey's master's thesis, "Lost in the Rush: the Forgotten Women of the Klondike Gold Rush," (Victoria, B.C.: University of Victoria, 1987), pp. 91-142.
19 Rosen, *The Lost Sisterhood,* p. xvii.
20 Trelawney-Ansell, E. C. *I Followed Gold.* London: Peter Davies, 1938, p. 171.
21 Martin, Cy. "Klondike Gold Rush Girlies," *Real West,* vol. XI, no. 60 (June 1968), p. 45.
22 Wickersham, James A. *Old Yukon.* Washington, D. C.: Washington Law Book Co., 1938, p. 408.
23 Parrish, Maud. *Nine Pounds of Luggage.* J. B. Lippincott, 1939. Erwin, Carol "Tex." *The Orderly Disorderly House.* New York: Doubleday, 1960.
24 Reporter/biographer R. N. DeArmond came across this quote in *Yukon Star,* Feb. 2, 1912, *after* his wonderful collection of Elmer John "Stroller" White's columns and editorials was published in *Klondike Newsman,* Lynn Canal Publishing, 1989. We thank him for sharing it with us, for it neatly sums up the spirit of the day.

1. PIONEERING PROSTITUTES
1 Hayne, M. H. E. *Pioneers of the Klondike: Being an Account of Two Years Police Service on the Yukon.* London: Sampson Low, Marsten, & Co., 1897, p. 45.
2 Gates, Michael. *Gold at Fortymile Creek: Early Days in the Yukon.* Vancouver: University of British Columbia Press, 1994, p. 83.
3 Cody, H. A. *An Apostle of the North.* New York: E. P.

Dutton & Company, 1908, p. 268.

4 Brooks, Alfred. *Blazing Alaska Trails*. Fairbanks: University of Alaska, 1953. On p. 333 Brooks cites the notes of "William McFee of Fairbanks" in crediting Kate with traveling the pass in 1888. The two sources that follow place her in the country a year earlier.

5 *The Daily Alaskan*, November 23, 1889, Editorial, p. 3.

6 Shalkop, Antoinette. "Stepan Uskin: Citizen by Purchase," *Alaska Journal*, Spring 1977, p. 103. Her citation of the Russian source is Ushin, Stepan, *Journal 1874-1895*, ms. in the Alaska Church Collection, Library of Congress.

7 Wright, Allen A. *Prelude to Bonanza*. Whitehorse: Studio North Ltd., 1992, copyrighted 1976, p. 121.

8 Hunt, William. *North of 53°: The Wild Days of the Alaska-Yukon Mining Frontier 1870-1914*. New York and London: Macmillan Publishing Company and Collier Macmillan, 1974, p. 7.

9 Senate Report 457, April 21,1881, 47th Congress, First Session. Source: Andersen, Thayne I. *Alaska Hooch: The History of Alcohol in Early Alaska*. Fairbanks: Hoo-Che-Noo, 1988, p. 79.

10 McCarley, Laura. *Histories of Downtown Buildings in Juneau, Alaska*. Juneau, 1978. File .0004VF, Alaska State Library, Juneau.

11 Simpson, Sherry, "Women on the Last Frontier," *Juneau Alaska Empire*, March 20, 1991.

12 Wright, *Prelude to Bonanza*, pp. 135-139.

13 Gates, *Gold at Fortymile Creek*, p. 8.

14 Wright, *Prelude to Bonanza*, p. 162.

15 Gates, *Gold at Fortymile Creek*, p. 38.

16 Bettles, Gordon. "Why I came to Alaska," *Heartland*, *Fairbanks Daily News-Miner*, July 21, 1996, p. H-8.

17 Gates, *Gold at Fortymile Creek*, p. 38.

18 Bettles, "Why I came to Alaska," p. H-10.

19 *The Daily Alaskan*, Nov. 23, 1889, Editorial, p. 3.

20 Simpson, "Women on the Last Frontier."

21 Wickersham Collection, Alaska State Library, Scrapbook #1, photo of the "Dutch Kid."

22 Gates, Michael, personal correspondence, Feb. 1, 1998.

23 Gates, *Gold at Fortymile Creek*, p. 80.

24 Ibid., p. 81.

25 DeGraf, Anna. *Pioneering on the Yukon: 1892-1917*. Hamden, Connecticut: The Shoestring Press, Inc., Archon Books, 1992, p. 21.

26 Ibid., pp. 30-31.

27 Evans, *Frontier Theatre*, p. 229.

28 Cole, Terrence. *Swiftwater Bill Gates*. Unpublished manuscript, 1994, pp. 9-10.

29 Davids, Henry. "Recollections." In *Sourdough Sagas*, edited by Herbert L. Heller. Cleveland: World Publishing, 1967, p. 76.

30 Wright, *Prelude to Bonanza*, p. 293.

31 Beebe, Iona. *The True Story of Swiftwater Bill Gates*. Iona Beebe, 1908, pp. 14-19.

32 Berton, Pierre. *Klondike: The Last Great Gold Rush 1896-1899*. Toronto/ Ottawa: McClelland and Stewart, p. 79.

33 Evans, *Frontier Theatre*, p. 232.

34 Tewkesbury, David and William. *Tewkesbury's Who's Who in Alaska and Alaska Business Index*. Juneau: Tewkesbury Publishers, 1947. Atwood, Evangeline. *Who's Who in Alaska Politics*. Portland, Oregon: Binford and Mort, 1979.

35 Gates, *Gold at Fortymile Creek*, p. 125.

36 Backhouse, Frances. *Women of the Klondike*. Vancouver/ Toronto: Whitecap Books, 1995, p. 64.

37 The verse was first presented by George Snow's group of dance hall girls, searching desperately for new material after miners, bored with viewing the same play, badly acted, night after night, began to howl malamutes from the audience. Hamlin, C. H. *Old Times on the Yukon*. Los Angeles: Wetzel Publishing Co., Inc., 1928, p. 5. Wickersham credits this verse to Hamlin, who was a federal lawman.

38 "Lotta Burns in Seattle: Mother of the Klondike Returns to Civilization," *Seattle- Post Intelligencer*, September 29, 1898.

2. THE GREAT KLONDIKE STAMPEDE

1 Parrish, Maud. *Nine Pounds of Luggage*. Philadelphia, New York, London, Toronto: J.B. Lippincott Company, 1939, p.23.

2 Johnson, James Albert. *Carmack of the Klondike*. Fairbanks, Alaska: Epicenter Press, 1990, pp. 65-86, 96. Just who in the party actually discovered the gold has been long debated, but all official documentation definitely names Carmack himself. And it is to Carmack's credit that he made certain his Native partners had legal claims they could profit from. This was not the case with the Native prospectors who started the rush at Circle but were cheated out of their discovery claims because they didn't do the proper paperwork.

3 Innis, Harold A. *Settlement and the Mining Frontier*. Toronto: The Macmillan Company of Canada Limited at St. Martin's House, 1936, p. 183.

4 The *Australian Mining Record*, August 19, 1897, published excerpts from San Francisco newspapers reporting the arrival of the *Excelsior* and the *Portland* with their gold-laden miners. James Albert Johnson cites this clipping in *Carmack of the Klondike*, p. 113-4.

5 Stampede figures are debatable. Estimates range from 30,000 to 100,000 actual participants. I've chosen to go with Alfred Brooks, a no-nonsense scientist who was present not only in Dawson but also in Skagway, Wrangell, and Juneau, as well as

for subsequent rushes in Nome and Fairbanks. Brooks, Alfred Hulse. *Blazing Alaska's Trails.* Fairbanks: University of Alaska Press, 1953, p. 346. Brooks reasoned it would "be conservative to assume that every Klondiker had at least two dependents or financial backers. About 60,000 were thought to have started for the Klondike in 1897 and 1898. Therefore, there would be nearly 200,000 who had more or less direct financial interest in the gold rush."

6 Parrish, *Nine Pounds of Luggage,* pp. 22-26.

7 "She Reached Dawson and Sang Her Way to Fame and Fortune," *Daily Klondike Nugget,* Oct. 24, 1900. Robinson's account of the storm is corroborated by Edward Lung as told to Ella Lung Martinsen. *Black Sand and Gold.* New York: Vantage Press, 1956, pp. 43-44.

8 Oliver, Lillian Agnes. "My Klondike Mission," *Wide World Magazine,* Apr.-Sept. 1899, p. 48.

9 McKeown, Martha Ferguson. *The Trail Led North: Mont Hawthorne's Story.* Portland, Oregon: Binford and Mort, 1960, p. 118.

10 Meadows, Mae McKamish. Letter of September 28, 1897, printed in the (Santa Cruz, California) *Daily Sentinel,* Oct. 24, 1897, p. 1. Her account is confirmed by her husband's diaries in an account published by his niece, Jean Beach King. *Arizona Charlie: A Legendary Cowboy, Klondike Stampeder and Wild West Showman.* Phoenix, Arizona: A Heritage Publisher's Book, 1989.

11 Secretan, J. H. E. *To the Klondyke and Back.* New York: Hurst and Blackett, 1898, p. 52.

12 Wold, Jo Anne. *The Andrew Nerland Legacy,* from Nerland's diary, August 20, 1898. Privately printed, 1988.

13 Stevens, Gary L. "Gold Rush Theater in the Alaska-Yukon Frontier." Dissertation for the Department of Speech and the Graduate School of the University of Oregon, 1984. Ann Arbor Michigan: University Microfilms International, 1985, p. 63.

14 Sinclair, John. Papers, Provincial Archives of British Columbia, May 30, 1898.

15 Hartshorn, Mrs. H. (Florence). *Along the Golden Trail, Being the Chronicles of the Hartshorn Family.* Edited by Janet Monro. National Archives, MG 30 D 46, vol. 2, p. 13.

16 Trelawney-Ansell, E. C. *I Followed Gold.* London: Peter Davies, 1938, pp. 140-141.

17 O'Connor, Richard. *High Jinks on the Klondike.* Indianapolis, New York: The Bobbs-Merrill Company, Inc., 1935, p. 72.

18 Black, Martha. *My Seventy Years.* London, Edinburgh, Paris, Melbourne, Toronto, and New York: Thomas Nelson and Sons Ltd., 1938, p. 94.

19 McKeown, *The Trail Led North,* p. 98.

20 Armstrong, Nevill A. D. *Yukon Yesterdays: Thirty Years of Adventure in the Klondike.* London: John Long Ltd., 1936, pp. 20-21.

21 Gates, Michael. *Gold at Fortymile: Early Days in the Yukon.* Vancouver: University of British Columbia Press, 1994, pp. 142-3.

22 Innis, *Settlement,* pp. 190-1.

23 Brooks, *Blazing Alaska's Trails,* p. 346.

24 Riggs, Thomas, Christmas Collection 1873-1945, #61. Alaska and Polar Regions Department, Elmer E. Rasmuson Library, University of Alaska Fairbanks, University of Alaska Archives.

25 Armstrong, *Yukon Yesterdays,* p. 26-27.

26 Hunt, William. *North of 53°: The Wild Days of the Alaska-Yukon Mining Frontier 1870-1914.* New York and London: Macmillan Publishing Company and Collier Macmillan, 1974, p. 80.

27 Armstrong, *Yukon Yesterdays,* p. 44.

28 Innis, *Settlement,* p. 194.

29 McKay, Mrs. J. J. "How I Went Through Chilkoot Pass in the Dead of Winter," *Examiner Sunday Magazine,* February 20, 1898, pp. 1-2. McDonald, Alice. "As Well as Any Man: A Swedish Immigrant in Alaska," *The Alaska Journal,* Summer 1984, p. 41.

30 "Of More Value Than Gold," *Atlin News Miner,* May 25, 1973, p. 6.

31 Romig, Emily Craig. *A Pioneer Woman in Alaska.* Caldwell, Ohio: The Caxton Press, 1948, p. 109.

32 Evans, Chad. *Frontier Theatre.* Victoria: Sono Nis Press, 1983, p. 236.

33 Sinclair, John Alexander. Papers, Provincial Archives of British Columbia, Letter to his wife from Skagway, Jan. 5, 1899. His suggestion of "respectable jobs dancing" was an oxymoron in 1899.

34 McKeown, *The Trail Led North,* p. 170.

35 Ibid., p. 198-9.

36 *Klondike Nugget,* August 6, 1898.

37 DeGraf, Anna. *Pioneering on the Yukon: 1892-1917.* Hamden, Connecticut: The Shoestring Press, Inc., Archon Books, 1992, p.79.

38 Riggs, Christmas Collection 1873-1945, #61.

39 Clark, John A. Collection, Correspondence, KOC-4, Jan. 29, 1923. Alaska and Polar Regions Department, Elmer E. Rasmuson Library, University of Alaska Fairbanks.

40 If one pan produced this much gold, miners considered the area worth pursuing.

41 DeArmond, R. N. *Klondike Newsman: "Stroller" White.* Skagway: Lynn Canal Publishing, 1989, pp. 168-9. The "long, juicy waltz" was a favorite Klondike expression and one used by square dance callers of the era.

42 Wickersham, James A. *Old Yukon.* Washington, D. C.: Washington Law Book Co., 1938, p.409.

43 Johnson, *Carmack of the Klondike*, pp. 29-49.

44 *Seattle Times*, July 27, 1899, from an undated clipping in the *Bennett Sun*.

45 Johnson, *Carmack of the Klondike*, pp. 112-115.

46 Johnson, *Carmack of the Klondike*, p. 113. LeGrande later purchased property in the Fairbanks red light district and was subsequently arrested for running a house of ill fame (May 4, 1908, Case #305) and for bootlegging (September 4, 1906, Case #724). Marguerite's testimony is from the record of the Supreme Court of the State of Washington, "In the Matter of the Estate of George Washington Carmack," Case #18829, Brief of Respondent, pp. 14-15.

47 Johnson, *Carmack of the Klondike*, pp. 115-116 and 146-151.

3. MINING THE KLONDIKE KINGS

1 Hunt, William. *North of 53°: The Wild Days of the Alaska-Yukon Mining Frontier, 1870-1814*. New York: Macmillan Publishing Co., Inc.; London: Collier Macmillian Publishers, 1974, p. 80. (A good summation of many other accounts.)

2 Lucia, Ellis. *Klondike Kate: The Life of the Queen of the Klondike*. New York: Ballantine Books, Inc., 1962, pp. 12-13.

3 Ryley, Bay. "The Bawdy Language of Gold Digging: Regulating Prostitution in Dawson City, Yukon, 1898-1903." Paper for Nancy Forestell and Ian McKay, Kingston, Canada: Queen's University, July 14, 1993.

4 Brooks-Vincent, La Belle. *The Scarlet Life of Dawson and the Roseate Dawn of Nome*. Seattle: M. R. Mayor, 1900, pp. 66 and 68.

5 Lucia, Ellis. *Klondike Kate*. New York: Ballantine Books, 1982, p. 98.

6 Tigstad, Karl Johan Andersson. "Lucky Swede," produced for *Hemmets Journal* Vol. 30 24 7 75 from a manuscript in the Dawson Museum.

7 "Charley Anderson Writes his Troubles with his Mercenary Wife." *Daily Klondike Nugget*, March 9, 1901.

8 *Vancouver Providence*, Feb. 15, 1939. Tigstad, "Lucky Swede," produced for *Hemmets Journal* Vol. 30 and 31, the Dawson Museum. The latter is backed by numerous newspaper accounts on the feuding Andersons.

9 An undated article from the *Skagway Daily Alaskan* that was picked up by an area newspaper, Jan. 3, 1901. I have the clipping but the name of the paper is missing.

10 "Are All Marriages Void?" Editorial Page, *Dawson Daily News*, Dec. 9, 1899.

11 "Protected from Himself," *Dawson Daily News*, December 9, 1899, p. 1.

12 Porsild, Charlene. "Culture, Class and Community: New Perspectives on the Klondike Gold Rush, 1898-1905." Thesis, Ottawa, Ontario: Carleton University, 1994, p. 205.

13 *The Klondike News*, April 1, 1899, p. 1.

14 *The Dawson Daily News*, Mining Edition, Sept. 1899, p. 14.

15 Berton, Pierre. *Klondike: The Last Great Gold Rush, 1896-1899*. Toronto, Ontario: Penguin Books Ltd., 1958, revised 1972, pp. 230, 507, and 524.

16 *Klondike News*, April 1, 1898.

17 Berton, *Klondike*, pp. 507 and 524. Berton quotes the *Examiner*.

18 DeArmond, R. N. Interview with the author in Sitka, April 1995.

19 McCurdy, H. W. *The H. W. McCurdy Marine History of the Pacific Northwest, 1969-1976*, p. 130.

20 "End of the Trail," *Alaska Sportsman*, Oct. 1963, p. 45.

21 *Alaska Life*, Feb. 1942, p. 10.

22 McCurdy, *Marine History*, p. 130.

23 *Klondike Nugget*, August 31, 1898.

24 Thacker, Jan. *Heartland, Fairbanks Daily News Miner*, July 14, 1966. The caption under the photo of Ester Duffy's whorehouse, University of Alaska Archives, notes that Babe Wallace bought her prized piano when Ester went broke. A note on a photo of Babe Wallace in the Wickersham Collection, Alaska State Library, Juneau, notes Wallace married Capt. Barrington and later died of tuberculosis. In an interview with Hill's son, Bill Barrington, in Anchorage on June 22, 1996, he questioned the Dawson record of Sid's marriage to Dirty Maud, believing officials might have confused the sisters. However, the family was not aware of Hill's marriage to Babe Wallace, which was well documented, so the brothers may not have been completely open with their heirs about their early history.

25 Thacker, *Fairbanks Daily News Miner*, July 14, 1966.

26 Interview with Bill Barrington, June 22, 1996.

27 Beebe, Iola. *The True Life Story of Swiftwater Bill Gates*. Iola Beebe, 1908; Seattle: Facsimile Reproduction, 1967, p. 22.

28 Ibid., pp. 23-24.

29 Evans, Chad. *Frontier Theatre*. Victoria: Sono Nis Press, 1983, pp. 235.

30 "The Girl Who Danced at Dawson," *San Francisco Examiner*, Sept 26, 1897, p. 7.

31 *Seattle Daily Times*, Feb. 2, 1898.

32 Ibid.

33 *Daily Klondike Nugget*, Nov. 14, 1898.

34 Berton, *Klondike*, p. 413.

35 Clark, John. A. "Nicknames," in *Random Reminiscences of 22 Years in Alaska*, Vol. 1. Alaska and Polar Regions Department, Elmer E. Rasmuson Library, University of Alaska Fairbanks, Box 1.

36 Lung, Edward, as told to Ella Lung Martinsen.

Black Sand and Gold. New York: Vantage Press, 1956, pp. 43-44.

37 *Dawson Daily News,* Jan. 11, 1900, p. 2.

38 Berton, Laura Beatrice. *I Married the Klondike.* Ontario: McClelland & Steward, Inc., 1993, p. 122.

39 *Dawson Daily News,* March 1, 1917.

40 Martinsen, Ella Lung, as told to her by her mother, Velma D. Lung. *Trail to North Star Gold: True Story of the Alaska-Klondike Gold Rush.* Portland, Oregon: Metropolitan Press, 1969, p. 77.

41 Helen Wilson in Skagway to her sister Alice Wilson Bair in Pennsylvania, (undated) written at close of World War I in 1918. Alaska State Library, Alaska Historical Collections.

42 Porsild, "Culture, Class and Community," pp. 202-3.

43 *Dawson Klondike Nugget,* Nov. 16, 1901.

44 Berton, Laura, *I Married the Klondike,* p. 40.

45 National Archives Yukon Territorial Records, RG 91, vol. 74, file 78.

46 *Vancouver Daily Providence,* Oct. 30, 1918.

47 Alaska State Library, US District Court, Commissioner's Probate Records RG 506, Series 58, Box 4635.

48 Evans, *Frontier Theatre,* p. 243.

49 Martinsen, *Trail to North Star Gold,* p. 187. The author, who calls her Diamond Tooth Gertie, has a right to be confused because there were not only two headliners with diamond fillings but also "Diamond Lil" Davenport, who was a high-profile hooker.

50 *Alaska Sportsman,* June 1961. *Seattle Post Intelligencer,* June 20, 1975.

51 *Klondike Nugget,* Oct. 5, 1898.

52 Sheet music courtesy of Jean Murray of Clear, Alaska, who is writing the definitive book on gold rush music. Written and composed by Arthur Sheldon. Words revised by Hattie Anderson, copyright 1892 by Charles Shard & Co.

53 McKeown, Martha Ferguson. *The Trail Led North: Mont Hawthorne's Story.* Portland, Oregon: Binford and Mort, 1960, p. 171.

54 Ibid., p. 176.

55 *Klondike Nugget,* April 19, 1899.

56 McKeown, *The Trail Led North,* p. 176.

57 Berton, Pierre, *Klondike,* p. 488.

58 *Klondike Nugget,* Oct. 14, 1899.

59 *Dawson Daily News,* Jan. 9, 1900.

60 *Herald Tribune,* undated clip; *Elizabeth Daily Journal,* October 28, 1932; and *Herald Tribune,* February 3, 1939. In Esther Lyons file, Theatre Library, The New York Public Library for the Performing Arts, Lincoln Center, New York City.

61 Clips in files of Esther Lyon and Essie Lyons, Theatre Library, The New York Public Library for the Performing Arts, Lincoln Center, New York City.

62 *Dawson Daily Nugget,* Jan. 17, 1900.

63 *Dawson Daily Nugget,* November 8, 1890.

64 *Dawson Daily News,* March 13, 1900.

65 *Nome News,* Aug. 7, 1900.

66 *Nome News,* September 8, 1900.

67 Stroller's Column, *Daily Klondike Nugget,* March 2, 1901.

4. THE REAL WORKING GIRLS

1 Yukon Archives, King Vs. Benoit, GR Series 11, Vol. 1455, File 214.

2 Stevens, Gary L. "Gold Rush Theater in the Alaska-Yukon Frontier." Dissertation, Department of Speech, University of Oregon, August 1984, p. 533.

3 Booth, Michael R. "Gold Rush Theaters of the Klondike," *Beaver,* Spring 1962, pp. 33-34.

4 Trelawney-Ansell, E. C. *I Followed Gold.* New York: Lee Furman, Inc., 1939, p.171.

5 During this period my grandfather in Vermont paid his farm workers one dollar per day. For Dawson prices I used correspondence from John Clark to James Oliver, Jan. 29, 1923. Clark, John A., Collection, Alaska and Polar Regions Department, Elmer E. Rasmuson Library, University of Alaska Fairbanks, Box 1, #44. The letter agrees with several published accounts.

6 McKeown, Martha Ferguson. *The Trail Led North: Mont Hawthorne's Story.* Portland: Binford & Mort, 1960, p. 183.

7 Hunt, William. *Distant Justice: Policing the Alaskan Frontier.* Norman and London: University of Oklahoma Press, 1987, pp. 60-61. *Seattle Times,* June 3, 1898.

8 Martin, Cy. *Whisky and Wild Women: An Amusing Account of the Saloons and Bawds of the Old West.* New York: Hart Publishing Co., 1986, p. 223.

9 Collier, William Ross, and Westgate, Edwin Victor. *The Reign of Soapy Smith.* Garden City, N.J.: Doubleday, Doran & Company, 1935, p 248.

10 Martinsen, Ella Lung, as told to her by her mother, Velma D. Lung. *Trail to North Star Gold: True Story of the Alaska-Klondike Gold Rush.* Portland, Oregon: Metropolitan Press, 1969, pp. 11-12, 16-17.

11 Collier and Westgate, *Reign of Soapy Smith,* pp. 248-49.

12 *Klondike Nugget,* Nov. 4, 1899.

13 Martin, *Whisky and Wild Women,* p. 230.

14 Porsild, Charlene L. "Culture, Class and Community: New Perspectives on the Klondike Gold Rush: 1896-1905." Thesis, Ottawa, Ontario: Carleton University, 1994, p. 170.

14 Coates, Kenneth, and Morrison, William R. *Land of the Midnight Sun: A History of the Yukon.* Edmonton: Hurtig Publishers, 1988, p. 107.

15 Porsild, "Culture, Class and Community," p. 193.

16 Black, Martha, as told to Elizabeth Bailey Price.

My Seventy Years. London, Edinburgh, Paris, Melbourne, Toronto, and New York: Thomas Nelson and Sons Ltd., pp. 134-5.

[17] Yukon Archives, Series 11, Vol. 1447, File 67. *Klondike Nugget,* August 12, 1899.

[18] *Klondike Daily Nugget,* March 16 and 18, 1901.

[19] "Frugal Pearl Mitchell," *Klondike Nugget,* Oct. 24, 1900. "Bleeker Objects to the Testimony of Josie Gordon in the Slorah Murder Trial," *Klondike Nugget,* Nov. 16, 1900.

[20] Black, *My Seventy Years,* p. 134.

[21] *Dawson Daily News,* Nov. 14, 1899.

[22] *Klondike Nugget,* April 22, 1899 and November 18, 1899.

[23] *Daily Klondike Nugget,* May 11, 1903. National Archives of Canada, RCMP RG 18 D4, v. 1. *Dawson Goal Register,* May 12, 1903.

[24] National Archives of Canada, RCMP RG 18 D4, v. 1, Police Goal Record, 1902. *Klondike Daily Nugget,* May 11, 1903. *Dawson Daily News,* May 12, 1903.

[25] *Klondike Nugget,* July 3, 1903.

[26] *Dawson Daily News,* May 27, 1903.

[27] Parrish, Maud. *Nine Pounds of Luggage.* Philadelphia, New York, London, Toronto: J.B. Lippincott, 1939, p. 25.

[28] Trelawney-Ansell, *I Followed Gold,* pp. 176-179.

[29] "She Blew Out Her Brains," *Klondike Nugget,* Dec. 14, 1898. "The Stroller's Column," *Klondike Nugget,* Oct. 21, 1899.

[30] *Klondike Nugget,* March 29, 1899.

[31] Evans, Chad. *Frontier Theatre.* Victoria: Sono Nis Press, 1983, p. 243. Evans quotes an article in the *Klondike Nugget.*

[32] *Klondike Nugget,* Nov. 4, 1899.

[33] DeGraf, Anna. *Pioneering on the Yukon, 1892-1917.* Edited by Roger S. Brown. Hamden, Connecticut: The Shoestring Press, Inc., Archon Books, 1992, pp. 79-81.

[34] Berton, Laura Beatrice. *I Married the Klondike.* Toronto, Ontario: McClelland & Stewart Inc., 1954, pp. 65-7. Whyard, Flo, "It Must Have Been Quite A Party," *Yukon News,* Feb 8, 1995, p. 20 from undated Dawson police records.

[35] Backhouse, Frances. "Women of the Klondike," *The Beaver,* Dec. 1988, p. 32.

[36] Walkowitz, Judith. *Prostitution and Victorian Society: Women, Class and the State.* Cambridge: Cambridge University Press, 1980, p.1.

[37] Guest, Hal J. *A History of the City of Dawson, Yukon Territory, 1896-1920.* Microfiche Reporter Series No. 7, Canadian Parks Service, 1981, pp. 221. Cites PAC, RCMP Records, v. 3055, Oct. 12, 1898.

[38] Letter from Ogilvie to officer commanding NWMP, Jan. 15, 1900. Yukon Archives, YTR,

CLB v.77, pp. 738.

[39] Anonymous. *Madeleine: An Autobiography.* New York: Persea Books, 1986 (Original edition 1919), p. 180.

[40] DeGraf, *Pioneering,* pp. 81-82.

[41] John H. McDougal to W. C. E. Stewart, Sept. 10, 1899. W. C. E. Stewart Papers NA MG29 C 90 File # 4,Canadian National Archives, Ottawa.

[42] *Klondike Nugget,* June 25, 1902 (A reprint from the *Seattle Washingtonian*). DeArmond, R. N. *Klondike Newsman: "Stroller" White.* Skagway: Lynn Canal Publishing, 1989, pp. 125-130.

[43] National Archives of Canada, RCMP RG 18 D4, v.1. *Dawson Goal Register,* July 11, 1902. Riggs, Thomas C., Collection, Alaska and Polar Regions Department, Elmer E. Rasmuson Library, University of Alaska Fairbanks, #61.

[44] Yukon Archives, Royal Northwest Mounted Police Town Station, Dawson, Y.T., July 25, 1905.

[45] Backhouse, "Women of the Klondike," p. 31.

[45] Black, *My Seventy Years,* p. 138.

[47] Hamlin, C. S. *Old Times on the Yukon.* Los Angeles: Wetzel Publishing Co, Inc., 1928, pp. 14 and 18.

[48] "Where The Great Fire Started," *Klondike Nugget,* May 6, 1899.

[49] Report of S. B. Steele, May 1899, PA, RCMP Records, Vol. 1444, f 181, p. 3.

[50] *Klondike Nugget,* April 12, 1899.

[51] *Klondike Nugget,* Oct. 29, 1898.

[52] "The New Tenderloin," *Klondike Nugget,* May 12, 1899. "Third Street Girls Given Twenty-four Hours in Which to Get Into the Confines of the Tenderloin District," *Klondike Nugget,* August 9, 1899.

[53] A number of researchers have unsuccessfully attempted to discover who actually profited from this venture: Guest, *History of the City of Dawson,* pp. 223-4. Also Ryley, Bay. "The Bawdy Language of Gold Digging: Regulating Prostitution in Dawson City, Yukon, 1898-1903." Paper for Nancy Forestell and Ian McKay, Kingston: Queen's University, 1993, pp. 34-35. Steele never revealed with whom he made the arrangements for the move, but they must have been major political and economic players in Yukon Territory.

[54] Armstrong, Nevill A. D. *Yukon Yesterdays: Thirty Years of Adventure in the Klondike.* London: John Long Ltd., 1936, pp. 53-54. His figures agree with other independent accounts including La Belle Brooks-Vincent's *Scarlet Life of Dawson and the Roseate Dawn of Nome.* Seattle: M.R. Mayor, 1900, p. 77.

[55] McPhail Report, Provincial Archives of Alberta, RCMP Records, v. 1445, f181, pt. 6.

[56] "Yesterday's Big Fire: Correct Story of How the Fire Originated," *Dawson Daily News,* Jan. 12, 1900.

[57] Booth, "Gold Rush Theaters of the Klondike," p. 33. Stevens, "Gold Rush Theater in the Alaska-Yukon Frontier," pp. 66-7.

[58] *Dawson Daily News*, March 8, 1900.

[59] *Klondike Nugget*, Oct. 21, 1902.

[60] Guest, *History of the City of Dawson*, p. 232.

[61] *Klondike Nugget*, March 18, 1901.

[62] Berton, Laura, *I Married the Klondike*, pp. 76-7.

5. MAE FIELD

[1] Berg, Helen. "The Doll of Dawson." *Alaska Sportsman*, Feb. 1944, pp. 8-9.

[2] Berg, "Doll of Dawson," p. 9.

[3] Hot Springs Docket Books 1890-98, researched by Helen Magee, Hot Springs, S.D.

[4] *Rapid City Tri Star Weekly*, March 19, 1895.

[5] Marriage License issued September 6, 1897, on file with Clerk of Courts, Hot Springs, South Dakota. *Hot Springs Star*, Sept. 10, 1897.

[6] Northwest Mounted Police records at Lake Bennett, May 31, 1898. "Pan For Gold" database, Yukon Territory: Http://www.goldrush. org/ghost-07.htm. Berg, "Doll of Dawson," p. 25.

[7] Berg, "Doll of Dawson," pp. 25-26.

[8] Berg, "Doll of Dawson," p. 26. *Hot Springs Star*, Jan. 21 and July 21, 1899.

[9] Berg, "Doll of Dawson," p. 30.

[10] Peterson, Art, and Williams, D. Scott. *Murder, Madness and Mystery: An Historical Narrative of Mollie Walsh Bartlett From the Days of the Klondike Gold Rush.* Williams, Oregon: Castle Peak Editions, pp. 25-26 and 32-33.

[11] Berg, "Doll of Dawson," p. 26.

[12] Ibid., p. 30.

[13] Ibid., p. 29.

[14] *Klondike Nugget*, Oct. 28, 1899.

[15] *Klondike Nugget*, Nov. 8, 1899.

[16] Berg, "Doll of Dawson," p. 29. *Klondike Nugget*, Nov. 11, 1899.

[17] Berg, "Doll of Dawson," p. 30.

[18] Polk Directories, 1901-1912. The Fairbanks Genealogical Society database, http://www.polarnet.com/users/fgs/db/polk.htm.

[19] "In Territorial Court: May Fields Compelled to Pay Her Laundry Bill. A Case That Was Not Devoid of Funny Incidents," *Klondike Nugget*, February 15, 1900, p. 5.

[20] *Hot Springs Star*, November 11, 1900 and July 5, 1901.

[21] Hot Springs Land Records, researched by Helen Magee. Polk Directories, 1901-1912.

[22] *Klondike Nugget*, Feb. 2-3, 1903.

[23] *Dawson Daily News*, June 18, 1903. *Klondike Nugget*, June 18, 1903.

[24] Letter from J.W. Falconer to Chief Inspector, May 2, 1904, Yukon Archives Gov 1619 XRG1, Series Vol 9, 1443, folder 2/3in.

[25] Research by Helen Magee, Hot Springs, S.D. Polks Directories for Dawson, 1903-1911.

[26] *Rex v May Fields*, Yukon Archives, Series ll, Vol 1431, File #10.

[27] Post office worker Clary Craig's list of people dying or leaving the Klondike. "Pan for Gold" database.

[28] Berg, "Doll of Dawson," p. 30-31.

[29] Ibid., p. 27.

[30] Polk Directories database. Charles, Pat, of Ketchikan. Interview with the author, Jan. 1997.

6. CORRINE B GRAY

[1] 1880 U.S. Census, Stark County, Ohio. Letter from Miss Laureen K. Landis, Genealogy Div. Head, to Neal Thompson Gardner, Stark County District Library, Canton, Ohio, Jan. 8, 1966, Ohio Historical Society, Columbus.

[2] "Corrine Has More Trouble: Two of Her Favorites Clash at Bennett." *Dawson Daily News*, Nov. 22, 1899, p. 1.

[3] Berton, Pierre. *Klondike: The Last Great Gold Rush, 1896-1899.* Toronto, Ontario: Penguin, 1990, p. 476 and 549.

[4] *Dawson Daily News*, Nov. 22, 1899.

[5] *Klondike Nugget*, Oct. 14, 1899.

[6] *Dawson Daily News*, Nov. 22, 1899.

[7] *Klondike Nugget*, Oct. 18, 1899.

[8] *Klondike Nugget*, Nov. 18, 1899.

[9] Original reprinted undated in the *Dawson Daily News*, Nov. 22, 1899.

[10] *The Dawson Daily News*, March 27, 1900. Also the *Klondike Nugget* of the same date.

[11] *Annual Report of the North-West Mounted Police*, 64 Victoria, A, 1901, p. 38, National Archives of Canada.

[12] Letter from William Ballou to his brother Walt, Dec.10, 1901, William Ballou Collection, University of Alaska Archives.

[13] Ibid., June 19, 1899.

[14] Ibid., Sept. 25, 1901. Population figure comes from Orth, Donald J. *Dictionary of Alaska Place Names*. Washington, D.C.: U.S. Government Printing Office, 1986, p. 791.

[15] Letter from William Ballou to his mother, Sept. 25, 1901, William Ballou Collection, University of Alaska Archives.

[16] Letter from William Ballou to his brother Walt, Nov. 1, 1901, William Ballou Collection, University of Alaska Archives.

[17] Ibid.

[18] Ibid., May 28, 1902.

[19] Obituary of William Ray Durfee, *Ashland Daily Press*, May 4, 1915. Obituary of Eugenia Durfee, *Ashland Daily Press*, April 10, 1930. *The Descendants of Thomas Durfee of Portsmouth, R. I.* Washington, D.

C.: Press of Gibson Brothers, 1905, pp. 372-3.

20 Letter from William Ballou to his brother Walt, May 28, 1902, William Ballou Collection, University of Alaska Archives.

21 Ibid., November 3, 1902.

22 Letter from William Ballou to his mother, December 3, 1902.

23 Letter from William Ballou to his brother Walt, February 13, 1903.

24 *The Alaska Forum*, March 14, 1903.

25 Letter from William Ballou to his brother Walt, May 15, 1903.

26 *The Alaska Forum*, March 14, 1903.

27 Rampart Probate Records, March 18, 1903, now in the Record's Office, Fairbanks, Alaska.

28 Letter from William Ballou to his brother Walt, May 19, 1903.

29 Undated clipping in the William Ballou collection.

30 Letter from William Ballou to his brother Walt, May 19, 1903.

31 Undated clipping in the William Ballou collection. *The* (Skagway) *Daily Alaska*, July 9, 1903.

32 Hudson, Sally. Interview with the author in Fairbanks, Alaska, March 1995.

33 Rampart Probate Records, March 18, 1903, now in the Records Office, Fairbanks, Alaska.

34 (Rampart) *Yukon Valley News*, August 3, 1904. Hunt, William R. "Judge Ballou of Rampart." *The Alaska Journal*, Winter 1972, pp. 41-47.

7. KLONDIKE KATE ROCKWELL

1 Evans, Chad. *Frontier Theatre: A History of Nineteenth-Century Theatrical Entertainment in the Canadian Far North West and Alaska*. Victoria, British Columbia: Sono Nis Press, 1983, p. 241.

2 Matson, Kate Rockwell, as told to Mary Mann. "I Was Queen of the Klondike." *Alaska Sportsman*, Aug. 1944, p. 10. Lucia, Ellis. *Klondike Kate, 1873-1957*. New York: Ballantine Books, Inc., 1962, pp. 74-75.

3 Lucia, *Klondike Kate*, pp. 21-28.

4 Schillios, Rolv. "Dance Hall Girl." *Alaska Magazine*, March 1956, p. 9. Matson, "I Was Queen," pp. 9-11.

5 Matson, "I Was Queen," p. 44 and 53-56. Schillios, "Dance Hall Girl," pp. 10-11. Obituary for Danny Allmon, *Vancouver Daily Province*, Nov. 2, 1901, taken from Kate Rockwell's personal scrapbook, Archives, University of Alaska Fairbanks.

6 Interview with Laura McCarley, 1949. Notes 0004VF included in *Histories of Downtown Buildings*, "The Imperial Saloon," Juneau, Alaska, 1978, State Historical Library.

7 Lucia, *Klondike Kate*, p. 76.

8 Matson, "I Was Queen," p. 29.

9 Lombard, Charles. "The Little Parson. . . ." *Alaska Life*, December 1939.

10 NWMP Records at Chilkoot Checkpoint, June 4, 1900. "Ghosts of the Gold Rush" database, Yukon Territory: http://www.gold-rush.org/ghost-07.htm.

11 Schillios, "Dance Hall Girl," p. 11.

12 Matson, "I Was Queen," p. 29. Lucia, *Klondike Kate*, p. 69. Kate saved photos of Allmon and his obituary until her own death.

13 King, Jean Beach. *Arizona Charlie: A Legendary Cowboy, Klondike Stampeder and Wild West Showman*. Phoenix, Arizona: A Heritage Publishers Book, 1989, p. 219.

14 Schillios, "Dance Hall Girl," pp. 30-31.

15 Lucia, *Klondike Kate*, pp. 74-5.

16 Martinson, Ella Lung, as told to her by her mother, Velma D. Lung. *The Trail to North Star Gold: True Story of the Alaska-Klondike Gold Rush*. Portland, Oregon: Metropolitan Press, 1996, p. 186-7.

17 Matson, "I Was Queen," p. 31.

18 "The Queen of the Klondike." *Frontier Days in the Yukon*. Edited by Garnet Basque. Dawson City, 1902.

19 Schillios, "Dance Hall Girl," p. 31.

20 Lucia, *Klondike Kate*, pp.79-80.

21 Saloutos, Theodore. "Alexander Pantages, Theater Magnate of the West." *Pacific Northwest Quarterly*, Oct. 1966, pp. 237-38. Saloutos cites an interview with Rodney Pantages, Dec. 3, 1965; Morgan, Murray, *Skid Row*, New York: 1951, p. 151-2; Crane, Warren E. "Alexander Pantages," *System*, Vol. 28, March 1920, p. 502; *Los Angeles Times*, Nov. 28, 1929.

22 *Seattle Post-Intelligencer*, April 9, 1926.

23 King, *Arizona Charlie*, p. 209.

24 Schillios, "Dance Hall Girl," p. 32.

25 Matson, "I Was Queen," p. 30. Martinsen, *Trail to North Star Gold*, p. 187-9.

26 Matson, "I Was Queen," p. 31.

27 Elliott, Eugene Clinton. *A History of Variety-Vaudeville in Seattle from the Beginning to 1914*. Seattle: University of Washington Press, 1944, p. 107.

28 Hall, Warren. *Esquire*, May 1951, p. 145.

29 Alexander Pantages Letters 1902-3 and 1922, University of Washington Archives, ACC 331-001.

30 Lucia, *Klondike Kate*, p. 106.

31 Letters from Alexander Pantages to Kate Rockwell, March 4, 1903, and July 12, 1903.

32 Post office worker Clary Craig's list of people dying or leaving the Klondike, "Pan For Gold" database.

33 Matson, "I Was Queen," p. 30.

34 Lucia, *Klondike Kate*, pp. 108-9.

35 Ibid., p. 111.

36 Schillios, "Dance Hall Girl," p. 32. Docket No.

47,301, King County, Washington.

37 Lucia, *Klondike Kate*, p. 121.

38 Schillios, Rolv. "Dreams and Reality." *The Alaska Sportsman*, April 1956, p. 16.

39 Lucia, *Klondike Kate*, pp. 117-120.

40 Saloutos cites *Seattle Argus*, Feb. 12 and 19, 1910, and April 2, 1910.

41 Schillios, "Dreams and Reality," p. 16.

42 Ibid., p. 17.

43 Lucia, *Klondike Kate*, p. 137-41.

44 Schillios, "Dreams and Reality," p. 17.

45 Letter from Rockwell to lawyer Thomas D. Page, from Princeville, Oregon, Jan. 30, 1920 and May 27, 1922, University of Washington.

46 Saloutos, "Alexander Pantages," pp. 141 and 146.

47 Lucia, *Klondike Kate*, pp. 145 and 153.

48 Saloutos, "Alexander Pantages," p. 146. Lucia, *Klondike Kate*, p. 173.

49 Lucia, *Klondike Kate*, p. 186.

50 Schillios, "Dreams and Reality," p. 39.

51 Ibid., p. 19.

52 *New York Times*, Feb. 1, 1943.

53 Schillios, "Dreams and Reality," p. 39.

54 Lucia, *Klondike Kate*, pp. 222-23. Schillios, "Dreams and Reality," pp. 39-40.

55 Schillios, "Dreams and Reality," p. 40.

56 Matson, "I Was Queen," p. 31. Lucia, *Klondike Kate*, p. 191.

8. NOME'S CROOKED GOLD RUSH

1 Berton, Pierre. *Klondike: The Last Great Gold Rush 1896-1899*. Toronto, Ontario, Canada: Penguin, 1958, p. 486.

2 "Blanche Lamonte Murder/Suicide." *Klondike Nugget*, Aug. 12, 1899.

3 Porsild, Charlene L. "Culture, Class and Community: New Perspectives on the Klondike Gold Rush, 1896-1905." Thesis, Carleton University, Ottawa, Ontario, 1994, p. 199. Cites R. W. Cauley Papers, Yukon Territory Archives.

4 Riggs, Thomas, Christmas Collection, 1873-1945, #61. Alaska and Polar Regions Department, Elmer E. Rasmuson Library, University of Alaska Fairbanks.

5 *Dawson Daily News*, Sept. 20, 1899.

6 Cole, Terrence. *Nome: City of the Golden Beaches*. Anchorage, Alaska: Alaska Geographic, Vol 11, No. 1, 1894, pp. 20-23.

7 Brooks, Alfred Hulse. *Blazing Alaska's Trails*. Second Edition. Fairbanks: University of Alaska Press, 1973, pp. 387-89.

8 Denison, Merrill. *Klondike Mike: An Alaskan Odyssey*. New York: William Morrow & Co., 1943, pp. 260 and 275-6.

9 Evans, Chad. *Frontier Theatre: A History of Nineteenth-Century Theatrical Entertainment in the Canadian Far*

North and Alaska. Victoria, B.C.: Sono Nis Press, 1983, p. 249. Major P.H. Ray to the Commanding Officer, Fort Gibbon, 10 November 1899, National Archives, Washington, D. C., District of North Alaska-Letters of P. H. Ray, Part 3, Engry 533, RG 393.

10 *Dawson Daily News*, Dec. 28, 1899.

11 Hunt, William. *Distant Justice: Policing the Alaska Frontier*. Norman and London: University of Oklahoma Press, 1987, pp. 87-88.

12 Ibid., p. 85.

13 Brooks, *Blazing Alaska's Trails*, pp. 376-77.

14 Dunham, Samuel C. *The Yukon and Nome Gold Regions*. U.S. Department of Labor, Vol. 5, Bulletin no. 29, July 1900, p. 845.

15 Brooks, *Blazing Alaska's Trails*, p. 379. Hunt, William R. *Golden Places: The History of Alaska-Yukon Mining with Particular Reference to Alaska's National Parks*. Anchorage: National Park Service, 1990, p. 118.

16 Brooks, *Blazing Alaska's Trails*, p. 389.

17 *Nome News*, Aug. 30, 1900.

18 Trelawney-Ansell, E. C. *I Followed Gold*. New York: Lee Furman, Inc., 1939, pp. 223-224.

19 Wallace, John B. "Three Strikes Was Out!" *The Alaska Sportsman*, Nov. 1939.

20 *Nome Weekly News*, Oct. 6, 1901. Trelawney-Ansell, *I Followed Gold*, p. 224.

21 Brooks, *Blazing Alaska's Trails*, p. 385.

22 Letter from William Ballou to his brother Walt, June 22, 1900, William Ballou Collection, Alaska and Polar Regions Department, Elmer E. Rasmuson Library, University of Alaska Fairbanks.

23 Brooks, *Blazing Alaska's Trails*, p. 397.

24 Hunt, *Distant Justice*, p. 348, Chapter 7, note 2.

25 Ibid., p. 126.

26 Hunt, William. *North of 53°: The Wild Days of Alaska-Yukon Mining Frontier 1870-1914*. New York and London: Macmillan Publishing Co., Inc. and Collier Macmillan Publishers, 1974, p. 126. Reed, Elmer. "The Mayor." *The Alaska Sportsman*, Dec. 1948, p. 11.

27 Hunt, *Distant Justice*, p. 137.

28 Trelawney-Ansell, *I Followed Gold*, pp. 221-224.

29 Ibid., p. 228.

30 Parrish, Maud. *Nine Pounds of Luggage*. New York, London, Toronto: J.B. Lippincott Company, 1939, pp. 28.

31 Wallace, John B. "Nome Was Like That." *Alaska Sportsman*, Oct. 1939, p. 33.

32 *Fairbanks Sunday Times*, Oct. 1, 1911, courtesy of the Rex Fisher Collection.

33 Reed, "The Mayor," p. 10-11.

34 Ibid., p. 26. Evans, Chad. *Frontier Theatre: A History of Nineteenth-Century Theatrical Entertainment in the*

Canadian Far West and Alaska. Victoria, B.C.: Sono Nis Press, 1983, p. 249.

35 Trelawney-Ansell, *I Followed Gold*, pp. 227-8.

36 *Dawson Daily Nugget*, Jan. 17, 1900. Earp, Josephine Sarah Marcus. *I Married Wyatt Earp*. Collected and edited by Glenn C. Boyer. Tucson, Arizona: University of Arizona Press, 1990, pp. 148 and 199.

37 Earp, *I Married Wyatt Earp*, pp. 198-9.

38 Ibid., pp. 160-1 and 200-20.

39 Cole, *Nome*, p. 95.

40 *Nome Daily Chronicle*, Aug. 21, 1900.

41 *Nome Daily News*, July 31, 1900.

42 Hunt, *North of 53°*, p. 248.

43 *Nome Daily Chronicle*, Aug. 23, 1900.

44 *Nome Daily Chronicle*, Aug. 22, 1900.

45 *Nome Daily Chronicle*, Aug. 23, 1900.

46 *Nome Daily Chronicle*, Sept. 8, 1900.

47 *Nome Daily Chronicle*, Sept. 10, 1900.

48 *Nome Daily Chronicle*, Sept. 21, 1900.

49 *Nome Gold Digger*, Sept. 26, 1900.

50 *Nome Gold Digger*, Aug. 28, 1901.

51 Stevens, Gary L. "Gold Rush Theater in the Alaska-Yukon Frontier." Doctor of Philosophy dissertation, University of Oregon. Ann Arbor, Michigan: University Microfilms International, 1985, p. 244.

52 Atwood, Evangeline. *Frontier Politics: Alaska's James Wickersham*. Portland, Oregon: Binford & Mort, 1979, pp. 31-34.

53 Ibid., p. 90.

54 James Wickersham Diary, December 11, 1900, Wickersham Collection, Alaska State Library, Juneau.

55 *Nome Nugget*, July 12, 1901.

56 Hunt, *North of 53°*, p. 197.

57 Dufresne, Klondy, with Cory Ford. "Daughter of the Gold Rush." *Alaska* magazine, p. 11-13.

58 *Nome Nugget*, July 26, 1901.

59 Hunt, *Distant Justice*, p. 141. Hunt cites *U.S. v. John J. Jolley*, court record Case 216 FRC.

60 *Nome Chronicle*, Dec. 15, 1900. Hunt, *North of 53°*, p. 197.

61 *The Nome Nugget*, May 14, 1904.

62 Nome Criminal Docket Fee Book OS 636, Alaska State Library, RG 507, 345.

63 Ibid.

64 *Nome Nugget*, May 4, 1904.

65 Nome Ordinance #146, passed June 1, 1904, and #148, passed June 28, 1904.

66 *Nome Nugget*, March 22, 1905.

67 *Nome Weekly Nugget*, Sept. 20, 1905. Neilson, Jon. "Sourdough Sirens and Cheechako Chippies: Alaska's Other Gold Rush." *Alaska Today*, May 1981, p. 16.

68 Wallace, John B. "We Settled Disputes With Fists." *The Alaska Sportsman*, Aug. 1939, p. 17.

69 *Nome Nugget*, Sept. 16 and 20, 1905.

70 *Daily Gold Digger*, March 22, 1907.

71 *Pioneer Press*, June 2 and 3, 1908.

72 Wallace, John B. "The People of Nome Were Scandalized." *Alaska Sportsman*, December 1939, p. 16.

73 Ibid., pp. 16-17. *Nome Gold Digger*, July 8, 1908. Walsh, Jim. Interview with the author, Nome, summer of 1995.

74 Osborne, Alice. "The Glory that Was Nome." *Heartland, Fairbanks Daily News-Miner*, June 25, 1995, H-13.

9. FAIRBANKS BATTLING THE ODDS

1 Hunt, William. *North of 53°: The Wild Days of the Alaska-Yukon Mining Frontier 1870-1914*. New York: Macmillan Publishing Company and London: Collier Macmillan Publishers, 1974, p. 139. *Fairbanks Daily News Miner*, Pioneer Edition, June 30, 1958. Nielson, Jon. "Sourdough Sirens and Cheechako Chippies," *Alaska Today*, May 1981 and April 1982, pp. 14 and 17.

2 Cole, Terrence. *E. T. Barnette: The Strange Story of the Man Who Founded Fairbanks*. Anchorage: Alaska Northwest Publishing Co., 1981, p.vii.

3 Robe, Cecil F. "The Penetration of an Alaskan Frontier: The Tanana Valley and Fairbanks." Ph. D. dissertation, Yale University, 1943, p. 118.

4 Cole, *E. T. Barnette*, pp. 20-25.

5 C. W. Adams. "I Hauled Fairbanks on a Sternwheeler." *Fairbanks Daily News Miner*, Special Golden Days Edition, July 22, 1952.

6 "RICH STRIKE MADE IN THE TANANA," *Yukon Sun*, Jan. 17, 1903.

7 *Klondike Daily Nugget*, March 31, 1903.

8 *Klondike Daily Nugget*, July 1, 1903.

9 Cole, *E. T. Barnette*, pp. 63-68. "Birthday Was 1902," *Fairbanks Daily News Miner*, Pioneer Edition, June 30, 1958.

10 "Hall Opens In Fairbanks," *Klondike Nugget*, May 8, 1903.

11 Letter from Sara Gibson to her son Tom, Sarah Ellen Gibson Collection, Box 1, Folder 71, Alaska and Polar Regions Department, Elmer E. Rasmuson Library, University of Alaska Fairbanks.

12 James Wickersham Diary, April 16, 1903, James Wickersham Collection, Alaska State Library.

13 *Yukon World*, Oct. 9, 1904.

14 *US v William B. Duenkel*. National Archives, Pacific Alaska Region RS Criminal Cases, 1900-1920 Box 8 RG 21 Case #205 4th Judicial District.

15 Robe, "Penetration of an Alaskan Frontier," p. 168.

16 Atwood, Evangeline. *Frontier Politics: Alaska's James Wickersham*. Portland, Oregon: Binford & Mort,

1979, p. 120.

[17] Stephens, Gary L. "Gold Rush Theater in the Alaska-Yukon Frontier." Dissertation for the Department of Speech and the Graduate School, University of Oregon, 1984, pp. 498-9.

[18] Dean, David M. *Breaking Trail: Hudson Stuck of Texas and Alaska*. Athens, Ohio: Ohio University Press, 1988, p. 73. Quotes letter from Stuck to John Wilson Wood, Sept. 7, 1904, and Dec, 12, 1904.

[19] *Valdez News*, Oct. 8, 1904 (Rex Fisher Collection).

[20] *Alaska Prospector*, April 13, 1905 (Rex Fisher Collection).

[21] *The Fairbanks Daily Times*, June 25, 1906.

[22] *Alaska Prospector*, Sept. 14, 1905 (Rex Fisher Collection).

[23] *Fairbanks Daily Times*, Dec. 24, 1906.

[24] *Fairbanks Evening News*, Sept. 23, 1905 (Rex Fisher Collection).

[25] "Wallace Woman Feared for Life." *Fairbanks Evening News*, July 18, 1905. Hunt, *North of 53°*, p. 160.

[26] *Tanana Weekly Miner*, January 18 and 19, 1907. Richard Geoghegan diary of January 12, 1907, translated by David Richardson, Richard Geoghegan Collection, Alaska and Polar Regions Department, Elmer E. Rasmuson Library, University of Alaska Fairbanks.

[27] Fairbanks City Council records, April 9, 1907, Alaska and Polar Regions Department, Elmer E. Rasmuson Library, University of Alaska Fairbanks.

[28] Dean, *Breaking Trail*, p. 72. Quotes letter from Stuck to John Wilson Wood, Sept. 7, 1904.

[29] Warren, Father William.Interview with author, Fairbanks Episcopal Church, spring 1972. Warren had read Stuck's diaries, and was struck by the churchman's deep concern for the young miners and observed he might well have been a latent homosexual. Warren also said that the diary covering Stuck's early years in Fairbanks had been destroyed by a church elder who was shocked by it. Stuck's biographer, David Dean, notes the churchman's unease with women in *Breaking Trail*, p. x, and later via telephone agreed the brilliant churchman had a much stronger love of his fellow man than womankind.

[30] Robe, "The Penetration of an Alaskan Frontier," p. 187.

[31] Affidavit by James Benjamin Daniels, Georgia Lee's cousin, December 15, 1955, Probate Records of Georgia Lee, Alaska State Library.

[32] Sneddeker, Duane R. "Regulating Vice: Prostitution and the St. Louis Social Evil Ordinance, 1870-1874." *Gateway Heritage*, Vol. 11, No. 2, Fall 1990, pp. 20-46.

[33] Warren, interview. According to Father Warren,

Stuck's diary was quite specific about the arrangements and his request to Andrew Nerland for help. Unlike St. Louis, in Fairbanks there appears to have been no city ordinance to establish the red light district, but once established the city council's open references to it and those of the press show it to have been a well-sanctioned institution.

[34] *Klondike Nugget*, Oct. 21, 1902.

[35] Wold, Jo Anne. *The Andrew Nerland Legacy*. Fairbanks: Nerland Family, 1984, p. 39.

[36] Jones, Albert N. Letter to the author, April 5, 1972.

[37] *Fairbanks Daily News Miner*, Sept. 13 and 19, 1906.

[38] Snapp, Tom. "Fourth Ave. 'Line' Was Quite a Place; Prostitution Condoned." *All-Alaska Weekly*, Friday, Feb. 2, 1973. Corroborated by just about any old-timer I ever interviewed.

[39] Ibid.

[40] Redding, Robert H. "The Line Offered Fairbanks Men Discreet Entertainment." *Fairbanks Daily News-Miner*, April 28, 1991.

[41] Nordale, LaDessa, a former Fairbanks judge. Interview with the author, at the Pioneer Home, May 1992.

[42] *Fairbanks Daily Times*, March 28, April 2, 1907 (Rex Fisher Collection). *Tanana Weekly Miner*, April 12, 1907 (Rex Fisher Collection).

[43] *Fairbanks Evening News*, Dec. 12, 1906.

[44] *Fairbanks Evening Alaskan*, April 23, 1907.

[45] *Fairbanks Daily Times*, Aug. 24, 1907.

[46] *Fairbanks Daily Times*, Dec. 10, 1907.

[47] *Fairbanks Daily Times*, Dec. 11, 1907.

[48] *Fairbanks Daily News*, Dec. 12, 1907. *Fairbanks Daily Times*, Dec. 12, 1907.

[49] *Fairbanks Daily Times*, April 30, 1908.

[50] *Fairbanks Daily Times*, May 1, 1908.

[51] *Fairbanks Daily Times*, May 6, 7, 8, 9, and Dec. 27, 1908.

[52] *The Tanana Tribune*, May 9, 1908 (Rex Fisher Collection). *Fairbanks Daily Times*, June 6, 1906.

[53] Langum, David J. *Crossing Over the Line: Legislating Morality and the Mann Act*.Chicago and London: The University of Chicago Press, 1994, pp. 23 and 28-29.

[54] I am most grateful to historian Clause M. Naske, who originally discovered Krauczunas's files in the National Archives and used them to write an intriguing piece, "The Red Lights of Fairbanks," for the *Alaska Journal*, Spring 1984. He kindly provided me with notes and photos for this chapter. Much of the following comes from letters from Krauczunas to Commissioner-General of Immigration, Aug. 22 and 28,1909, National Archives, R.G. 85, File 52484-28, White Slave Traffic.

[55] Dawson Gaol Register, May 12, 1902, National Archives, Ottawa. *Daily Klondike Nugget,* March 25, 1902.

[56] *Klondike Nugget,* Sept. 18, 1902.

[57] *Seward Gateway,* Sept. 25, 1909. *Fairbanks Daily News Miner,* Oct. 15,1909.

[58] "Random Reminiscences of Years in Alaska," Volume II, Chapter titled, "Mail Order Wife." John A. Clark Collection, Box 1, Alaska and Polar Regions Department, Elmer E. Rasmuson Library, University of Alaska Fairbanks.

[59] Wickersham, James. *Old Yukon.* Washington,D.C.: Washington Law Book Co., 1938, pp.208-216. It offers a reproduction of Fairbanks's first newspaper, *The Fairbanks Miner,* May 1903.

[60] Ito, Kazuo. *Issei: A History of Japanese Immigrants in North America.* Translated by Shinichiro Nakamura and Jean S. Gerard. Seattle, Washington: Executive Committee for Publication of Issei: A History of Japanese Immigrants in North America, c/o Japanese Community Service, 1973, p. 387-88.

[61] Case Number 140, Alaska State Archives, District 4, Series 509 # 514, OS 22.

[62] *Fairbanks Daily Times,* Aug. 24, 1907.

[63] Letter from the Rev. Albert N. Jones, Truro Parish, Lorton, VA, to author, April 5, 1972.

[64] Ibid. The Rev. Jones noted that the collection "made by a Japanese photographer dealing with a syndicate who imported Japanese prostitutes to Alaska," ended up in the estate of Charles Thompson, where it was purchased by Rev. Elson Eldridge and George Loudoun, a welfare worker. Eldridge denied ownership, but Loudoun's widow acknowledged her husband had bought photographs from the estate. This unique collection purchased (probably from Loudoun) by the late Fabian Carey in the 1950s now belongs to his son, Michael Carey of Anchorage. It is evident from a reflection of the photographer in the mirror of two of the portraits that he was not Japanese. Nor does he appear to be a Fairbanks-based professional.

[65] Fairbanks Title Insurance Co., Penny Champagne, researcher, Jan. 1997.

[66] Letter from B.S. Rodney to the Attorney General, Aug. 12, 1913, and to the Acting Secretary to the Attorney General, Sept. 12, 1913, National Archives, R.G. 85, File 52484-28, White Slave Traffic.

[67] *The Socialist Press,* Sept. 5, 1914. *Fairbanks Daily News Miner,* Oct. 5, 1914 (Rex Fisher Collection).

[68] *Fairbanks Daily News Miner,* Oct. 8, 1914.

[69] *Fairbanks Daily News Miner,* Oct. 12, 1914.

[70] Autopsy Notes, Mrs. William Harp a.k.a. Alice Astor, April 8, 1915, Alaska State Library, 509, Location 4359, Box 3, Assent #81-13.

[71] *Fairbanks Daily Times,* April 6, 10, and 11, 1915 (Rex Fisher Collection).

[72] Butrovich, John. Interview with the author, Fairbanks, July 1996.

10.GEORGIA LEE

[1] Notes on affidavit of James Ben Daniels in Georgia Lee file of Attorney Lewis Grigsby, Pittsfield, Illinois, made December 15, 1957. Probate record of Georgia Lee, Probate Court of Fairbanks Precinct, Fourth Division, Case # 1767, Alaska State Library.

[2] Ibid. Tombstone of Nancy Eldridge Daniel, Georgia Lee's sister, in Blue River Cemetery says she was born Dec. 13. Milton, Pike County Illinois, #430 Book A, p. 149, June 8, 1867. Grigsby, Lewis, interview with the author in Milton, Illinois, summer 1994. Letter to Lewis Grigsby by Minnie Yaeger, March 15, 1953.

[3] Letter to Lewis Grigsby by Minnie Yaeger, March 15, 1953.

[4] Marriage License, Pike County, Illinois, #594, Dec. 27, 1875. Minnie Yaeger, recalling family history, cites J. P. Book A, page 270, in probate records.

[5] Letter from Minnie Yaeger to Lewis Grigsby, March 15, 1955.

[6] Pike County Record 843, recorded by W. V. Grimes of Milton, Dec. 30, 1880. Letter from Minnie Yaeger to Lewis Grigsby, March 15, 1953, and notes in her file.

[7] Pike County Book 3, page 14, by A. N. Hess, April 18, 1881. Minnie Yaeger Records. Letter from Minnie Yaeger to Lewis Gribsky, March 15, 1953, and notes in her file.

[8] Pike County Records #1149, Minnie Yaeger, Nov. 6, 1881. Probate Court, Fairbanks, in the matter of the estate of Georgia Lee, #1767, May 28, 1955.

[9] Davis, Dora. Interview with the author, Pittsfield, Illinois, summer of 1993.

[10] Ibid. Affidavit of James Ben Daniels.

[11] Lewis Grigsby's notes on Daniels's affidavit.

[12] Davis, interview.

[13] Affidavit of James Ben Daniels.

[14] Gould's St. Louis Directory of 1906, p. 676. The St. Louis Police have no records for Georgia Lee or Georgia Eldredge.

[15] James Ben Daniels affidavit. Hayden, Cliff, interview with the author, North Pole, Alaska, October 8, 1994. Atwood, Evangeline, and DeArmond, Robert N. *Who's Who In Alaskan Politics: A Biographical Dictionary of Alaskan Political Personalities, 1884-1974.* Portland, Oregon: Binford and Mort, 1997, p. 44.

16 Richard Geoghegan diary, November 24, 1907, Alaska and Polar Regions Department, Elmer E. Rasmuson Library, University of Alaska Fairbanks.

17 Davis, Dora. Letter to author, Aug. 7, 1997.

18 Butrovich, John. Interview with the author, Fairbanks, 1994. Stroeker, William. Interview with the author, Fairbanks, Aug. 11, 1994.

19 *U.S. vs. Charles Thompson*, File Criminal Case #305. National Archives Anchorage, RG 21, Box 13, 3rd Divison, Fairbanks Criminal Cases 1900-20 293-321, #298.

20 Probate Court File on Charles Thompson, Alaska State Library, Juneau, Alaska.

21 *Fairbanks Evening News*, July 18, 1905.

22 Hansen, A. H. *Tundra: Romance and Adventure on American Trails*. New York: The Century Press, 1930, pp. 190-191.

23 *Fairbanks Daily Times*, May 24, 1910. Account was corraborated and expanded by John Butrovich on July 2, 1996.

24 *Fairbanks Daily Times*, Sept. 30, 1910 (Rex Fisher Collection).

25 Hayden, Orea. "Gold Rush Pioneer Leaves Her Mark." *Heartland, Fairbanks Daily News Miner*, Jan. 31, 1993, pp. H8-H13.

26 Hayden, Orea and Cliff. Interview with the author, North Pole, Feb. 25, 1995.

27 Coghill, Jack. Interview with the author in Nenana, Oct. 14, 1995.

28 Cashen, William R. *Farthest North College President: Charles E. Bunnell and the Early History of the University of Alaska*. Fairbanks: University of Alaska Press, 1972, p. 169.

29 Herbert, Chuck. Phone interview with author from Anchorage, 1993.

30 Alaska State Library, RC 509, Series 414, District 4, Civil Docket 1920-27, OS 22 915. Cases # 2609, 2674, 2675, 2785-2802 and 2807-8. Also Butrovich interviews.

31 Stroeker, Bill, and John Butrovitch. Interview with the author, Aug. 11, 1994.

32 Gull, Marge. Interview with the author in Anchorage, fall of 1993.

33 Stonefield, Rosa (McCoy's sister). Interview with the author, Eugene, Oregon, March 1995.

34 *Alaska Sportsman*, Feb. 1943, p. 43. *Fairbanks Daily News Miner*, Sept. 24, 1942.

35 *San Diego Sun*, Jan. 30, 1933. *San Diego Union*, Feb. 2, 1933.

36 *San Diego Union*, Feb 2, 1933.

37 *San Diego Union*, March 18, 1933.

38 *San Diego Union*, Feb. 11, 1933.

39 Charles Thompson Probate Records.

40 Herbert, Chuck. Phone interview with the author from Anchorage, 1993.

41 Hayden, Orea and Cliff, interview.

42 Zucchini, Albert. Interview with the author in Fairbanks, May 25, 1995.

43 Murray, Ken. Interview with the author in Fairbanks, spring 1994.

44 Yukon Territory Certificate of Registration of Death #001047054, Oct. 21, 1954.

45 *Fairbanks Daily News Miner*, Oct. 27 and Nov. 2, 1954. *Jessen's Weekly*, Oct. 28, 1954.

46 Davis, Dora. Letter to the author, Sept. 15, 1992.

47 *Democrat Times*, Dec. 1, 1954.

11. RICHARD HENRY GEOGHEGAN

1 Richard Geoghegan diary, translated by David Richardson, June 23, 1942, Richard Geoghegan Collection, Alaska and Polar Regions Department, Elmer E. Rasmuson Library, University of Alaska Fairbanks.

2 Richardson, David. "The Geoghegan Brothers of Alaska." *Alaska Journal*, Winter, 1976, p. 17.

3 Ibid., p. 18.

4 Riley, Burke. Interview with the author, Juneau, Alaska, April 1996.

5 Richardson, David. Unpublished Biography of Richard Geoghegan and personal correspondence, May and April 1991. Richardson performed the incredible feat of translating the linguist's surviving diaries, written in a combination of American Pitman shorthand and miscellaneous foreign languages, some of which were kept on the back of check stubs.

6 Richardson, "Geoghegan Brothers," p. 21.

7 *Fairbanks Weekly News*, April 16, 1904.

8 Richardson, "Geoghegan Brothers."

9 Ibid.

10 Geoghegan diary, 1907.

11 Riley, interview.

12 *Fairbanks Daily Times*, Feb. 11, 1915 (Rex Fisher Collection).

13 Richardson, Unpublished Biography, pp. 269-70.

14 Ibid., p. 271. Letter to Geoghegan's cousin, March 5, 1937, Richard H. Geoghegan Collection, Alaska and Polar Regions Department, Elmer E. Rasmuson Library, University of Alaska Fairbanks.

15 Richardson, Unpublished Biography, p. 272.

16 "To My Darling Little Mate, Ella." Oversized Scrapbook, Richard H. Geoghegan Collection, C14 D4.

17 *Record* Group 504, Location 4359, Box 3, Ass. #81-13, State of Alaska Library. *Nome Nugget*, May 14, 1904.

18 *Fairbanks Daily News Miner*, May 23, 1921.

19 *Fairbanks Daily News Miner*, Sept. 19, 1922.

20 *Fairbanks Daily News Miner*, March 13 and 15, 1922, and Feb. 8, 1923.

21 *Fairbanks Daily News Miner*, Aug. 8, 1922.

22 Richardson, "Geoghegan Brothers," p. 24.
23 Letter from Richard Geoghegan to a cousin, March 5, 1937, Richard Geoghegan Collection, Alaska and Polar Regions Department, Elmer E. Rasmuson Library, University of Alaska Fairbanks.
24 Letter from Richard Geoghegan to James Wickersham, April 14, 1936, Richard Geoghegan Collection, Alaska and Polar Regions Department, Elmer E. Rasmuson Library, University of Alaska Fairbanks.
25 Martin, Frederika I. "Richard Henry Geoghegan." Richard Geoghegan Collection, Alaska and Polar Regions Department, Elmer E. Rasmuson Library, University of Alaska Fairbanks.
26 Widow of George Loudoun. Phone conversation with the author, in 1992.
27 Geoghegan diary, 1942.
28 Ibid.

12. THE CALLAHANS
1 Callahan, Erinia Pavloff Cherosky. "A Yukon Biography." *The Alaska Journal*, Spring 1975, p. 127.
2 Gates, Michael. *Gold at Fortymile Creek: Early Days in the Yukon.* Vancouver: University of British Columbia Press, 1994, p. 65-6.
3 Callahan, "A Yukon Biography."
4 Atwood, Evangeline, and DeArmond, R. N. *Who's Who in Alaska Politics: A Biographical Dictionary of Alaskan Political Personalities, 1884-1974.* Portland, Oregon: Binfort and Mort, 1977, p. 14.
5 Dan Callahan Criminal Case #17. National Archives Anchorage, RG 21 U.S. District Court Div. Fairbanks Criminal Cases 1900-20, Box 01 of 19.
6 (Rampart) *Alaska Forum*, Sept. 27, 1900.
7 (Rampart) *Alaska Forum*, Jan. 3, 1901, p. 3.
8 Ibid.
9 Letter from District Attorney R. F. Roth to Attorney General, June 10, 1916. NA, RG 6, Letters Received.
10 Butrovich, John. Interview with the author, Fairbanks, July 12, 1994.
11 *Fairbanks Daily Times*, Dec. 29, 1906.
12 *Fairbanks Daily Times*, Jan. 24 and 29, 1907.
13 *Fairbanks Daily News Miner*, Dec. 12, 1907.
14 Office of the City Clerk. *City of Fairbanks Elections, 1903-1994.* Edited by Bernard A. Smith, Dec. 21, 1994.
15 Davis, Mary Lee. *We Are Alaskans.* Boston, Massachusetts: W. A. Wilde, 1931, pp. 172-73.
16 Circle old-timers who prefer their names to be left off this note recall Grandma Callahan was very proud of her heritage.
17 Office of the City Clerk, *City of Fairbanks Elections.*
18 National Archives Anchorage, Records 504, Location 4359, Box 509, Assent 81-13. Case #835, Jan. 7, 1919. Decision January 19, 1916.

19 *Fairbanks Daily Times*, March 22, 1916.
20 *Fairbanks Daily Times*, March 15, 1916.
21 *Fairbanks Daily Times*, March 26, 1916.
22 *Fairbanks Daily News Miner*, Sept. 23, 1922 and November 18, 1922.
23 Murray, Ken. Interview with the author, Fairbanks, spring 1993.

13. TOM MARQUAM
1 Oregon Historical Society, Scrapbook 60, p. 180.
2 *All Alaska Weekly*, Dec. 4, 1931. *Samuels Directory,* Portland, Oregon, 1881, p. 190, researched by Arlaine Borich of the Marquam family.
3 *All Alaska Weekly*, Dec. 4, 1931.
4 Oregon Historical Society, Scrapbook 122, p. 251.
5 *All Alaska Weekly*, Dec. 4, 1931.
6 Hunt, William R. *Distant Justice: Policing the Alaskan Frontier.* Norman and London: University of Oklahoma, 1987, pp. 29-32. Among his most interesting citations are Bennett to Attorney General, June 17, July 3, 1898, NA, RG 60, Letters Received; and *U.S. v. W. E. Crews, Thomas Marquam, et al,* court record, Case 999, FRC.
7 *Douglas Island News*, Jan. 10, 1900.
8 *Skagway Daily Alaskan*, May 29, 1900.
9 *Daily Alaska Dispatch*, Oct. 2 and 23, 1902.
10 *Daily Alaska Dispatch*, Nov. 25, 1903.
11 "Hearings Before Subcommittee of Committee on Territories Appointed to Investigate Conditions in Alaska," U.S. Senate, U.S. Government Printing Office, 1904.
12 According to Alaska Pioneer Records, Allman arrived in Skagway on June 15, 1900. According to her obituary in the *Seattle Post Intelligencer*, Feb. 28, 1917, she had family in Perry and Waterloo, Iowa, and a sister in Seattle. According to Jack Allman's obituary in the *Anchorage Times*, July 11, 1953, Jack came to Alaska at age seven with his mother.
13 Atwood, Evangeline. *Frontier Politics: Alaska's James Wickersham.* Portland, Oregon: Binford & Mort, 1979, pp. 156-7.
14 *Fairbanks Evening News*, Aug. 31, 1906.
15 Ginger Carroll, a distant relative of Marquam, in an interview with Frank Young of Fairbanks shortly before his death in 1992.
16 Case #305, State Library #905, 4th District Criminal Register OS 1029. Criminal Case #314, *U.S. v Thomas A. Marquam*, National Archives Record Group 21 (U.S. District Court), Box 13, 3rd Division Fairbanks Criminal Cases 1900-1920, 2930-321 (no 298).
17 Atwood, *Frontier Politics*, pp. 165-66.
18 Hunt, *Distant Justice*, p. 318.
19 *Fairbanks Times*, Jan. 7, 1909.
20 *Fairbanks Daily News*, Jan. 7, 1909.

21 *Fairbanks Daily News*, Aug. 23, 1910. *Dawson Daily News*, Sept. 10, 1910. *Douglas Island News*, Oct. 5, 1910.

22 Oregon Historical Society, Scrapbook 60, p. 180. *The Oregonian*, March 5, 1921. Personal Scrapbook 1911, A. H. Hansen Collection, Alaska and Polar Regions Department, Elmer E. Rasmuson Library, University of Alaska Fairbanks.

23 *Fairbanks Weekly Times*, Nov. 6, 1911. *Weekly Alaska Dispatch*, Jan. 13, 1911.

24 Hunt, *Distant Justice*, p. 318-19. He cites Clegg's affidavit, March 23, 1912, NA RG 60, Letters Received.

25 *Fairbanks Daily News Miner*, Feb. 21, 1917. *Seattle Post Intelligencer*, Feb. 28, 1917.

26 Naske, Claus M., and Rowinski, L.J. *Fairbanks: A Pictorial History*. Norfolk/ Virginia Beach: The Donning Company, 1981, pp. 57-58.

27 Dalton, Kathleen. Interview with the author, Jan. 1991. Verified by other pioneers.

28 Marriage license #54021, State of Alaska Registrar.

29 James Wickersham diary, Jan. 8, 1921, James Wickersham Collection, Alaska State Library.

30 Atwood, *Frontier Politics*, pp. 31-34.

31 DeArmond, Robert N. Letter to the author, Dec. 17, 1997.

32 Ginger Carroll following an interview with the late Frank Young and Marquam family members.

33 *Fairbanks Daily News Miner*, Aug. 30, 1923.

34 *Fairbanks Daily News Miner*, March 19, 1925. Atwood and DeArmond, *Who's Who*, p. 61.

35 *Fairbanks Daily News Miner*, May 7, 1925.

36 Solka, Paul. Interview with the author in Eugene, Oregon, March 5, 1995. Solka was at the *Fairbanks Daily News Miner* when Sutherland's people offered Mrs. W. F. Thompson, principal stockholder, $2,000 in commercial campaign printing orders for her support. Marquam offered her $10,000 to be paid after the election. When he lost, she received nothing. Letter from Solka to author from Eugene, Oregon, Aug. 19, 1994.

37 *Stroller's Weekly*, Oct. 30, 1926.

38 *Stroller's Weekly*, July 24, 1926. *Anchorage Daily Times*, Nov. 5, 1926.

39 Letters to Mary dated Oct. 3 and 17, 1928. Herbert Heller Collection, University of Alaska Archives, Lynn Smith, Box 1 Folder 20.

40 *Fairbanks Daily News Miner*, Dec. 15, 1928.

41 Butrovich, John, of Fairbanks. Interview with the author, July 1994. Rogge, Pat Hering, a former neighbor. Interview with the author in 1995.

42 *Alaska Weekly*, Dec. 4, 1931. *Fairbanks Daily News Miner*, Nov. 24 and 30, 1931. Also clippings without citations from Arlaine Borich, a distant relative in Tigard, Oregon, who is working on

Marquam geneology.

43 Rogge, interview. Fairbanks Recorders Office, May 5, 1935, 74142V26 p. 485.

44 *Juneau Alaska Empire*, July 10, 1953. Atwood, *Frontier Politics*, pp. 397-97.

14. SIN IN SOUTHERN ALASKA

1 *U.S. v Fred Rassmussen*. National Archives, Alaska Region RG 21, Box 10, 1st Division Juneau Criminal Case Files 1900-1911, 344B-393B, File 381B.

2 *U.S. v Fred Rassmussen*, File 336B.

3 "Rassmussen Gets Severe Sentence This Morning." *Alaska Dispatch*, Jan. 26, 1903. "The Judge Severe: Two Other Douglas City Men Will Get Six Months Each . . . Moral Wave Fierce." *Nome Nugget*, April 15, 1903. "Judge Brown Gives A Very Severe Sentence." *Alaska Dispatch*, January 27, 1903.

4 *Fred Rassmussen v US*, Supreme Court of the United States 516-536, 197 U.S.

5 Gruening, Ernest. *The State of Alaska: A Definitive History of America's Northernmost Frontier*. New York: Random House, 1954, p. 44. Naske, Clause M., and Slotnick, Herman E. *Alaska: A History of the 49th State*. Second Edition, Norman, Oklahoma: University of Oklahoma Press, 1987, p. 92.

6 Post office worker Clary Craig's list of people dying or leaving the Klondike: Fred Rassmussen, Jan. 22, 1909, Tanana. Pan For Gold database, Yukon Territory: http://www.gold-rush.org/ghost-07.htm.

7 Letter from R. N. DeArmond from Sitka, October 21, 1991. Dearmond, Bob. "Juno's Days of Yore," Info Alaska, The Weekly T.V. Guide, *Juneau Alaska Empire*, March 14, 1987, p. 4.

8 Gaddis, Thomas E. *Birdman of Alcatraz: The Story of Robert Stroud*. Mattituk, N.Y.: Aeonian Press, 1955, pp. 16-17.

9 Babyak, Jolene. *Bird Man: The Many Faces of Robert Stroud*. Berkeley: Ariel Vamp Press, 1994, p. 16.

10 Gaddis, *Birdman of Alcatraz*, pp. 17-19.

11 Price, Susan. "Juneau's Most Infamous Murder Case." *Juneau Empire*, October 8, 1995.

12 National Archives, RG 21, U.S. District Court Records, 1st Divison Criminal Case Files, 1900-1911, Box 29 # 603 B - 632 B.

13 Gaddis, *Birdman of Alcatraz*, p. 23-24.

14 "Surgeon Who Witnessed Dan McGrew Incident in Juneau Tells of Famous Lou," *Juneau Empire*, April 12, 1923.

15 Letter written at close of World War I by Helen Wilson to her sister Alice Wilson Bair in Pennsylvania, from Skagway (undated) in 1918. Alaska Historical Collections, Alaska State Library.

[16] Steele, Sam. *Forty Years in Canada.* London: Jenkins, 1915, p. 292.

[17] Berton, Pierre. *Klondike: The Last Great Gold Rush, 1896-1899.* Toronto, Ontario: Penguin Books Ltd., 1958, revised 1972, p. 281.

[18] Earp, Josephine Sarah Marcus. *I Married Wyatt Earp: The Recollections of Josephine Sarah Marcus Earp.* Collected and edited by Glenn G. Boyer. Tucson, Arizona: The University of Arizona Press, 1990, p. 160.

[19] Steele, *Forty Years in Canada*, p. 297.

[20] Clifford, Howard. *The Skagway Story.* Anchorage: Alaska Northwest Publishing Co., 1975/1983, p. 81.

[21] *Seattle Times*, June 3, 1898. Hunt, William R. *Distant Justice: Policing the Alaskan Frontier.* Norman and London: University of Oklahoma Press, 1987, pp. 60-61.

[22] Choate, Glenda J. *Skagway, Alaska, Gold Rush Cemetery.* Skagway: Lynn Canal Publishing, 1989, p. 9.

[23] Clifford, Howard. *The Skagway Story.* Anchorage: Alaska Northwest Publishing Co., 1975/1983, pp. 83-84. Spude, Catherine Blee, National Park Service, Denver. Correspondence with the author, Sept. 26, 1992.

[24] *Skagway News*, Jan. 13, 1899.

[25] Nakano, Mei. *Japanese American Women: Three Generations 1890-1990.* Sebastopol, Calif: Meva Press Publishers, Inc., 1990, p. 24. Yamazaki, Tomoko. *The Story of Yamada Waka: From Prostitute to Feminist Pioneer.* Tokyo, New York, San Francisco: Kodansha International, 1978, p 22-23.

[26] We are indebted to Tomoko Yamazako for her translation of "Myself and My Surroundings," an essay Waka wrote in 1914, p. 76. Indeed, without the English translation of Yamazako's fine biography of Waka, and the careful work of Yuji Ichioka, we would have little insight into the lives of the Japanese women who were enslaved as prostitutes during the gold rush era. Yamazako, *Story of Yamada Waka*, p. 73. Ichioka, Yuji. "Ameyuki-san: Japanese Prostitutes in Nineteenth-Century America." *Amerasia* 4:1 (1977) Vo. l #2, July 1971, pp. 7-11.

[27] Yamazako, *Story of Yamada Waka*, p. 88.

[28] Ito, Kazuo. *Issei: A History of Japanese Immigrants in North America.* Translated by Shinichiro Nakamura and Jean S. Gerard. Seattle, Washington: Executive Committee for Publication of Issei: A History of Japanese Immigrants in North America, c/o Japanse Community Service, 1973. p. 775.

[29] *Daily Alaskan*, April 10 and 23, 1901.

[30] Ito, *Issei*, p. 391.

[31] Lung, Edward B., as told to Ella Lang Martinsen. *Trail to North Star Gold: True Story of the Alaska-Klondike Gold Rush.* New York: Vantage Press, 1956, p. 384.

[32] Wisenbaugh, Vicki, Tenakee Historical Collection. Phone interview with the author, November 1993.

[33] Smythe, Gillian, of Anchorage. Interview with author, April 1994. *Valdez News*, September 1 and 11, 1901.

[34] Thompson, Homer S. Correspondence with the author from Homer, May 17, 1993. James Wickersham diary, James Wickersham Collection, Alaska State Library, January 8, 1921.

[35] Allen, June. *Spirit: Historic Ketchikan, Alaska.* Ketchikan: Lind Printing for Historic Ketchikan, Inc., 1992, pp. 47-52.

[36] Duncan, Thomas. "Alaska Broadcasting: 1922-1977." Thesis, University of Alaska.

[37] Allen, June. *Dolly's House.* Ketchikan: Tongass Publishing Co., 1976, p. 5.

[38] Ibid, p. 8.

[39] Ibid, pp. 11-14.

[40] Notes on Creek Street by Mark Wheeler, Tongass Historical Society Inc., Ketchikan, 1993.

[41] Williams, Lou. Phone interview with author from Ketchikan, July 4, 1996.

[42] Allen, *Historic Ketchikan*, p. 38.

15. TOUGH TIMES IN FAIRBANKS

[1] University of Alaska Museum, facts posted in a display on Fairbanks in 1910.

[2] Rasmuson Archives ACC 92-080, Tax Rolls Box 20 and Box 23. Also land records from the office of the Fairbanks District Recorder.

[3] Researching Barnette is murky business at best. The best job of it is Terrence Cole's *E. T. Barnette: The Strange Story of the Man who Founded Fairbanks.* Anchorage: Alaska Northwest Publishing Company, 1981. Chapter 8 details his colorful Oregon career and Chapter 9 his final financial dealings in Alaska.

[4] Naske, Clause M. and Rowinski, L. J. *Fairbanks: A Pictorial History.* Norfolk/Virginia Beach: The Donning Company/Publishers, 1981, p. 29.

[5] Robe, C. F. "The Penetration of an Alaskan Frontier: The Tanana Valley and Fairbanks." Ph. D. dissertation, Yale University, 1943, p. 12.

[6] Naske and Rowinski, *Fairbanks*, p. 57.

[7] Gull, Marge. Interview with the author at Pioneer Home in Anchorage, September 1993. Riley, Burke. Interview with the author, March 4, 1994.

[8] Young, Frank. Interview with the author two months before Young's death.

[9] Richard Geoghegan diary, March 3, 1942, Richard Geoghegan Collection, Alaska and Polar Regions Department, Elmer E. Rasmuson Library, University of Alaska Fairbanks. Undated obituary

found in the scrapbook of Ruth McCoy, now in the same archives.

10 *Fairbanks Daily News Miner*, May 29, 1922.

11 *Fairbanks Sunday Times*, March 23, 1913 (Rex Fisher Collection).

12 Young, S. Hall. *Hall Young of Alaska: The Mushing Parson*. New York and Chicago: Flemming H. Revell Company, 1927.

13 *Fairbanks Daily News Miner*, July 18, 1957.

14 Lewis, Bill. Interview with the author, Fairbanks, July 12, 1996.

15 Murie, Margaret E. *Two in the Far North*. Anchorage: Alaska Northwest Publishing Co, 1978, p. 31. Carter, Debbie. "Ladies of the Line." *Fairbanks Daily News Miner*, July 17, 1982.

16 Stroeker, Bill. Interview with the author, Fairbanks, September 1994. Young, Frank. Interview with the author, Fairbanks, April 1992.

17 Letter from Tom Gibson to Aunt, August 27, 1908, Sarah Ellen Gibson Collection, Alaska and Polar Regions Department, Elmer E. Rasmuson Library, University of Alaska Fairbanks, Box 1, Gor 313.

18 Loftus, Audrey. "Tom Gibson—Meat Hunter." *Alaska Sportsman*, June 1967, pp. 18-21, 59; July 1967, pp. 6-8; and August 1967, pp. 20-21.

19 "She Arrived as a Bride," *Fairbanks News-Miner*, Golden Days, July 27, 1959.

20 A 1922 city plate shows only fifteen houses.

21 *Polk Directory*, 1915-1916. Fairbanks Title Insurance Co., Penny Champagne researcher, January 1997. Akimoto's photographs and personal effects were auctioned off with the rest of Charles Thompson's estate in September of 1942 with a good part of the town in attendance.

22 Marshall, Robert. *Arctic Village*. New York: Literary Guild of New York, 1993, p. 161. James Wickersham diary, Jan. 8, 1921, James Wickersham Collection, Alaska State Library.

23 Marshall, *Arctic Village*, pp. 43 and 267-8.

24 Blaekley, Geoffrey. "Murder on the Koyukuk: The Hunt for the Blueberry Kid." *Alaska History*, spring 1996, p. 15.

25 "A Sporting Woman." *Hot Springs Echo*, Jan. 14, 1909. "Fire Scare when Dutch Marie's Place Burned." *Hot Springs Echo*, Dec. 31, 1910.

26 *Seattle Post Intelligencer*, May 24, 1914.

27 Blaekley, "Murder on the Koyukuk," pp.15-16.

28 *The Ruby Record-Citizen*, August 2, 1914.

29 Blaekley, "Murder on the Koyukuk," pp. 22-3.

30 Herns, Ruby and Frederick. "Memories of Iditarod," *Alaska Sportsman*, February 1965, pp. 35-37.

31 Correspondence with Rolfe Buzzell, Alaska Department of Natural Resources, Office of History and Archeology, September 1, 1993.

32 Naske and Rowinski, *Fairbanks*, p. 23.

33 Gates, Michael. *Gold at Fortymile Creek: Early Days in the Yukon*. Vancouver: University of British Columbia Press, 1994, p. 125.

34 Caption by Mrs. Pusly on photo of The Jewel, Ester Duffy's whorehouse at Fort Gibbon. University of Washington Archives.

35 Solka, Paul. Interview with the author in Eugene, Oregon, March 5, 1995.

36 Twogood, Ron and Dorothy. Interview with the author, Fairbanks, Feb. 9, 1997.

37 Tower, Dr. Elizabeth. *Big Mike Henry: Irish Prince of the Iron Trails*. Anchorage: Elizabeth Tower, 1990, pp. 46-47.

38 Memorandum from Assistant District Forester Charles H. Flory to District Forester, January 6, 1917. This correspondence is missing from the Forest Service national files at the Archives, but other correspondence there bears it out and the typeface matches. I obtained a much-xeroxed copy from a close friend who apparently knew someone who saved the embarrassing memo from destruction.

39 Memo from District Forester to the Forester, Washington, D. C., January 9, 1917. Letter to District Forester from Forest Supervisor W.G. Weigle, January 19, 1917.

40 McSmith, Blanche, close personal friend and executor of Swanson's estate. Interview with the author in Juneau, 1992, and by phone to Juneau in 1994.

41 *Anchorage Daily News*, Jan. 13, 1973. *Anchorage Daily Times*, Jan. 15, 1973.

42 *Fairbanks Daily News-Miner*, May 31, 1922.

43 *Fairbanks Daily News-Miner*, Oct. 1, 1925.

44 State Archives, Oct. 26, 1926. *Fairbanks Daily News Miner*, Oct. 25, 1926.

45 *Fairbanks Daily News Miner*, Oct. 1, 1925. "Insanity, Sabotage or 'Reform'?" *Fairbanks Daily News Miner*, Sept. 25 and Nov. 17, 1922.

46 *Fairbanks Daily News Miner*, Oct. 23 and Nov. 6, 1922.

47 *Fairbanks Daily News Miner*, Feb. 27 and 28, 1923.

48 Alaska State Library, RC 509, Series 414, District 4 Civil Docket 1920-27 OS 22 915. Cases # 2609, 2674, 2675. 2785, 2786, 2787, 2788, 2789, 2790, 1791, 2792, 2793, 2794, 2795, 2796, 2797, 2798, 2799, 2800, 2802, 2803, 2807, 2808. Lawyers for the Line included Charles Williams, John Clark, and Charles E. Sampson.

49 *Fairbanks Daily News Miner*, October 31, 1925.

50 *Fairbanks Daily News Miner*, January 5, 1926.

16. EDITH NEILE

1 Armstrong, Nevill A. D. *Yukon Yesterdays: Thirty Years of Adventure in the Yukon*. London: John Long Ltd., 1936, pp 50-53.

2 Trelawney-Ansell, E. C. *I Followed Gold*. London: Peter Davies, 1938, p. 189. Alder, Lee. Interview with the author, March 9, 1997.

3 Berton, Pierre. *Klondike: The Last Great Gold Rush, 1896-1899*. Toronto, Ontario: Penguin Books Ltd., 1958, revised 1972, p. 487.

4 Hamlin, C. S. *Old Times on the Yukon*. Los Angeles: Wetzel Publishing Co., Inc., 1928, pp. 27-28.

5 Sterling, Joe, Edith Neile's nephew. Interview with the author in Everett, Washington, Feb. 25, 1995.

6 Nixon, Richard J. Jr. "Vigilante Committee Visits Yreka." Siskiyou County Historical Society, courtesy of Ian D. Matheson of Seattle, Washington, to whom we are indebted for some fine research on the Radford family and on Edith Neile herself.

7 (Yreka) *Siskiyou News*, Oct. 16, 1897. From *Siskiyou Pioneer*, Vol. III, No. 8, 1965.

8 Sterling, interview.

9 Martinsen, Ella Lung, as told to her by her mother, Velma D. Lung. *Trail to North Star Gold: True Story of the Alaska-Klondike Gold Rush*. Portland, Oregon: Metropolitan Press, 1969, pp. 187-8.

10 Sterling, interview.

11 Hamlin, C.S. *Old Times*, p. 59-61. He writes of Neile's "half sister" who failed as a dance hall girl and also as a cook, depicting her with a drinking problem. Edna Radford did not drink and Edith had two half-sisters, one of whom might have come north. There are enough references to the "Colt" from old-timers to safely assume Edna also made a brief appearence.

12 Sterling, interview.

13 "Random Reminiscences of 22 Years in Alaska," Vol. 1. John. A Clark Collection, Alaska and Polar Regions Department, Elmer E. Rasmuson Library, University of Alaska Fairbanks, Box 1.

14 Alaska State Library, RG507, Fairbanks Case #282, July 11, 1907.

15 Interview with Rolfe Buzzell, History and Archeology, Alaska Department of Natural Resources in Anchorage, 1994.

16 Sterling, interview.

17 *Fairbanks Daily News Miner*, Oct. 7 and 8, 1918.

18 Sterling, interview. *Fairbanks Daily News Miner*, June 19, 1919.

19 Sterling, interview. Also Kennedy, Kay, a Fairbanks reporter who knew Neile well. Interview with the author, Nov. 1993. Both said that Neile was happiest when she was helping others, and spent everything she had to that end.

20 Richardson, Marilyn. "'Spanish Grippe' Grips Our Town," *Heartland, Fairbanks Daily News Miner*, May 20, 1920, reprinted in *Heartland, Fairbanks Daily News Miner*, Jan. 9, 1994.

21 Patty, Ernest. *North Country*. New York: D. McKay, 1969, pp. 44-5.

22 Richardson, "Spanish Grippe." Sterling, interview.

23 National Archives, Anchorage, RG #21, Box 52, Alaska 4th Division, Files 19060-55, 2565-2584. File # 2574, May 9, 1922.

24 Ibid.

25 Sterling, interview.

26 *Fairbanks Daily News Miner*, Feb. 9 and 10, 1962.

27 Letter from Joe Sterling to the author, postmarked August 18, 1994.

28 *Fairbanks Daily News Miner*, Feb 10, 1962.

EPILOGUE

1 Hunt, William R. *Golden Places: The History of Alaska-Yukon Mining*. Anchorage, National Park Service, Alaska Region, 1990, pp. 143-4. Stroeker, William. Interview with the author, Aug. 11, 1994.

2 Murie, Margaret E. *Two in the Far North*. Anchorage: Alaska Northwest Publishing Co, 1978.

3 Nordale, LaDessa, a former Fairbanks judge. Interview with the author at the Pioneer Home, May 1992.

4 Casey, Bob. Interview with the author, Circle Hot Springs, July 1995.

5 Tillion, Clem. Interview with the author, Juneau, winter 1992.

6 Gull, Marge. Interview with the author at the Pioneer Home in Anchorage, September 1993. Hudson, Sally, of Fairbanks, who worked in Lucille's Apparel as a girl. Interview with the author, March 1995.

7 Moody, Jim, of Fairbanks. Interview with the author, July 1994.

8 Herbert, Chuck. Phone interview with the author from Anchorage, Aug. 30, 1992.

9 *Jessen's Weekly*, October 8, 1943.

10 Bayer, Lawrence, and Drayton, Wayne. *Prostitution in Fairbanks*. Anchorage Museum of History and Art, collection of William C. Ray, pp. 4-5.

11 Ibid., pp. 1-2.

12 Ibid., p. 8.

13 *Jessen's Weekly*, October 8, 1943. *Fairbanks Daily News Miner*, October 8, 1943.

14 *Jessen's Weekly*, October 22 and November 19, 1943.

15 Cook, Pat, of Fairbanks. Interview with the author, summer of 1992. Young, Frank, of Fairbanks. Interview with the author, April 1992.

16 Carter, Debbie. "Ladies of the Line," *Fairbanks Daily News-Miner*, July 17, 1962. Zaverl, Stan, former Fairbanks Police Chief. Interview with the author, February 10, 1997.

17 Redding, Robert H. "The Line offered Fairbanks men discreet entertainment." *Fairbanks Daily News Miner, Heartland*, April 28, 1991. Cook, Earl, who collected rents for real estate clients. Interview with the author.

[18] Erwin, Carol, with Miller, Floyd. *The Orderly Disorderly House*. Garden City, New York: Doubleday & Company, pp. 270-271.

[19] Iris Woodcock Collection, Anchorage Museum of History and Art.

[20] Cook, interview.

[21] Ferguson, Thorne. Interview with the author in Anchorage, June 22, 1996.

[22] Hulk, Bernie. Interview with the author in Juneau, March 21, 1996. *Juneau Alaska Empire*, Aug. 15 and 16, 1956.

[23] Tillion, Clem. Interview with the author in Juneau, winter 1967.

[24] Carman, Lee, of Fairbanks. Interview with the author, spring 1992.

[25] Myers, John P., who was an M.P. on the Line at age nineteen in 1943. Phone interview with the author from Cave Creek, Arizona, summer 1994.

[26] Casey, interview.

[27] Baker, Marge, who worked for the U.S. Commissioner during this period. Interview with the author in Fairbanks, June 18, 1996.

[28] Carter, "Ladies of the Line."

[29] Baker, interview.

[30] Erwin, *Orderly Disorderly House*, p. 61.

[31] *Fairbanks Daily News Miner*, March 6, 1952.

[32] Nordale, interview. *Fairbanks Daily News Miner*, June 9, 1952.

[33] Erwin, *Orderly Disorderly House*, p. 272 and 275.

[34] Nordale, interview.

[35] Redding, Robert H. "Compass." *Heartland, Fairbanks Daily News-Miner*, Aug. 22, 1993.

[36] Redding, Robert H. 'The Line offered Fairbanks men discreet entertainment." *Heartland, Fairbanks Daily News-Miner*, April 28, 1991.

[37] Erwin, *Orderly Disorderly House*, p.275.

[38] Cook, interview.

[39] O'Connor, Richard. *High Jinks on the Klondike*. Indianapolis, N.Y.: The Bobbs-Merrill Co., 1954 (Fifth edition), p. 192.

[40] Brooks, Alfred Hulse. *Blazing Alaska's Trails*. Fairbanks: University of Alaska Press, 1973, First Edition 1953, p. 351.

[41] Erwin, *Orderly Disorderly House*, p. 253.

Selected Bibliography

Allen, June. *Dolly's House: No. 24 Creek Street.* Ketchikan, Alaska: Tongass Publishing Co., Second Edition, 1982.

Allen, June. *Spirit: Historic Ketchikan, Alaska.* Ketchikan, Alaska: Lind Printing for Historic Ketchikan Inc., 1992.

Anonymous. *Madeleine: An Autobiography.* Introduction to 1919 Edition by Judge Ben. B. Lindsey. New Introduction by Marcia Carlisle. New York: Persea Books, 1986.

Armstrong, Nevill A. D. *Yukon Yesterdays: Thirty Years of Adventure in the Klondike.* London: John Long Ltd., 1936.

Atwood, Evangeline. *Frontier Politics: Alaska's James Wickersham.* Portland, Oregon: Binford & Mort, 1979.

Atwood, Evangeline and DeArmond, Robert N. *Who's Who in Alaska Politics: A Biographical Dictionary of Alaskan Political Personalities, 1884-1974.* Portland, Oregon: Binford & Mort, 1977.

Babyak, Jolene. *Bird Man: The Many Faces of Robert Stroud.* Berkeley, California: Ariel Vamp Press, 1994.

Backhouse, Frances. *Women of the Klondike.* Vancouver/Toronto: Whitecap Books, 1995.

Beebe, Mrs. Iola. *The True Life Story of Swiftwater Bill Gates.* Copyright 1908 by Mrs. Beebe. Seattle, Wash: The Shorey Book Store, Facsimile Reproduction 1967 SJS# 163.

Berton, Laura Beatrice with Foreword by Pierre Berton and Preface by Robert W. Service. *I Married the Klondike.* First published in 1954, Boston: Little Brown. Ontario: McClelland & Stewart, Inc., 1993.

Berton, Pierre. *Klondike: The Last Great Gold Rush, 1896-1899.* Revised Edition, A Penguin Books Canada/McClelland and Stewart Book, Ontario, 1990.

Black, Martha, as told to Elizabeth Bailey Price. *My Seventy Years.* London, Edinburgh, Paris, Melbourne, Toronto, and New York: Thomas Nelson and Sons Ltd., 1938.

Blee, Catherine Holder (now Spude). *Sorting Functionally-Mixed Artifact Assemblages With Multiple Regression: A Comparative Study in Historical Archeology.* Doctoral thesis, University of Colorado, 1991.

Brooks, Alfred Hulse. *Blazing Alaska's Trails.* Second Edition. Fairbanks: University of Alaska Press, 1973. (First Edition 1953.)

Brooks-Vincent, La Belle. *The Scarlet Life of Dawson and Roseate Dawn of Nome.* Seattle: M.R. Mayor, 1900.

Bullough, Vern and Bonnie. *Prostitution, An Illustrated Social History.* New York: Crown Publishers, Inc., 1978.

Butler, Anne M. *Daughters of Joy, Sisters of Misery: Prostitutes in the American West, 1865-90.* Urbana and Chicago, Illinois: University of Illinois Press, 1985.

Carberry, Michael and Lane, Donna. *Patterns of the Past, An Inventory of Anchorage's Historic Resources.* The Municipality of Anchorage, Community Planning Department, 1986.

Choate, Glenda J. *Skagway, Alaska, Gold Rush Cemetery.* Skagway, Alaska: Lynn Canal Publishing, 1989.

Clifford, Howard. *The Skagway Story.* Anchorage: Alaska Northwest Publishing Co., 1975, 1983.

Coates, Ken S. and Morrison, William R. *Land of the Midnight Sun: A History of the Yukon.* Edmonton, Canada: Hurtig Publishers, 1988.

Coates, Ken, and Morrison, William R. *The Sinking of the Princess Sophia: Taking the North Down With Her.* Fairbanks, Alaska: University of Alaska Press, 1991.

Cody, H. A. *An Apostle of the North.* New York: E. P. Dutton & Company, 1908.

Cole, Terrence. *E. T. Barnette: The Strange Story of the Man Who Founded Fairbanks.* Anchorage: Alaska Northwest Publishing Co., 1981.

Cole, Terrence. *Ghosts of the Gold Rush: A Walking Tour of Fairbanks.* Fairbanks, Alaska: Tanana-Yukon Historical Society, 1977.

Cole, Terrence Michael. *A History of the Nome Gold Rush: The Poor Man's Paradise.* A dissertation. Seattle, Washington: University of Washington, 1983.

Cole, Terrence. *Nome: City of the Golden Beaches.* With Jim Walsh, Editorial Consultant. Anchorage, Alaska: Alaska Geographic, Volume 11, Number 1, 1984.

Collier, William Ross and Westgate, Edwin Victor. *The Reign of Soapy Smith: Monarch of Misrule.* Garden City, N.J.: Doubleday, Doran & Co., 1935.

Connelly, Mark Thomas. *The Response to Prostitution in the Progressive Era.* Chapel Hill: University of North Carolina Press, 1980 (UA Juneau HQ144).

Croft, Toni and Bradner, Phyllice. *Touring Juneau.* Juneau, 1973.

Curtin, Walter R. *Yukon Voyage: Unofficial Log of the Steamer Yukon.* The Caxton Printers, Ltd., 1983.

Davids, Henry. "Recollections," *Sourdough Sagas*

edited by Herbert L. Heller, 28-83. Cleveland: World Publishing, 1967.

Dean, David M. *Breaking Trail: Hudson Stuck of Texas and Alaska*. Ohio University Press, Athens, 1988.

DeArmond, R.N. *Stroller White: Tales of a Klondike Newsman*. Vancouver: Mitchell Press Limited, 1969. Reprint Skagway, Alaska: Lynn Canal Publishing, 1989.

DeGraf, Anna. *Pioneering on the Yukon, 1892-1917*. Edited by Roger S. Brown. Hamden, Connecticut: The Shoestring Press, Inc., Archon Books, 1992.

Duncan, John Thomas. *Alaska Broadcasting, 1922-77: An Examination of Government Influence*. Thesis, University of Oregon, 1982.

Earp, Josephine Sarah Marcus. *I Married Wyatt Earp*. Collected and edited by Glenn C. Boyer. Tucson, Arizona: University of Arizona Press, 1990.

Erwin, Carol. *The Orderly Disorderly House*. Garden City, N.J.: Doubleday, 1960.

Evans., Chad. *Frontier Theatre: A History of Nineteenth-Century Theatrical Entertainment in the Canadian Far North and Alaska*. Victoria, B.C.: Sono Nis Press, 1983.

Ferrell, Ed. *Strange Stories of Alaska and the Yukon*. Fairbanks/Seattle: Epicenter Press, 1995.

Gaddis, Thomas E. *Birdman of Alcatraz: The Story of Robert Stroud*. Mattituk, N.Y.: Aeonian Press, 1955, 1958, 1962.

Gates, Michael. *Gold at Fortymile Creek: Early Days in the Yukon*. Vancouver: University of British Columbia Press, 1994.

Green, Lewis. *The Gold Hustlers*. Anchorage: Alaska Northwest Publishing Co., 1977.

Guest, Hal J. *A History of the City of Dawson, Yukon Territory, 1896-1920*. Microfiche Report Series No. 7. Chapter 8, "Languorous Lilies of Soulless Love," p. 219- 246. Ottawa: Canadian Parks Service, 1981.

Hamlin, C. S. *Old Times on the Yukon*. Los Angeles: Wetzel Publishing Co., Inc., 1928.

Haskell, William B. *Two Years in the Klondike and Alaskan Gold-Fields*. Hartford, Conn.: Hartford Publishing Company.

Hedrick, Basil and Savage, Susan. *Steamboats on the Chena: The Founding and Development of Fairbanks, Alaska*. Fairbanks, Alaska: Epicenter Press, 1988.

Hosokawa, Bill. *Nisei: The Quiet Americans*. Niwot, Colorado: University of Colorado Press, 1992.

Hunt, William R. *Distant Justice: Policing the Alaskan Frontier*. Norman and London: University of Oklahoma Press, 1987.

Hunt, William R. *Golden Places: The History of Alaska-Yukon Mining With Particular Reference to Alaska's National Parks*. Anchorage: National Park Service, 1990.

Hunt, William R. *North of 53°: The Wild Days of the Alaska- Yukon Mining Frontier, 1870-1914*. New York: Macmillan Publishing Co., Inc.; London: Collier Macmillan Publishers, 1974.

Innis, Harold A. *Settlement And The Mining Frontier*. Canadian Frontiers of Settlement. Volume IX, *Settlement and the Forest Frontier in Eastern Canada*. Toronto: The Macmillan Company of Canada Limited, at St. Martin's House, 1936.

Ito, Kazuo. *Issei: A History of Japanese Immigrants in North America*. Translated by Shinichiro Nakamura and Jean S. Gerard. Seattle, Washington: Executive Committee for Publication of Issei c/o Japanese Community Service, 1973.

Johnson, James Albert. *Carmack of the Klondike*. Fairbanks, Alaska: Epicenter Press, 1990.

Kelcey, Barbara. *Lost in the Rush: The Forgotten Women of the Klondike Gold Rush*. Master's thesis. Victoria, B.C.: University of Victoria, 1987.

Ketz, James A. and Arundale, Wendy H. *Rivertown*. Fairbanks, Alaska: Department of Transportation and Public Facilities, 1986.

King, Jean Beach. *Arizona Charlie: A Legendary Cowboy, Klondike Stampeder and Wild West Showman*. Phoenix, Arizona: A Heritage Publishers Book, 1989.

Lucia, Ellis. *Klondike Kate: The Life & Legend of Kitty Rockwell, The Queen of the Yukon*. New York: Ballantine Books, 1962.

Lynch, Jeremiah. *Three Years in the Klondike*. Chicago: R. R. Donnelley & Sons, 1967.

Marshall, Robert. *Arctic Village*. New York: Literary Guild of New York, 1933.

Martin, Cy. *Whiskey and Wild Women: An Amusing Account of the Saloons and Bawds of the Old West*. New York: Hart Pub. Co., 1974.

Martinsen, Ella Lung. *Trail to North Star Gold: True Story of the Alaska-Klondike Gold Rush*. (As told to her by her mother, Velma D. Lung.) Portland, Oregon: Metropolitan Press, 1969.

McKee, Lanier. *The Land of Nome*. New York: The Grafton Press, 1902.

McKeown, Martha Ferguson. *The Trail Led North: Mont Hawthorne's Story*. Portland, Oregon: Binford & Mort, 1960.

Mayer, Melanie J. *Klondike Women: True Tales of the 1897- 1898 Gold Rush*. Swallow Press, Ohio University Press, 1989.

Meier, Gary and Gloria. *Those Naughty Ladies of the Old Northwest*. Bend, Oregon: Maverick Publishers, 1990.

Naske, Clause M. and Rowinski, L.J. *Fairbanks: A Pictorial History*. Norfork: The Donning Company, 1981.

Nakano, Mei. *Japanese American Women: Three Generations, 1890-1990*. Sebastopol, California: Meva Press Publishers, Inc., 1990.

O'Connor, Richard. *High Jinks on the Klondike*.

Indianapolis, New York: The Bobbs-Merrill Co., 1954 (5th edition).

Patty, Ernest. *North Country*. New York: D. McKay, 1969.

Parrish, Maud. *Nine Pounds of Luggage*. Philadelphia, New York, London, Toronto: J. B. Lippincott Company, 1939.

Peterson, Art and Williams, D. Scott. *Murder, Madness, and Mystery: An Historical Narrative of Mollie Walsh Bartlett From the Days of the Klondike Gold Rush*. Williams, Oregon: Castle Peak Editions, 1991.

Peterson, Gail, Editor. *A Vindication of the Rights of Whores*. Preface by Margo St. James. Seattle, Washington: The Seal Press, 1989.

Porsild, Charlene L. "Culture, Class and Community: New Perspectives on the Klondike Gold Rush, 1896-1905." Thesis, Carleton University, Ottawa, Ontario, 1994.

Richardson, David. Unpublished Biography of Richard Geoghegan.

Robe, Cecil Francis. "The Penetration of an Alaskan Frontier: The Tanana Valley and Fairbanks." Dissertation for Doctorate of Philosophy, Yale University. Ann Arbor, Michigan: University Microfilms, 1973.

Romig, Emily Craig. *A Pioneer Woman in Alaska*. Caldwell, Ohio: The Caxton Press, 1948.

Rosen, Ruth. *The Lost Sisterhood: Prostitution in America, 1900-1918*. Baltimore: The Johns Hopkins University Press, 1982.

Ryley, Bay. *The Bawdy Language of Gold Digging: Regulating Prostitution in Dawson City, Yukon, 1898-1903*. Paper for Nancy Forestell and Ian McKay. Kingston: Queen's University, 1993.

Seagraves, Anne. *Soiled Doves: Prostitution in the Early West*. Hayden, Idaho: Wesanne Publications, 1994.

Secretan, J. H. E. *To the Klondyke and Back*. New York: Hurst and Blackett, 1898.

Solka, Paul Jr. with Bremer, Art. *Adventures in Alaska Journalism Since 1903*. Fairbanks, Alaska: Commercial Printing Co., 1980.

Spotswood, Ken. *Klondike Gold Rush Information Kit*. Whitehorse, Yukon: Klondike Gold Rush Centennial, 1996.

Steele, Harwood. *Policing the Arctic: The Story of the Conquest of the Arctic by the Royal Canadian* [formerly Northwest] *Mounted Police*. London: Jarrolds Publishers, 1936.

Steele, Col. S. B. *Forty Years in Canada*. London: Jenkins Press, 1915.

Stevens, Gary L. "Gold Rush Theater in the Alaska-Yukon Frontier." A Dissertation for Doctorate of Philosophy, University of Oregon. Ann Arbor, Michigan: University Microfilms International, 1985.

Stone, Thomas. *Miners' Justice: Migration, Law and Order on the Alaska-Yukon Frontier, 1873-1902*. New York, Bern, Frankfurt, Paris: Peter Land Publishing, Inc., 1988.

Tewkesbury, David and William. *Who's Who in Alaska*. Juneau: Tewkesbury Publishers, 1947.

Tollemarche, Stratford. *Reminiscences of the Yukon: 1898-1909*. London: Edward Arnold, 1912.

Tower, Dr. Elizabeth. *Big Mike Henry: Irish Prince of the Iron Trails*. Anchorage: Elizabeth Tower, 1990.

Trelawney-Ansell, E. C. *I Followed Gold*. New York: Lee Furman, Inc., 1939.

Wagner, Roland Richard. "Virtue Against Vice: A Study of Moral Reformers and Prostitution in the Progressive Era." Thesis for Doctorate of Philosophy (History), University of Wisconsin, 1971.

Walkowitz, Judith. *Prostitution and Victorian Society: Women, Class and the State*. Cambridge: Cambridge University Press, 1980.

Wickersham, James A. *Old Yukon*. Washington, D.C.: Washington Law Book Co., 1938.

Wold, Jo Anne. *Wickersham: The Man At Home*. Fairbanks: Tanana Yukon Historical Society, 1981.

Wold, Jo Anne. *The Andrew Nerland Legacy*. From Nerland's Diary, August 20, 1898. Privately printed 1988.

Woolston, Howard B. *Prostitution in the United States Prior to the Entrance of the United States in World War*. (Originally published by Century Press, 1921.) Reprinted in Publication No. 29, Patterson Smith Reprint Series in Criminology, Law Enforcement and Social Problems. Montclair, N.J.: Patterson Smith, 1969.

Wright, Allen A. *Prelude to Bonanza*. Whitehorse, Yukon: Studio North Ltd., 1992, Copyright 1976.

Yamazaki, Tomako. *The Story of Yamada Waka: From Prostitute to Feminist Pioneer*. New York, San Francisco: Kodansha International, 1985.

ACADEMIC JOURNALS

Saloutos, Theodore. "Alexander Pantages, Theater Magnate of the West." *Pacific Northwest Quarterly*, October 1966.

Yubi, Ichiioca. "Ameyusi-San Japanese Prostitutes in 19th Century America." *Amerasia Journal*, Vol. 4 #1, 1977, pp. 1-21. Los Angeles and London, 1982.

ARCHIVES

Krauczunas, Kazis, to Commissioner-General of Immigration, August 22, 1909, File 52484-28, White Slave Traffic, R.G. 85 National Archives.

McCarley, Laura. "Histories of Downtown Buildings, Juneau," Alaska State Library, Utility number 19685, Historical Vertical File 1978.0004VF 1978.

MAGAZINES

Alaska Churchman 1904.

Avery, George. "Klondike Mike's Knockout Fight." *Alaska Sportsman*, September 1955, pp. 12-13, 33-36.

Alberts, Laurie. "Petticoats and Pickaxes." *Alaska Journal*, Summer 1977 Vol. 7 #3, pp. 146-159.

Backhouse, Frances H. "Women of the Klondike: Some Came to Do the Work of the Lord—Others Came only to Mine the Miners." *The Beaver*, Vol. 68 #6, December 1988/Jan 1989, pp. 30-36.

Berg, Helen. "The Doll of Dawson." *Alaska Sportsman*. Feb. 1944, pp. 8-9.

Bettles, Gordon. "Why I came to Alaska." *Heartland, Fairbanks Daily News-Miner*, July 21, 1996, p. H-8.

Betts, William James. "Klondike Photographer." *Alaska Sportsman*, Dec. 1964, pp. 16-19.

Booth, Michael R. "Gold Rush Theatres of the Klondike." *Beaver*, Spring 1962, p. 32-37.

Carey, Michael. "Mystery of the Photos." *We Alaskans, Anchorage Daily News*, May 16, 1993, p. M-8 and M-14.

Davis, Edby. "Alaska As I Knew It: Part II." *Alaska Sportsman*, Nov. 1964, pp. 16-19.

Dufresne, Klondy, with Ford, Corey. "Daughter of the Gold Rush, Chapter One." *Alaska Magazine*, September 1972, pp. 9-13.

Lung, Edward B. with Martinson, Ella Lung. "Glittering Fortunes and Empty Pokes." *Alaska Sportsman*, February 1952, pp. 18-23, 28-35.

Holloway, Sam. "Sporting Women of the Klondike." *The Yukon Reader*, Vol. 1, No 3. pp. 7-29.

Herbert, Chuck. "He Truly Loved the Yellow Metal." *Alaska Miner*, Feb. 1992, p. 15.

Jepson, Jill. "Frontier Theatre in the Alaska Gold Rush." *Heartland, Fairbanks Daily News Miner*, Oct. 24, 1993, pp. 9-14.

Martin, Cy. "Klondike Gold Rush Girlies." *Real West*, Vol. XI, No. 60, June 1968, p. 45.

Matson, Kate Rockwell with Mann, May. "I was Queen of the Klondike." *Alaska Sportsman*, August 1944, pp. 10, 11, 28, 29, 30, 31, 32.

Morgan, Lael. "Whores with a Heart." *We Alaskans, Anchorage Daily News*, May 16, 1993, pp. 7 and 10-14.

Naske, Claus, "The Red Lights of Fairbanks." *The Alaska Journal*, Spring 1984, Vol. 14, #2, pp 27-32.

Nielson, Jon. "Sourdough Sirens and Cheechako Chippies: Alaska's Other Gold Rush." *Alaska Today*, May 1981-April 1982, pp. 14-18.

Reed, Elmer. "The Mayor." *Alaska Sportsman*, December 1948, pp 10-11, 25-27.

"Sourdough Sweethearts." *Life*, May 19, 1958.

Schillios, Rolv. "Dance Hall Girl: Memories of Klondike Kate." *The Alaska Sportsman*, March 1956, pp. 8-11, 30-32.

Schillios, Rolv. "Dreams and Reality: Memories of Klondike Kate." *The Alaska Sportsman*, April 1956, pp. 16-19, 39, 40.

Shalkop, Antoinette. "Stepan Uskin: Citizen by Purchase." *Alaska Journal*.

Wallace, John B. "The People of Nome Were Scandalized," *The Alaska Sportsman*, December 1939; "Three Strikes Was Out!," Nov. 1939; "We Settled Disputes With Fists," August 1939; and "Nome Was Like That," October 1939.

SPECIAL COLLECTIONS

Ballou, William, Collection. Alaska and Polar Regions Department, Elmer E. Rasmuson Library, University of Alaska Fairbanks.

Clark, John A., Collection. Alaska and Polar Regions Department, Elmer E. Rasmuson Library, University of Alaska Fairbanks.

Geoghegan, Richard, Collection. Alaska and Polar Regions Department, Elmer E. Rasmuson Library, University of Alaska Fairbanks.

Smith, Lynn, Herbert Heller Collection. Alaska and Polar Regions Department, Elmer E. Rasmuson Library, University of Alaska Fairbanks, Box 1 Folder.

Riggs, Thomas, Christmas 1873-1945. Alaska and Polar Regions Department, Elmer E. Rasmuson Library, University of Alaska Fairbanks, #61.

Wickersham, James. Alaska State Library.

ELECTRONIC DATABASES

Pan For Gold Database, Yukon Territory Http://www.gold-rush.org/ghost-07.htm.

Polk Directories, 1901-1912. The Fairbanks Genealogical Society database, Http://www.polarnet.com/users/fgs/db/polk.htm.

INTERVIEWS

Marge Baker in Fairbanks, June 18, 1996.

Bill Barrington, the son of Hill Barrington, in Anchorage, spring of 1996.

Renee Blahuta of Fairbanks, April 1993 and earlier.

Arlaine Borich, a descendent of Tom Marquam, by phone from Tigard, Oregon, winter of 1995 and January 1998.

Rolfe Buzzell, History and Archeology, Alaska Department of Natural Resources in Anchorage, 1994.

John Butrovich, Fairbanks, July 1996 and earlier.

Lee Carman of Fairbanks, spring of 1992.

Ginger Carroll of Fairbanks by phone, 1993.

Bob Casey, Circle Hot Springs, July 1995.

Jack Coghill in Fairbanks, Oct. 14, 1995.

Earl and Pat Cook of Fairbanks, summer of 1992 and February 1997.

Kathleen Dalton in Fairbanks, January 1991.

Dora Davis in Milton, Illinois, summer of 1994.

S E L E C T E D   B I B L I O G R A P H Y

Don "Bucky" Dawson of Ketchikan by phone, March 1997.
R. N. DeArmond in Sitka, April 1995 and earlier.
Thorne Ferguson in Anchorage, June 22, 1996.
Ed Ferrell of Juneau by phone, spring 1995.
Michael Gates, Yukon historian of Dawson, January 1998 and earlier.
Marge Gull, Anchorage Pioneer Home, September 1993.
Orea and Cliff Hayden, North Pole, Feb. 25, 1995.
Chuck Herbert in Anchorage by phone, Aug. 30, 1992.
James Albert Johnson of Seattle, spring 1995 and earlier.
Bernie Hulk in Juneau, March 21, 1996.
Kay Kennedy, a Fairbanks reporter who knew Edith Neile well, in November 1993.
Bill Lewis of Fairbanks, July 12, 1996.
Ian Matherson of Seattle, spring of 1994.
Helen McGee, Hot Springs, South Dakota, September 1997.
Blanche McSmith, close personal friend and executor of Zula Swanson's estate, in Juneau in 1992 and by phone in 1994.
Jim Moody of Fairbanks, July of 1994.
Ken Murray in Fairbanks, spring 1994.
John P. Myers, Cave Creek, Arizona, in the summer of 1994.
Jerry Nerland, grandson of Andrew Nerland, in Anchorage, spring of 1996.
David Neufeld, Yukon historian of Whitehorse, May 1996 and earlier.
LaDessa Nordale, a former Fairbanks judge, at the Pioneer Home, May 1992.
Ruth and Roy Olson in Fairbanks, Feb. 1997.
Alice Osborne of Nome and Sequim, WA, in spring of 1995.

Rob Pegues of Tenakee in April of 1996.
Burke Riley, Juneau, Alaska, April 1996 and earlier.
Pat Hering Roggie, a former neighbor of the Tom Marquams, in a 1995 interview.
Sally Hudson, who lived in Rampart as a girl and later worked in Lucille's Apparel in Fairbanks, March 1995.
G. June Rust Sidars, April 1994.
Jill Smythe of Anchorage, April of 1994.
Paul Solka, Eugene, Oregon, March 5, 1995 and earlier.
Olga Steger of Fairbanks, fall of 1996.
Joe Sterling, Edith Neile's nephew, in Everett, Washington, Feb. 25, 1995.
Rosa Stonefield, McCoy's sister, Eugene, Oregon, March 1995.
Bill Stroeker, Fairbanks, August, 11, 1994 and earlier.
Clem Tillion in Juneau, winter 1967 and earlier.
Ron and Dorothy Twogood of Fairbanks, Feb. 9, 1997.
James Walsh of Nome and Seattle, January 1998 and earlier.
Peter Walsh of Nome and Fairbanks, spring of 1996.
Fred Wilkinson in Circle, July 1997.
Madalin Wilkinson via phone in Seattle, February 1997.
Father William Warren, Fairbanks Episcopal Church, in spring 1972 and earlier.
Lou Williams, Ketchikan Daily News, Ketchikan, July 4, 1996.
Vicki Wisenbaugh, Tenakee Historical Collection, November 1993.
Frank Young of Fairbanks, April 1992.
Stan Zaverl, former Fairbanks Police Chief, February 10, 1997.
Albert Zucchini in Fairbanks May 25, 1995.

$\mathcal{P}hoto\ \mathcal{C}redit\ \mathcal{A}bbreviations$

AMHA: Anchorage Museum of History and Art, Alaska.
ANA: Alaska National Archives Regional Branch, Anchorage, Alaska.
ASL: Alaska State Library, Juneau, Alaska.
BCARS: British Columbia Archives and Records Services, Victoria, B.C.
NA: National Archives and Records Administration, Washington, D.C.
NAC: National Archives of Canada, Ottawa, Ontario.

NAPAR: National Archives, Pacific Alaska Region (Anchorage).
THS: Tongas Historical Society, Ketchikan Museum, Ketchikan, Alaska.
UAF: Alaska and Polar Regions Dept., University of Alaska Fairbanks.
UW: Special Collections Division, University of Washington Libraries, Seattle.
YA: Yukon Archives, Whitehorse, Yukon Territory.

$\mathscr{Index}$

Women Writers Offer Insights from the FAR NORTH

- **Seven Words for Wind: Essays and Field Notes from Alaska's Pribilof Islands,** Sumner MacLeish. Beautifully written stories that invite the reader into a landscape and culture like none other on earth. $16.95, hardbound.

- **Cold Starry Night,** Claire Fejes. The heartwarming memoir of a New York artist who moves to remote Fairbanks, Alaska, in 1946. $19.95, softbound.

- **Girl in the Gold Camp,** Peggy Rouch Dodson. A teenager rafts down the Yukon River in 1909 to live in a gold camp, where she is courted by lonely miners and comes to love outdoor adventure. $14.95, trade paperback.

- **Two Old Women: An Alaska Legend of Betrayal, Courage, and Survival,** Velma Wallis. An inspirational Athabascan Indian legend about two courageous elders who survive a brutal winter famine. $16.95, hardbound.

- **Bird Girl and the Man Who Followed the Sun,** Velma Wallis. A legend retold about two Indians who pay a heavy price for their independence. $19.95, hardbound.

To order a book, write Epicenter Press, Box 82368, Kenmore, WA 98028, or phone 800-950-6663. WA residents must include 8.6% sales tax. Add $5 shipping for the first book, $2 for each additional book. Visa, MC accepted.

The Good Time Girls come alive on VIDEO

You'll find an astonishing treasure of historic photographs, gold rush sound effects, and the absorbing story of **Good Time Girls of the Alaska - Yukon Gold Rush** in this 34-minute video from KAKM Video, affiliated with KAKM-TV, Anchorage, Alaska's public television station. **$19.95.**

To place a video order, write KAKM Video, 3877 University Dr., Anchorage, AK 99508, or call toll-free 800-684-3368. Add $4 shipping for the first video, $1 for each additional video. Visa, MC accepted.

MIDNIGHT HOUR
OSHIWORA, OR "WH